Turbo Pascal 6.0

The Nuts and Bolts of Program Construction

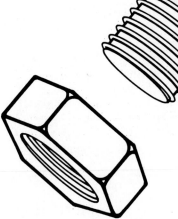

John DiElsi

McGraw-Hill, Inc.
New York St. Louis San Francisco Auckland Bogotá
Caracas Lisbon London Madrid Mexico Milan
Montreal New Delhi Paris San Juan Singapore
Sydney Tokyo Toronto

TURBO PASCAL 6.0: The Nuts and Bolts of Program Construction

Copyright © 1991 by McGraw-Hill, Inc. All rights reserved. Printed in the United States of America. No part of this publication may be reproduced or distributed in any form or by any means or stored in a data base or retrieval system without the prior written permission of the publisher.

4 5 6 7 8 9 0   **DOH   DOH**   9 4 3 2

ISBN 0-07-557790-9

This book was set in Garamond type by Advanced Presentations.
The editor was David M. Shapiro;
production coordination was done by Linda Hauck and Simmon Factor.
The cover was designed by Seventeenth Street Studios.
Interior design and illlustrations were done by Advanced Presentations.
Development and production management were provided by Cole and Associates.
R. R. Donnelley & Sons Company was printer and binder.

Library of Congress Cataloging-in-Publication Data

DiElsi, John J.
      Turbo Pascal 6.0: the nuts and bolts of program construction /
      John DiElsi.
          p.   cm.
      ISBN 0-07-557790-9
      1. Pascal (Computer program language) 2. Turbo Pascal (Computer program) I. Title. II. Title: Turbo Pascal 6.0
QA76.73.P35D54 1991
005.369—dc20   90-44654

Turbo Pascal is a registered trademark of Borland International, Inc.

Table of Contents

Chapter 2: Components of a Pascal Program

Chapter 3: Fundamental Input and Output

Chapter 6: Functions

Chapter 7: Selection Structures

Chapter 8: Iteration Structures

Chapter 9: Arrays

Chapter 10: Records, Searching, and Sorting

Chapter 11: Data File Techniques

Chapter 12: An Introduction to Advanced Pascal Structures and Object-Oriented Programming

Preface

This text is meant for an introductory course in structured programming using Turbo Pascal 6.0 and its integrated development environment (IDE) called the Programmer's Platform. Version 6.0, the most recent version of Turbo Pascal, is a significant improvement over the previous two versions, 5.0 and 5.5. This programming system offers tools that make it easier to learn proper programming skills and use them in creating well-written programs. Although other texts claim to be Turbo Pascal compatible, this one incorporates the programming tools provided by the IDE into the programming topics in a natural way, not as a special section in a chapter or an appendix.

The text also can be used for instruction in Microsoft's QuickPascal. All the program solutions written for Turbo Pascal compile and execute, *without modification,* in QuickPascal. Although QuickPascal and Turbo Pascal perform essentially the same functions, the programming environment for QuickPascal (menus, menu choices, windows, etc.) differs from the Turbo Pascal IDE.

To be productive, any language must conform to a set of rules governing its use. But this is not enough. You may be able to discern the meaning of an English sentence even though it is ungrammatical, but a computer cannot interpret the statements in a programming language unless they are "grammatically" correct. And though most people can write grammatically correct sentences in English or some other human language, very few are professional writers. In computer languages, the need to write programs that are not only "grammatically" correct but polished as well is even more important.

This text emphasizes the creation of understandable, reliable, and maintainable Pascal programs. It also provides the tools to do the job. Its informal writing style will help the reader understand important programming concepts while minimizing the jargon and technical language that can cause misinterpretation. The numerous examples provided are explained in detail. In addition, there are completely developed problem solutions that show how to apply these concepts in practical ways. This emphasis on detail—*the nuts and bolts of program construction*—is vital to the creation of well-designed, well-written solutions to practical problems. Turbo Pascal is a vehicle; the problem-solving skills are the goal.

Summary of Contents

Chapter 0 introduces those portions of the Turbo Pascal 6.0 programming environment that are needed to create, edit, and execute a program. It also includes a sample programming session that acquaints the reader with the Turbo Pascal integrated development environment.

A six-step method for designing and implementing solutions to programming problems is detailed in Chapter 1—and applied throughout the text.

Chapter 2 discusses string, character, Boolean, and numeric data types; program documentation; and the fundamental components common to all Pascal programs. These concepts form the basis for a sample program that ends the chapter.

Pascal statements that create output and accept input are the essence of Chapter 3. These include how the Turbo Pascal environment can display output on a monitor screen, print it, and store it in a text file as well as how it can accept input from a keyboard and a text file. The chapter also highlights how the Turbo Pascal environment assists in finding and correcting program errors.

Chapter 4 introduces the fundamentals of processing numeric data. It also develops a strategy for testing programs that can be used as part of the software development methodology presented in Chapter 1.

Using system-defined procedures as a guide, Chapter 5 illustrates how parameters pass information between programmer-defined procedures and stresses the importance of the modular independence that can result. Chapter 6 distinguishes between Pascal procedures and functions, and shows how to create programmer-defined functions using system-defined functions as models.

Chapters 7 and 8 present, respectively, selection structures and iteration structures that, along with the sequential processing in earlier chapters, complete the repertoire of basic structures from which all programs are constructed. In addition to introducing single-option and multiple-option selection structures, Chapter 7 shows how these structures can be utilized to create menu-driven software. In Chapter 8, both definite and indefinite loop (iteration) structures are discussed and used to introduce simulation.

Array and record structures as well as their application in searching and sorting operations are detailed in Chapters 9 and 10.

Chapter 11 introduces the fundamentals of creating, reading from, adding to, and changing a data file composed of record data types.

Chapter 12, the final chapter, gives a brief introduction to advanced programming topics, including enumerated data types, pointer data types, linked lists, recursion, and object-oriented programming.

Several appendices serve as handy reference tools for both the Turbo programming environment and the Pascal language. Answers to selected exercises and programming assignments also are included.

General Features

Each chapter opens with both a list of key terms introduced in that chapter and a set of learning objectives. And each chapter ends with (1) a "Store and Forward" section that summarizes the concepts presented in that chapter and links them to the new topics presented in the next chapter, (2) a "Snares and Pitfalls" section that details errors commonly encountered by new programmers, (3) exercises to test comprehension of concepts, and (4) programming assignments covering a wide range of interests, to test the ability to apply concepts in a practical way.

An easy-to-read style enhanced by simple notational conventions regarding the use of **boldface** and *italic* type make it easy to understand concepts and work independently. The many figures included enhance the detailed explanations of programming concepts. Examples and their interpretations appear side by side, to eliminate sifting through text to find those explanations. Style tips for producing well-documented programs are presented throughout in special highlighted sections. These emphasize the importance of establishing good programming habits at an early stage.

An instructor's manual providing guidelines for effective instruction and answers for selected text exercises and assignments not found in the text is available, as is a computer disk containing the solutions to all chapter application programs and selected programming assignments.

Course of Study

Chapter 0, which introduces the integrated development environment, can be either omitted or covered independently if desired. To emphasize structure and modularization techniques, procedures are introduced early and used throughout the text. The creation and use of text files presented in Chapter 3 is optional; sections 3.6 through 3.8 can be omitted without affecting the study of topics appearing later in the text. Chapter 11 ("Data File Techniques") assumes no knowledge of text files in Chapter 3 and is self-contained. Beyond that, the book is organized so each chapter builds on concepts developed in the previous chapters. Chapter 12 ("An Introduction to Advanced Pascal Structures and Object-Oriented Programming") introduces topics likely to be found in a second course in programming and should be covered if time permits.

Acknowledgments

Many things contributed to the creation of this text, not the least of which was the understanding and moral support offered by both my family and my friends. Even though, at times, "the book" seemed to be more important than they, it was not. I would also like to thank Professor Joseph Bergin, Pace

University; Professor Roger Bielefeld, Cleveland State University; Professor George Converse, Southern Oregon State College; Associate Professor Maria C. Kolatis, County College of Morris (New Jersey); and Dr. Barbara Owens, St. Edwards University, for taking the time to suggest improvements, many of which have been incorporated; the copy editor Elliot Simon, for his valuable assistance in clarifying content; my colleagues at Mercy College, Dobbs Ferry, New York, for their encouragement; and Alan Held, Ginette Voldman, and Jim Hendricks for their assistance in providing many of the solutions. Special thanks are due to Barbara Pickard, Annette Gooch, Linda Hauck, Simmon Factor, and Brete Harrison at Cole and Associates, and David Shapiro at McGraw-Hill, all of whom helped produce the final product despite changes in publishers and five versions of Turbo Pascal. Their guidance and support were greatly appreciated.

John DiElsi

Dedicated to Dad
For a lifetime of love, support, and friendship

CHAPTER 0

The Turbo Pascal 6.0 System

Key Terms

About	operating system
bug	**Options**
Close	**Output**
Compile	output device
compiler	**Print**
cursor	processor
Debug	program
desktop	Programmer's Platform
dialog box	**Restore line**
disk drive	**Run**
DOS shell	**Save**
Edit	**Save as**
File	scroll
hardware	**Search**
hot key	secondary storage
input device	software
integrated development	source code
environment (IDE)	status line
main memory	System (≡)
menu bar	TPTOUR
monitor	**Trace into**
New	**User screen**
object code	window
Open	**Window**

Objectives

- To introduce hardware and software terminology and fundamentals
- To present the essential components of the Turbo Pascal Programmer's Platform
- To provide hands-on experience for the programming process through a step-by-step exercise

0.1 Introduction

Mention the term *computer* and you're likely to get a wide range of responses, from awe to disgust. Some people think computers can do everything, while others think they should do nothing.

A computer is nothing more than a sophisticated tool, a collection of devices—*hardware*—that can be instructed to perform a variety of tasks. It is difficult to talk to a computer on its own terms, since all it basically understands is a series of on/off states, a combination of switches whose values are either on or off. To make the task of communicating with a computer easier and more efficient, we have to write a set of instructions—a *program*—in a high-level, or Englishlike, language and have it translated into a low-level language, one the computer understands. The translator, called a *compiler,* takes the program's instructions (*source code*) and puts them in a form the computer can execute (*object code*). Turbo Pascal is a language presented in an *integrated development environment (IDE),* called the *Programmer's Platform,* that simplifies the creation, correction, and production of programs.

This chapter introduces the fundamental concepts common to all computer systems. It summarizes the basic operation of the Turbo Pascal Programmer's Platform and provides a step-by-step guide for creating and running a sample program. More detailed explanation of the IDE can be found in the Turbo Pascal User's Guide that accompanies the software.

0.2 Hardware and Software Fundamentals

Every computer system consists of both a set of devices (the hardware) and instructions (*software*) for using that hardware. The major hardware components of a computer system include a *processor, main memory,* one or more *disk drives,* a printer, a *monitor,* and a keyboard. Figure 0.1 shows these components and how they're interrelated.

The processor performs all the calculations and makes all the decisions. It receives data and instructions from main memory and stores results there. *Secondary storage devices,* such as disk drives, store information that is not immediately required by the processor. They hold data and instructions, which are transferred to and from main memory as needed. The printer and monitor are *output devices* that receive results from main memory; the keyboard is an *input device* that enters data into main memory. Since secondary storage devices send data to and receive data from main memory, they also can be considered input and output devices.

The most powerful hardware in the world is useless without software to tell it what to do, and the most important piece of software is the operating system. An *operating system* is a collection of programs that control all the resources in a computer system, from hardware through programming

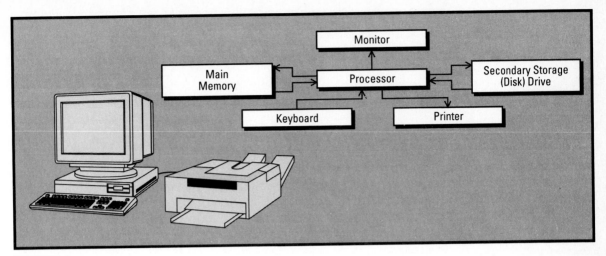

Figure 0.1
Components of a
Computer System

languages and service programs. Turbo Pascal 6.0 is a programming language that was designed to work with IBM or IBM-compatible microcomputer systems with either fixed (hard) or removable (floppy) disks, using the MS-DOS or PC-DOS operating system. Although there is also a version available for Macintosh microcomputers, that version will not be discussed here.

If the Programmer's Platform is not already installed on your computer, the Turbo Pascal User's Guide provides detailed instructions.

0.3 The Turbo Pascal Programmer's Platform

The Turbo Pascal Programmer's Platform is an integrated development environment (IDE) that consists of a text editor for entering and editing program instructions, an integrated debugger to help locate errors (*bugs*) in the program, and a compiler to translate the instructions into machine-readable form. Pull-down menus, windows, and Help facilities simplify its use.

The main screen appears immediately after you load Turbo Pascal (see Figure 0.2). The main screen is divided into three sections: the menu bar at the top, the desktop (middle portion), and the status line at the bottom. The *menu bar* gives access to the commands in the IDE. If you press function key F10 to get to the menu bar, one of the ten menu choices will be highlighted. (All menu titles and menu choices in this text are displayed in **boldface** type.) To move from one menu item to another, you can either use the left- and right-arrow keys on the keyboard or press the first letter in the menu name (for example, F for **File**). If a menu item is highlighted, you can display the menu associated with that choice by pressing the down-arrow key or the Enter key. You can also display a menu in one step, by holding

Figure 0.2
Main Screen with
Opened Edit Window

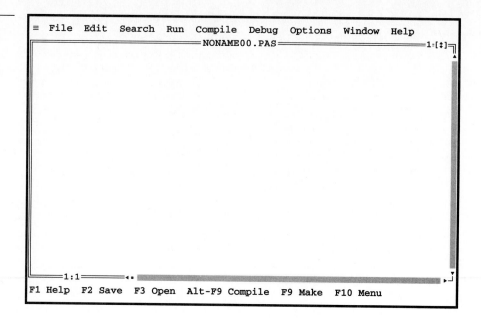

down the Alt key and pressing the first letter in the name of the menu item. To go to the **Run** menu, for example, hold down the Alt key and press R, the first letter in **Run**.

The *desktop* is designed to contain *windows*—special-purpose rectangular areas with boundaries that isolate them from the rest of the desktop. Windows must be activated before they can be seen on the desktop. One of these windows, the Edit window, must be activated in order to enter the instructions for a Pascal program. To create an Edit window for a new program, press the Alt and F keys simultaneously (Alt-F) to reveal the **File** menu, then highlight the **New** option from that menu by using the down-arrow key, and finally press the Enter key. The IDE creates the first Edit window automatically when the Turbo System is started. This results in an Edit window entitled **NONAME00.PAS** that fills the entire desktop. See Figure 0.2.

The *cursor*, the blinking underscore symbol (_) in the upper left corner of this window, indicates where the next entered character will appear on the screen. The cursor must be in the Edit window to enter the instructions for a Pascal program. In the bottom left corner of this window are two numbers separated by a colon. The first number represents the program line number for the current position of the cursor in the window, while the second represents the cursor position's column number. For example, 7:11 indicates that the cursor is at the intersection of the 7th row and 11th column of this Edit window.

The *status line* indicates what keystroke shortcuts (*hot keys*) activate relevant menu choices and provides descriptions of what actions the system is doing or ready to do. The status line at the bottom of Figure 0.2 shows six hot-key options. For example, to activate the menu bar, press the F10 function key; to compile the program in the Edit window, hold down the Alt key and simultaneously press the F9 function key (Alt-F9). Additional hot-key options appear to the right of the items in activated menus. Table 0.1 summarizes selected hot-key options, which are also listed in Appendix A.

Hot Key	Menu Equivalent	Function
F1	Help	Displays a Help screen
F2	File/Save	Saves active editor file
F3	File/Open	Opens file
F4	Run/Go to cursor	Executes to cursor location
F5	Window/Zoom	Zooms the active window
F6	Window/Next	Cycles through open windows
F7	Run/Trace into	Traces into subroutines
F8	Run/Step over	Steps over subroutine calls
F10		Activates the menu bar
Alt-F1	Help/Previous topic	Displays previous Help screen
Alt-F3	Window/Close	Closes active window
Alt-F5	Window/User screen	Displays User screen
Alt-F9	Compile/Compile	Compiles active program
Alt-Spacebar	≡ menu	Goes to ≡ (System) menu
Alt-C	Compile menu	Goes to **Compile** menu
Alt-D	Debug menu	Goes to **Debug** menu
Alt-E	Edit menu	Goes to **Edit** menu
Alt-F	File menu	Goes to **File** menu
Alt-H	Help menu	Goes to **Help** menu
Alt-O	Options menu	Goes to **Options** menu
Alt-R	Run menu	Goes to **Run** menu
Alt-S	Search menu	Goes to **Search** menu
Alt-W	Window menu	Goes to **Window** menu
Alt-X	File/Exit	Exits Turbo Pascal to DOS
Ctrl-F1	Help/Topic search	Gives language-specific help while in editor
Ctrl-F2	Run/Program reset	Resets running program
Ctrl-F7	Debug/Add watch	Adds a watch expression
Ctrl-F8	Debug/Toggle breakpoint	Clears or sets conditional breakpoint
Ctrl-F9	Run/Run	Executes active program

Table 0.1
Turbo Pascal 6.0 Hot Keys

A program called TPTOUR, which is included in the Turbo Pascal 6.0 software package, guides you through the fundamentals of the Programmer's Platform (IDE). To use this program, place the disk containing it in the active disk drive, type TPTOUR, and press the Enter key. Follow the directions on the screen to learn more about the IDE's features.

0.4 Turbo Pascal Menus

Making a selection from the menu bar displays a list of options related to a menu heading. The options in a menu listing can be selected by first displaying the listing using function key F10. Next, either use the down-arrow key to highlight the choice and press Enter, or press the highlighted letter in the option name. If an option is followed by an ellipsis (. . .), its selection displays a *dialog box*—a window that lets you confirm or change data relevant to that option. Some options have hot-key equivalents, which are shown to the right of the option's name when its menu is displayed. You can back out of any selection by continuing to press the Esc key until you activate the Edit window. This chapter discusses a few of the fundamental menu options you will be using; others are presented later in the text.

System (≡) Menu

The system menu, represented on the screen by ≡, is shown in Figure 0.3. This menu provides three general system options, including the **About** option, which displays the version/copyright box shown in Figure 0.4.

Figure 0.3
System (≡) Menu

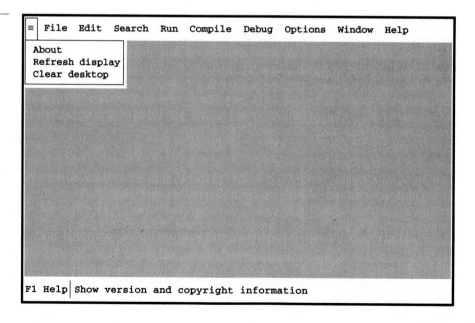

6

File Menu

The **File** menu, shown in Figure 0.5, provides options that open existing files and save files. The **Open** option gets an existing file from the disk and displays it in an Edit window. It can be activated either by selecting **Open**

Figure 0.4
"About" Dialog Box

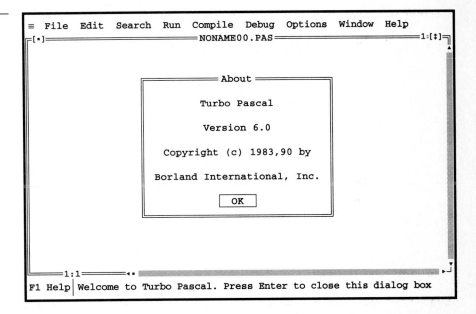

Figure 0.5
File Menu

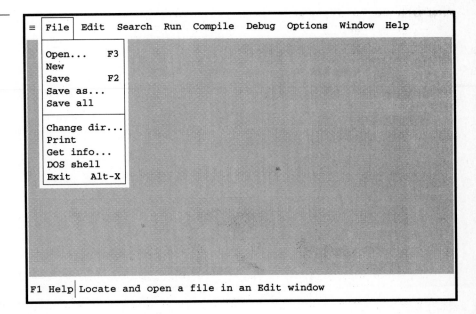

from the **File** menu or by pressing the function key F3 (the hot key for **Open**). The IDE then displays an "Open a File" dialog box, with the cursor flashing in the area below Name (Figure 0.6).

A file name usually consists of up to eight letters, a period, and the extension PAS. Often, a descriptive name is chosen to help remember the contents or purpose of a program file. If you can't remember the name of the file to load, press the Tab key to activate the Files area of this box, which lists all the Pascal files in the current directory. To open a file, use the arrow keys to highlight the desired file name in the Files area and then press Enter. When the name of the desired file appears in the Name area, press the Enter key again to transfer a copy of the file to the Edit window.

The **File** menu option **New** opens a new Edit window. To choose **New**, display the **File** menu and either highlight **New** and press Enter or press N, the highlighted letter in the option name. There is no hot-key option for **New**. If a program file is already in an existing Edit window, the IDE creates a new, clear Edit window and places it in front of the existing one.

The **Save** option, which can be chosen from the **File** menu or by using the F2 hot key, copies the file in the active Edit window to a disk. If you have not assigned a name to the file, a "Save File As" dialog box appears. See Figure 0.7. Just type a descriptive name (no more than eight letters) for the file, preceded by the letter designation of the drive on which the file is to be saved, including a colon and a complete directory path, and then press Enter. After the file has been saved, the IDE returns you to the Edit window. If the file already has a name, a dialog box does not appear and the file is saved under the current name. (Additional information concerning directories can be found in your computer's DOS manual.)

If you choose the **Save as** option from the **File** menu rather than **Save**, a "Save File As" dialog box always appears, whether you have saved the file

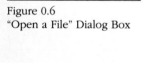
Figure 0.6
"Open a File" Dialog Box

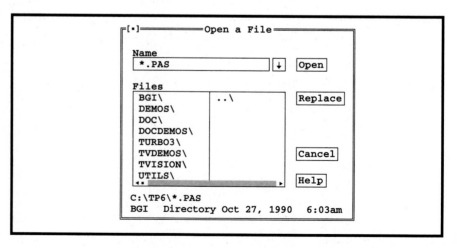

Figure 0.7
"Save File As" Dialog Box

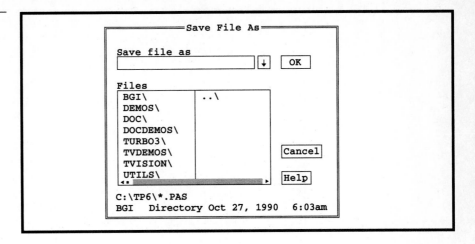

under another name or not. This gives you the opportunity to save the active file under a different name.

The **Print** option enables you to print a copy of the file in the active Edit window.

The **DOS shell** option permits you to leave Turbo Pascal temporarily and takes you to DOS, where you can execute any DOS command. To return to your departure point, just type the word *exit* and press the Enter key.

If you select the **Exit** option, the IDE is closed for business and you return to the operating system. The hot-key option for **Exit** is Alt-X.

Edit Menu

Options in the **Edit** menu (see Figure 0.8) allow you to cut, copy, and paste sections of programs in the active Edit window. Choosing **Restore line** from this menu negates the *last* editing command made.

Search Menu

With the options in the **Search** menu (see Figure 0.9) you can search for program text and errors in program files.

Run Menu

The **Run** menu contains options that let you execute a program or move through it one step at a time. As Figure 0.10 shows, most of these options have equivalent hot keys.

Use the **Run** option from this menu (Ctrl-F9) to translate a program in the Edit window into machine-readable form (compile the program) and execute it. If there are any errors in the compile phase, a description of the error is shown at the top of the Edit window. Pressing the Esc key removes the description and moves the cursor to the error position.

The **Trace into** option also is very useful for finding program errors. Details of its operation are given in Chapter 3.

Figure 0.8
Edit Menu

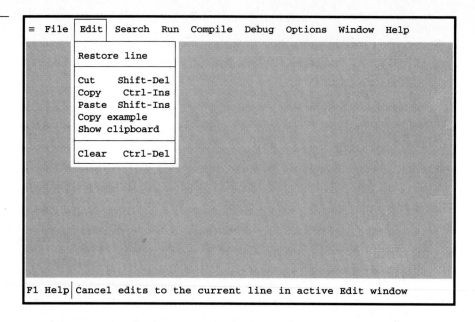

Figure 0.9
Search Menu

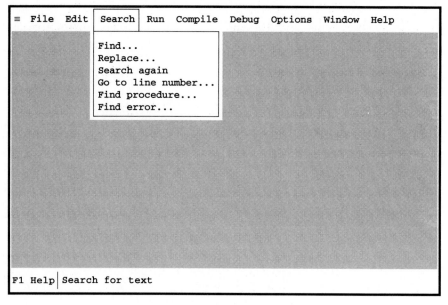

Compile Menu

The **Compile** menu, shown in Figure 0.11, includes the **Compile** option (Alt-F9), which translates the source code in the Edit window to object code. The program is not executed, but relevant error messages are displayed.

Debug Menu

The **Debug** menu (see Figure 0.12) supplies options that help detect and correct errors in programs. Its use will be featured in Chapter 3.

Options Menu

The **Options** menu, given in Figure 0.13, provides facilities that allow you to specify new defaults for compiler options.

Figure 0.10
Run Menu

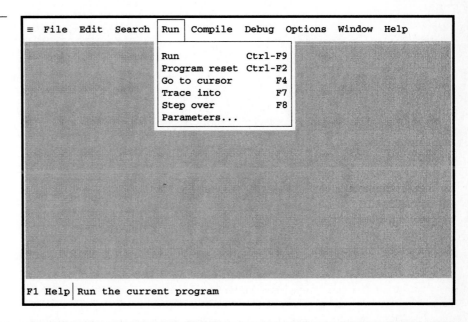

Figure 0.11
Compile Menu

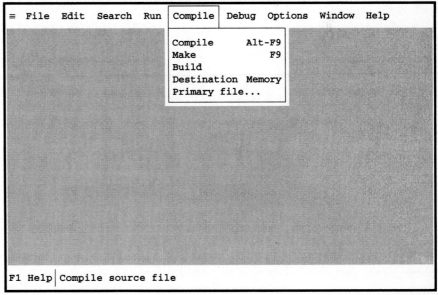

Window Menu

The **Window** menu (see Figure 0.14) manages the windows that appear on the desktop. The **Output** option of this menu opens a window at the bottom of the desktop where program output can be displayed. Selecting the **Close** option (Alt-F3) removes the active window from the desktop

Figure 0.12
Debug Menu

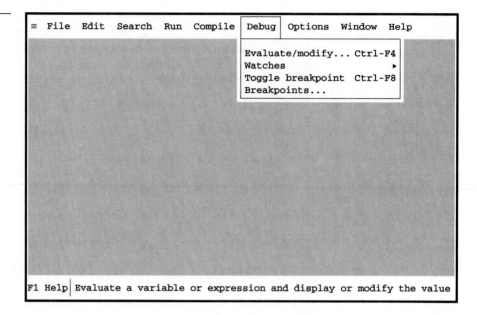

Figure 0.13
Options Menu

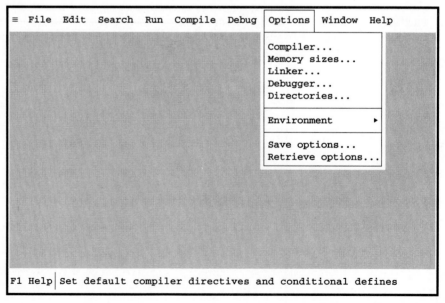

Figure 0.14
Window Menu

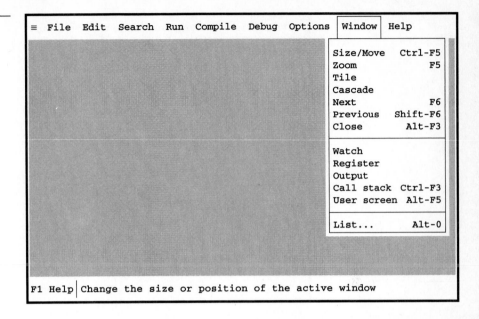

```
≡  File   Edit   Search   Run   Compile   Debug   Options   Window   Help

                                              Size/Move    Ctrl-F5
                                              Zoom              F5
                                              Tile
                                              Cascade
                                              Next              F6
                                              Previous     Shift-F6
                                              Close         Alt-F3

                                              Watch
                                              Register
                                              Output
                                              Call stack   Ctrl-F3
                                              User screen   Alt-F5

                                              List...        Alt-0


F1 Help│Change the size or position of the active window
```

(including an Output window if it is active). The **User screen** option (Alt-F5) shows a program's full-screen output, covering the entire Programmer's Platform. Pressing any key returns you to the Platform.

The windows on the desktop can be moved and sized for convenient arrangement on the desktop. Refer to the User's Guide for further details.

Help Menu

The **Help** menu (Figure 0.15) provides on-line assistance for virtually all components of the Programmer's Platform and Turbo Pascal.

You don't have to use the **Help** menu to get help. Pressing the F1 hot key at any time opens a relevant Help window that provides information on the active part of the main screen. For example, pressing F1 when the **File** option on the menu bar is highlighted shows a description of the function of each of its menu choices (as in Figure 0.16).

0.5 The Turbo Pascal Editor

To enter or alter program code, you must be able to move around the Edit window. This can be done with the four arrow keys, but this method sometimes proves quite tedious. A number of cursor movement commands make it easier to navigate in the Edit window. For example, instead of repeatedly using the left-arrow key to move the cursor to the beginning of the existing line, you can press the Home key.

The Turbo Pascal Editor also includes commands for inserting text, deleting text, and performing operations on blocks of text. For example, to delete the

Figure 0.15
Help Menu

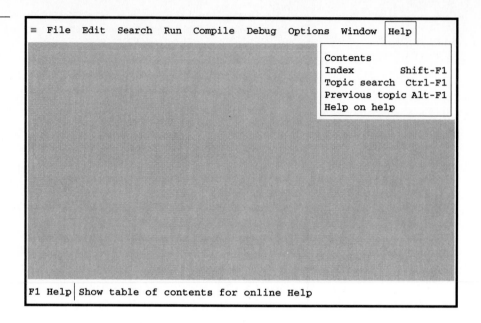

Figure 0.16
Help Window for **File**

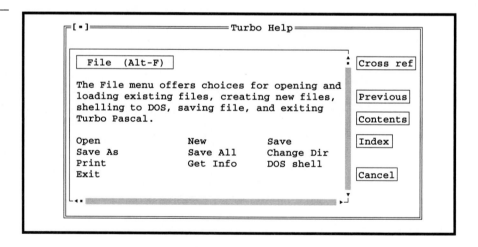

character to the left of the cursor, you press Ctrl-H or the Backspace key. To delete an entire line, you move the cursor to that line and press Ctrl-Y.

A summary of the more common editor commands is given in Table 0.2 and in Appendix B. Complete detailed descriptions can be found in the Turbo Pascal User's Guide. A little practice with the more powerful features of the Turbo editor can save you many keystrokes.

Table 0.2
Turbo Pascal 6.0
Editor Commands

Function	Keystroke
Movement Commands	
Character left	Ctrl-S or left arrow
Character right	Ctrl-D or right arrow
Word left	Ctrl-A or Ctrl-left arrow
Word right	Ctrl-F or Ctrl-right arrow
Line up	Ctrl-E or up arrow
Line down	Ctrl-X or down arrow
Page up	Ctrl-R or PgUp
Page down	Ctrl-C or PgDn
Beginning of line	Ctrl-Q/S or Home
End of line	Ctrl-Q/D or End
Top of window	Ctrl-Q/E or Ctrl-Home
Bottom of window	Ctrl-Q/X or Ctrl-End
Beginning of program	Ctrl-Q/R or Ctrl-PgUp
End of program	Ctrl-Q/C or Ctrl-PgDn
Insert and Delete Commands	
Delete line	Ctrl-Y
Delete block	Ctrl-K/Y
Delete to end of line	Ctrl-Q/Y
Delete character left of cursor	Ctrl-H or Backspace
Delete character under cursor	Ctrl-G or Delete
Insert line	Ctrl-N
Block Commands	
Copy block to edit file	Ctrl-K/C
Copy block to Clipboard	Edit/Copy or Ctrl-Ins
Delete block (not saving to Clipboard)	Edit/Clear or Ctrl-Del
Delete block (saving to Clipboard)	Edit/Cut or Shift-Del
Hide/display block	Ctrl-K/H
Mark block begin	Ctrl-K/B
Mark block end	Ctrl-K/K
Mark single work	Ctrl-K/T
Move block from Clipboard	Edit/Paste or Shift-Ins
Move block to edit file	Ctrl-K/V
Read block from disk	Ctrl-K/R
Write block to disk	Ctrl-K/W
Miscellaneous	
Find	Ctrl-Q/F or Search/Find
Find and replace	Ctrl-Q/A or Search/Replace
Invoke main menu	F10
Language help	Ctrl-F1
Open file	F3 or File/Open
Save file	Ctrl-K/S or F2 or File/Save

0.6 Running a Sample Pascal Program: A Step-By-Step Guide

The following exercise should acquaint you with the basics of using the Turbo Pascal Programmer's Platform to create, edit, and execute a simple program. At this point you need not be concerned about understanding the Pascal code; it is discussed in later chapters.

1. Enter the Turbo Pascal IDE by typing *turbo* at the DOS prompt and pressing the Enter key. A new Edit window is created automatically. The cursor location prompt at the bottom of the Edit window should read 1:1, indicating that the cursor is on line 1, column 1 of that window.

2. Enter the following program exactly as written:

```
program Countdown;
   var
      count : integer;
   begin
     for count = 10 downto 1 do
       Writeln (count:5)
     Writeln ('Blastoff!')
   end.
```

3. Attempt to run the program by pressing Ctrl-F9. The system responds by displaying the following error message at the top of the Edit window:

```
Error 91: ":=" expected.
```

The cursor should be underlining the equal sign in the *for* statement. A program does not produce any output unless all errors of this type are corrected.

4. Press the Esc key to remove the error message, then press the colon symbol (:) to change = to :=.

5. Again, try to run the program by pressing Ctrl-F9. This time the system responds with another error message:

```
Error 85: ";" expected.
```

Even though the cursor is under the *W* in the second *Writeln* statement, the error occurred because a semicolon was missing at the end of the first *Writeln* statement.

6. Press the Esc key to remove the error message, press the up-arrow key once to move the cursor to the preceding line, and press the End key to move the cursor to the end of that line. Then enter a semicolon. The edited program becomes:

```
program Countdown;
   var
      count : integer;
   begin
     for count := 10 downto 1 do
       Writeln (count:5);
     Writeln ('Blastoff!')
   end.
```

7. Run the program by pressing Ctrl-F9. After a brief period of time (and some activity), you're back in the Edit window. It looks as though nothing has happened, but the output from the program is waiting for you to uncover it.

8. Select **User screen** from the **Window** menu (or press Alt-F5) and you'll see the following output:

```
10
 9
 8
 7
 6
 5
 4
 3
 2
 1
Blastoff!
```

9. Press any key to return to the main screen.

10. To see both the program listing and its output on the same screen, press Alt-W to activate the **Window** menu, and press O to reveal an Output window at the bottom portion of the desktop. The cursor now appears in the Output window at the end of the output. As indicated in the status line, the arrow keys allow you to move through the text (*scroll*) to see all the output.

11. To remove the Output window, press Alt-F3 (or select **Close** from the **Window** menu) to close this window and activate the previous window—the Edit window.

12. Press Alt-F9 to compile the program. This translation process does not execute the program but, if there are no errors, displays a window giving information about the file (see Figure 0.17). Press any key to remove this dialog box from the desktop.

13. Now it's time to save the correct version of this program. Press F2 to activate **Save** from the **File** menu. A window appears on the screen asking you to name the program, since you have not yet done so. Type the file name BLASTOFF preceded by its complete path name, for example,

      A:\BLASTOFF

Figure 0.17
"Compiling" Dialog Box

```
═══════════════ Compiling ═══════════════

  Main file: NONAME00.PAS
  Compiling: NONAME00.PAS

  Destination: Memory      Line number:      8
  Free memory:   256k      Total lines:      8

        Compile successful: Press any key
```

and press the Enter key. (The system automatically adds the PAS extension.) After a brief period of disk activity, the Edit window becomes active and the file name **BLASTOFF.PAS** is displayed at the top of it.

14. Since a copy of the file is saved on disk, you can remove the program from the Edit window by pressing both Alt-F to activate the **Window** menu and C to close the window. The desktop is now ready for another program.

If looking at a blank desktop reminds you that you should have made a printed (hard) copy of the program before erasing it, you can quickly call up a file copy from the disk on which it was just saved:

15. Press F3 to open a file and copy it from the disk back into the editor. The system responds by asking for the name of the program to load. Press the Tab key, use the arrow keys to highlight **BLASTOFF.PAS**, and press Enter to select that file and place its name in the Name area. Press the Enter key again to copy the program's source code into the Edit window.

16. Make sure your printer is turned on. Press Alt-F to reveal the **File** menu, and press P to print the contents of the active Edit window.

17. The IDE Help facility also gives assistance with Pascal vocabulary. Put the cursor under the Pascal word *begin* in the Edit window, and press Ctrl-F1. The Help window that appears (see Figure 0.18) explains how *begin* is used in a Pascal program. If the help screen is too small to hold all the necessary help information, press the PgDn (page down) key to display more. Press the Esc key to remove this Help window from the desktop.

18. Leave the Turbo Pascal Programmer's Platform and return to DOS by either pressing Alt-X or choosing **Exit** from the **File** menu.

This exercise samples the more common functions of the Turbo Pascal Programmer's Platform. Additional features are discussed throughout the text. More detailed information on these and other features can be found in the Turbo Pascal User's Guide that accompanies the software.

Figure 0.18
Help Window for begin

```
┌─[■]══════════════ Help ══════════════2:[↑]┐
│                                            ▲
│ ┌──────────────────────────┐              │
│ │ begin ... end construct   │              │
│ └──────────────────────────┘              │
│  This construct is a compound statement. The│
│  "begin" and "end" keywords serve as state-│
│  ment brackets.                            │
│                                            │
│  Syntax:                                   │
│    begin                                   │
│       statement;                           │
│       statement;                           │
│       ...                                  │
│       statement                            │
│    end                                     │
│  When bracketed in this way, any number of │ ▼
└◄■ ▒▒▒▒▒▒▒▒▒▒▒▒▒▒▒▒▒▒▒▒▒▒▒▒▒▒▒ ►┘
```

Store and Forward

[Note: The Store and Forward section at the end of each chapter in this text summarizes the important points presented in that chapter and tells how they prepare you for the topics in succeeding chapters.]

A computer system has hardware components that store, calculate, display, and accept data; it also must have software to tell the hardware what to do. Because computers do not understand human languages and most humans find it difficult to understand the computer's language, compilers were developed to translate instructions from a high-level human language to the object code the computer understands.

The Turbo Pascal integrated development environment (IDE), called the Programmer's Platform, provides the tools and a comfortable atmosphere for creating, editing, and executing programs written in the high-level language called Pascal. An elementary knowledge of how the IDE works is necessary before you can write programs.

The next step is to learn some general strategies for solving problems and apply these strategies to work out problems requiring computer solutions.

Exercises

1. Explain, in general terms, the purpose of the following components of the Turbo Pascal integrated development environment:
   a. **File** menu
   b. Hot keys
   c. Output window
   d. **Save as** option from the **File** menu
   e. Help window

2. Answer the following questions in paragraph form.
   a. What are secondary storage devices, and why are they needed in a computer system?
   b. Distinguish between high-level and low-level computer languages.
   c. What is the purpose of an operating system?
   d. Cite an advantage and a disadvantage of a development environment that uses menus.
   e. What is the difference between the compile and run options in the IDE?

3. Explain, in paragraph form, how each of the following tasks is performed:
   a. Print a program listing.
   b. Cancel the last command chosen in the IDE.
   c. Get help with Pascal vocabulary.
   d. Create an Output window at the bottom of the desktop.
   e. Move the cursor in the Edit window to the beginning of a program.

4. Users often must consult the manuals that accompany software to find out how to perform certain tasks. Using the Turbo Pascal User's Guide, describe how to do each of the following:
   a. Block a portion of text in the Edit window.
   b. Delete a blocked portion of text from the Edit window.
   c. Display the previous Help screen.
   d. Move the cursor to the last error position.
   e. Pick a file from a list of the previous eight files opened.

CHAPTER 1

Elements of Software Design

Key Terms

algorithm	output
debugging	pseudocode
decision structure	software engineering
decomposition	structure chart
documentation	submodule
input	top-down design
iteration structure	walkthrough
module	

Objectives

- To develop a method of creating easy-to-understand, reliable software
- To apply the software methodology to the solution of problems
- To introduce sequential, decision, and repetition structures

1.1 Introduction

In less than 50 years computers have become an integral part of our daily lives: They keep track of bank accounts, control automobiles, and help publish newspapers and periodicals. The decrease in the price of hardware has made computers available to almost everyone. The best hardware in the world, however, is as productive as an expensive paperweight unless the proper operating instructions tell the hardware what to do and how to do it. A collection of such instructions, designed to perform a particular task, is called a program. Both hardware (the computer) and software (the programs) must work together if computers are to become effective in solving problems.

The dictionary defines *problem* as a question proposed for solution. Changing a flat tire, handling an unruly child, and completing an income tax form are all examples of everyday problems requiring solution. Computers cannot solve all problems, of course, but they can provide solutions for certain types of problems.

You can find solutions by a hit-or-miss process, that is, by trying a number of possible methods and hoping to find one that solves the problem. More often than not, this approach leads to a greater expenditure of time and effort than is necessary. A more reasoned approach would be to devise an *algorithm*—a set of rules for solving the problem. And if you expect a computer to help implement your solution, you must have a way to translate the algorithm into a programming language understood by the computer.

Just as there are many spoken languages, so are there many high-level programming languages. If you had to learn another spoken language, how would you choose one? The factors determining your selection might include the number of people who speak that language and whether that language enables you to express your ideas clearly, succinctly, and in an organized fashion. It is for precisely these reasons that Pascal, which allows you to express an algorithm in an organized, concise manner, was chosen for this text.

Our task then is to create a program that produces the correct results demanded by a problem statement. The destination is known; we just need a good road map to get there. This chapter presents the fundamental steps to create road maps that bridge the gap between a problem and its solution.

The link between the input supplied by the problem statement and the output required of its solution can be likened to a trip you might take to a relative's new house. You start the trip with only the input data (the address), and you have no idea how long it will take to get there or whether there are any obstructions or detours. Yet you must reach the new house with the solution—the results asked for in the problem statement.

The roads may be short and straight, or may have curves and potholes. You can't just start the trip without any advance planning. For example, if the trip is a long one, you must make sure to have enough gas before departing, for you may not find many gas stations along the way. A little planning, such as checking a local transportation report and consulting a road map, may save you from wasting time in a traffic backup.

Let's consider a practical example that outlines a process that can be used to create valid, well-written programs. Suppose you want to change the flat tire on a car. Without a plan, nothing would get done. If your plan is to simply call an auto club or service station and have a mechanic change the tire, you still have to know whom and where to call. If, on the other hand, you want to change the tire yourself, you have to know all the steps in the changing process. In either case, you must follow some procedure to get the job done.

The first thing to do is analyze the problem: What is causing your car to slow down, tilt to one side, and make a thumping noise? You pull over to the side of the road, get out of the car, and discover that one of the tires is flat.

Now that you have determined what the problem is, you must consider possible solutions and outline a plan to implement one of them. You may know the steps for changing a tire or be able to find them in the owner's manual. If you decide to call a mechanic, your outlined plan consists of nothing more than getting to a phone, looking up a phone number, calling, and waiting. After reviewing your outline to see whether it is correct, you follow the steps in your plan to make sure the tire is changed.

Even if an outline is correct, however, you can make mistakes in following it. You may have no spare tire, forget to jack up the car before trying to remove the tire, or give the service station the wrong location of the car. To avoid repeating the mistake, you have to recall your original plan and revise it.

The final test is whether you can drive the car with the changed tire. If the lug nuts holding the tire to the axle were not tightened enough and the tire wobbles when you drive, you should retrace the steps in your solution, find out where you went wrong, make appropriate corrections, and try again.

Obviously, there is more than one way to have a flat tire changed, and similarly, there may be many different solutions to any given problem. Some solutions may be easier to understand than others, and some may make more efficient use of available resources, but all must have one thing in common—the solutions must produce the results called for by the problem.

A set of operating procedures similar to the one just discussed can be used to create software that will solve specific problems. (A methodology of this type is an important part of a field called *software engineering*, whose activities also include the conceptualization and implementation of entire software systems.)

1.2 A Software Design Methodology

The following steps can be used to design and construct the computer solution to a problem:

Step 1: Analysis of the problem
Step 2: Modular design of the solution
Step 3: Design of the structure of the modules
Step 4: Production of code
Step 5: Verification of the solution
Step 6: Documentation of the solution

Of the six steps, only Step 4 depends on a particular programming language. The other five steps can be used for computer solutions using any language.

Analysis of the Problem   In order to design the solution to a problem, you must have a clear statement of the problem, including what data is to be entered (*input*) and what results are to be produced (*output*). After a careful reading of the problem,

Figure 1.1
Sample Input/Output
Chart

Input	Output

the input and output quantities specified by the problem statement should be determined. A chart similar to the one in Figure 1.1 can be used to list those quantities.

Suppose, for example, you want to design a problem solution that determines the distance your car can travel on a single full tank of gas (range), given the average miles-per-gallon (mpg) rating of the car and the capacity of the tank, in gallons. The word *given* is a key word in the problem statement, for it implies that the quantities that follow it must be supplied, or input. Other problem statement words indicating that input quantities are being asked for are *input* and *accept.* In this problem, the mpg rating and tank capacity are input values.

Although such clue words often assist in alerting you to needed input quantities, they may not be present in the problem statement. Sometimes you have to read between the lines. The range problem can be restated as follows: "The miles-per-gallon (mpg) rating of a car can be used to find the range of a car, that is, the distance a car can travel on a full tank of gas. Determine this range." Not only does this statement lack any input key words, it does not explicitly state that the size of the tank must be known, information that must be drawn or inferred from the statement of the problem. This is often a difficult task, but it does become easier after solving many problems.

Deciding what results are needed is not as difficult as discovering input quantities, since the desired outcome should be stated explicitly in the statement of the problem. If it is not, the statement requires clarification and rephrasing. Some of the key words that can indicate what results are to be produced are *determine, find, output, calculate, decide,* and *discover.* In this problem, the range is the desired result.

Figure 1.2 summarizes the input and output quantities for this problem.

Modular Design of
the Solution

Although it is possible to write a term paper without any previous planning, this often leads to a poorly constructed composition, with no clear path from the beginning to the end—and a grade that reflects that lack. It is better to construct an outline by listing the major topics and their corresponding subtopics in the order in which they will appear. There should be enough information to give a general idea of the structure and content of the paper. This process gives the writer a chance, before beginning the writing, to

Figure 1.2
Car Range Input/Output
Chart

Input	Output
mpg rating	Range
Tank capacity	

review the organization of the entire paper and make appropriate changes.

You should follow a similar process when designing and constructing a computer solution to a problem: Subdivide it into smaller, more manageable subproblems. The solution is represented by a main *module* and the subproblems are represented by *submodules*. This *decomposition* process, known as *top-down design*, can be graphically represented by a *structure chart* similar to the one in Figure 1.3.

The solution to the car-range problem can be divided into three submodules: one that accepts the required data (mpg rating and tank capacity), a second that determines the range, and a third that displays this result. Figure 1.4 shows the structure chart outlining the solution.

The complexity of the problem and the method of solution may require further decomposition of some or all modules. If constructed properly, the inverted treelike structure that results gives an overall view of the structure of the solution.

You can design the solution entirely on your own, or you can use methods and techniques developed by others to help you. Such outside assistance may come in the form of solution designs to similar problems or from books, articles, or periodicals that supply information on the subject of the given problem. For example, if you wanted to devise the solution to a problem involving mortgage payments, you might look in a business text or speak with someone who works at a bank or mortgage company.

Each successfully solved problem adds to the library of methods and techniques you can call on to solve future problems. Thus, the design and construction of solutions is a cumulative process: The more problems you

Figure 1.3
Sample Structure Chart

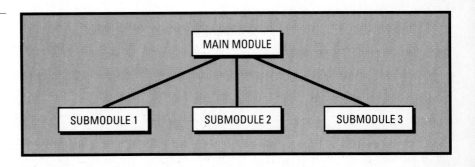

Figure 1.4
Car-Range Structure Chart

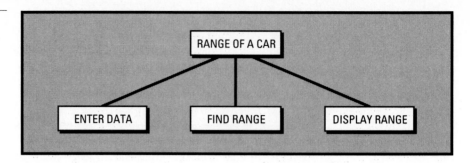

solve, the stronger your background and the easier it is to solve newly posed problems.

Design of the Structure of the Modules

The modules in the previous step were defined in very general terms. In this stage of the design process, you create a detailed outline of the solution for each submodule and combine them to form the complete solution.

Although the outline of a solution for each module may be in diagram form, such as a flowchart, this text utilizes *pseudocode*, an Englishlike outline form similar to the one you might use for a term paper. This informal outline style is chosen because it is relatively simple to learn and easy to understand. It takes minimal space, requires no special equipment such as rulers or templates, and can be transformed into Pascal syntax in a natural, instinctive way.

Returning to the car-range problem, we use English-like descriptions to represent the process for each of the three submodules we want to outline:

```
RANGE OF A CAR
    ENTER DATA
    FIND RANGE
    DISPLAY RANGE

ENTER DATA
    enter a car's mpg rating
    enter its tank capacity in gallons

FIND RANGE
    find the range

DISPLAY RANGE
    output the range
```

The first line in the description of each module is its title, written in all uppercase letters. The steps in a module are indented from the title and written in lowercase letters, unless they represent a call to a submodule, in which case they are written in uppercase letters, as shown in the outline.

Submodule titles are indented further to indicate that they are called by the main module.

In this case the steps (submodules) in the RANGE OF A CAR module are executed in order. The ENTER DATA submodule is called first. The processing continues at that submodule, where it accepts values for mpg rating and tank capacity. Control is then returned to the main module's next step, in which the FIND RANGE submodule is called. The range is calculated in that submodule and processing continues with the last step in RANGE OF A CAR, the call to the DISPLAY RANGE submodule. After following the steps in this submodule, the program returns to the last statement in the main module and stops.

Taking the time to create an outline for a solution that is so obvious may seem unnecessary, but you must practice this process on such simple problems before you can attempt to apply it to larger, more complicated problems. It is in the design of these more sophisticated problems that outlining really pays dividends.

Production of Code

The completed outline is used as a guide in producing code, or writing the instructions to implement the plan. In this text, the module outline written in pseudocode can easily be translated into the structured language Pascal, although other languages can be used.

Verification of the Solution

Unfortunately, reviewing the outline and code of a solution is no guarantee that the solution is correct. Before a program is used with real data, you should make a *walkthrough* of the solution, step by step, using data typical for the problem. The results of these manual calculations should be compared to the results produced by the computer. If there is a match, the solution may be correct; if there is no match, you must find and correct any errors.

Let's walk through the solution to our range problem with some representative data.

ENTER DATA
    enter a car's mpg rating 25
    enter its tank capacity in gallons..13

FIND RANGE
    find the range

        range = mpg rating × tank capacity
             = 25 × 13 = 325 miles

DISPLAY RANGE
    output the range..325 miles

If errors have been detected, they must be removed before the program can be used. The process of removing errors from a program is called *debugging.* It is important to remove errors, or bugs, from a solution as early in the design process as possible. Generally, the later in the process an error is discovered, the more costly—and difficult—it is to correct.

Two types of errors you are likely to find in the debugging process are errors in syntax and errors in logic. Syntax errors result from a misuse of the programming language; they can be as simple as errors in the spelling of essential words and the omission of program punctuation. For example, it is a syntax error if the Pascal word **begin** is spelled **began**.

You do get some assistance in correcting syntax errors. Your program is checked by the Pascal compiler as it is translated into machine-usable code. If the compiler doesn't understand a particular word or punctuation mark, it displays a message to that effect and often indicates the position of the error. Errors of this type are corrected by returning to the coding step in the design process and making the appropriate adjustment.

Logic errors produce incorrect or unexpected results. An example of a logic error would be the use of an improper formula to calculate a particular quantity. You'll still get an answer, but it will not be the correct one.

Logic errors are more difficult to detect and correct than are syntax errors. You may be able to find logic errors by comparing the computed results with those obtained during a manual walkthrough of the solution. Compilers offer little assistance in correcting these errors; you may have to go back to the analysis of the problem to find and correct the error. Unfortunately, this means that all the steps following analysis must also be revised, a time-consuming process. Tools and techniques, such as selecting appropriate test data and top-down testing, are helpful in detecting and correcting logic errors; they are detailed in later chapters.

Documentation of
the Solution

You may find it difficult to construct a model airplane or sew a dress unless you are familiar with all the parts and know how they are to be assembled. Fortunately, most model kits contain directions, and you can buy a pattern that shows you in detail how to make a dress. The designers of the model and the dress recorded what they did so that others could build the model and make the dress. The recording of the steps taken to produce a result is known as *documentation.* Good documentation gives good results: a model that looks good and a dress that fits well. So too it is in software design. Clear, concise, and complete documentation of all the steps in the design process makes a software solution easier to understand, use, and modify.

Documentation can be classified as external or internal. External documentation involves the recording of any part of the design process that is not part of the program. It helps you understand what the program is supposed to do, how it was constructed, and how it operates. Input/output charts and structure charts are examples of external documentation.

Internal documentation describes the program code and aids in understanding the logic of the solution. When you read a textbook, you may write helpful notes in the margins of some pages; internal documentation is the marginal notes of a program. (More details on specifications and implementation of internal documentation are presented in succeeding chapters.)

Don't think that because this step is listed last you can delay documenting the solution until all the other steps are completed. Each step in the process should be recorded as it is done. That way, if you have to return to a previous step, you will have something to help you.

Now let's see how this approach to finding the solution to a problem can be used to set up computer solutions to other problems. Although you can't yet translate our outlines into code, you can practice the other steps in the process.

1.3 Application of Sequential Structures: Heart of the Matter

The heart is a muscle that works 24 hours a day, 7 days a week, every week we live. Given a person's average heartbeat rate, in beats per minute, determine and output how many times his or her heart beats in 1 hour.

Our solution to this problem consists of a sequential structure, since it starts with the input of data, calculates the number of heart beats per hour, and ends with the display of the answer.

STEP 1:
ANALYSIS OF THE PROBLEM

The key word *given* indicates what quantity is to be input (heartbeat rate), and the term *output* signifies the result desired (heartbeats per hour). Figure 1.5 summarizes these findings.

STEP 2:
MODULAR DESIGN OF
THE SOLUTION

The problem can be divided into three subtasks: entering the heartbeat rate, calculating the total number of heartbeats per hour, and displaying that total. A structure chart outlining a solution is shown in Figure 1.6.

The purpose of this step is to get an overall view of how the modules work together. You do not have to specify the structure of each module at this stage.

STEP 3:
DESIGN OF THE STRUCTURE
OF THE MODULES

A sequence of steps for each of the modules follows.

```
HEARTBEAT
    ENTER HEART RATE
    FIND TOTAL BEATS
    OUTPUT TOTAL BEATS
```

Figure 1.5
Heartbeat Input/Output
Chart

Input	Output
Heartbeat rate	Total heartbeats

Figure 1.6
Heartbeat Structure Chart

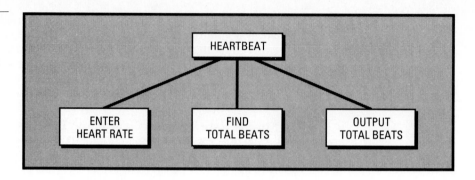

ENTER HEART RATE
   enter number of beats per minute

FIND TOTAL BEATS
   find heartbeats per hour
      (rate per minute × number of minutes per hour)

OUTPUT TOTAL BEATS
   output heartbeats per hour

The number of heartbeats per hour in FIND TOTAL BEATS is the product of the number per minute and the number of minutes in an hour. For example, if a heart beats at 70 beats per minute, the number of beats in an hour is 70 × 60 (the number of minutes in an hour), or 4200.

STEP 4:
PRODUCTION OF CODE

The pseudocode produced in the previous step is readily translated into any programming language. The production of code from the pseudocode would be completed once you have learned Pascal.

STEP 5:
VERIFICATION OF
THE SOLUTION

Let's walk through the solution with some representative data.

ENTER HEART RATE
   enter number of beats per minute 72

FIND TOTAL BEATS
   find heartbeats per hour
      = 72 × 60 = 4,320

OUTPUT TOTAL BEATS
   output heartbeats per hour..4,320

The answer could be determined by hand or by calculator. After the program is coded and executed, the result could be compared with the one produced by the computer to determine the accuracy of the solution. If errors were found in any of the previous steps, they would have to be corrected and the process restarted.

STEP 6:
DOCUMENTATION OF
THE SOLUTION

The structure chart in Step 2 (Figure 1.6) and the pseudocode in Step 3 serve as external documentation for the solution.

1.4 Application of Decision Structures: Checking Your Account

Keeping accurate data on the activity of a checking account can save you from the embarrassment and cost of bouncing a check. Suppose you are given the current balance in a checking account and the amount of a check to be drawn against the account. If there is enough money in the account to cover the check, determine and output the new balance with a "transaction processed" message. If there is not enough money in the account, do not change the balance; output that balance with an "insufficient funds" message.

Our solution to this problem includes a decision, since its output depends on an updated value for the account balance that is determined by the initial balance and the amount of the check to be cashed.

STEP 1:
ANALYSIS OF THE PROBLEM

The input quantities are the current balance and a check amount. The specifications for this problem do not allow negative balances; therefore, the output consists of the new balance and a message indicating whether or not the transaction was processed. Figure 1.7 summarizes the input and output quantities for this problem.

STEP 2:
MODULAR DESIGN OF
THE SOLUTION

The solution design in Figure 1.8 contains six modules on three levels, with a module on the second level calling two on the third level. The main module (CHECK TRANSACTION) first calls a module (ENTER DATA) that accepts the current balance and the amount of a check. After receiving that data, the main module calls TRANSACTION TEST to determine whether there are sufficient funds in the account. The outcome of the decision indicates whether INSUFFICIENT FUNDS or DEDUCT AMOUNT is called. Each of these modules determines the new balance and stores an appropriate message. The last module outputs the results.

STEP 3:
DESIGN OF THE STRUCTURE
OF THE MODULES

Since modules that are called by others should appear in the outline following their calling modules, the outlines for INSUFFICIENT FUNDS and DEDUCT AMOUNT should immediately follow the outline for TRANSACTION TEST.

Figure 1.7
Check Transaction
Input/Output Chart

Input	Output
Current balance	New balance
Amount of check	Message

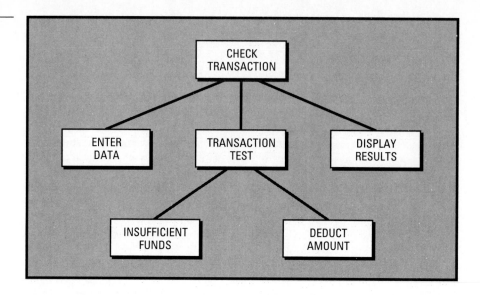

Figure 1.8
Check-Transaction
Structure Chart

The indentation on the lines following *if* and *otherwise* makes it easier to understand this decision structure.

    CHECK TRANSACTION
        ENTER DATA
        TRANSACTION TEST
        DISPLAY RESULTS

    ENTER DATA
        enter the current balance
        enter a check amount

    TRANSACTION TEST
        if check amount is greater than current balance then
            INSUFFICIENT FUNDS
        otherwise
            DEDUCT AMOUNT

    INSUFFICIENT FUNDS
        new balance = current balance
        message is "insufficient funds"

    DEDUCT AMOUNT
        new balance = current balance – check amount
        message is "transaction processed"

DISPLAY RESULTS
    output the new balance
    output the message

In the TRANSACTION TEST module, if the check amount is greater than the current balance, the module INSUFFICIENT FUNDS is called and the *otherwise* sequence is skipped. If the current balance is greater than or equal to the amount of the check, the *then* sequence (INSUFFICIENT FUNDS module) is skipped and the DEDUCT AMOUNT module is called to update the balance and save an appropriate message. After either INSUFFICIENT FUNDS or DEDUCT AMOUNT is executed, the results are output using the last module.

STEP 4:
PRODUCTION OF CODE

As in the previous application, this step would be completed once you have learned Pascal.

STEP 5:
VERIFICATION OF
THE SOLUTION

Using the outline for the main module as a guide, let's walk through the solution with one set of data.

ENTER DATA
    enter the current balance $451.32
    enter a check amount..$170.01

TRANSACTION TEST
    the check amount is *not* greater than current balance
        (skip the *then* part)
    otherwise

    DEDUCT AMOUNT
        new balance = current balance – check amount
            = \$451.32 – \$170.01 = \$281.31
        message is "transaction processed"

DISPLAY RESULTS
    output the new balance $281.31
    output the message ....transaction processed

This data set tests the *otherwise* part of the decision structure. Choose some data to test the *then* part.

ENTER DATA
    enter the current balance $692.45
    enter a check amount..$901.22

TRANSACTION TEST
    the check amount is greater than current balance then

INSUFFICIENT FUNDS

new balance = $692.45

message is "insufficient funds"

(skip the *otherwise* part)

DISPLAY RESULTS

output the new balance $692.45

output the message ....insufficient funds

We have now tested both possibilities in the decision structure; if the computer results agree, we can be reasonably certain of the correctness of the solution.

If any errors were found in any of the previous steps, they would have to be corrected and the process restarted.

STEP 6:
DOCUMENTATION OF
THE SOLUTION

The structure chart in Step 2 and the pseudocode in Step 3 serve as external documentation for the solution.

1.5 Application of Repetition Structures: Feeding the Hungry

Suppose that every 10 years the population of a city doubles and that the available food supply is capable of feeding only 2,000 additional residents. Given an initial population of a city and how many people that city can feed, find the year in which the population outgrows its food supply.

The solution to this problem contains a repetition structure, since the process of doubling the population and increasing the food supply must be repeated until population overtakes the food supply.

STEP 1:
ANALYSIS OF THE PROBLEM

The input quantities are the starting year, the initial population, and the population that could be supported by the food supply in that year. Every 10 years, the population doubles while the potential to feed 2,000 is added to the food supply. When the population is larger than the food supply, stop and output the year. Figure 1.9 shows the input and output quantities.

Figure 1.9
Population Food Supply
Input/Output Chart

Input		Output
Population		Year
Food supply		
Year		

STEP 2:
MODULAR DESIGN OF
THE SOLUTION

The problem can be divided into three subtasks: entering the necessary data (year, population, and food supply), updating that data, and displaying the year when the population outgrows the food supply. A structure chart outlining the solution is shown in Figure 1.10.

STEP 3:
DESIGN OF THE STRUCTURE
OF THE MODULES

POPULATION/FOOD SUPPLY
    ENTER DATA
    UPDATE DATA
    DISPLAY YEAR

ENTER DATA
    enter the initial year
    enter the initial population
    enter the initial food supply

UPDATE DATA
    repeat
        add 10 to the year
        double the population
        add 2,000 to the food supply
    until the population > food supply

DISPLAY YEAR
    output the last value of year

The indentation on the lines following *repeat* makes it easier to see which steps are to be repeated. Repetition structures such as these are sometimes called *iteration structures* or *loops*. If the population is less than or equal to the food supply, the indented steps must be repeated with the most recent values of the year, population, and food supply. When the population exceeds the food supply, the iteration structure ends and the final value of the year is output.

Figure 1.10
Population Food Supply
Structure Chart

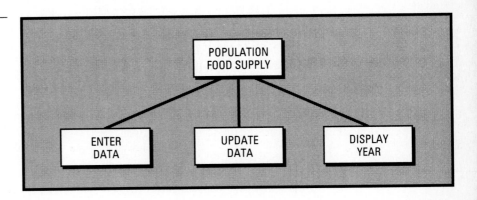

STEP 4:
PRODUCTION OF CODE

The pseudocode is translated into a programming language to determine the solution.

STEP 5:
VERIFICATION OF
THE SOLUTION

Let's walk through the solution with one set of data, using the execution order provided by the main module.

ENTER DATA
    enter the initial year 1990
    enter the initial population 1,000
    enter the initial food supply 30,000

UPDATE DATA
  repeat
    add 10 to the year..2000
    double the population 2,000
    add 2,000 to the food supply 32,000
  2,000 is not greater than 32,000

  repeat
    add 10 to the year..2010
    double the population 4,000
    add 2,000 to the food supply 34,000
  4,000 is not greater than 34,000

  repeat
    add 10 to the year..2020
    double the population 8,000
    add 2,000 to the food supply 36,000
  8,000 is not greater than 36,000

  repeat
    add 10 to the year..2030
    double the population 16,000
    add 2,000 to the food supply 38,000
  16,000 is not great then 38,000

  repeat
    add 10 to the year..2040
    double the population 32,000
    add 2,000 to the food supply 40,000
  32,000 is not greater than 40,000

repeat
    add 10 to the year 2050
    double the population 64,000
    add 2,000 to the food supply 42,000
64,000 is greater than 42,000

DISPLAY YEAR
    output the last value of year 2050

The steps in the loop were repeated six times, until the population became greater than the food supply. Again, the results should be compared to those produced by the computer to check for accuracy.

If errors were found in any of the steps, they would have to be corrected and the process restarted.

STEP 6:
DOCUMENTATION OF
THE SOLUTION

The work done in the previous steps serves as external documentation for the solution.

These examples illustrate the three fundamental structures used in the creation of a program solution to a problem: a simple sequence of steps (the heartbeat problem); a *decision structure*, in which only one of two or more options is executed (the checking account problem); and an *iteration structure*, in which a sequence of steps is repeated until a specified condition is met (the food supply problem).

Store and Forward

Solving problems is a necessary and sometimes difficult process. If you take enough time in the planning stage, however, the solution is generally reliable, logical, and easy to understand. With this in mind, this chapter has presented a six-step process for planning and implementing problem solutions: (1) analyze the problem, (2) create a modular design for the solution, (3) design the modules' structure, (4) produce code from the module structures, (5) test the solution, and (6) ensure that the solution process is completely documented.

The next step is to create Pascal code from the design. Chapter 2 introduces the structure and basic components common to all Pascal programs. The succeeding chapters will increase your knowledge of Pascal and help you to learn techniques that can improve your problem-solving skills.

Exercises

1. Answer the following questions.
   a. The software design methodology described in this chapter is language independent except for Step 4 (Production of Code). Explain what this means.
   b. Why are errors in the specifications determined in the analysis phase of the software design methodology generally more costly to correct if not caught early?
   c. What is an advantage of decomposing a problem solution into submodules?
   d. What are two advantages of using an English-like pseudocode for the design of individual modules?
   e. Distinguish between syntax errors and logic errors.
   f. Distinguish between internal and external documentation.
   g. At which stage of the software design methodology should documentation take place? Justify your answer.

Elementary Problems

For each of the following exercises, decide which of the fundamental programming structures (sequential, decision, and repetition) are used in the solution, then employ steps 1, 2, 3, and 5 of the software design methodology to obtain a solution. These steps are repeated here for your convenience:

Step 1: Analysis of the problem
Step 2: Modular design of the solution
Step 3: Design of the structure of the modules
Step 5: Verification of the solution

2. A census report indicated that there were 9,453,000 boys aged 5 and under in the United States in 1985. If the expected growth rate for this age group between 1985 and 1990 is 4% over the 5-year period, find the expected population in 1990.

3. The English Department of a midwestern college awards departmental honors for students achieving a grade point average (GPA) of 3.65 or above in all major-level English courses. Accept a student's name and English GPA, and output a message indicating whether a student has gained honors or not.

4. Determine the total cost of a purchase of video cassette tapes given the cost of a single tape and the number of tapes purchased.

5. Lefty Romero hit 12, 8, 15, 20 and 17 home runs during his first 5 years in the major leagues. Find the average number of home runs hit by Lefty over that period.

6. The following formula converts Fahrenheit temperatures (F) to Celsius temperatures (C):

$$C = \frac{5(F-32)}{9}$$

Given a Fahrenheit temperature, output its corresponding Celsius temperature.

7. One method of determining whether someone is overweight is to find the ratio of that person's weight (in pounds) to height (in inches). For example, the average weight-to-height (wh) ratio for women is 2.42. Given a man's height and weight, calculate and output his wh ratio.

8. For a genetic laboratory experiment, a student starts out with two fruit flies. The fly population doubles every day. Determine how many days it would take for the fly population to reach 80.

9. In the same genetic laboratory experiment as in Exercise 8, find the fly population if the experiment starts with two flies and is allowed to continue for 14 days.

10. Find the straight-line depreciation value for an item, given the purchase price, the salvage value, and the number of years over which the item is to be depreciated. The straight-line value is the difference between the purchase price and the salvage value, divided by the number of years.

11. If an input value consists of the time of day in 24-hour notation, output that time in the standard AM/PM form. For example, if the time 14:32 were entered, the solution would be 2:32 PM.

Challenging Problems

12. A cord of wood occupies a volume of 128 ft³. Find the number of cords contained in a box-shaped pile of wood, given the length, width, and height of the pile.

13. The nature of the roots of a quadratic equation in the form $ax^2 + bx + c = 0$ is determined by the value of its discriminant, $b^2 - 4ac$. Find the number and type of roots of an equation whose coefficients are a, b, and c.

14. Given a series of positive integers, or whole numbers, find the largest in the series. The number of integers in the series is not known in advance. Enter −1 to end the input phase of the process.

15. It costs a company $850,000 to manufacture color monitors for computers. The selling price of a single monitor is $450. Determine the average number of monitors the company would have to sell every month in order to break even for the year.

16. The Continental Basketball League awards points to competing teams using the following criteria: A team receives one point for each quarter in which it outscores an opponent and receives three points for outscoring the opponent

for the entire game. For example, if Team A outscores Team B in three of the four quarters, but Team B wins the game, Team A would receive 3 points (1 for each quarter it outscored Team B) and Team B would receive 4 points (1 for the only quarter it outscored Team A and 3 for winning the game). Find the number of points awarded to each team, given the number of points each team scored in a quarter.

17. The numbers on the jerseys of basketball players can be at most two digits, each of which must be an integer from 0 to 5. Accept a possible jersey number for a basketball player and determine whether that number is legal or not.

18. A union has accepted a 6% increase in pay 4 months after its contract expired. The company must now reimburse all employees for the 4 months they worked under their previous salaries. As part of the agreement, this retroactive pay is to be spread out over the next 6 months. Given an employee's yearly salary before the increase, find his or her monthly salary for the 6 months following the settlement.

19. In the children's game Rock, Paper, and Scissors, two participants simultaneously throw out a fist (rock), two fingers (scissors), or four fingers (paper). Rock "smashes" scissors, scissors "cut" paper, and paper "covers" rock. Accept a throw by players A and B and determine the winner.

20. Find the number of guesses needed to determine someone's weight in a game in which the guesser is told whether his or her prediction is too high or too low and continues to guess until the correct weight is deduced.

21. Determine the cost of gasoline used in an automobile trip, given a car's miles-per-gallon rating, the distance traveled, and the average price per gallon paid for the gas.

CHAPTER 2
Components of a Pascal Program

Key Terms

begin	**integer**
binary number	keyword
bit	**longint**
boolean	**procedure**
char	**program**
const	**real**
constant	reserved word
data type	**string**
end	**type**
e-notation	**var**
identifier	variable

Objectives

- To introduce the concept of a data type
- To describe different Pascal data types and show how to define them
- To distinguish between constants and variables
- To describe the basic components of all Pascal programs and how they work together
- To apply documentation principles to Pascal programs
- To give an example of a complete Pascal program

2.1 Introduction

In the previous chapter we developed a six-step method for designing software to solve a given problem. This process left out one important step—the production of code. In this chapter you will learn how to add this step to the design methodology and implement it using the structured programming language Pascal.

The Pascal language, named after the seventeenth century French mathematician Blaise Pascal, was developed in the early 1960s by Niklaus Wirth. His intention was to create a language suitable for solving problems via an organized methodology rather than a hit-or-miss approach. This makes Pascal a fitting vehicle for the software design process described in Chapter 1.

In order to learn any language, you must first start with an understanding of its basic vocabulary and a set of rules governing grammar and syntax; that is, you must understand how the words in the vocabulary are combined to form coherent, comprehensible sentences and paragraphs.

In general, a Pascal program consists of a collection of statements that direct the computer to perform specific tasks. For the most part, each statement contains at least one *keyword* that is predefined by the creator of the language. Some of these keywords are called *reserved words* because they cannot be used for anything but their intended purpose. In this text, Pascal keywords consist of all lowercase letters and are presented in **boldface** type.

Each program statement may also contain identifiers that have been defined by the programmer for the purpose of referencing particular data items. In specifying these identifiers, the programmer must determine the type of data each references so that the system interprets the data properly.

2.2 Simple Data Types

There are two basic *data types*. Early computers were developed to accept numeric data only, perform calculations, and produce results. More recent applications have made increasing use of nonnumeric data, consisting of keyboard characters, words, and the logical values true and false.

Numeric Data Types

Numbers with no fractional or decimal parts are called *whole numbers*, or *integers*, while those with fractional or decimal parts are called *real numbers*, or *reals*. The numbers 34, –456, and 1024 are all examples of integers. Because –43.56 has a decimal part, it is not an integer. The legal (acceptable) range for integer values varies from system to system. In Turbo Pascal, for example, integers may range from –32768 to 32767. Although plus (+) and minus (–) signs precede integers to indicate positive or negative values, an integer with no sign preceding it is presumed to be positive; 234 is therefore equivalent to +234. Minus signs must be used to indicate negative values.

Commas or decimal points may *not* be used in expressing integer values in Pascal. The value 1,204, for example, must be expressed as 1024, and 76.0 as 76, if an integer specification is desired. In ordinary arithmetic, commas often make large integers easier to understand. Commas in the representation of a single integer value in Pascal, however, are likely to cause the computer to misinterpret it.

Turbo Pascal also defines a numeric data type called **longint** (for "long integer") that allows you to work with integers larger or smaller than normal integer types. The range for long integers is from –2147483648 to 2147483647.

Real numbers, or reals, are those with decimal or fractional parts. Thus, 12345.678, –6.123, and –0.000583 are examples of real numbers.

Scientific notation, or *e-notation*, simplifies the representation of very large numbers, very small numbers, and numbers requiring many decimal positions to produce precise results. In this notation, a value is expressed as a real multiplied by a power of 10. Very large (positive) or very small (negative) real numbers are those with many digits to the left of the decimal point. 546730.354 and 91503200.111 are examples of reals with large values; –5429678.1 and –7223987.4567 are examples of reals with small values. The real value 1234000000.0 can be entered or displayed as 1.234e+9, or 1.234 times 10^9. (Again, as with integers, you may *not* use commas to express a large value.) The 1.234 (called the *mantissa*) comes from the significant digits in the original number, and the +9 (the *exponent*) represents the number of positions the decimal point is moved to the *left* from its place in the original representation (after the last 0) to its position in the e-notation representation (between the 1 and the 2). In similar fashion, –456700000000 can be represented as –4.567e+11. If no sign precedes either the mantissa or the exponent, it is assumed to be positive. Here are some examples.

Standard notation	Scientific notation (e-notation)	Mantissa	Exponent
76321.489	7.6321489e+4	7.6321489	4
8631000.0	8.631e+6	8.631	6
–91400000.0	–9.14e+7	–9.14	7

A real number that requires a large number of positions following the decimal point can also be represented using e-notation. The real number 0.00000000007654 can be expressed as 7.654e–11, with the –11 indicating the number of positions the decimal point is moved to the *right* from its place in the original representation to its position in e-notation (between the 7 and the 6). For example:

Standard notation	Scientific notation (e-notation)	Mantissa	Exponent
–0.00000121	–1.21e-6	–1.21	–6
0.0000000426	4.26e-8	4.26	–8
0.000191567	1.19567e-4	1.19567	–4

Pascal requires at least one digit to the left of the decimal point for expressing real numbers. An error results if this convention is not followed. For example, the number .000135 is not acceptable; it must be written as 0.000135 before it is interpreted properly.

The range of acceptable real numbers varies from one version of Pascal to another. Turbo Pascal allows real values from 2.9e–39 through 1.7e38, with a mantissa of up to 12 places to the right of the decimal point.

Nonnumeric Data Types

The character data type consists of one letter, number, or special character that can be produced by a keyboard, such as @, a, H, 9, *, and]. If a single digit is of type **char** (short for *character*), you cannot perform any numerical operations on that digit (for example, adding it to any integer).

The **string** data type (available in nonstandard versions of Pascal) is a collection of characters; it can be thought of as an extension of the **char** data type. Turbo Pascal permits a single string to contain up to 255 characters. Some examples of string data are *SSN*, *@$2.75*, *George Washington*, and *666 Fifth Avenue*.

Although you can define numeric values as type **string**, you cannot then use them in mathematical calculations. To perform calculations with numeric values, they must be defined as either type **integer**, **longint**, or **real**.

Quantities of type **boolean** have only the values true or false. Boolean data is used when the computer is called on to make decisions.

2.3 Identifiers

Identifiers are names that represent quantities linking them to specific locations in main memory. In Turbo Pascal, identifiers must start with a letter or an underscore character (_) and can be followed by a combination of 62 additional letters, digits, and underscore characters. Not all combinations are possible, since Pascal reserved words can be used only for specific purposes.

Identifiers must be unique; that is, you should never use identical identifiers to represent different quantities in the same program, even if the quantities are of different types.

Table 2.1 lists examples of some acceptable and unacceptable identifier names.

Table 2.1
Examples of Identifier Names

Acceptable	Unacceptable (and Reason Why)	
netpay	amount$	($ not allowed)
side2	7up	(Cannot begin with a number)
total	low value	(Blank not allowed)
wordcount	case	(Reserved word)

Constants

Quantities with values that do not change in a program are called *constants* and are represented by constant identifiers. For example, if you need a fixed tax rate for many calculations in a program, you can declare that value to be a constant. Make sure such values do not change, since any attempt to change them results in an error.

Variables

Quantities that can have different values are called *variables* and are represented by variable identifiers. For example, the variable identifier *wholeprice*, representing the wholesale price of an item, can take on several values during the execution of a program. Since Pascal treats constants and variables differently, you must specify whether this identifier is a constant or a variable.

2.4 Data Definitions

All data are eventually transformed into the *binary number* system by the Pascal compiler. In this system, quantities are represented by bit strings, or collections of 0s and 1s. (The word *bit* is an abbreviation for *binary digit.*) A bit string can be interpreted by the computer in many different ways. For example, 1000001 can represent the letter A, the decimal value 65, or a true followed by five falses and another true. Since you are the only one who determines how the data is to be interpreted, you must inform the computer in the declaration section of a program.

Constant Declaration

Identifiers that represent quantities whose values do not change must be specified in a constant declaration.

FORMAT: **const**
    `<identifier> = <value>;`
    `<identifier> = <value>;`
          `...`

The declaration starts with the reserved word **const** (short for constant), followed by the identifier name you have chosen, the equal sign (=), and the constant value assigned to the location represented by the name. A semicolon concludes the declaration. In general, semicolons end every Pascal statement (in the same way a period marks the end of an English sentence). When this statement is executed, an appropriate amount of memory is allocated for the storage of the data found in the declaration statement.

In this text, certain notation and placement conventions are followed when illustrating Pascal statement formats and program instructions. For example, `<identifier>` represents any acceptable identifier name; the angle brackets (`<`, `>`) are not part of the name. In a similar fashion, `<value>` represents the value assigned to `<identifier>` and also does not include `<` and `>`. The square brackets enclosing the last two lines of the format signify that this part of the format is optional; that is, one or more additional constants may be defined in the same **const** section.

Example

```
const
  e = 2.71;
  switch = true;
  yes = 'y';
  maxsize = 100;
```

The value 2.71 is assigned to the real constant *e*; *true*, to the Boolean constant *switch*; the letter *y*, to the character constant named *yes*; and 100, to the integer constant *maxsize*.

The names chosen for identifiers should indicate what each represents. The data types for constant identifiers are not explicitly specified but are determined by the values assigned to those identifiers. For example, *e* is a real constant since it is assigned a real value.

You may be wondering why constant identifiers are used at all, and why you can't just put the constant value in the program where you need it. There are several reasons for declaring identifiers for constants. The first involves generality and flexibility. Suppose a tax rate is part of several statements in a program. If the rate is changed, you have to modify all occurrences of it. If you assign that value to a constant identifier called *taxrate*, however, you would have to change only the value assigned in the declaration. A second reason is related to processing efficiency. Before processing can take place, all data must be translated into a bit string and stored in a location represented by an identifier. Each time that identifier is referenced, the binary value is used. If a constant value is placed in many parts of the program and not in the declaration section, each occurrence of that value must be translated to binary form each time it is referenced, a time-consuming process. Finally, using an identifier for a constant value gives a clearer indication of the purpose of that value. The constant identifier *interestrate* suggests that its value represents an interest rate, whereas the value 0.065 does not.

STYLE TIP	Although you can choose any name for your identifier, it is good practice to select a name that symbolizes what the constant represents. For example, the identifier *rebate* might be appropriate for a fixed amount of money returned to a buyer for a purchase. Constant identifiers should be used whenever they are needed to improve a program's executing efficiency and maintainability.

Variable Declaration

Identifiers that represent quantities whose values are expected to change are defined in a variable declaration.

FORMAT:
```
var
   <identifier list> : <type>;
   <identifier list> : <type>;
          ...
```

A variable declaration starts with the reserved word **var** (an abbreviation for "variable"), followed by a list of identifiers separated by commas, the colon (:), and the value type for each item in the preceding list. A semicolon ends each declaration type. The Pascal keywords and the built-in data types they represent are shown in Table 2.2. When the **var** statement is compiled, an appropriate amount of memory is allocated for the storage of the data types specified by the declaration statement.

The **string** type in Turbo Pascal should include the maximum number of characters it can contain, enclosed in the square brackets [and]. For example, **string[20]** sets aside enough space to accommodate 20 characters; more than 20 characters in the string results in an error.

The same notation and placement conventions established for constant

Table 2.2
Turbo Pascal Type
Identifiers

Identifier	Type
boolean	Boolean
char	character
integer	integer
longint	long integer
real	real
string[ ]	string

declarations are followed for variable declarations: `<identifier list>` represents any acceptable list of identifiers separated by commas; the angle brackets (`<` and `>`) are not part of the identifier names. The data type assigned to `<identifier>` is represented by `<type>`; the `<` and `>` are not included. The square brackets enclosing the last two lines of the format signify that this part of the format is optional; that is, one or more additional identifier lists may be defined if needed.

Example

```
var
  name : string[20];
  state : string[10];
  payment : real;
  answer : boolean;
  count, total : integer;
```

The identifier called *name* is designated for string storage with a maximum capacity of 20 characters, while the **string** type *state* can store a maximum of 10. Real data can be stored in *payment*, only true or false for *answer*, and integer values for both *count* and *total*.

STYLE TIP

Although you can choose any name for an identifier, it is good practice to select a name that symbolizes what the variable represents. Several identifier lists may be defined in a single variable declaration. For example, one **var** section can be used to declare identifiers to represent both someone's name and corresponding address. The two-space indentation of each variable list declaration under the reserved word **var** simplifies recognition of identifiers defined as variables.

Type Declaration

The type declaration allows you to create a data type or to give a different name to an existing one.

FORMAT: **type**

```
<identifier list> = <definition>;
<identifier list> = <definition>;
                 . . .
```

The declaration starts with the reserved word **type,** followed by a type identifier name, the equal sign (**=**), the definition of the type represented by the identifier, and a semicolon. Several identifiers may be defined under a single type declaration.

A **type** statement declaration defines a data type not already known by the system and must be defined *before* the variable declaration statement using it. Storage is not allocated when a type declaration is compiled; only when the variable declaration using that declared type is compiled.

STYLE TIP	Although you may choose any name for your identifier, it is good practice (1) to select a name that is representative of the type definition and (2) to end that name with the word *type*. Using this convention, you can always clearly distinguish type identifiers from constant and variable identifiers. For example, you can define a type called *employeetype* and not worry about having it mistaken for a constant or a variable called *employee*.

Example

```
type
  digittype = 0..9;
  moneytype = real;
  nametype = string[20];

var
  price, salary : moneytype;
  phonebutton : digittype;
  name : nametype;
```

The **type** declaration defines legal values for any variable of type *digittype* to range from 0 through 9. The two dots in this statement indicate that all the integers between the values preceding and following the dots are to be included. The type *moneytype* is identical to the type **real**. A variable of type *nametype* is a string with maximum capacity of 20 characters. At this stage, no memory is allocated since no variables have been defined.

In the next step, the variable declaration defines and allocates memory for the identifiers *price* and *salary*, of type *moneytype*, the identifier *phonebutton*, of type *digittype*, and the identifier *name*, of type *nametype*.

2.5 Key Components of a Pascal Program

Each Pascal program must have a name as well as indications of where the program begins and ends. The top-down approach to program design also points out the need for a way to code submodules, and Pascal obliges by providing subprograms called *procedures* for this purpose. This section introduces enough about procedures to use them in solving basic programming problems. Additional information about the use of procedures is presented in later chapters.

Program Names

The first line of each program should be a program header containing the reserved word **program** and an identifier that represents the name assigned to the program.

FORMAT: `program <identifier>;`

The reserved word **program** is followed by a legal identifier, and the statement ends with a semicolon. (As a matter of convention in this text, all program names start with an uppercase letter.)

Example

`program Population;`	`Population` identifies the program that follows this line.

The begin-end Pair

The reserved word **begin** signifies the beginning of the body of code comprising the program; the reserved word **end** followed by a period (.) indicates the termination of that body of code. Although it doesn't do anything, here's an example of the most fundamental Pascal program:

```
program Fundamental;
begin
end.
```

Procedures

The instructions that make up submodules in top-down design can be included in a Pascal structure called a *procedure*. Procedures can be thought of as small programs, subprograms, within or called by the main program. In fact, the main program might consist only of calls to subprograms.

FORMAT: `procedure <identifier>;`

This statement begins with the reserved word **procedure**, followed by a legal identifier; it ends with a semicolon. A procedure takes the same form as an entire program in that it can have its own declaration section and must start with **begin**. The last statement in a procedure is **end**, followed by a semicolon. (As previously indicated, the last statement for a main program is **end**, followed by a period.)

STYLE TIP	Begin a procedure name with an uppercase letter. If the name consists of more than one word, the first letter of each word is also uppercase, with no space between words. This convention will make it easier to spot procedure names when examining a program.

Example

```
procedure DoNothing;
begin
end;
```

DoNothing identifies a procedure that contains no other statements and whose last statement is **end** followed by a semicolon.

2.6 Program Documentation

Documentation of the solution is one of the steps discussed earlier in the software design methodology. It includes a written record of all phases of the process. Certain symbols in Pascal allow you to make comments about a part of a program without affecting program execution.

An opening brace ({) signifies the beginning of a comment and a closing brace (}) the end. For systems whose keyboards lack braces, the beginning of a comment is denoted by an opening parenthesis followed immediately by an asterisk: (*. The end of the comment is indicated by an asterisk followed immediately by a closing parenthesis: *). Mistakenly leaving a space between an asterisk and a parenthesis can cause entire sections of code to be treated as a single comment.

Example

```
{ This is a comment. }
(* So is this. *)
```

Both of these expressions can serve as comments in a Pascal program.

Anything enclosed within the comment opener and closer is ignored when a program is executed, with the exception of another comment. In general, you should not put one comment inside another, since the end of the inner comment will be interpreted as the end of the outer one.

Example

```
{ outer { inner } comment }
```

The brace following *inner* is interpreted as the end of the outer comment. The compiler does not know how to translate *comment* }.

Every program should contain enough documentation to allow someone who understands programming (but who did not write the program) to understand what the program is designed to do and how it is done. A properly documented program includes:

The title of the program
The name of the creator of the program
The date the program was completed
A description of the system on which the program was designed
    to execute
A brief description of the purpose of the program
A summary of the input data the program accepts
A summary of the results to be output
A description of the function of each identifier in the program
Any other information that would help someone understand the
    logic of the solution

An example of documentation that might be used at the beginning of a program follows.

```
{------------------------------------------------------------ }
{  PROGRAM:      Property Tax                                 }
{  PROGRAMMER:   John Q. Public                               }
{  DATE:         February 2, 1990                             }
{                                                             }
{  This program determines the amount of tax owed by          }
{  a home owner based on the assessed value of that           }
{  owner's home and a tax rate of 5.25%.                      }
{                                                             }
{  INPUT:        the assessed value of a house                }
{                                                             }
{  OUTPUT:       the amount of tax owed                       }
{------------------------------------------------------------ }
```

STYLE TIP

Separate introductory documentation from the rest of a program by surrounding it with a "comment box," thus making it easier to pick out the executable and nonexecutable portions of the program. The information in this comment box is neatly organized, with blank lines inserted to emphasize important information.

It is easy to become overambitious and provide too much documentation. Sometimes this is worse than providing too little, since the logic of the program easily can get lost.

This text, especially in its initial chapters, stresses the placement, type, and amount of documentation for a program.

2.7 Putting the Parts Together

Every Pascal program has three major sections: the program header section, the declaration section, and the processing section. The program header section consists of the **program** statement naming the program. This is followed by the declaration section, which starts with the constant declaration, followed, in order, by the type declaration, the variable declaration, and any procedures. A procedure must appear before the statement that calls it. The processing section contains the body of the main program. Figure 2.1 shows the fundamental structure of a Pascal program.

2.8 A Sample Pascal Program

So far this discussion has been largely theoretical. The structure of a program and a small collection of Pascal statements have been discussed, but you haven't yet written a working program. The completely documented Pascal program in Figure 2.2 illustrates structure and form and shows a sample of the output.

Figure 2.1
Structure of a
Pascal Program

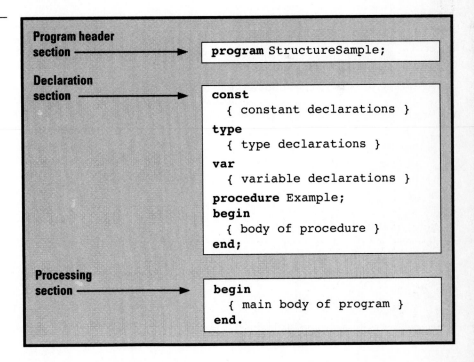

```
program StructureSample;

const
   { constant declarations }
type
   { type declarations }
var
   { variable declarations }
procedure Example;
begin
   { body of procedure }
end;

begin
   { main body of program }
end.
```

Figure 2.2
TaxCalculation
Program Listing and
Sample Output

```pascal
program TaxCalculation;
{--------------------------------------------------------------------}
{ PROGRAM:        Property Tax                                       }
{ PROGRAMMER:     John Q. Public                                     }
{ DATE:           February 2, 1990                                   }
{                                                                    }
{ This program determines the amount of tax owed by a home owner in one }
{ year based on the assessed value of that owner's home and an annual }
{ tax rate of 5.25%.                                                 }
{                                                                    }
{ INPUT:          value: assessed value of a house                  }
{                                                                    }
{ OUTPUT:         taxamount: amount of tax owed                      }
{--------------------------------------------------------------------}
  const
    taxrate = 0.0525;                                    { tax rate }
  type
    moneytype = real;                            { monetary amounts }
  var
    value,                                { assessed value of house }
    taxamount                                 { amount of tax owed }
      : moneytype;

  procedure EnterAssessedValue;
  {------------------------------------------------------------------}
  { Accept assessed value of house                                  }
  {------------------------------------------------------------------}
  begin
    Write ('Enter assessed value of house: $');
    Readln (value)
  end;

  procedure FindTaxAmount;
  {------------------------------------------------------------------}
  { Find the amount of tax owed                                     }
  {------------------------------------------------------------------}
  begin
    taxamount := value * taxrate
  end;
```

```
procedure OutputTax;
{------------------------------------------------------------------}
{ Output amount of tax owed                                        }
{------------------------------------------------------------------}
begin
   Writeln ('Amount of tax to be paid: $', taxamount:9:2)
end;

begin
   EnterAssessedValue;
   FindTaxAmount;
   OutputTax
end.
```

──────── **Output** ────────

```
Enter assessed value of house: $185000
Amount of tax to be paid: $   9712.50
```

Although a sample programming session was presented in Chapter 0, enter and execute this program on your system to get additional practice in entering and executing a program.

Store and Forward

Programs are designed to process different types of data: integer, long integer, real, character, string, and Boolean. Names, or identifiers, can represent the name of a program, procedures, or quantities whose values vary or remain constant. Identifiers are essential elements in the three fundamental components of all Pascal programs: the program header section, the declaration section, and the processing section. Even though the identifiers may be good reminders of what they represent, they are not enough; internal documentation should be included to record all important information needed to understand a program. The output of a program also should be documented to explain the displayed results.

This basic understanding of the structure of a Pascal program now can be incorporated into the software design method and used to produce accurate computer solutions to practical problems. The next steps are: determine how to enter data into the computer (input data), and display results of the calculations it performs (output data).

Snares and Pitfalls

All programming languages have strict sets of rules that govern their use. If you don't follow the rules, you may not get what you expect. Even though the Pascal compiler provides assistance in detecting some of these errors, it is better to develop good skills and thus avoid errors whenever possible.

- *Using improper characters in an identifier name:* Turbo Pascal allows only letters, numerals, and the underscore character (_) for identifier names. Characters other than these, including spaces, produce errors.

- *Using a reserved word as an identifier.* An error results if an attempt is made to use a reserved word as an identifier in a Turbo Pascal program.

- *Forgetting to end Pascal statements with semicolons:* The semicolon indicates the end of a Pascal statement. Its omission often leads to errors.

- *Attempting to change the value of a constant identifier.* No statement in a program can modify the value assigned to a constant identifier. A programmer can change the value by rewriting the **const** declaration for the identifier.

- *Omitting the period after* **end** *at the end of the program:* The period following **end** indicates the end of a program. If it does not appear, Pascal expects additional code.

- *Omitting the semicolon after* **end** *in a procedure:* The semicolon following **end** indicates the end of a procedure. If it does not appear, Pascal expects additional code in the procedure.

- *Improperly closing a comment:* All statements and instructions enclose between comment characters are ignored during execution. If you open a comment but forget to close it, your entire program becomes a comment. If one comment is contained within another, the end of the inner comment is interpreted as the end of the outer comment.

- *Omitting a* **begin** *or an* **end**: The reserved words **begin** and **end** must occur in pairs. Leaving one or the other out can produce errors.

- *Improperly ordering declaration statements:* Declarations for the main program or a procedure should occur in the following order: **const**, **type**, then **var**.

Exercises

1. Answer the following questions.
   a. Why are declaration statements used in a Pascal program?
   b. How does the computer determine how a sequence of bits is to be interpreted?
   c. Why should the **type** declaration come before the **var** declaration in a program?
   d. Why is program documentation an important part of software design?
   e. Why is too much program documentation just as bad as too little?

2. Each part of this exercise represents a single data value. Classify each as **real**, **integer**, **longint**, **char**, **string**, or **boolean**. If the value does not fit in any of these categories, say so. String and character values are enclosed in single quotation marks; for example, 'printer' would be considered a string.
   a. 123e–4
   b. 0.456
   c. 23197
   d. 'word'
   e. –1.23e–4
   f. false
   g. .956
   h. 'x'
   i. 'false'
   j. '62500'
   k. –1.23e+4
   l. 62500
   m. 1.23e4
   n. 0.011235
   o. 62,500
   p. 'letter'

3. Classify each of the following Pascal statements as valid or invalid. If the statement is invalid, explain why it is.
   a. **program;**

   b. **type**
      `wholenumber = integer;`

   c. **end.**

   d. **var**
      `first;`

   e. **procedure** EnterData

   f. `(* remarkable *)`

   g. `{ remarkable }`

   h. **const**
      `a, b = 4;`

   i. **var**
      `first,`
      `second`
      `   : char;`

   j. **type**
      `hours : integer;`

4. Write a Pascal statement to implement each of the following:
   a. Terminate a program.
   b. Define the identifier *sonic* to be real.
   c. Define *e* to have the value 2.71.
   d. Define the identifier *test* to have values true or false.
   e. Define the identifier *grade* to contain single-letter grades.
   f. Define a type called *twodigittype* to have values from 10 to 99, inclusive.
   g. Define a procedure called **DisplayResults**.
   h. Start a program.
   i. Enter your name as a comment.
   j. Define identifiers *i* and *j* to have integer values.

5. The program in Figure 2.3 finds the average of two real numbers. Recopy the program, filling in the empty boxes with appropriate Pascal reserved words and symbols.

```
┌──────────┐ Average;
└──────────┘
┌─┐ This program finds the average of two real numbers ┌─┐
└─┘                                                    └─┘
    ┌──────┐
    └──────┘
       two = 2;                    ┌─┐ number of scores ┌─┐
    ┌──────┐                       └─┘                  └─┘
    └──────┘
      first,                       ┌─┐      first number ┌─┐
                                   └─┘                   └─┘
      second,                      ┌─┐     second number ┌─┐
                                   └─┘                   └─┘
      average                      ┌─┐ average of numbers ┌─┐
         :┌──────┐;                └─┘                    └─┘
          └──────┘


       ┌───────────┐ EnterData;
       └───────────┘
       ┌─────────┐
       └─────────┘
    Write ('Enter the first real number: ');
    Readln (first);
    Write ('Enter the second real number: ');
    Readln (second)
       ┌──────┐
       └──────┘


       ┌───────────┐ FindAverage;
       └───────────┘
       ┌──────┐
       └──────┘
    average := (first + second) / two
       ┌──────┐
       └──────┘


       ┌───────────┐ DisplayAverage;
       └───────────┘
       ┌──────┐
       └──────┘
    Writeln ('Average: ',average)
       ┌──────┐
       └──────┘


    ┌──────┐
    └──────┘
    EnterData;
    FindAverage;
    DisplayAverage
    ┌──────┐
    └──────┘
```

Figure 2.3
Program for Exercise 5

CHAPTER 3

Fundamental Input and Output

Key Terms

Assign	**Rewrite**
Close	run-time error
external file	**text**
file pointer	text file
hard copy	trace
internal file structure	unit
Lst	**uses**
Printer	**Write**
Readln	**Writeln**
Reset	

Objectives

- To produce program output on the monitor screen
- To generate both printed program listings and program results
- To enter data from the keyboard
- To introduce text files for the storage and retrieval of data
- To introduce tracing and show how it can be used as part of the problem-solving process

3.1 Introduction

Chapter 1 introduced a language-independent process for designing good software, including the basic steps in creating a program: input, output, and processing. Chapter 2 presented the basic components of a Pascal program. The entire design process, including the coding step (which was mentioned but not shown), can now be used to create and test a Pascal program. Before we can do this, however, we must know the Pascal statements that input data and output results.

There are many ways to input and output data in a computer system. You can enter data by typing at a keyboard or transferring it from a disk file. Data can be output to a monitor screen, a printer, or a disk file. Instructions for using printers and disks for input or output vary from system to system.

This chapter presents the fundamental Pascal input and output statements needed to accept data from a keyboard or a file, and output data on a screen, at a printer, or to a file.

3.2 Screen Output

There are two statements that can be used to send output to a monitor screen and a printer: **Writeln** and **Write**.

The **Writeln** Statement When the instruction **Writeln** is followed by a list of items, output is displayed on the screen.

FORMAT: **Writeln (<output list>);**

The values in the list are separated by commas and enclosed in parentheses, with a semicolon following the closing parenthesis. When a **Writeln** statement is executed, the quantities in the output list are shown in the order specified. After the last value in the list is displayed, the cursor moves to the next screen line to display any subsequent output. It might help to think of **Writeln** as "*Write* the values in parentheses and move to the next screen *line*."

The output list can consist of constants or identifiers. If string constants are to be displayed, the computer shows *exactly* what is contained within the apostrophes (or single quotation marks) enclosing the constant.

Example

```
procedure OutputExample1;
begin
  Writeln ('Strong');
  Writeln ('C')
end;
```

OutputExample1 displays the word *Strong* on the first available screen line, moves the cursor to the next line, displays the letter *C*, and moves the cursor to a new line. The output appears as:

```
Strong
C
```

There is no semicolon following the second **Writeln** statement. In general, no semicolon is necessary when a statement precedes an **end** statement. And even if you put one in, it will not affect the execution of the program.

Since apostrophes mark the beginning and the end of string constants, how are apostrophes that are parts of strings indicated? Wherever you want an apostrophe to appear, enter two consecutive apostrophes in a string constant in the **Writeln** statement. When this statement is executed, only one of the apostrophes is shown.

Example

```
procedure OutputExample2;
begin
  Writeln ('He''s tall!')
end;
```

When executed, `OutputExample2` produces the following:

```
He's tall!
```

Using the double apostrophes in the **Writeln** statement ensures that one apostrophe will appear on the screen.

Unless otherwise specified, Pascal outputs numeric constants in a standard format. Real numbers are displayed in an 18-character field as scientific notation, or e-notation, values. The first character of the field is reserved for a plus or a minus sign and the last character for the third digit in a three-place exponent. With the exception of leading zeroes, integer values are displayed exactly as they are written in the **Writeln** statement; you can specify other output formats.

Example

```
procedure OutputExample3;
begin
  Writeln (42.7);
  Writeln (976)
end;
```

The output produced by this procedure is:

```
4.2700000000E+01
976
```

When identifiers are used in **Writeln** statements, the values stored in the locations represented by the identifiers are displayed.

Example

```
procedure OutputExample4;
begin
  Writeln (name);
  Writeln (initial);
  Writeln (age);
  Writeln (salary)
end;
```

If *Washington* were stored in **name**; *G*, in initial; *35*, in **age**; and *135.67*, in **salary**, the output would be:

```
Washington
G
35
1.3567000000E+02
```

Although the output for *42.7* and *salary* in the previous two examples are correct, their representation in e-notation is not suitable for most applications. Fortunately, Pascal provides some control over where and how the output is placed on the screen, by allowing each item in the output list to be displayed according to your specifications. Output format is determined by one or two integer values following an item in the output list.

```
<output list item> : <field width> : <decimal places>
```

An item in the output list is followed by a colon and the number of characters in the field displaying the item. The item is right-justified in this field. If the field you specify is not large enough for the value, Turbo Pascal displays the entire value, throwing off the spacing scheme for the remainder of the output list.

If a real value is output, the number of digits following the decimal point may also be specified following the field width and a second colon. A maximum of 11 digits after the decimal point is allowed for a real value. An error message is displayed if you specify a decimal-place field for integers, characters, or strings.

Example

```
procedure OutputExample5;
begin
  Writeln ('1234567890');
  Writeln (35:7);
  Writeln ('c':8);
  Writeln ('string':9);
  Writeln (12345:3);
  Writeln (1.234567:10:3);
  Writeln (11234.567:5:1)
end;
```

OutputExample5 produces:

```
1234567890
     35
       c
   string
12345
     1.235
11234.6
```

The first output line labels the display columns. For example, 35 is right-justified in a field of width 7. The entire value 12345 is shown even though a field width of 3 is specified for this five-digit value, since Turbo Pascal displays an entire value even if the field specification isn't large enough to display it. 1.234567 is rounded to three decimal places for display purposes and becomes 1.235; 11234.6 is shown with the one decimal place indicated.

STYLE TIP	Inserting a space following the **Writeln** instruction in all the examples is not necessary, but it does make the program easier to read. This convention is continued for the remainder of the text.

Although only one item was displayed in each of the **Writeln** statements in the preceding examples, you can output many items in a single statement. All you have to do is insert a comma between items in the list, even if you have field specifiers. The field size defined for any item is measured from the end of the field of the preceding item.

Example

```
procedure OutputExample6;
begin
  Writeln ('Last name: ', name);
  Writeln ('Initial: ', initial);
  Writeln ('Age: ', age);
  Writeln ('Salary: $', salary:7:2)
end;
```

If `name` contained *Washington*, `initial` contained *G*, `age` contained *35*, and `salary` contained *135.67*, the output would be:

```
Last name: Washington
Initial: G
Age: 35
Salary: $ 135.67
```

Each output list has two fields: a descriptive string constant and an identifier. For example, the first field in the first **Writeln** statement has a width of 11 (8 letters, 2 spaces, and a colon), and that description is left-justified. Since no field specification is present, the value for `name` is displayed left-justified or immediately following the first field. The remaining three statements are interpreted similarly.

The **Write** Statement

The **Write** statement also displays output on the screen.

FORMAT: **Write (<output list>);**

As with the **Writeln** statement, the instruction **Write** is followed by a list of items to be shown on the screen. The quantities in the list are separated by commas and enclosed in parentheses; a semicolon follows the closing parenthesis. When a **Write** statement is executed, the values in the output list are displayed according to their specifications, with the cursor remaining on the same screen line as the last item displayed, rather than moving to the next screen line. The formatting rules are the same as those for the **Writeln** statement.

Example

```
procedure OutputExample7;
begin
  Write ('Strong');
  Write ('C')
end;
```

OutputExample7 displays the word *Strong* on the first available screen line and then displays the letter *C* immediately after it. The cursor stays on the same line.

```
StrongC
```

The **Write** and **Writeln** statements can be used together in the same procedure.

Example

```
procedure OutputExample8;
begin
  Write ('Item: ');
  Writeln (appliance);
  Write ('Cost: $');
  Writeln (cost:7:2)
end;
```

If *blender* is stored in **appliance** and *37.95* is stored in **cost**, the output is:

```
Item: blender
Cost: $   37.95
```

The cursor stays on the same line after the **Write** statements are executed, so values are displayed immediately following their respective descriptions.

3.3 Printed Output

So far, program output and listings have been displayed on the monitor screen. Suppose you want a printed copy of the results of a program to be included as part of a written report or that you need a printed copy of a long program for review? Turbo Pascal provides facilities that allow you to produce printed output (*hard copy*) of both program listings and results, although the processes used to obtain each of these are different.

The **uses** Statement

Turbo Pascal contains libraries of useful procedures that are grouped into categories called *units*. You must notify a program that you are using a particular unit by including a **uses** statement immediately after the program header.

FORMAT: **uses**
      < library name list >;

The reserved word **uses** is followed by one or more of these library names separated by commas. The statement ends with a semicolon.

The **Printer** unit simplifies printing from inside a Pascal program, using a predefined identifier called **Lst** (for list device) to indicate that output is to be sent to a printer.

STYLE TIP
Indent the reserved word **uses** from the program header and any defined units from **uses**, as in:

```
program IndentSample;
   uses
      Printer;
   const
      . . .
```

Program Results

The **Write** and **Writeln** statements that output results on the screen can produce a hard copy of program results. When data is displayed on the screen, only the output data and specifications are contained in the parentheses following either of these reserved words. When data is to be sent to the printer, the predefined identifier **Lst** follows the opening parenthesis and is separated from the output list by a comma. All output following the comma in the **Write** or **Writeln** statement containing **Lst** is printed.

Example

```
program OutputExample9;
  uses
    Printer;

  procedure PrintOutput;
  begin
    Writeln (Lst,'Strong');
    Writeln (Lst,'C')
  end;

begin
  PrintOutput
end.
```

The **Printer** unit is defined following the program header, and the main program calls procedure **PrintOutput**. Since **Lst** follows the left parenthesis in the first statement in that procedure, *Strong* is printed on the first available line. The statement is **Writeln** and not **Write**, causing the print head to move to the next line on the paper. Since **Lst** also appears in the second **Writeln** statement, *C* is printed on that line and the print head moves to a new line on the paper. The printed output is:

```
Strong
C
```

This procedure is similar to **OutputExample1** earlier in Chapter 3 except that output is produced at the printer instead of on the screen.

The same rules that govern the formatting of data displayed on the screen can govern output data at a printer. If you want output on both the screen and at the printer, you must have one output instruction with **Lst** and another without it.

STYLE TIP	Use two procedures to separate output on the monitor and at the printer. This convention facilitates debugging a program if the output is displayed incorrectly.

Example

```
program OutputExample10;
  uses
    Printer;
  var
    name : string[20];
    age : integer;

  procedure ScreenOutput;
  begin
    Writeln ('Name: ', name);
    Writeln ('Age: ', age:3)
  end;

  procedure PrintOutput;
  begin
    Writeln (Lst,'Name: ', name);
    Writeln (Lst,'Age: ', age:3)
  end;

begin
 ScreenOutput;
 PrintOutput
end.
```

If **name** has the value *Davis* and **age** the value *44*, the output produced by both these procedures would appear identical, except that the output from **ScreenOutput** is on the screen and that from **PrintOutput** is at the printer.

```
Name: Davis
Age:   44
```

Program Listing

As discussed in Chapter 0, in the Turbo Pascal integrated development environment, you can obtain a printed copy of the program in the active Edit

Figure 3.1
File Menu

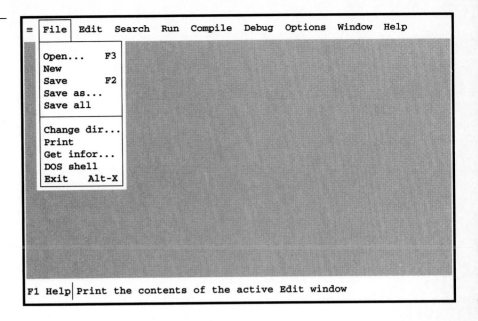

Figure 3.2
"Save File As" Dialog Box

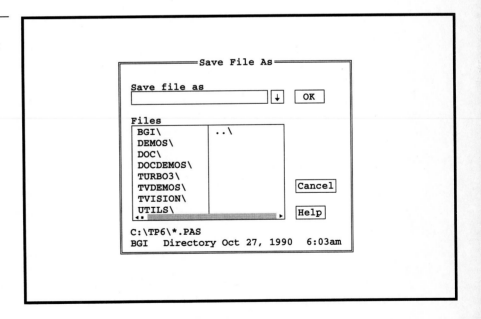

window by using the **Print** option from the **File** menu (see Figure 3.1). A brief summary of the instructions for printing a program listing is repeated here for completeness and your convenience.

1. Save a copy of your program to disk by selecting the **Save** option from the **File** menu and filling in the resulting dialog box (see Figure 3.2). Then press function key F10 to activate the menu line at the top of the screen.
2. Press F to select **File** from that menu line.
3. Press P to choose the **Print** option and transfer a copy of your program to the printer.

3.4 Keyboard Input

Both the **Readln** and **Read** statements can be used to accept data from the keyboard.

The **Readln** Statement   The **Readln** instruction places data into main memory locations for processing.

FORMAT: **Readln (<identifier list>);**

The instruction **Readln** is followed by a list of variable identifiers representing locations for incoming data. The identifiers in the list are separated by commas and enclosed in parentheses, with a semicolon following the closing parenthesis. When this statement is executed, the computer stops and waits for appropriate value(s) to be entered at the keyboard. The identifier must be defined in the declaration section of the program. This definition determines which type of data the program will expect. Entering a data type that does not match the data type of the identifier causes an error. Except for **string** and **char** types, if there is more than one identifier in the list, you can press the space bar or the Enter key after entering the value for one identifier before entering data for the next one. If a character is specified, the system accepts the first keyboard character entered as the value and assumes that all subsequent characters belong to the next variable identifier in the input list.

If a string is specified, the system accepts the number of characters declared for the identifier and again assumes that all succeeding characters belong to the next variable identifier in the input list. After entering the data for all the identifiers in the list, press the Enter key, to signal the computer to place the data in the location(s) set aside for the identifier(s), and the cursor moves to the next line on the screen.

Example

```
procedure InputExample1;
begin
  Readln (a, b);
  Writeln (a:10, b:10)
end;
```

Assume *a* and *b* are declared integers. When this procedure is executed, the cursor appears on the screen and waits for you to enter data. If you enter *25*, press the space bar, enter *79* and press the Enter key. The following appears on the screen:

```
25 79
        25        79
```

The first line is a result of the **Readln** statement, and the second, the **Writeln** statement.

If you press the Enter key after entering both *a* and *b*, the input values appear on separate lines and the output is:

```
25
79
        25        79
```

Example

```
procedure InputExample2;
begin
  Readln (a, b);
  Writeln (a:10, b:10)
end;
```

If *a* is declared as a **string** [5] identifier (a string with no more than 5 characters) and *b* is declared to be a character, when this procedure is executed the cursor appears on the screen and waits for you to enter data. The first five characters entered are stored in *a* and the next character in *b*, even though no space is entered. The actual storage takes place after pressing Enter. If you enter *abcdef* and press the Enter key, the output is:

```
abcdef
        abcde           f
```

The first line is entered by you, prompted by the **Readln** statement, and the second is produced by the **Writeln** statement.

Most programs are not written for use by the original programmer. They generally are written for someone with little or no knowledge of programming. For that reason, the program must specify exactly which data and which types of data are to be entered. It is very disconcerting to see a flashing cursor on the screen and not know what to do.

STYLE TIP	Every **Readln** statement should be preceded by **Write** or **Writeln** statements describing what data to enter at the keyboard and, if necessary, any special format required for their entry.

Example

```
procedure InputExample3;
begin
  Writeln ('Enter a name using all 10');
  Writeln ('characters, an age, then');
  Writeln ('press the Enter key.');
  Readln (name, age);
  Writeln;
  Writeln ('Name: ', name);
  Writeln ('Age: ', age:3)
end;
```

Suppose *name* is declared to be a string of length 10 and *age* is declared an integer. The first three **Writeln** statements describe how to input the desired data. The **Readln** accepts the first ten characters for *name* and the next two for *age*. When the Enter key is pressed, a blank line is displayed (**Writeln;**), and the entered data is output in a different form. If you forget to enter a value for *age* before pressing Enter, an arbitrary value is displayed for it.

```
——————— Output ———————
Enter a name using all 10
characters, an age, then
press the Enter key.
Benny     39

Name: Benny
Age:  39
```

Example

```
procedure InputExample4;
begin
  Writeln ('Enter your age;');
  Writeln ('press Enter.');
  Readln (age);
  Writeln;
  Writeln ('Age: ', age:3)
end;
```

After the *age* prompt, suppose you enter *2*, a space, and *1* instead of *21*. The space acts to separate data items in a **Readln** statement, so only the *2* is stored in age.

```
——————— Output ———————
Enter your age;
press Enter.
2 1

Age:  2
```

You must be very careful entering data for a **Readln** statement. Not supplying enough data, typing extra spaces, or not including required spaces can cause the incorrect data to be stored or can lead to incorrect results. Errors of this type, called *run-time errors* since they are not detected until a program is executed, can occur even with precise data-entry directions. You might not detect their presence unless you do a thorough walkthrough and check the program's produced results against the expected ones.

STYLE TIP

To minimize the chance of entering erroneous data, avoid multiple inputs for variable identifiers in a single **Readln** statement. Type a separate **Readln** statement for each entered data value. Immediately precede each **Readln** with a **Write** statement so the description of what is to be entered is on the same line as the entered value. The practice of having entered data immediately follow a description makes it easier to detect the entry of invalid data. With these style conventions in mind, the procedure `InputExample3` might instead be recoded as:

```
procedure InputExample3;
begin
  Writeln ('Press the Enter key following each entry.');
  Write ('Enter your name: ');
  Readln (name);
  Write ('Enter your age: ');
  Readln (age);
  Writeln;
  Writeln ('Name: ', name);
  Writeln ('Age: ', age:3)
end;
```

Its output:

```
Press the Enter key following each entry.
Enter your name: Benny
Enter your age: 39

Name: Benny
Age:  39
```

3.5 Application: "Hello, My Name Is . . . "

Once you know the Pascal statements that can enter data and output results, you can add the coding step to the solution process. Write a program that accepts a person's full name and outputs a name badge with "Hello My

Name Is" on one line and the entered name on the next line. Include modules to output both on a screen and at a printer.

ANALYSIS OF THE PROBLEM   The statement of the problem indicates that the input is a name and output is a name badge. Figure 3.3 summarizes this information.

MODULAR DESIGN
OF THE SOLUTION   The problem can be divided into three steps: Enter the name, show the badge information on the screen, and print the badge information. A structure chart outlining the solution is shown in Figure 3.4.

DESIGN OF THE
STRUCTURE OF THE
MODULES

NAME BADGE
    ENTER NAME
    DISPLAY NAME BADGE
    PRINT NAME BADGE

ENTER NAME
    enter a name

DISPLAY NAME BADGE
    output "Hello, My Name Is"
    output name

PRINT NAME BADGE
    print "Hello, My Name Is"
    print name

Figure 3.3
Name Badge Input/Output
Chart

Input	**Output**
Name	Name badge

Figure 3.4
Name Badge Structure
Chart

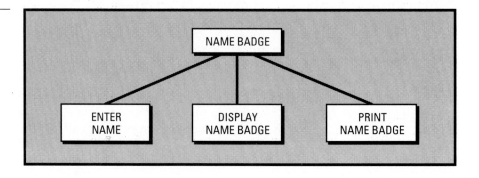

PRODUCTION OF CODE

You should only enter the program into the computer after the complete translation from pseudocode has been made on paper. This allows you to review the translation twice: once when it is written and a second time when it is keyed into the editor. In the long run you'll end up spending less time in front of the computer screen thinking, entering code, and correcting errors.

The program starts with the program header:

```
program NameBadge;
```

This is followed by a declaration of the string variable called *name* that can store up to 20 characters:

```
var
  name : string[20];
```

As previously explained, all program and procedure names in the text begin with an uppercase letter. If names consist of two or more words, the words are run together (leaving no spaces), with the beginning of each word capitalized.

The outline specifies the order in which the main module calls three submodules or procedures: ENTER NAME, followed by DISPLAY NAME BADGE and PRINT NAME BADGE. The coding for each follows the variable declaration. Although the pseudocode for a submodule follows its call in the design outline, the actual code for a submodule must appear before its call in a program.

The **Write** statement in the module ENTER NAME requests a name, and the Readln accepts a value for the variable defined as *name*.

```
procedure EnterName;
begin
  Write ('Enter a name: ');
  Readln (name)
end;
```

The DISPLAY NAME BADGE module comes next and contains two **Writeln** statements: one for "Hello, My Name Is" and a second for the name:

```
procedure DisplayNameBadge;
begin
  Writeln ('Hello, My Name Is');
  Writeln (name)
end;
```

PRINT NAME BADGE is the last module to be coded. Because the same output is sent to the printer, it is almost identical to DisplayNameBadge; the difference is that the output in each **Writeln** statement is preceded by **Lst**, sending that output to the printer:

```
    procedure PrintNameBadge;
    begin
      Writeln (Lst, 'Hello, My Name Is');
      Writeln (Lst, name)
    end;
```

Since **Lst** is defined only in the Turbo Pascal unit **Printer**, a **uses** statement calling that unit should follow the program header:

```
uses
    Printer;
```

The main program follows the three procedures and (as indicated by the outline) consists of calls to each in order:

```
begin
  EnterName;
  DisplayNameBadge;
  PrintNameBadge
end.
```

VERIFICATION OF THE
SOLUTION

These components are assembled and the program is executed to determine if the correct output is produced. A more detailed verification process that can be used for larger, more complicated programs is introduced in the next chapter.

DOCUMENTATION OF
THE SOLUTION

After the program is verified, it is documented to produce the final product, as shown, along with sample output, in Figure 3.5.

Figure 3.5
NameBadge Program
Listing and Sample Output

```
program NameBadge;
{------------------------------------------------------------------- }
{ PROGRAM:       Name Badge                                          }
{ PROGRAMMER:    J. E. Hoover                                        }
{ DATE:          March 15, 1990                                      }
{                                                                    }
{                                                                    }
{ This program accepts a name and shows the text for a name badge    }
{ both on the screen and at the printer.                             }
{                                                                    }
{ INPUT          name of person                                      }
{                                                                    }
{ OUTPUT         name badge                                          }
{------------------------------------------------------------------- }
```

```pascal
uses
   Printer;                              { utilities for printer output }
var
   name                                            { person's name }
     : string[20];

procedure EnterName;
{--------------------------------------------------------------- }
{ Accept name to appear on name badge.                           }
{--------------------------------------------------------------- }
begin
   Write ('Enter a name: ');
   Readln (name)
end;

procedure DisplayNameBadge;
{--------------------------------------------------------------- }
{ Display name badge on monitor.                                 }
{--------------------------------------------------------------- }
begin
   Writeln ('Hello, My Name Is');
   Writeln (name)
end;

procedure PrintNameBadge;
{--------------------------------------------------------------- }
{ Print name badge.                                              }
{--------------------------------------------------------------- }
begin
   Writeln (Lst, 'Hello, My Name Is');
   Writeln (Lst, name)
end;

begin
  EnterName;
  DisplayNameBadge;
  PrintNameBadge
end.
```

———————————— **Output** ————————————

```
   Hello, My Name Is
   Abraham Lincoln
```

Brief summaries of the purpose of the program and of its individual procedures are enclosed in comment boxes following the program or procedure name. The comment box for the main program also contains a title for the program, the name of the programmer, the date the program was completed, and a list of input and output values. Each identifier is followed by a brief description of what each represents.

3.6 Text File Output

Program output also can be stored as a text file on a disk. A *text file* is a collection of keyboard characters grouped by lines, where each line in the file ends with an invisible end-of-line marker. Text editors such as the one employed by Turbo Pascal produce similar text files.

Pascal file operations require communication between data in an *internal file structure* stored in main memory and a corresponding *external file* stored on disk. The internal file structure, in this case a text file, must be defined by a program and is represented by an identifier. A name for the disk file must be associated with this identifier before data can be transferred.

A file identifier that specifies the structure of the internal file should be defined to be of type **text** in the declaration section of a program.

Example

```
var
  movies
    : text;
```

The file identifier *movies* is defined as a text file and represents its internal file structure.

The **Assign** Statement

The **Assign** statement establishes a link between an internal file structure and an external or disk file.

FORMAT: **Assign (<file identifier>, <external file name>);**

The file identifier for the internal file structure must have been declared as a file of type **text** before appearing in **Assign**. The external file name is a string that consists of the disk drive designation and a colon, a back-slash, and a file name. If no drive is specified, the active one is used for the file.

Example

```
Assign (movies, 'comedy.txt');
```

The internal file defined in the previous example is associated with the external file called *comedy.txt*. Since the external file name is a string constant, it must be enclosed in single quotation marks.

STYLE TIP	Using a *txt* extension for names of text files, as in the previous example, helps to distinguish these disk files from program files.

Assume that the internal file structure contains movie titles. Since movies can fall into different categories (comedy, drama, adventure, etc.), you might want to specify in which of a series of files a title is to be stored. A variable identifier can be defined to store an external file name associated with a particular category and that identifier used as the second parameter in the **Assign** statement.

Example

`Assign (movies, category);`

Assume that *category* is defined as a string and *movies* as a text file. A call to procedure `GetExtFileName` accepts the name of the movie category and uses it as the external file name in the **Assign** statement. Entering a different name for *category* will store movie data in a different file.

The **Assign** statement is the only Pascal statement that contains the external file name. After the connection between an internal file structure and an external file is made, the program need only refer to the internal identifier. Pascal takes care of the transfer of data to and from the external file at the appropriate times.

After the connection is established, data is sent either from the internal structure to the external file or vice versa. The **Assign** statement establishes the link, but it does not determine the direction of the data flow.

The **Rewrite** Statement

The **Rewrite** statement prepares the system to send data from the internal structure to the external file by creating and opening a new file to receive output from the computer.

FORMAT: **Rewrite (<file identifier>);**

When this statement is executed, the external file associated with the file identifier is created and a *file pointer* is set to the beginning of the file. The file pointer indicates where the next data written to the file is to be placed. If an external file with that name already exists, the old file is deleted, with a new, empty file replacing it. **Rewrite** establishes a one-way path from the internal file structure to the external file.

Example

```
Assign (movies, category);
Rewrite (movies);
```

A file pointer is set to the beginning of the defined internal file structure called *movies*, which is now ready to receive data from the program. It will store data in the external file *category* linked to it by the **Assign** statement.

The **Writeln** Statement for Text Files

Rewrite determines the data path direction, whereas the **Writeln** statement for text files actually stores data in the internal file structure.

```
Writeln ( <file identifier>, <output identifier> );
```

If the first identifier in a **Writeln** statement is a file identifier, then the output identifier must be a variable parameter. When this statement is executed, output data is stored in the internal file structure, followed by an end-of-line marker, and the file pointer is advanced to the next line to prepare for any subsequent data transfer. No screen output is seen as a result of the execution of this statement.

Example

```
Assign (movies, category);
Rewrite (movies);
Writeln (movies, movie1);
Writeln (movies, movie2);
Writeln (movie1);
Writeln (movie2);
```

The internal structure *movies* is linked to the file *category* in the **Assign** statement. The **Rewrite** statement prepares the file to receive output and sets the file pointer at the beginning of the file. The contents of *movie1* is written to *movies*, an end-of-line marker attached, and the file pointer advanced so the data for *movie2* follows it in the file. Since the last two **Writeln** statements do not contain file identifiers, their output is sent to the screen. If the two movie names entered were *Stagecoach* and *Blue Gardenia*, respectively, the file would look like this:

```
Stagecoach
Blue Gardenia
```

Because data must be stored in a variable identifier before being transferred to the internal file structure, you cannot use a constant or constant identifier as the output identifier in a **Writeln** statement for files.

Example

`Writeln (intfile, 35);`	If *intfile* is a file identifier, this statement produces an error message, since a variable identifier, not 35, is required as the output identifier.

Once a file is opened for receiving output data with a **Rewrite** statement, it must be closed before data can be read from that file.

The **Close** Statement

The **Close** statement removes access to an open file. Once the file is closed, no processing can be done on it until it is reopened.

FORMAT: **Close** (<file identifier>);

When a **Close** statement is encountered, the external file associated with the internal identifier receives data, and access to that external file is ended. All the steps involved in the creation of a file must be enclosed between a **Rewrite** statement and a **Close** statement.

Even though text files are composed of keyboard characters, you can use them to store numeric values. The Pascal system automatically converts numeric values to characters when they are output to a text file and converts the characters back to numeric values when they are input from a text file.

Example

```
procedure CreateTextFile;
begin
  Assign (movies, category);
  Rewrite (movies);
  Write ('Enter movie title: ');
  Readln (title);
  Writeln (movies, title);
  Write ('Enter gross income from showing: $');
  Readln (income);
  Writeln (movies, income);
  Close (movies)
end;
```

```
var
  movies
    : text;
  category
    : string[20];
  title
    : string[30];
  income
    : real;

  ...

GetExtFileName;
CreateTextFile;
```

Assume the declarations for program variables are as shown. After the procedure `GetExtFile-Name` accepts a string representing a category, the procedure `CreateTextFile` is called. The **Assign** statement links the internal file *movies* with the external file name stored in *category*, and **Rewrite** opens *movies* to send data to the external file. The next two statements request and receive a value for the title of a movie, and **Writeln** stores that title in the internal file structure. Subsequent statements request and accept a value for the gross income generated by the movie and store that value in the internal file. Finally, the internal file structure is closed, and the entered data transferred to the external file.

Using the Turbo Pascal Editor to Create a Text File

Text files also can be created using the same Turbo Pascal editor as for entering a program. To create a text file in this manner, clear the Edit window and enter the data to be stored in the file, one line at a time, making sure to press the Enter key at the end of each line. When the file is complete, press F2 (**Save**) and use *.txt* to end the file name.

For example, to create a text file of famous books, start by clearing the Edit window, using **New** from the **File** menu, if necessary. Type the name of the first book and press Enter, the name of the second book followed by Enter, etc. When all data has been entered, press F2 (**Save**), type *books.txt* in the Name area of the "Save File As" dialog box, and press Enter.

3.7 Text File Input

After data is stored in an external file, it can be returned to an internal file structure. The **Assign** statement again can be used to establish a link, but the **Rewrite** statement is unsuitable, since it specifies a one-way data movement *from* the internal structure *to* an external file. Another statement is needed to transfer data in the other direction.

The Reset Statement

The **Reset** statement uses the link instituted by **Assign** to open an existing file for the purpose of transferring data *from* the external file *to* its corresponding internal file structure.

FORMAT: **Reset (<file identifier>);**

When this statement is executed, the external file associated with the file identifier is opened and the file pointer is set to point to the first record of the file. If there is no external file with the given name, an error results. This statement establishes a one-way data path from the external file to the internal structure.

Example

Assign (movies, category);
Reset (movies);

A file pointer is set to the beginning of *movies* and is now ready to receive data from the external file designated by *category*. The incoming data is stored in the internal file structure.

The **Readln** Statement for Text Files

The **Reset** statement serves only to establish the direction of the data flow. The **Readln** statement for text files accepts data from an external file for storage in an internal file structure.

FORMAT: **Readln (<file identifier>, <input identifier>);**

If the first identifier in a **Readln** statement is an internal file identifier, the record at the current file pointer position is transferred to the location represented by the input identifier. The file pointer then is advanced to the next line in the file. The input identifier must be a variable identifier.

Example

Assign (movies, category);
Reset (movies);
Readln (movies, movie1);
Readln (movies, movie2);

The internal structure *movies* is linked to *category* in the **Assign** statement. The **Reset** statement prepares the system to receive input from the external file and sets the file pointer at the beginning of that file. If the file has at least two data items, the first is read into the variable *movie1* and the file pointer advanced to the next line in the file so that the next **Readln** accepts the second for the variable *movie2*.

Example

```
procedure ReadTextFile;
begin
  Assign (movies, category);
  Reset (movies);
  Readln (movies, title);
  Readln (movies, income);
  Close (movies)
end;
```

```
var
  movies
    : text;
  category
    : string[20];
  title
    : string[30];
  income
    : real;

  . . .

GetExtFileName;
ReadTextFile;
```

Assume the declarations for program variables are as shown. After the procedure `GetExtFileName` accepts a string representing a category, the procedure `ReadTextFile` is called. The **Assign** statement links the internal file *movies* with the external file name stored in *category*, and **Reset** opens *movies* to receive data from the external file. The first **Readln** statement receives the first item in the data file and stores it in the location *title*, and the second stores the second data item in the location *income*. An error results if there is a type mismatch. The **Close** statement breaks the connection between *movies* and *category*.

3.8 Application Using Text Files: "Hello" Revisited

Consider again the program that accepts a person's name and creates a name badge for that person. Suppose the name appearing on the name badge is stored in an existing text file called *guest.txt*, and rather than entering the name from the keyboard, it is read from this file. To adapt the program to accept this different form of input, the **EnterName** procedure would have to be altered and an internal file structure identifier declared. If *namefile* is the identifier for this structure, **EnterName** now becomes:

```
procedure EnterName;
begin
  Assign (namefile, 'guest.txt');
  Reset (namefile);
  Readln (namefile, name);
  Close (namefile)
end;
```

Except for minor changes in the documentation, the rest of the program would remain intact. The file-based solution to the Name Badge problem is shown, along with its output, in Figure 3.6.

Figure 3.6
NameBadge Program
Listing and Sample Output

```
program NameBadge;
{-------------------------------------------------------------------- }
{ PROGRAM:       Name Badge                                           }
{ PROGRAMMER:    J. E. Hoover                                         }
{ DATE:          March 16, 1990                                       }
{                                                                     }
{ This program reads a name from the file 'guest.txt' and shows the   }
{ text for a name badge both on the screen and at the printer.        }
{                                                                     }
{ INPUT          name of person                                       }
{                                                                     }
{ OUTPUT         name badge                                           }
{-------------------------------------------------------------------- }
  uses
    Printer;                              { utilities for printer output }
  var
    name                                         { person's name }
      : string[20];
    namefile                              { internal file for name }
      : text;

  procedure EnterName;
  {-------------------------------------------------------------------- }
  { Read name to appear on name badge from file.                        }
  {-------------------------------------------------------------------- }
  begin
    Assign (namefile, 'guest.txt');
    Reset (namefile);
    Readln (namefile, name);
    Close (namefile)
  end;

  procedure DisplayNameBadge;
  {-------------------------------------------------------------------- }
  { Display name badge on monitor.                                      }
  {-------------------------------------------------------------------- }
  begin
    Writeln ('Hello, My Name Is');
    Writeln (name)
  end;
```

```
procedure PrintNameBadge;
{------------------------------------------------------------ }
{ Print name badge.                                           }
{------------------------------------------------------------ }
begin
   Writeln (Lst, 'Hello, My Name Is');
   Writeln (Lst, name)
end;

begin
  EnterName;
  DisplayNameBadge;
  PrintNameBadge
end.
```

─────────────────────── **Output** ───────────────────────

```
   Hello, My Name Is
   Abraham Lincoln
```

3.9 Tracing a Program with the Turbo Pascal IDE

One of the features of the integrated development environment is that it can step through, or *trace*, a program by highlighting each line of the program in the order in which it is executed. To use this facility, you must make sure that the program to be traced is active (it should be the one in the active Edit window) and that certain system options are properly set.

The **Integrated debugging** selection from the **Debugger** option of the **Options** menu must be active, as shown in Figure 3.7. If it is off, use the Tab key to highlight the **Integrated** option in the "Debugger" dialog box, press the spacebar until **X** appears in the square brackets, [ ], and press the Enter key.

When you select the **Compiler** option from the **Options** menu, a different dialog box appears (see Figure 3.8). Make sure the **Debug information** and **Local symbols** choices in the Debugging section of that box are both on; if either one is off, then highlight that option, press the spacebar until **X** appears in the square brackets, [ ], next to each of these options, and press Enter.

Initiate tracing by selecting **Trace into** from the **Run** menu or by pressing function key F7, as shown in Figure 3.9. Press F7 to start a trace. The **begin** statement in the main program is highlighted. Pressing F7 again moves the highlight bar to the next statement to be executed. This process continues until the tracer reaches the **end** statement in the main program. Each time

Figure 3.7
"Debugger" Dialog Box

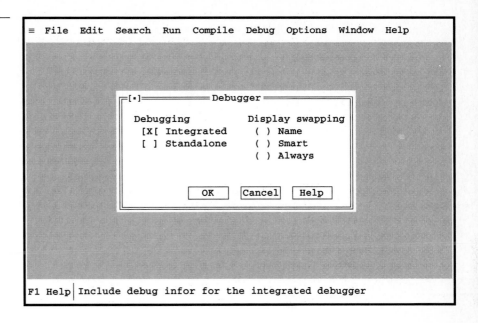

Figure 3.8
"Compiler Options"
Dialog Box

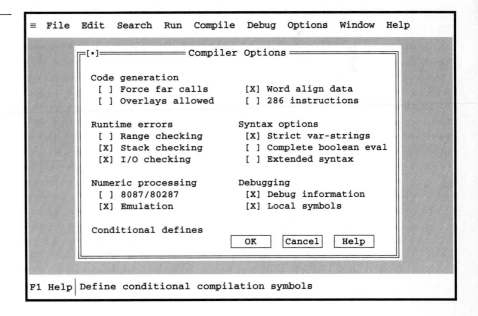

Figure 3.9
Run Menu with
Trace into

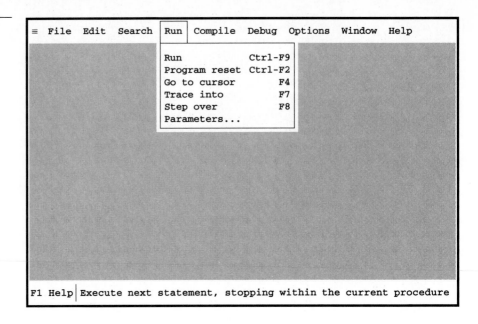

input is required, the system switches to the Output window for data entry and automatically returns to the Edit window when that entry is completed.

An undocumented version of the program **NameBadge** is shown in Figure 3.10, with reference numbers enclosed in parentheses to the left of particular lines of code to indicate the order of execution.

Figure 3.10
Numbered **NameBadge**
Program Listing

```
      program NameBadge;

         uses
           Printer;
         var
           name
             : string[20];

         procedure EnterName;
(3)      begin
(4)        Write ('Enter a name: ');
(5)        Readln (name)
(6)      end;
```

```
         procedure DisplayNameBadge;
 (8)  begin
 (9)     Writeln ('Hello, My Name Is');
(10)     Writeln (name)
(11)  end;

         procedure PrintNameBadge;
(13)  begin
(14)     Writeln (Lst, 'Hello, My Name Is');
(15)     Writeln (Lst, name)
(16)  end;

 (1)  begin
 (2)     EnterName;
 (7)     DisplayNameBadge;
(12)     PrintNameBadge
(17)  end.
```

Execution starts at **begin** in the main program. After the procedure **EnterName** is called in the main program, control jumps to **begin** in **EnterName**, where its four statements are executed before control returns to a call for **DisplayNameBadge** in the main program. The trace for the remainder of the program proceeds in a similar fashion.

Store and Forward

The main function of a computer is to communicate with the outside world. It receives data, processes that data, and produces results. Since a programming language is the interface between a user and the computer, it must be capable of accepting data (input) and returning information (output).

This chapter has presented Turbo Pascal processes to receive input from the keyboard and a text file as well as to send output to a monitor, a printer, and a text file—processes that were included in the software design methodology in Chapter 1.

The programs presented thus far have behaved like water pipes—with data entering at one end and coming out unchanged at the other. To be useful, the flow of water through the pipe should generate power or nothing has been gained by its passage through the pipe. Similarly, we have to process the input to produce more "powerful" results. The next chapter gives us the processing tools to make use of the data flow.

Snares and Pitfalls

- *Failing to enclose input or output quantities in parentheses:* The output list in **Write** and **Writeln** statements or the input list in a **Readln** statement must be enclosed in parentheses.

- *Omitting apostrophes* (single quotation marks) *to enclose string constants in* **Write** *and* **Writeln** *statements:* String constants in output statements not enclosed in single quotes are treated as variable identifiers.

- *Failing to separate items in an input or output list with commas:* If two input or output quantities are not separated by commas, the quantities are considered a single item.

- *Omitting a* **uses** *statement when sending output to a printer:* Because **Lst** is defined only in the **Printer** unit, that unit must be called by a **uses** statement in the main program.

- *Omitting the* **Assign** *statement when working with text files:* The **Assign** statement establishes a link between an internal file structure and its corresponding external file on a disk. No file operations can occur unless this link has been made.

- *Failing to close a text file after its use:* If access to a text file is not removed with a **Close** statement, additional operations on the file can produce unpredictable results.

- *Using the wrong "direction" statement for the transfer of data between an internal file structure and its corresponding external file:* The **Rewrite** statement allows data transfers from the internal file structure to the external file while the **Reset** statement allows data transfers from the external file to the internal structure.

- *Using a constant or a constant identifier as an output identifier in a* **Writeln** *statement for text files:* Data must be stored in a variable identifier before it can be transferred to the internal file structure.

Exercises

1. Answer the following questions in paragraph form.
   a. What is the difference between a **Write** statement and a **Writeln** statement? Cite examples to justify your answer.
   b. Why is it advisable to precede a **Readln** statement with a **Write** or **Writeln** statement?
   c. Give an advantage to using one **Readln** statement for each input value instead of one for all the inputs required by a program.
   d. Explain how a **Writeln** statement that sends output to the monitor screen can be modified to send data to a text file.
   e. What is a Turbo Pascal unit?

2. Classify each of the following Pascal statements as valid or invalid. If invalid, explain why. Unless otherwise stated, assume all identifiers have been properly declared.
   a. **Write ('Oranges');**
   b. **Accept (intfile, extfile);**
   c. **Rewrite (intfile, extfile);**
   d. **Readln (d);**
   e. **Close (intfile);**

3. Write a Pascal statement that corresponds to the given descriptions.
   a. Output the values of the integer variable identifiers *a*, *b*, and *c* on a single line in fields 12 characters wide.
   b. Indicate that the internal file structure *cars*, which is already linked to an external file, is to receive data from that external file.
   c. Accept a value for the variable identifier *base*.
   d. Move the contents of the variable *phone* to the internal file structure *phonebook*.
   e. Display the real value stored in the location *rebate* preceded by an appropriate message. The value should follow a $ and be displayed in a field of 9 characters, with two digits following the decimal point.

4. Consider the file program **NameBadge** in Section 3.8.
   a. Write a procedure for that program called **CreateGuestFile** that creates the text file called *guest.txt* containing the name of a person for whom a name badge is to be printed.
   b. Use the Turbo Pascal text editor to create the same text file described in part a.

Programming Assignments

1. Write a program that displays the heading "Table of Contents" in the center of the screen and underlines it with hyphens (-) as follows:

   ```
   Table of Contents
   -----------------
   ```

2. Write a program that displays the heading "Table of Contents" in the center of a printed page as shown in Assignment 1.

3. Write a program that displays on the monitor an enlarged letter X composed of individual X characters as follows:

```
   X         X
    X       X
     X     X
      X   X
       X X
        X
       X X
      X   X
     X     X
    X       X
   X         X
```

4. Write a program to create an external file called *x.txt* that stores the X shown in Assignment 3.

5. Write a program that displays a rectangle composed of asterisks (*) in the center of a monitor screen.

```
* * * * * * * *
*             *
*             *
* * * * * * * *
```

6. Write a program that prints the asterisk box in Assignment 5.

7. Write a program that reads the following limerick from a text file called *limerick.txt* and displays it on the screen.

   There was a young lady name Betty
   Whose programs looked like spaghetti.
   They jumped all around,
   No structure was found,
   So they ended up being confetti.

8. Write a program that stores a first name and a last name in two distinct variables. Display, on a single line, the first name followed by a space and the last name.

9. Write a program that stores a first name and a last name in two distinct variables. Display, on a single line, the last name followed by a comma, a space, and the first name.

10. Write a program that stores a person's first name and a last name in an external text file called *name.txt*.

11. Write a program that accepts a person's name and displays a message saying hello to that person.

12. Write a program that displays the following tree:

```
     / \
    /   \
   /     \
  /       \
 /_____\
    | |
```

13. Write a program that stores a message enclosed in a box (as in the following example) in a text file called *message.txt*.

```
---------------------------------
|                               |
|      Programmed for Success   |
|                               |
---------------------------------
```

14. Write a program that centers the title box in Assignment 13 on a printed page.

15. Write a program that reads a recipe from a text file called *recipe.txt* and displays it on the screen.

16. Write a program that accepts a person's name and complete address and prints it in a form that could be used to address an envelope.

17. Write a program that reads the lyrics to a song from a text file called *lyrics.txt* and prints them.

18. Write a program that prints the title page of this textbook.

19. Write a program that prints a form that could be used as a calendar for weekly appointments.

20. Write a program that prints the title page from a magazine.

CHAPTER 4

Processing Numeric Data and Testing Solutions

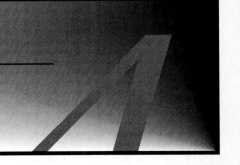

Key Terms

Add watch
assignment operator
breakpoint
div
expression
mod
operand
operator
order of precedence

precedence
Run
Run menu
stub
Toggle breakpoint
top-down testing
Trace into
Watches window

Objectives

- To create valid arithmetic expressions using the Pascal arithmetic operators
- To use arithmetic expressions in the problem-solving methodology
- To check problem solutions with a top-down testing process
- To employ the Turbo Pascal integrated development environment (IDE) in the top-down testing process

4.1 Introduction

Butter, sugar, eggs, flour, milk, baking powder, and salt combined in different proportions and processed in different ways can produce coffee cakes, pancakes, or muffins. In a similar fashion, a computer program can accept the same set of inputs, process them differently, and produce different results. (The "compute" in a computer comes from its ability to process entered data and generate desired results.)

Processing of any kind involves executing certain operations in a particular order. A recipe determines the order in which to perform cooking "operations," such as measure, mix, stir, heat, boil, fry, and bake, so as to produce the desired outcome. To make pancakes, for example, you don't cook the egg before combining it with the other ingredients, but you do cook the final pancake batter. In Pascal, a program determines the order in which to perform arithmetic operations, such as addition, subtraction, multiplication, and division, so as to produce the desired results.

This chapter introduces fundamental concepts regarding the manipulation of numeric data: arithmetic operations, their use in the formulation of arithmetic expressions, and the storage of the results of calculations in specific memory locations. It also extends your knowledge of the problem-solving process by providing details on top-down testing, a method that aids in the verification of solutions.

4.2 Operations

Operators perform actions on objects called *operands*. For example, when you add two numbers, addition is the numeric operation, the numbers that are added are the operands, and the plus sign (+) represents the operator. Operators that require two operands, such as addition, subtraction, multiplication, and division, are called binary operators. Those that require a single operand are termed unary operators.

Although Pascal operations are similar to arithmetic operations, there are some major differences.

A list of Pascal operators and their arithmetic counterparts is given in Table 4.1. Notice that there is no exponentiation operator in Pascal.

Addition, Subtraction, and Multiplication

Negation is used to represent negative quantities such as −3.4 and −6; since it requires only one operand, it is a unary operation. Addition, subtraction, and multiplication behave as in arithmetic. If both operands for these operations are integers, the result is an integer; if both operands are reals, the result is a real. If one operand is a real and the other an integer, the result is a real. Table 4.2 gives some examples of these Pascal operations.

Table 4.1
Pascal Operators and Their Arithmetic Counterparts

Operation	Pascal Operator	Arithmetic Operator
Negation	−	−
Addition	+	+
Subtraction	−	−
Multiplication	*	x
Real division	/	÷
Integer division	div	(none)
Modulo	mod	(none)

Table 4.2
Examples of Addition,
Subtraction, and
Multiplication Operations
in Pascal

```
3 + 4 = 7
7.0 - 3.0 = 4.0
6 * 1.5 = 9.0
1.5 - 1 = 0.5
2.25 * 1.5 = 3.375
5.8 + 3 = 8.8
```

Table 4.3
Examples of Division
Operations in Pascal

```
9 / 2 = 4.5
9 div 2 = 4
9 mod 2 = 1
18 mod 2 = 0
-14 div 3 = -4
-14 mod 3 = -2
14 mod -3 = 2
18.2 / 2 = 9.1
18.2 div 2 gives an error
```

Division

There are two types of division in Pascal, real and integer. The real division operator (/) always produces a real result, even if both operands are integers. For example, 4/5 equals 0.8, as does 4.0/5 and 4/5.0. The **div** and **mod** operators act only on integer operands. An error results if either operand is a real.

The **div** operation gives the quotient that results when one integer is divided by another. Since 7 divided by 3 gives a quotient of 2 with a remainder of 1, the value of 7 **div** 3 is 2; the remainder is ignored.

The **mod** operation returns only the remainder when one integer is divided by another; the quotient is ignored. The sign of the result of **mod** is the same as the sign of the first operand. For example, 7 **mod** 3 = 1, whereas −7 **mod** 3 = −1.

Additional examples of Pascal division operations are shown in Table 4.3. All real results include a decimal point.

4.3 Expressions

An *expression* is a combination of operands and operators. Each of the expressions in Tables 4.2 and 4.3 contains a single operator and two operands. The following expression contains two operators and three operands: 12 + 6/3.

When you have more than one operator in an expression, you have to decide which operation should be performed first: 12 + 6, or 6/3. If the addition is done first, the result is

$$12 + 6/3 = 18/3 = 6$$

If the division is done first, the answer becomes

$$12 + 6/3 = 12 + 2 = 14$$

Clearly, the computer does not have a choice; only one of these interpretations is correct.

To avoid any confusion in interpretation, some operations must take *precedence*, that is, have a higher priority than others. Table 4.4 summarizes the *order of precedence* for numeric operations, that is, the order in which they are performed.

Higher-precedence operations are performed before lower-precedence operations. If two operations have the same order of precedence, e.g., *, /, **div**, and **mod**, the one on the *left* takes precedence.

Examples

```
5 + 7 div 3 - 4 mod 3
5 +   2    - 4 mod 3
5 +   2    - 1
    7      - 1
           6
```

The **div** and **mod** operations have a higher precedence than + and –; since **div** is to the left of **mod**, it is performed first. In the remaining expression, **mod** has the highest precedence and is performed next. Since + is to the left of – in the remaining expression, it is done next, followed by –.

```
7.5 - 10 / 4 * 2 + 3
7.5 -   2.5  * 2 + 3
7.5 -      5.0   + 3
    2.5          + 3
               5.5
```

The real division (/) is to the left of the multiplication (*) and is performed first. Even though both operands of / are integers, their result is a real. The * operation in the resulting expression has both a real and an integer operand; its result is also real. The evaluation of the expression is completed by doing the subtraction followed by the addition. In general, an expression that contains a mixture of real and integer values has a real result.

What happens if you want to change the standard order of operations? For example, suppose you want the average of two numbers. For the result

Table 4.4
Precedence of Numeric
Operations in Pascal

Operation	Operators	Precedence
Negation	–	Highest
Multiplication, division	*, /, div, mod	High
Addition, subtraction	+, –	Lowest

to be correct, the addition of the two numbers must take place *before* the division of the result by 2. As in arithmetic and algebra, parentheses are used to override the established order or precedence. If an expression contains more than one set of parentheses, they are evaluated from left to right. If one set is contained within another, the inner set is evaluated before the outer set. The following examples have the same operators and operands as in the previous examples, but parentheses have been included to change the order of operations.

Examples

```
(5 + 7) div 3 - 4 mod 3
   12   div 3 - 4 mod 3
         4    - 4 mod 3
         4    -   1
               3
```

The parentheses indicate that the + is done first, followed by **div**, **mod**, and –.

```
7.5 - 10 / 4 * (2 + 3)
7.5 - 10 / 4 *     5
7.5 -   2.5 *      5
7.5 -         12.5
      -5.0
```

Because of the parentheses, + is performed first, followed by /, *, and –, in that order.

```
7.5 - 10 / (4 * (2 + 3))
7.5 - 10 / (4 *     5   )
7.5 - 10 /    20
7.5 -     0.5
      7.0
```

The inner parentheses are evaluated first, and the result (5) is an integer. The outer parentheses indicate that multiplication is the next operation to be performed, and the result (20) is still an integer. In the remaining expression, the / operation takes precedence and yields a real result. The subtraction then gives the final answer.

Although you must know how to evaluate given expressions, you must also be able to write and code the expressions that represent relationships in your solutions. Proper Pascal expressions are expressed on a single line with

Table 4.5
Comparison of Algebraic
and Pascal Expressions

Algebraic	Pascal
$\dfrac{a+b}{c-d}$	`(a + b)/(c - d)`
$3x + 5y + 8z$	`3*x + 5*y + 8*z`
$4x^2$	`4*x*x`

no operations implied. For example, in algebra the value for one-half may be expressed as

$$\frac{1}{2}$$

occupying two lines. In Pascal, the same expression is coded in a single line as 1/2. In algebra, multiplication is often implied, as when *ab* is understood to mean the value of *a* multiplied by the value of *b*. In Pascal, however, the multiplication must be clearly stated. The expression **ab** in Pascal is interpreted simply as a single identifier, **ab**. To represent the product correctly, you must use the multiplication operator and write **a * b**.

Another rule of thumb that helps avoid errors is to enclose the numerator and denominator of any division operation in parentheses. For example, the expression **a * b / c * d** is not equivalent to **a * b / (c * d)**. In the former, the product of **a** and **b** is divided by **c** and the result multiplied by **d**, while in the latter the product **a * b** is divided by the product **c * d**. Although enclosing both the numerator and denominator in parentheses may be unnecessary, using them does not invalidate the expression, and it averts any possible misinterpretation. When in doubt, parenthesize to clarify your intent. Table 4.5 contains additional algebraic expressions and their Pascal equivalents.

4.4 Assignment Statements

Assignment statements store the value of an expression in a variable location.

FORMAT: `<identifier> := <expression>;`

The assignment statement begins with a declared variable identifier, followed by the *assignment operator* (`:=`) and a proper expression. (You must *never* leave a space between the colon and the equal sign.) When this statement is encountered, the value of the expression on the right side of the assignment operator is stored in the location represented by the declared variable identifier on the left side of the assignment operator. It may be useful for you to think of **:=** as a left-facing arrow (←), since it "moves" data from right to left.

In general, the value of the expression must be of the same type as the one declared for the variable identifier; that is, you cannot store a character type in a location defined as a real variable. An exception is that you can store an integer value in a real location, in which case the system converts the integer to decimal form by adding a decimal point and using 0 for the fractional part. The reverse is not true, however. You cannot store a real value in an integer location; attempting to do so will cause an error.

Examples

`pay := rate * hours;`

Assume that *pay*, *rate*, and *hours* are declared reals, and *rate* and *hours* have been previously assigned the values *5.50* and *10.5*, respectively. The value of **rate * hours** (10.5 × 5.50, or 57.75) is stored in the real location represented by *pay*. If *pay* were a declared integer, an error would result, since a real value cannot be stored in an integer location.

`range := high - low;`

Assume that *range*, *high*, and *low* are declared integers, with *high* and *low* assigned values of *89* and *56*, respectively. The value of **high - low** (89 − 56, or 33) is stored in the integer location *range*. If *range* were a declared real, 33 would be converted to a real (33.0) and then stored in *range*.

`average := sum / number;`

Regardless of whether *sum* and *number* are integers or reals, the division produces a real result. If *average* were a declared real, the value of the expression **sum / number** would be stored in *average*. If *average* were a declared integer, an error would result.

`count := count + 1;`

If *count* were a declared integer, 1 would be added to the current value of count (the right side of **:=**) and that value stored in *count*, replacing the previous value. This statement has the effect of adding 1 to the value of *count* each time it is executed.

STYLE TIP	An expression may be included and its value output in the same **Write** or **Writeln** statement, as in

```
Writeln ('4 + 5 = ', 4 + 5);
```

for which the following output is produced:

```
4 + 5 = 9
```

The string constant defining the problem is output, and since the expression **4 + 5** is not enclosed in single quotation marks, its value (**9**) is shown. This practice of performing calculations in output statements is avoided in this text, and **Write** and **Writeln** are used solely for output. Separating output and processing in this manner further emphasizes the modular approach to problem solving by utilizing **Write** and **Writeln** statements solely for output while performing calculations in statements designed for that purpose.

4.5 Top-Down Testing with the Turbo Pascal IDE

Top-down testing is a structured method designed to verify the solution to a problem. It may prove cumbersome in testing the solutions to problems with relatively simple solutions, but it can be very useful when authenticating the design process for more complex problems.

The same structure that resulted from separating a problem into components in the modular design phase of the methodology is used to test the solution in the verification phase. The top module is the first one to be coded and should consist primarily of calls to other modules. Temporary modules, or *stubs*, are inserted for each of the procedures in the design. At this stage, verification of the code in the main program consists of testing whether the program jumps to each of the stubs to continue execution and whether those stubs return control back to the main program. Turbo Pascal's integrated development environment provides facilities that easily test the interconnections between a module and its submodules even though the final coding for the submodules has not been completed.

The best way to illustrate the testing process is by walking through it with an example such as the heartbeat example in Chapter 1, which is repeated here.

PROBLEM STATEMENT   The heart is a muscle that works 24 hours a day, 7 days a week, every week we live. Given a person's average heartbeat rate, in beats per minute, determine and output how many times his or her heart beats in 1 hour.

ANALYSIS OF THE PROBLEM   Figure 4.1 presents the input/output chart.

Figure 4.1
Heartbeat Input/Output
Chart

Input	Output
Heartbeat rate	Total heartbeats

MODULAR DESIGN OF
THE SOLUTION

The structure chart is shown in Figure 4.2.

DESIGN OF THE
STRUCTURE OF THE
MODULES

HEARTBEAT
    ENTER HEART RATE
    FIND TOTAL BEATS
    OUTPUT TOTAL BEATS

    ENTER HEART RATE
        enter number of beats per minute

    FIND TOTAL BEATS
        find heartbeats per hour
        (rate per minute × number of minutes per hour)

    OUTPUT TOTAL BEATS
        output heartbeats per hour

PRODUCTION OF CODE
AND VERIFICATION OF
THE SOLUTION

The program header, declarations, and code for the main module of a possible solution follow:

```pascal
program Heartbeat;

const
  minsperhour = 60;
var
  heartrate,
  totalbeats
    : integer;
```

Figure 4.2
Heartbeat Structure Chart

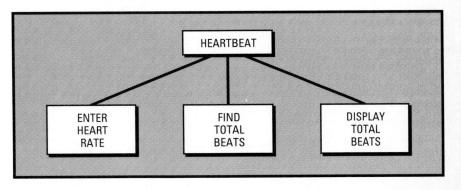

```
     procedure EnterHeartRate;
     begin
     end;

     procedure FindTotalBeats;
     begin
     end;

     procedure DisplayTotalBeats;
     begin
     end;

 begin
   EnterHeartRate;
   FindTotalBeats;
   DisplayTotalBeats
 end.
```

The constant defines the number of minutes in an hour. The variable identifiers *heartrate* and *totalbeats* are declared as integers.

The main program consists of calls to procedures, each representing a submodule in the structure chart. For testing purposes, stubs similar to those shown are inserted for each procedure.

After entering this version of the solution into the editor, the **Trace into** option from the IDE can be used to test whether the main program is properly connected to its procedures. Repeatedly pressing function key F7 highlights each statement in the order in which it is executed, jumping from main program to procedure and back to the main program. The trace is completed after the **end** statement in the main program is highlighted. Since all statements were highlighted in order, you can assume that the main program does what it is supposed to do—that is, goes to and returns from each of the called procedures.

Since each module can be verified after it is coded, you do not have to wait until the entire program is coded to test a module, so the production of code and the verification of the solution take place concurrently.

The next step in the testing process is to replace the **EnterHeartRate** stub with the actual code for that procedure. The outline of the solution for this module appears in the previous step of the design process. With this outline as a guide, replace the **EnterHeartRate** stub with the following:

```
     procedure EnterHeartRate;
     begin
       Write ('Enter heartbeat rate: ');
       Readln (heartrate)
     end;
```

The IDE Watches window follows the activity of any variable you designate by tracking the values attained by the variable in the course of execution of a program. Select the **Watch** option from the **Window** menu to activate a Watches window at the bottom of the screen. To track the value of *heartrate,* press Ctrl-F7 or select **Add watch** from the **Watches** submenu of the **Debug** menu. In the "Add Watch" dialog box that appears (see Figure 4.3), type the identifier name *heartrate* and press the Enter Key. The identifier now appears in the Watches window at the bottom of the screen.

To test the `EnterHeartRate` procedure, you have to tell the Pascal system to stop after returning to the main program from that procedure. The IDE comes to the rescue by allowing you to make lines in a program *breakpoints.* When a program comes to a breakpoint, it stops so you can examine the Edit and Watches windows. With this is mind, temporarily hide the Watches window and activate the Edit window by pressing Shift-F6 or choosing **Previous** from the **Window** menu. Now move the cursor to the `FindTotalBeats` line in the main program, and place a breakpoint there by pressing Ctrl-F8 or selecting **Toggle breakpoint** from the **Debug** menu. Pressing Ctrl-F8 a first time inserts a breakpoint at the location of the cursor. Pressing it a second time removes that breakpoint. This keystroke alternates between setting and removing breakpoints. The `FindTotalBeats` line in the main program is highlighted. Uncover the Watches window by pressing Shift-F6 to display the previous screen—the one that contained the Watches window. You can now execute the program by choosing **Run** from the **Run** menu or typing Ctrl/F9. After you enter a value for *heartrate,* the system returns to the Edit screen and the program stops at the breakpoint. Since the value for *heartrate* in the Watches window matches the input value, you can continue by replacing the next stub, `FindTotalBeats`. If the input value did not match the value in

Figure 4.3
"Add watch" Dialog Box

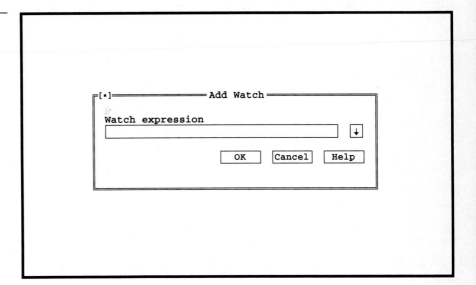

the Watches window, you would have to review the code and correct any inconsistencies before proceeding.

Since a calculation is performed in `FindTotalBeats`, an assignment statement is used in the solution:

```
procedure FindTotalBeats;
begin
  totalbeats := heartrate * minsperhour
end;
```

Add the variable *totalbeats* to the Watches window by moving the cursor under one of the letters in *totalbeats* and typing Ctrl/F7 (**Add watch**). After you press the Enter key, the Watches window is set to show the contents of both *heartrate* and *totalbeats*.

The next breakpoint should be set at the `DisplayTotalBeats` procedure call in the main program. Hide the Watches window (Shift-F6), press Ctrl-F8 (**Toggle breakpoint**) to remove the breakpoint from the call to `Find-TotalBeats`, move the cursor to call `DisplayTotalBeats`, and press Ctrl-F8 again to insert a new breakpoint there. Redisplay the Watches window (Shift-F6), and run the program again by pressing Ctrl-F9 (**Run**). A dialog box appears on the screen, indicating that the source code has been modified (the stub was replaced), and asks if you want to rebuild. Type *Y* or press Enter. This time the program execution stops at the `DisplayTotalBeats` procedure call in the main program. If a check of the Watches window shows the correct value for *totalbeats,* you can add the code for the `DisplayTotal-Beats` procedure. If not, review your coding, make the appropriate changes, reset the breakpoint, and retest the program before continuing.

The final step is to enter the correct code for the last procedure, `DisplayTotalBeats`:

```
procedure DisplayTotalBeats;
begin
  Writeln ('Total heartbeats per hour: ', totalbeats)
end;
```

Selecting **Output** from the **Window** menu opens an Output window and places it on top of the Watches window. A sample run of the program (with this procedure replacing its corresponding stub) shows the following in the Output window:

```
Enter heartbeat rate: 72
Total heartbeats per hour: 4320
```

When you have finished with the Watch variables, clear the Watches window by pressing Alt-F3 while that window is active.

Table 4.6 summarizes the Turbo Pascal IDE commands used for debugging in this exercise.

Table 4.6
Selected Turbo Pascal IDE
Debugging Commands

Command	Key Implementation
Add watch	Ctrl-F7
Previous (screen)	Shift-F6
Run	Ctrl-F9
Toggle breakpoint	Ctrl-F8
Trace into	F7

DOCUMENTATION OF
THE SOLUTION

After the code in the final module has been verified, enter the necessary internal documentation. The input/output chart, structure chart, and pseudocode comprise the external documentation. The final program listing and a sample output are shown in Figure 4.4.

STYLE TIP

Variable identifiers in the declaration section of a program should be listed on separate lines, even if they are of the same type. Adopting this convention makes it easier to find these identifiers. It also allows you to describe the purpose of each identifier by placing documentation to its right and not interfering with the program readability, as shown by the following declaration from the **Heartbeat** program:

```
var
   heartrate,                      { heartbeat rate }
   totalbeats            { total heartbeats per hour }
      : integer;
```

The top-down testing method just illustrated verifies the design of the software solution to a problem by first coding the top module (main program) and substituting program stubs for all the submodules in the solution. The stubs are replaced individually by properly coded procedures, and the program is tested. If an error is detected, the last procedure coded is a likely cause for the failure; it must be corrected before coding the next module. After all the procedures have been verified, the program and all its procedures are documented. The entire design methodology, including testing, must be mastered with elementary problems before it can be used to solve more challenging problems.

A detailed explanation of the entire software design methodology is shown in the solutions of the following problems. Because our emphasis is on learning Pascal, some of the more obvious steps are not shown. This should not diminish their importance; nor does it mean that you should stop using them.

Figure 4.4
Heartbeat Program
Listing and Sample Output

```
program Heartbeat;
{-------------------------------------------------------------------}
{ PROGRAM          Heartbeats                                       }
{ PROGRAMMER:      C. Barnard                                       }
{ DATE:            May 3, 1990                                      }
{                                                                   }
{ This program finds the total number of heartbeats made in one hour, }
{ given a person's heartbeat rate.                                  }
{                                                                   }
{ INPUT            heartbeat rate                                   }
{                                                                   }
{ OUTPUT           total heartbeats per hour                        }
{-------------------------------------------------------------------}
  const
    minsperhour = 60;                               { minutes in an hour }
  var
    heartrate,                                        { heartbeat rate }
    totalbeats                            { total heartbeats per hour }
      : integer;

  procedure EnterHeartRate;
  {-------------------------------------------------------------------}
  { Accept heartbeat rate.                                           }
  {-------------------------------------------------------------------}
  begin
    Write ('Enter heartbeat rate: ');
    Readln (heartrate)
  end;

  procedure FindTotalBeats;
  {-------------------------------------------------------------------}
  { Find total heartbeats per hour.                                  }
  {-------------------------------------------------------------------}
  begin
    totalbeats := heartrate * minsperhour
  end;
```

```
procedure DisplayTotalBeats;
{--------------------------------------------------------------------}
{ Display total heartbeats per hour.                                 }
{--------------------------------------------------------------------}
begin
  Writeln ('Total heartbeats per hour: ', totalbeats)
end;

begin
  EnterHeartRate;
  FindTotalBeats;
  DisplayTotalBeats
end.
```

─────────────────────── **Output** ───────────────────────

```
Enter heartbeat rate: 60
Total heartbeats per hour: 3600
```

4.6 Application Using Top-Down Testing: Dr. Celsius, I Presume

The following formula converts Fahrenheit (F) temperatures to Celsius (C) temperatures:

$$C = \frac{5(F - 32)}{9}$$

Write a program that accepts a Fahrenheit temperature and outputs its corresponding Celsius temperature.

ANALYSIS OF THE PROBLEM   The term *accept* indicates that the input quantity is the Fahrenheit temperature; *output* indicates that the desired result is the Celsius temperature. This is shown in Figure 4.5.

MODULAR DESIGN OF THE SOLUTION   The problem can be divided into three subtasks: entering the Fahrenheit temperature, calculating its Celsius equivalent, and displaying that equivalent. A structure chart outlining a solution is shown in Figure 4.6.

Figure 4.5
Temperature Conversion
Input/Output Chart

Input	Output
Fahrenheit temperature	Celsius temperature

Figure 4.6
Temperature Conversion
Structure Chart

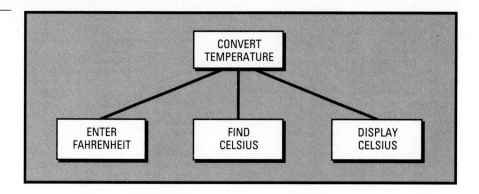

DESIGN OF THE
STRUCTURE OF THE
MODULES

CONVERT TEMPERATURE
   ENTER FAHRENHEIT
   FIND CELSIUS
   DISPLAY CELSIUS

ENTER FAHRENHEIT
   enter the Fahrenheit temperature

FIND CELSIUS
   find the Celsius temperature

DISPLAY CELSIUS
   output the Celsius temperature

PRODUCTION OF CODE
AND VERIFICATION OF
THE SOLUTION

The first step is to design the solution for the main module, with program stubs in place of all the submodules:

```
program ConvertTemperature;
  var
    ftemp,
    ctemp
      : real;

  procedure EnterFahrenheit;
  begin
  end;

  procedure FindCelsius;
  begin
  end;

  procedure DisplayCelsius;
  begin
  end;
```

```
begin
  EnterFahrenheit;
  FindCelsius;
  DisplayCelsius
end.
```

The identifiers *ftemp* and *ctemp* are declared reals, since temperature values need not be integer values. Follow the execution path of this initial version by using the IDE trace facility (F7).

The **EnterFahrenheit** procedure is first to replace its stub:

```
procedure EnterFahrenheit;
begin
  Write ('Enter Fahrenheit temperature: ');
  Readln (ftemp)
end;
```

Use **Add watch** (Ctrl/F7) to put *ftemp* into the Watches window, set a breakpoint at the **FindCelsius** procedure call in the main program (Ctrl/F8), and test **EnterFahrenheit**. Once verified, you can add the **FindCelsius** procedure by translating the formula given in the statement of the problem to its Pascal equivalent:

```
procedure FindCelsius;
begin
  ctemp := 5 * ftemp - 32 / 9
end;
```

Add *ctemp* to the Watches window (Ctrl/F7), set a breakpoint at the **DisplayCelsius** procedure call in the main program (Ctrl/F8), and test **FindCelsius**. If *50.5* is entered for *ftemp,* the Watches window shows a value of approximately *248.94* for *ctemp*. A check of this value by hand shows that 10.28 is the correct answer, not 248.94. The error is probably in the **FindCelsius** module. Checking that module, we find that the formula was not coded properly, for *ftemp − 32* should have been enclosed in parentheses. After the correction is made, that module becomes:

```
procedure FindCelsius;
begin
  ctemp := 5 * (ftemp - 32) / 9
end;
```

Resetting the breakpoint and rerunning the program shows the correct value of *ctemp* in the Watches window.

In the last step, a procedure is added to show the converted Celsius temperature, rounded to two decimal places:

```
       procedure DisplayCelsius;
       begin
          Writeln ('Celsius equivalent: ', ctemp:6:2)
       end;
```

One last execution with all procedures in place serves to verify the results of the completed program.

DOCUMENTATION OF
THE SOLUTION

The input/output chart, structure chart, and pseudocode serve as external documentation for the solution. The internal documentation is added to the program for the final product, shown, along with sample output, in Figure 4.7.

Figure 4.7
ConvertTemperature
Program Listing and
Sample Output

```
program ConvertTemperature;
{------------------------------------------------------------------}
{ PROGRAM:       Temperature Conversion                            }
{ PROGRAMMER:    L. Kelvin                                          }
{ DATE:          May 4, 1990                                       }
{                                                                  }
{ This program accepts a Fahrenheit temperature, converts it to the }
{ Celsius scale and displays the result.                           }
{                                                                  }
{ INPUT:         Fahrenheit temperature                            }
{                                                                  }
{ OUTPUT:        Celsius temperature                               }
{------------------------------------------------------------------}

   var
     ftemp,                                    { Fahrenheit temperature }
     ctemp                                       { Celsius temperature }
        : real;

procedure EnterFahrenheit;
   {------------------------------------------------------------------}
   { Accept a Fahrenheit temperature.                                 }
   {------------------------------------------------------------------}
   begin
     Write ('Enter Fahrenheit temperature: ');
     Readln (ftemp)
   end;
```

```
procedure FindCelsius;
{------------------------------------------------------------------}
{  Find the Celsius equivalent of a Fahrenheit temperature.        }
{------------------------------------------------------------------}
begin
  ctemp := 5 * (ftemp - 32) / 9
end;
procedure DisplayCelsius;
{------------------------------------------------------------------}
{ Display a Celsius temperature.                                   }
{------------------------------------------------------------------}
begin
  Writeln ('Celsius equivalent: ', ctemp:6:2)
end;

begin
  EnterFahrenheit;
  FindCelsius;
  DisplayCelsius
end.
```

───────────────────────── **Output** ─────────────────────────

```
  Enter Fahrenheit temperature: 72
  Celsius equivalent:  22.22
```

When you are finished with the watch variables, close the Watches window.

4.7 Application Using Top-Down Testing: Where There's Smoke, There's Fire

A retailer pays $72 for each case of 24 smoke alarms she purchases for resale. Given the number of cases purchased and assuming she sells all she buys, determine the retailer's gross income from the resale of the alarms as well as her net profit if she sells them for $5.99 each and it costs her $15 (in overhead) to place an order.

ANALYSIS OF THE PROBLEM   The word *given* indicates that input quantity is the number of cases purchased, and *determine* indicates that the gross income and net profit are the desired results. See Figure 4.8.

MODULAR DESIGN OF   The problem can be divided into four parts: entering the number of cases
THE SOLUTION   purchased, calculating the gross income, calculating the net profit, and

Figure 4.8
Smoke Alarm Input/Output
Chart

Input	Output
Number of cases purchased	Gross income
	Net profit

displaying the results of the calculations. Since the two calculation modules are relatively simple and require few steps, both could have been included in the same module. Figure 4.9 shows a structure chart outlining the solution.

DESIGN OF THE
STRUCTURE OF THE
MODULES

SMOKE ALARM SALES
   ENTER CASES PURCHASED
   FIND GROSS INCOME
   FIND NET PROFIT
   DISPLAY INCOME AND PROFIT

ENTER CASES PURCHASED
   enter number of cases purchased

FIND GROSS INCOME
   find number of alarms (number of cases × 24)
   find the gross income (5.99 × number of alarms)

FIND NET PROFIT
   find cost of alarms (number of cases × 72)
   find expenses (cost of alarms + overhead)
   find net profit (gross income − expenses)

Figure 4.9
Structure Chart for Smoke
Alarm Sales

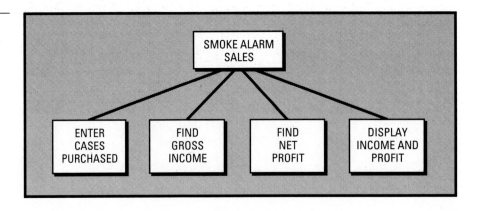

DISPLAY INCOME AND PROFIT
   output the gross income
   output the net profit

PRODUCTION OF CODE
AND VERIFICATION OF
THE SOLUTION

First design the solution for the main module and create program stubs for all the submodules:

```pascal
program SmokeAlarmSales;
  const
    costpercase = 72.00;
    alarmspercase = 24;
    unitsellprice = 5.99;
    overhead = 15.00;
  var
    quantity,
    alarmcount
      : integer;
    alarmcost,
    income,
    expenses,
    profit
    : real;

  procedure EnterQuantity;
  begin
  end;

  procedure FindGrossIncome;
  begin
  end;

  procedure FindNetProfit;
  begin
  end;

  procedure DisplayResults;
  begin
  end;

begin
  EnterQuantity;
  FindGrossIncome;
  FindNetProfit;
  DisplayResults
end.
```

Since the cost for each case (*costpercase*), the number of alarms in each case (*alarmspercase*), the unit selling price of each alarm (*unitsellprice*), and overhead cost for each purchase (*overhead*) do not change in the program, they are declared as constant identifiers. The values declared for each of these quantities determine their respective types.

The gross income (*gross*) and net profit (*profit*) are declared as real variable identifiers, since they represent monetary values. The total cost of the alarms (*alarmcost*) and the total expenses (*expenses*) are quantities that determine the gross income and net profit, respectively. They also have monetary values and are declared reals. The number of alarms purchased is an integer quantity that helps calculate the gross profit. You can follow the execution path of this initial version with the trace facility (F7) in the IDE.

The code replacing the stub for the **EnterQuantity** module is written first:

```
procedure EnterQuantity;
begin
  Write ('Enter number of cases purchased: ');
  Readln (quantity)
end;
```

Put *quantity* in the Watches window, set a breakpoint at the **FindGrossIncome** procedure call in the main program (Ctrl/F8), and test **EnterQuantity**. After it is verified, you can add the **FindGrossIncome** procedure by coding the two steps in the outline for that submodule:

```
procedure FindGrossIncome;
begin
  alarmcount := quantity * alarmspercase;
  income := unitsellprice * alarmcount
end;
```

Add *alarmcount* and *income* to the Watches window (Ctrl/F7), set a breakpoint at the **FindNetProfit** procedure call in the main program (Ctrl/F8), and test **FindGrossIncome**. If the number of cases purchased is *4*, a hand-check of the values of *alarmcount* and *income* shows that they match the values of *96* and *575.04* for these identifiers in the Watches window.

The next step is to substitute a procedure for the FindNetProfit stub:

```
procedure FindNetProfit;
begin
  alarmcost := quantity * costpercase;
  expenses := alarmcost + overhead;
  profit := income - expenses
end;
```

To test this procedure, add *alarmcost, expenses,* and *profit* to the Watches window, set a breakpoint at the **DisplayResults** procedure call in the main program, and test **FindNetProfit**. If *4* is entered for the number of cases purchased, the Watches window shows that *alarmcost* equals *288*, *expenses* equals *303*, and *profit* equals *272.04*, matching the results done by hand.

DisplayResults now replaces its stub:

```
procedure DisplayResults;
begin
   Writeln ('Gross Income: $', income:8:2);
   Writeln ('Net Profit: $', profit:8:2)
end;
```

One last execution with all procedures in place serves to verify the results of the completed program.

DOCUMENTATION OF
THE SOLUTION

The input/output chart, structure chart, and pseudocode serve as external documentation for the solution, and internal documentation is added for the final version, shown, along with sample output, in Figure 4.10.

Figure 4.10
SmokeAlarmSales
Program Listing and
Sample Output

```
program SmokeAlarmSales;
{--------------------------------------------------------------------------}
{ PROGRAM:        Smoke Alarm Sales                                         }
{ PROGRAMMER:     S.E. DeBear                                               }
{ DATE:           May 20, 1990                                              }
{                                                                          }
{ This program finds the gross income and net profit produced from the     }
{ sale of smoke alarms. The alarms are purchased in 24-unit cases          }
{ at a cost of $72 and sold at $5.99 each. There is an additional          }
{ expense of $15 for each order that is processed. It is assumed that      }
{ all alarms are sold.                                                     }
{                                                                          }
{ INPUT:          number of cases purchased                                }
{                                                                          }
{ OUTPUT:         gross income                                             }
{                 net profit                                               }
{--------------------------------------------------------------------------}
```

(continued)

```
const
  costpercase = 72.00;              { cost per case }
  alarmspercase = 24;              { alarms per case }
  unitsellprice = 5.99;           { unit selling price }
  overhead = 15.00;               { overhead per order }
var
  quantity,                    { number of cases purchased }
  alarmcount                  { number of alarms purchased }
    : integer;
  alarmcost,                        { total cost of alarms }
  income,                      { gross income from sales }
  expenses,                          { total expenses }
  profit                      { net profit from sales }
    : real;

procedure EnterQuantity;
{-------------------------------------------------------------- }
{ Accept the number of cases purchased.                         }
{-------------------------------------------------------------- }
begin
  Write ('Enter number of cases purchased: ');
  Readln (quantity)
end;

procedure FindGrossIncome;
{-------------------------------------------------------------- }
{ Find the gross income from all sales.                         }
{-------------------------------------------------------------- }
begin
  alarmcount := quantity * alarmspercase;
  income := alarmcount * unitsellprice
end;

procedure FindNetProfit;
{-------------------------------------------------------------- }
{ Find the net profit from all sales.                           }
{-------------------------------------------------------------- }
begin
  alarmcost := quantity * costpercase;
  expenses := alarmcost + overhead;
  profit := income - expenses
end;
```

```
procedure DisplayResults;
{-------------------------------------------------------------------- }
{ Output the gross income and net profit.                             }
{-------------------------------------------------------------------- }
  begin
    Writeln ('Gross Income: $', income:8:2);
    Writeln ('Net Profit: $', profit:8:2)
  end;

begin
  EnterQuantity;
  FindGrossIncome;
  FindNetProfit;
  DisplayResults
end.
```

──────────────────── **Output** ────────────────────

```
Enter number of cases purchased: 9
Gross Income: $ 1293.84
Net Profit: $ 630.84
```

Store and Forward

The power of a computer is evident from its ability to evaluate numeric expressions. Expressions consist of variables, constants, and operations that are combined according to specific rules. The assignment statement takes the value of an expression and stores it in a location from which it can be referenced when performing other calculations or when displaying results. With this ability, a program can accept data, do some work on that data, and output results.

As programs become more sophisticated, the need for proving them correct becomes increasingly important. The top-down testing process introduced in this chapter complements the top-down design method and allows us to test a program, module by module. The Turbo Pascal IDE provides facilities to help in this regard.

The procedures written for the decomposition process are cohesive in that they perform one particular task, but they depend on the main program for their variables and constants. The next chapter introduces a way to make procedures more independent of the main program or of each other. In this way, modules devised for one program can be used in another, with minimal changes.

Snares and Pitfalls

- *Omitting the multiplication operator:* Although multiplication is implied in algebra, it must be clearly indicated in Pascal; the product of *a* and *b* must be coded as **a * b**.

- *Using integer division instead of real division, and vice versa:* The real division operator (/) yields a real result, while the integer division operator (**div**) produces only an integer quotient, with the remainder discarded.

- *Omitting left or right parentheses:* In a numeric expression, the number of left parentheses should equal the number of right parentheses.

- *Improperly coding the assignment operator:* The assignment operator is a colon followed immediately by an equal sign; omitting either one or allowing a space between them produces an error.

- *Storing a real value in an integer location:* A real value cannot be stored in a location representing an integer. An integer value can, however, be stored in a location representing a real.

- *Using an improper location name on the left of an assignment operator:* Only a variable identifier can appear to the left of the assignment operator; expressions or constant identifiers are not allowed.

- *Dividing by zero:* An error results if an attempt is made to evaluate a fractional expression whose denominator is 0.

Exercises

1. Answer the following questions in paragraph form.
   a. Why is a method for overriding the order of operations necessary?
   b. Explain how breakpoints can help to debug a program.
   c. Why is a tracing utility useful?
   d. Explain how the assignment operator (:=) works.
   e. What is a program stub?

2. Classify each of the following Pascal statements as valid or invalid. If invalid, explain why. Unless otherwise stated, assume all identifiers have been properly declared.
   a. `average := total / count;`
   b. `c * c := a * a + b * b;`
   c. `double := double * 2;`
   d. `product = first * second;`
   e. `dividend mod divisor := remainder;`

3. Write a Pascal statement that corresponds to the given descriptions.
   a. Divide one integer (*first*) by another (*second*), and store the quotient in a location named *top*.
   b. Divide one integer (*third*) by another (*fourth*), and store the remainder in a location named *left*.
   c. Divide one integer (*fifth*) by another (*sixth*), and store the decimal result in a location named *float*.
   d. Calculate *rectarea*, the area of a rectangle, as a product of its length (*lngth*) and width (*wdth*).
   e. Triple the value stored in location *temp*, and store the new value in *temp*.

4. Find all the errors in the following program.

```pascal
program SimpleInterest;
  const
    rate : 0.115;
  var
    principal,
    interest
      : real

  procedure EnterData;
  begin
    Write ('Enter principal $')
    Readln (principal);
    Write (Enter time in years)
    Readln (time);
    Write ('Enter rate in decimal form: ')
    Readln (rate)
  end;

  procedure FindInterest;
  begin
    interest := (principal * rate * time)
  end;

  procedure DisplayInterest;
  begin
    Writeln ('Interest: '$, interest:8:2)
  end;

begin
  EnterData;
  FindInterest;
  DisplayInterest
end
```

5. Show the output produced by the following program.

```
program Example5;
  var
    a, b, c, d, e : real;
    i, j, k : integer;

  procedure Initialize;
  begin
    a := 2.0;
    b := 1.5;
    c := 0.5;
    i := 4;
    j := 10
  end;

  procedure Calculate1;
  begin
    d := a * b / c + i div j;
    k := j div i * i mod j;
    e := j / i
  end;

  procedure Calculate2;
  begin
    d := d / 4;
    k := k mod i;
    e := e + 1
  end;

  procedure Output;
  begin
    Write ('d = ', d:5:2);
    Write ('k = ', k:6);
    Writeln ('e = ', e:7:2)
  end;

begin
  Initialize;
  Calculate1;
  Output;
  Calculate2;
  Output
end.
```

6. The outline of a program that determines the circumference of a circle, given its radius, follows. Write a Pascal program to implement the outline.

   CIRCLE
       ENTER RADIUS
       FIND CIRCUMFERENCE
       OUTPUT CIRCUMFERENCE

   ENTER RADIUS
       enter the radius of a circle

   FIND CIRCUMFERENCE
       calculate the circumference
           (circumference = 6.28 × radius)

   OUTPUT CIRCUMFERENCE
       output the circumference

Programming Assignments

Some of the following assignments have appeared in previous exercises or programming assignments. Design and implement Pascal solutions for them.

Elementary

1. A 1985 census report indicated that there were 9,453,000 boys aged 5 and under in the United States. If the expected growth rate for this age group between 1985 and 1990 is 4% over the 5-year period, write a program to find the expected population in 1990.

2. Write a program to determine the total cost of a purchase of video-cassette tapes, given the cost of a single tape and the number of tapes purchased.

3. Lefty Romero hit 12, 8, 15, 20, and 17 home runs during his first 5 years in the major leagues. Write a program to find the average number of home runs hit by Lefty over that period.

4. Write a program that finds the straight-line depreciation value for an item, given the purchase price, the salvage value, and the number of years over which the item is to be depreciated. (The straight-line value is the difference between the purchase price and the salvage value, divided by the number of years.)

5. Write a program that accepts the measure of an angle in degrees and outputs its measure in radians. (3.1416 radians = 180 degrees)

6. Write a program that accepts a car salesperson's base weekly salary and the dollar value of the sales generated. Find and display the salesperson's total weekly salary (base salary + commission) if he or she receives a commission of 4.5% of the sales.

7. Write a program that outputs a person's age, given the current year and the year in which the person was born.

8. In addition to a flat monthly fee of $25, a computer information service charges $1 for each minute a customer's computer is connected. Write a program that determines the monthly charge for a customer, given the total number of minutes a customer has used the service in a month.

9. A nurse taking the pulse of a patient counts the number of heart beats in a 15-second period. Write a program that outputs the pulse rate per minute.

10. The energy E, in joules, possessed by a light wave is related to its wavelength L, in meters, by the following formula:

$$E = \frac{hc}{L}$$

where h is a constant whose value is 6.63×10^{-34} joule-seconds and c is the speed of light, with constant value 3.00×10^8 meters/second. Write a program that finds the energy of a photon of light whose wavelength is 5.35×10^{-8} meters.

Challenging

11. A cord of wood occupies a volume of 128 ft³. Write a program that finds the number of cords contained in a box-shaped pile of wood, given the length, width, and height of the pile.

12. It costs a company $850,000 to manufacture color monitors for computers. The selling price of a single monitor is $450. Write a program to determine the average number of monitors the company would have to sell every month in order to break even for the year.

13. A union has accepted a 6% increase in pay 4 months after its contract had expired. The company must now reimburse all employees for the 4 months they worked under their previous salaries. As part of the agreement, this retroactive pay will be paid over the next 6 months. Given an employee's yearly salary before the increase, write a program to find his or her monthly salary for the 6 months following the settlement.

14. A distributor that rents movies to local theaters receives $195 each time a movie is shown and keeps for operating expenses 20% of all it receives. Of the remainder, the studio that produced the movie receives 80%, and the actors' guild 20%. Write a program that determines how much the distributor, the movie studio, and the actors' guild receive in a week, given the total number of showings for three different theaters during that week.

15. The speed of light is approximately 3.00×10^8 meters per second. Write a program to find the speed of light in miles per hour if 1 foot = 0.305 meters.

16. A measure of inflation involves comparing the prices of an item at different times and finding the percentage change between these prices (the difference between the two prices divided by the earlier one). Write a program that accepts the name of an item, its price in January of a given year, and its price in April of the same year. Use the data to determine and output the percentage change for these first 3 months and for the entire year, assuming that the price continues to climb at the same rate. The program should also use the yearly figure to predict the price of the item at the end of the year.

17. Write a program that accepts a length of time in hours, minutes, and seconds and converts it to a decimal figure representing that time in days.

18. The volume of a sphere, in cubic feet, is given by the product of 4.19 and the cube of the radius (in feet). A spherical ball of putty has a radius of 1.25 feet. Write a program to find the additional volume of putty needed to increase the radius to 2.10 feet. Use a separate procedure to find the cube of the number.

19. Write a program that determines the cost of materials for the construction of a rectangular box, both with and without a cover, given the dimensions of the box and the cost per square foot of the materials used to construct the box.

20. A manufacturer sells its computers to dealers at 250% of the cost of the materials needed to assemble them. The computer's selling price is determined by adding markups ranging from 25% to 60% of the computer's cost to the dealer. Write a program that accepts the materials cost for a computer and outputs the cost of that computer to the dealer, a range of selling prices for it based on which markup is used, and a range of profits based on the markup.

CHAPTER 5

Procedures

Key Terms

actual parameter	**procedure**
black box	scope
Delete	side effect
formal parameter	**Str**
Insert	**Val**
local identifier	value parameter
module interface table (MIT)	variable parameter
parameter	

Objectives

- To introduce some Turbo Pascal system-defined procedures as models for programmer-defined procedures
- To pass values between program components by using parameters
- To define the scope of an identifier and demonstrate its consequences
- To create programmer-defined procedures and use them in the problem-solving methodology

5.1 Introduction

Chapter 2 introduced procedures as the basic building blocks of well-written structured programs: A problem is divided into blocks, or modules, each of which performs a single task. One of the major goals of top-down design is to produce a program whose modules are complete yet minimally dependent on each other, thereby simplifying program maintenance.

Even when a program is divided into separate blocks, however, each one still depends on and uses the identifiers declared in the main program. A greater degree of independence is possible if each module has its own set of identifiers. Then a module can be used in the solution of other problems, regardless of the identifiers declared for those problems. To achieve this independence, we must find a way to send the data required for calculations

Figure 5.1
The "Black Box" Concept

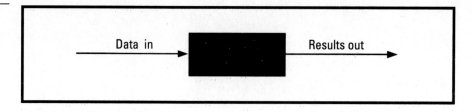

Data in   Results out

to the modules as well as receive results of calculations *from* the modules. An analogy might serve to clarify.

Suppose the manager of a automobile dealership wants a summary of the number of different types of cars sold in a given month. She could give all the sales reports to an employee (pass the data to him) and expect him to provide the results on a summary sheet she provided (receive information in return). The work of the employee is minimally dependent on the manager, requiring only that she deliver the sales reports and accept the sales summary. The manager would be aware not of how the employee produced the results, but only that the summary sheet was completed accurately.

Analogously, a procedure can be thought of as a *black box*, some unknown structure that accepts data from the main program or another procedure, does some processing, and returns results to the caller. See Figure 5.1. The box is termed "black" because the calling program does not have to "see" inside it to determine how the called procedure provides results, just as the manager did not have to "see" how the employee completed the summary.

This chapter starts by describing how built-in Pascal procedures utilize this capability of transferring data to and receiving results from calling statements, and gives some examples of how these procedures are used. With these examples as models, you can create your own procedures that provide the same data-transfer capabilities.

5.2 System-Defined Procedures

The Pascal language system defines its own procedures for some common tasks. The **Write**, **Writeln**, and **Readln** statements, for example, are actually all procedure calls. A constant or variable data item sent to a **Write** or a **Writeln** is displayed on a monitor screen or printed, while the **Readln** statement accepts data from the keyboard and stores it in memory locations. In all these statements, the data items sent to the procedure or received from it are called *parameters*. Calls to procedures start with the name of the procedure, followed by a list of parameters enclosed in parentheses. A semicolon signals the end of the calling statement.

The **Insert** Procedure

The **Insert** procedure places one string at a specified location in a second string.

FORMAT: **Insert (<source>, <destination>, <index>);**

This procedure takes the string constant or variable **<source>** and implants it in the string variable **<destination>**, starting at character number **<index>** in the destination string. Although the destination string has a new value, the source remains unchanged. You must know in which order to list the parameters. If parameters are placed in the wrong order, incorrect results or an error message will follow.

Examples

```
s := 'read';
d := 'unable';
i := 3;
Insert (s, d, i);
```

The string *read* is placed in *unable* starting at position 3. The letters to the right of *n* are moved to make room for *read*. After the insertion, *d* contains the string *unreadable*.

```
s := 'read';
d := 'unable';
i := 3;
Insert (d, s, i);
```

Regardless of its designation, the *s* is now the destination, and *unable* is inserted in *read* starting at position 3. The value of the string *d* does not change, but *s* becomes *reunablead*.

```
s := 'read';
d := 'unable';
i := 3;
Insert (i, s, d);
```

This implementation leads to an error, since the first parameter, *i*, is an integer instead of a string.

The **Delete** Procedure

The **Delete** procedure removes characters from a given string starting at an indicated location.

FORMAT: **Delete (<source>, <index>, <count>);**

The number of characters specified by **<count>** is removed from the string **<source>**, starting at position **<index>**. The source string is changed while the values of the other parameters remain unchanged. Even though they are both integers, the index must be the second parameter and the count the third.

Examples

```
s := 'character';
i := 5;
c := 2;
Delete (s, i, c);
```

Starting at *i*, the fifth letter, 2 letters are removed from *character*, resulting in the value of *s* changing to *charter*.

```
s := 'character';
i := 5;
c := 2;
Delete (s ,c, i);
```

Since *c* is the second parameter, it represents the index, and *i*, being the third, represents the count. As a result, 5 characters are removed from *s*, starting at position 2, leaving *s* as the string *cter*.

```
s := 'character';
i := 5;
c := 2;
Delete (i, c, s);
```

The **Delete** statement produces an error, since the first parameter should be a string and the last an integer.

The **Insert** and **Delete** procedures both contain three parameters enclosed in parentheses. **Insert** has two strings followed by an integer, where the first string must be the source and the second the destination. The **Delete** procedure has a string followed by two integers, where the first integer must be an index and the second a count.

The String Procedure

The **Str** (string) procedure converts a numeric value (integer or real) to its string representation.

FORMAT: **Str** (<number>, <string>);

The constant or variable represented by **<number>** is converted into a string and stored in variable **<string>**.

Example

```
i := 123;
Str (i, s);
Delete (s, 2, 1);
```

The integer *123* is converted into the string *123*. The **Delete** procedure then removes 1 character at position 2, changing the contents of *s* to the string *13*.

If the number parameter is real, the scientific notation (e-notation) representation of that number is stored as a string, unless field descriptors are included in the **Str** procedure.

Examples

```
r := 123.45;
Str (r, s);
```

Since no field descriptors are specified in **Str**, the real number *r*, whose value is 123.45, is converted to the string *1.2345000000E+02* and stored in *s*.

```
r := 123.45;
Str (r:6:2, s);
```

r is converted to the string *123.45* and stored in *s*, since field descriptors have been added to the first parameter in **Str**.

The Value Procedure

The **Val** (value) procedure converts a string containing numbers into its integer or real numeric equivalent.

FORMAT: **Val (<string>, <number>, <code>);**

The constant or variable **<string>** is converted into an integer if the variable **<number>** is a declared integer, or into a real number if **<number>** is a declared real. If the string contains only a numeric value, 0 is returned for **<code>**. If the string is invalid for any reason (for example, if it contains a letter), **<code>** gives the position of the first invalid character in the string and the variable **<number>** is assigned the value 0. If **<number>** is an integer, a decimal point is considered an invalid character.

Examples

```
s := '789';
Val (s, i, c);
i := i + 111;
```

If *i* is a declared integer, the string *789* is changed to the integer 789 and stored in *i*. 111 is added to 789, and the result, 900, replaces 789 as the value of *i*.

```
i := 632;
s := '789.54';
Val (s, i, c);
i := i + 111;
```

If *i* is a declared integer, the decimal point stored in string *s* is invalid. Consequently, 4 is stored in the code variable *c* and *i* is set to 0. In the last statement, 0 is added to 111, and that sum replaces 0 as the value of *i*.

```
s := '789abc';
Val (s, r, c);
Writeln ('code: ',c);
```

Assume *r* is a declared real. Since the string *789abc* contains letters, when **Val** is executed, the position of *a*, the first invalid character, is stored in *c*, 0.0 is stored in *r*, and 4 is displayed as the value of the code, since the first nonnumeric character *a* is in position 4 in string *s*.

5.3 Subprogram Communication

All four procedures discussed in the previous section contain parameters enclosed in parentheses, although the number of parameters, their types, and the order in which they are listed vary. Programmer-defined procedures also allow the transfer of values through parameters enclosed in parentheses.

The parameters in the call to a procedure are termed *actual parameters*, while those in the called procedure are called *formal parameters*. Thus, when employing a system-defined procedure, we specify the actual parameters. The formal parameters, which are designated and defined when the code for the procedure is written, are hidden.

There are two types of parameters used to transfer information between a procedure and its call: value parameters and variable parameters.

Value Parameters

A *value parameter* is similar to a one-way street, allowing the transfer of data from a call to its procedure but not permitting information to be returned to the calling statement. Copies of the values of the actual parameters, which may be variables or constants, are sent to memory locations represented by variable identifiers defined in and known by only the called procedure. See Figure 5.2. The identifiers that represent these locations in the procedure are called *local identifiers.*

There are two copies of the value for each value parameter: one in the main program or calling procedure and another that is local to the called procedure. If your program changes the value of the formal parameter in the called procedure, it does not cause a change in the value of the actual parameter in the calling statement.

Value parameters are used in **Write** and **Writeln** procedures, since values are only sent to these procedures and not changed by them. Consider the format of the **Insert** procedure rewritten as follows:

```
Insert ( <source>, <destination>, <index> );
```

The source string and index in the **Insert** procedure are value parameters, since they do not change or return any values to the calling statement. The same cannot be said for the destination string; its new value must be returned to the caller, using a variable parameter for this purpose.

Variable Parameters

The *variable parameter* is similar to a two-way street, allowing both the transfer of data from a call to its procedure and the return of information from the procedure to the calling statement. In this case, a single memory

Figure 5.2
Value Parameter
One-Way Action

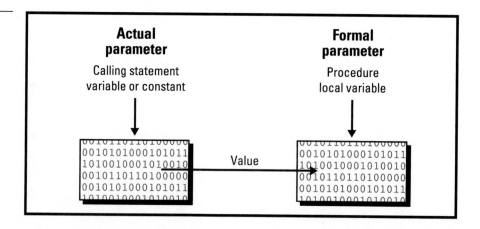

Figure 5.3
Variable Parameter
Two-Way Action

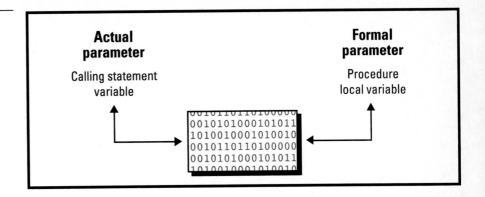

Actual parameter

Calling statement variable

Formal parameter

Procedure local variable

location is referenced by two variable identifiers: the actual parameter specified in the calling statement and a local one, the formal parameter, defined by the called procedure. See Figure 5.3.

Any change in the value of the local variable (formal parameter) automatically alters the actual parameter, since they both refer to the same physical memory location.

It is important to understand the distinction between value parameters and variable parameters, and when to employ each. Variable parameters are needed when a called procedure changes values that must be returned to a calling statement. If data sent to a procedure is not changed, a value parameter is the choice.

Procedure Declarations with Parameters

When a procedure is defined, formal parameters are enclosed in parentheses in the procedure statement following the name given to the procedure.

FORMAT: `procedure <identifier> (<formal parameter list>);`

Each formal parameter declaration must include an identifier, indicate whether it is a value parameter or a variable parameter, and specify its data type:

`[var] <identifier> : <data type>;`

To signify that a formal parameter is a variable parameter, **var** must precede the identifier. If **var** is not present, the identifier is a value parameter. The square brackets, [and], indicate that **var** may or may not be present, depending on whether the identifier is a value parameter or a variable parameter. As in a variable declaration, a colon separates the identifier name from its data type. Semicolons are used to delimit or separate formal parameters in the list.

Example

`procedure T (var x:real; y:integer);`	Procedure **T** has two formal parameters: x, a real variable parameter; and y, an integer value parameter.

The order in which the actual parameters appear in a procedure call must correspond to the order of the formal parameters in the procedure declaration, as Figure 5.4 illustrates.

The actual parameters *test1* and *test2* in the call to **Average** are value parameters and can pass data only one way, to the locations represented by

Figure 5.4
Communicating Using
Parameters

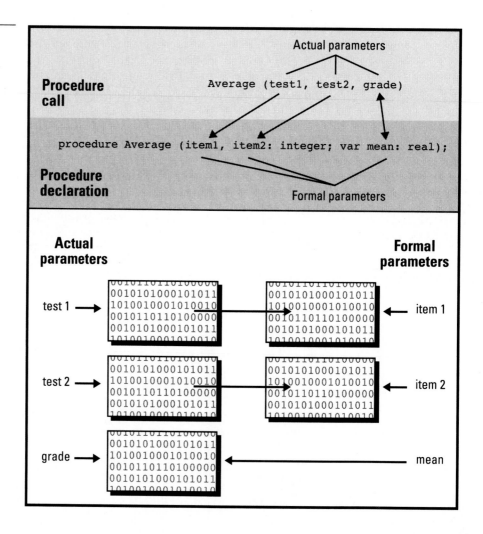

item1 and *item2*, respectively. Because *mean* is a variable parameter, both it and *grade*, its matching parameter in the call, refer to the same location in main memory. When a value for mean is calculated in procedure **Average**, that value is automatically accessible to *grade*.

Identifiers having the same parameter type *and* data type may be listed together, with their identifier names separated by commas, as in:

procedure Sample1 (**var** x, y : **real**);

and

procedure Sample2 (i, j : **integer**);

If identifiers are not of the same parameter type or data type, they must be declared independently, where each declaration is separated from the next by a semicolon, as in:

procedure Sample3 (**var** x : **real**; y : **real**);

and

procedure Sample4 (z : **real**; k : **integer**);

Only simple data types (**integer, longint, real, char,** and **boolean**) or programmer-defined data types are allowed as types in procedure header statements. You must define strings in **type** statements if string parameters are to be parts of procedure headers.

Example

```
type
  stringtype = string[20];
  . . .

  procedure R (s : stringtype);
```

For a string *s* to be passed to procedure R, a **type** statement defining *stringtype* should be present in the main program. The statement

procedure R (s : **string**[20]);

would result in an error.

5.4 The Scope of Identifiers

Programmer teams often design and implement large projects in which each team member may be assigned the responsibility of producing one module or set of modules, with these modules as independent of one another as possible. Individual programmers may use the same identifier names for the same or different quantities in different modules. Thus, a module created by one team member may affect a module created by another, adding another measure of dependency. To avoid problems of this type, Pascal allows—but strictly governs—identical identifier names in different modules.

An identifier that is declared in a main program has global scope and is valid in all procedures contained in that program. The *scope* of an identifier is the set of modules (programs or subprograms) in which the identifier is legally declared. If a subprogram contains an identical identifier name, however, the local declaration takes precedence; that is, an identifier declared in a subprogram overrides the global scope of that identifier. Parameters declared in a **procedure** statement are considered local to that procedure.

A program skeleton is shown in Figure 5.5. At the time of its call, the procedure **One** has three local variable identifiers: a variable parameter *w*

Figure 5.5
Program Skeleton

```
program Main;
  var
     w, x, y, z : ...

  procedure One (var w: ... ; a : ... );
     var
        x: ...;
     begin
        .
        .
        .
     end;

  procedure Two (c: ... ; y : ... ; var x ...);
     var
        z, w: ...;
     begin
        .
        .
        .
     end;

begin {Main}
     .
     .
     .
  One (y, z);
     .
     .
     .
  Two (w, y, x);
     .
     .
     .
end.
```

that shares a location with the global variable y declared in the main program, a value parameter a that receives a value from the global variable z, and a local variable x. There are two different locations labeled x, one global and the other local to procedure **One**. Figure 5.6 illustrates the memory relationship between **Main** and **One**.

Procedure **Two** in Figure 5.5 has five local variables: the value parameters c and y, which receive values from the global variables w and y, respectively; a variable parameter x that refers to the same location as the global variable x; and two local variables z and w. There are separate global and local variables for the identifiers w, x, y, and z. See Figure 5.7.

Figure 5.6
Memory Relationship
Between Program **Main**
and Procedure **One**

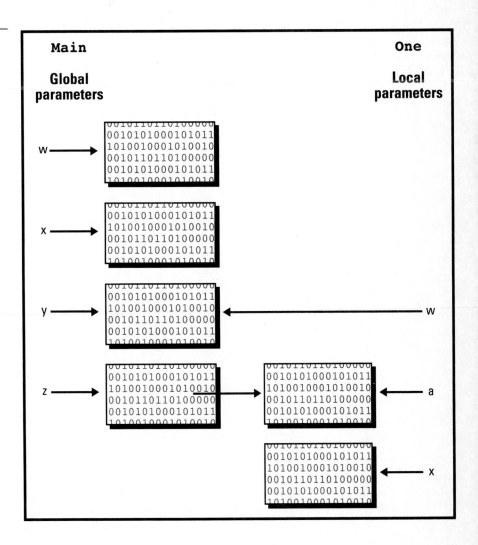

Figure 5.7
Memory Relationship
Between Program Main
and Procedure Two

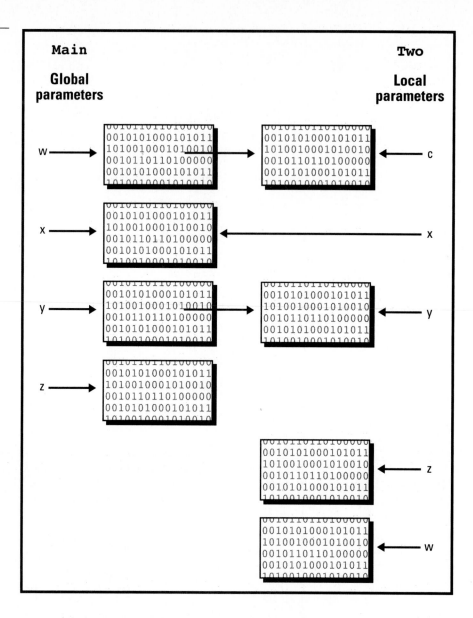

Side Effects

Since global variables defined in a program are valid for all its subprograms, their values can be altered by any statement in any of these subprograms. A change in a global variable that is not returned through a parameter is known as a *side effect*. Side effects can produce logic errors that are difficult to detect and debug.

Example

<table>
<tr>
<td>

```
program SideEffect;
  var
  gv : real;
   . . .

  procedure SE ( ... );
  var
   . . .
  begin
   . . .
  gv := gv + 1.2;
   . . .
  end;

begin
   . . .
  gv := 4.2;
  Writeln (gv:5:1);
  SE ( . . . );
  Writeln (gv:5:1);
   . . .
end.
```

</td>
<td>

After 4.2 is assigned to *gv* in the main program and displayed, a call is made to procedure **SE**. If **SE** has no local variable named *gv* that overrides the global *gv*, 1.2 is added to 4.2 and the result, 5.4, stored in the global *gv*. The **Writeln** statement in the main program following the call to **SE** then displays 5.4, the altered value of the global variable *gv*. Procedure **SE** has produced a side effect by changing the value of *gv*.

</td>
</tr>
</table>

There are no side effects with constant identifiers, because their values cannot be altered. An attempt to do so causes an error.

STYLE TIP	To eliminate possible side effects, avoid using global variables in subprograms or identical identifiers for different quantities.

5.5 Programmer-Defined Procedures with Parameters

A programmer-defined procedure has the same key components as a program: Both have names, and both contain declaration and processing sections. The only major difference is that the first line in a main program is a **program** header, whereas the first line in a procedure is a **procedure** header. Consider some examples, keeping in mind the types of parameters, the order in which the parameter identifiers are listed, and the data type for each of these identifiers.

Example

```
procedure Output (cost : real; qty : integer);
begin
  Writeln ('Number of items sold: ', qty);
  Writeln ('Total cost: $', cost:6:2)
end;
```

call:
```
    Output (cost, number);
```

Assume that *cost* and *number* have been declared in the main program. When `Output` is called, the current values for the global variables *cost* and *number* are passed to the local value parameters *cost* and *qty*. There are now two copies of each variable, even though the same identifier (*cost*) is declared in both the procedure `Output` and the main program. `Output` displays the local values with appropriate messages. There is no need for variable parameters, since neither of the passed values was changed by `Output`.

Example

```
procedure EnterCircle (var x, y, radius : real);
begin
  Writeln ('Enter circle values: ');
  Write (' x-coordinate of center: ');
  Readln (x);
  Write (' y-coordinate of center: ');
  Readln (y);
  Write (' radius: ');
  Readln (radius)
end;
```

call:
```
  EnterCircle (xc, yc, rad);
```

`EnterCircle` accepts values for its variable parameters *x*, *y*, and *radius*, and returns them through *xc*, *yc*, and *rad*, respectively.

Example

```
procedure Switch (var first, second : integer);
  var
    temp : integer;
begin
  temp := first;
  first := second;
  second := temp
end;
```

`Switch` exchanges the values stored in *a* and *b*. When it is called, 3 is passed to *first* and 5 to *second*. `Switch` takes the 3 in *first* and stores it in the local variable *temp* and takes 5, the value of *second*, and stores it in *first*. Both *first* and *second* now contain 5. Then the 3 stored in *temp* is copied into *second*, and control returns to the calling statement. The identifiers *first* and *second* are variable parameters, since the exchanged val-

call:
```
  a := 3;
  b := 5;
  Switch (a, b);
```

ues are to be sent back to the main program, where *a* is now 5 and *b* is 3.

Constants can also be used as actual parameters, but they must have the same type as their corresponding formal value parameter. The formal parameter that corresponds to a constant actual parameter *cannot* be a variable parameter, since a value calculated in a procedure cannot be passed back to a call and stored in a location represented by a constant.

Example

```
procedure Sum (x, y : integer; var ans : integer);
begin
  ans := x + y
end;
```

call:
```
  Sum (6, 7, total);
```

6 and 7 are passed to *x* and *y*, respectively. The procedure **Sum** adds these values and stores the result, 13, in *ans*. Since the global variable *total* has access to the same memory location as *ans*, *total* now also contains 13.

To minimize the interdependence between modules and to strengthen the modules themselves, the practice of passing values through parameters is used for the remainder of the text.

5.6 Application in Passing Data: Discount Prices

A computer outlet store sells hardware and allows customers to call for discounted prices. Write a program that outputs the discounted price, given the list price of the item to be purchased and the discount percentage.

ANALYSIS OF THE PROBLEM   Figure 5.8 lists the input and output quantities required for the solution.

Figure 5.8
Price-Quote Input/Output Chart

Input	Output
List price of item	Discounted price
Discount percentage	

141

Figure 5.9
Price-Quote Solution
Design

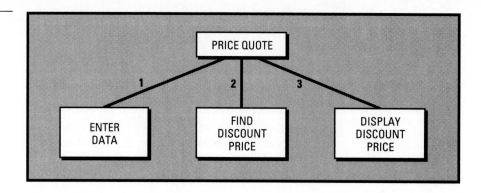

MODULAR DESIGN OF
THE SOLUTION

The basic design of the solution giving the relationships among the modules is shown in Figure 5.9.

Three lines, or interfaces (numbered 1, 2 and 3), connect related modules. A *module interface table* (*MIT*) specifies the actual parameters involved in each interface and specifies what quantities are sent to and received from each module. Figure 5.10 shows the MIT for this structure chart.

The first column gives the interface number shown on the design chart. The In column specifies the actual parameters whose values are needed by the called module, and the Out column shows the values that have been received by the calling statement as a result of the module's action. Interface 1 does not send any data from the main program to **ENTER DATA**, but it does receive values for *listprice* and *discountpct* from that module. The values of *listprice* and *discountpct* are sent to **DISCOUNT PRICE** via Interface 2, and a value for *discountprice* is returned. Interface 3 transmits the calculated value for *discountprice* to **DISPLAY DISCOUNT PRICE**, which returns nothing to the main program.

Creating an MIT helps you determine whether formal parameters are value parameters or variable parameters. All identifiers in the Out column must be variable parameters, while identifiers that only send data to a module are value parameters. For this problem, *listprice* and *discountpct* are variable parameters for Interface 1 and value parameters for Interface 2;

Figure 5.10
Price-Quote Module
Interface Table

Interface	In	Out
1	—	listprice, discountpct
2	listprice, discountpct	discountprice
3	discountprice	—

countprice is a variable parameter for Interface 2 and a value parameter for Interface 3.

DESIGN OF THE
STRUCTURE OF THE
MODULES

PRICE QUOTE
   ENTER DISCOUNT DATA
   FIND DISCOUNT PRICE
   DISPLAY DISCOUNT PRICE

   ENTER DISCOUNT DATA
     enter list price of item
     enter discount percentage

   FIND DISCOUNT PRICE
     calculate the discounted price
     [discountprice = (1 − discountpct) × listprice]

   DISPLAY DISCOUNT PRICE
     output the discounted price

The discounted price is calculated by changing the discount percentage to decimal form (dividing it by 100), subtracting it from 1, and multiplying the result by the list price. For example, if the discount percentage is 15, then 1 − 15/100, or 0.85, should be multiplied by the list price to obtain the discounted price.

PRODUCTION OF CODE
AND VERIFICATION
OF SOLUTION

The program skeleton with the stubs for procedures follows. The procedure headers and calls indicating the information that is passed between the main program and procedures are completed, but the code for the procedures themselves is not written until that module is added to the solution.

```
program PriceQuote;
  var
    listprice,
    discountpct,
    discountprice
      : real;

  procedure EnterData (var list, pct : real);
  begin
  end;

  procedure FindDiscountPrice (list, pct : real;
                               var price : real);
  begin
  end;
```

(continued)

143

```
    procedure DisplayDiscountPrice (dsctprice : real);
    begin
    end;

begin
  EnterData (listprice, discountpct);
  FindDiscountPrice (listprice, discountpct, discountprice);
  DisplayDiscountPrice (discountprice)
end.
```

The parameters for the main program calls are determined by the declared global identifiers; the identifiers for the formal parameters shown in the procedure headings may be the same as or different from their corresponding actual parameters, but they must match in type and placement.

You can use the **Trace into** option (F7) from the Turbo Pascal IDE to check whether the parameters in the main program correspond to their counterparts in each of the procedures. Any errors in matching either the number of parameters or their types are revealed during the trace and must be corrected before they are involved in calculations that might produce inaccurate results.

The next step is writing the code for the **EnterData** module and adding it to the program:

```
procedure EnterData (var list, pct : real);
begin
  Write ('Enter list price: $');
  Readln (list);
  Write ('Enter discount percentage (in %): ');
  Readln (pct)
end;
```

Use the IDE (1) to place the identifiers *discountpct, listprice, pct,* and *list* in the Watches window via **Add watch** (Ctrl/F7); (2) to install a breakpoint (Ctrl/F8) at the **FindDiscountPrice** call in the main program; and (3) to run the program (Ctrl/F9). If you enter 1299 for the list price and 20 for the discount percentage, these values appear next to their respective identifiers in the Watches window. "Unknown identifier" follows each of the local identifiers *pct* and *list,* since the breakpoint is in the main program and these identifiers are not defined in the main program.

If you had placed a breakpoint at the **end** statement in the **EnterData** procedure, 1299 would appear for both *list* and *listprice,* and 20 for both *discountpct* and *pct.* Since *listprice* and *discountpct* are declared in the main program, they are defined for all procedures in that program, including **EnterData**.

The `FindDiscountPrice` procedure is written next and added to the solution:

```
procedure FindDiscountPrice (list, pct : real;
                                      var price : real);
begin
  price := (1 - pct/100)*list
end;
```

Add *discountprice* and *price* to the Watches window, and set a breakpoint at the `DisplayDiscountPrice` procedure call in the main program. If the input values for *discountpct* and *listprice* are 20 and 1299, respectively, then 1039.2 is the calculated value for *discountprice*. Again, *price, pct,* and *list* are undefined, since the breakpoint is in the main program and they are not defined there. This value of discounted price should be compared to a hand-checked version to ensure the accuracy of the calculations.

Since 1039.2 is the correct value, the last module, DisplayDiscountPrice, is coded and added to the solution:

```
procedure DisplayDiscountPrice (dsctprice : real);
begin
  Writeln ('Discounted price: $', dsctprice:8:2)
end;
```

After this module is tested, comments are added to the program. The final version of the program and sample output are shown in Figure 5.11.

Figure 5.11
Price-Quote Program
Listing and Sample Output

```
program PriceQuote;
{--------------------------------------------------------------------}
{ PROGRAM:       Price Quotation                                     }
{ PROGRAMMER:    Ray Dioschak                                        }
{ DATE:          May 25, 1990                                        }
{                                                                    }
{ This program finds the discounted price of a computer hardware item }
{ given its list price and a discount percentage.                    }
{                                                                    }
{ INPUT          list price of computer hardware item                }
{                discount percentage                                 }
{                                                                    }
{ OUTPUT         discounted price of the item                        }
{--------------------------------------------------------------------}
```

(continued)

```
var
  listprice,                              { list price of a hardware item }
  discountpct,                                  { discount percentage }
  discountprice                                   { discounted price }
    : real;

procedure EnterData (var list, pct : real);
{------------------------------------------------------------------------}
{ Accept the list price and discount percentage from the keyboard.     }
{                                                                      }
{ IN            none                                                   }
{                                                                      }
{ OUT           list:       list price of a hardware item             }
{               pct:        discount percentage                       }
{------------------------------------------------------------------------}
begin
  Write ('Enter the list price: $');
  Readln (list);
  Write ('Enter the discount percentage (in %): ');
  Readln (pct)
end;

procedure FindDiscountPrice (list, pct : real; var price : real);
{------------------------------------------------------------------------}
{ Calculate the discounted price                                       }
{                                                                      }
{ IN            list:       list price of a hardware item             }
{               pct:        discount percentage                       }
{                                                                      }
{ OUT           price:      discounted price                          }
{------------------------------------------------------------------------}
begin
  price := (1 - pct/100)*list
end;

procedure DisplayDiscountPrice (dsctprice : real);
{------------------------------------------------------------------------}
{ Display discounted price                                             }
{                                                                      }
{ IN            dsctprice:  discounted price                          }
{                                                                      }
{ OUT           none                                                   }
{------------------------------------------------------------------------}
begin
  Writeln ('Discounted price: $', dsctprice:8:2)
end;
```

```
begin
  EnterData (listprice, discountpct);
  FindDiscountPrice (listprice, discountpct, discountprice);
  DisplayDiscountPrice (discountprice)
end.
```

──────────────────── **Output** ────────────────────

```
Enter the list price: $1349
Enter the discount percentage (in %): 17.5
Discounted price: $ 1112.92
```

The requirements for documentation for each procedure are similar to those for the main program. The In and Out sections indicate the identifiers representing the data received by the procedure and sent back to the main program, respectively. This data can be found in the In and Out columns of the MIT in Figure 5.10. Any other local variables used by a procedure also require descriptive documentation.

5.7 Application in Passing Data: Taxing Work

The amount of tax charged to a property owner is based on the assessed value of the property and the tax rate. Write a program that accepts the assessed value of a piece of property and determines the tax due if 80% of the assessed value is taxed at rate of 2.3%.

ANALYSIS OF THE PROBLEM   Since the 80% value assessment and 2.3% tax rate are true for all properties, they are declared as global constants and are not included in the specification of input and output variable identifiers in Figure 5.12.

MODULAR DESIGN OF
THE SOLUTION   The modular structure outlining the solution and its corresponding MIT are shown in Figure 5.13.

DESIGN OF THE   TAX PAYMENT
STRUCTURE OF THE   ENTER ASSESSED VALUE
MODULES   TAX DUE
                           DISPLAY TAX DUE

Figure 5.12
Tax Payment Input/Output
Chart

Input	Output
Assessed value	Tax

Figure 5.13
Tax Payment Solution
Design and Module
Interface Table

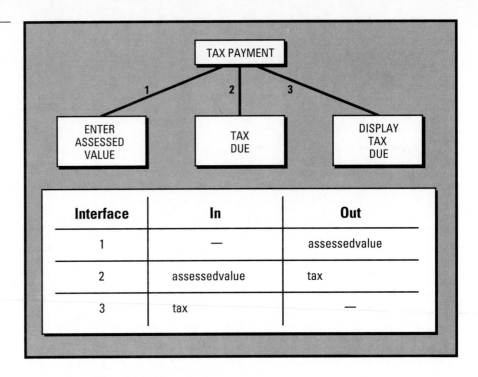

ENTER ASSESSED VALUE
    enter assessed value of property

TAX DUE
    determine tax due on property
        (assessed value × assessment percentage × tax rate)

DISPLAY TAX DUE
    output the tax due

PRODUCTION OF CODE
AND VERIFICATION OF
SOLUTION

```
program TaxPayment;
  const
    assessedpct = 0.80;
    taxrate = 0.023;
  var
    assessedvalue,
    tax
      : real;

  procedure EnterAssessedValue (var worth : real);
  begin
  end;
```

```
procedure TaxDue (propvalue : real; var tax : real);
begin
end;

procedure DisplayTaxDue (tax : real);
begin
end;

begin
  EnterAssessedValue (assessedvalue);
  TaxDue (assessedvalue, tax);
  DisplayTaxDue (tax)
end.
```

Use the **Trace into** option from the IDE to check if any errors result from a mismatch of the actual parameters in the main program and their corresponding formal parameters in each of the procedures. These errors must be corrected before adding `EnterAssessedValue` procedure.

```
procedure EnterAssessedValue (var worth : real);
begin
  Write ('Enter assessed value of property: $');
  Readln (worth)
end;
```

The actual parameter *assessedvalue* in the main program receives the input value from the formal variable parameter *worth*. Use the IDE to verify this by placing both these identifiers in the Watches window, installing a breakpoint at the `TaxDue` call in the main program, and running the program.

After testing the entry module, you can add the `TaxDue` procedure to the solution:

```
procedure TaxDue (propvalue : real; var tax : real);
begin
  tax := propvalue * assessedpct * taxrate
end;
```

The value of the global variable *assessedvalue* is passed to the local variable *propvalue* and used to find the correct value for tax. Add any new identifiers to the Watches window, install a new breakpoint, run the program, and compare the results in the Watches window with those calculated by hand.

The last module, `DisplayTaxDue`, is added to the solution after validating the results of the previous module:

```
procedure DisplayTaxDue (tax : real);
begin
  Writeln ('Tax due: $', tax:6:2)
end;
```

After a final run to check the validity and format of the output, comments are added to produce the final version shown, along with an output sample, in Figure 5.14.

Figure 5.14
TaxPayment Program
Listing and Sample Output

```
program TaxPayment;
{----------------------------------------------------------------------}
{ PROGRAM:       Tax Payment                                           }
{ PROGRAMMER:    Bosten T. Partee                                      }
{ DATE:          May 31, 1990                                          }
{                                                                      }
{ This program finds the amount of tax due on a property assessed at   }
{ 80% of its value with a tax rate of 2.3%.                            }
{                                                                      }
{ INPUT          assessed value of a property                          }
{                                                                      }
{ OUTPUT         tax due                                               }
{----------------------------------------------------------------------}
  const
    assessedpct = 0.80;                        { assessed percentage }
    taxrate = 0.023;                                    { tax rate }
  var
    assessedvalue,                      { assessed value of property }
    tax                                       { amount of tax due }
      : real;

  procedure EnterAssessedValue (var worth : real);
    {------------------------------------------------------------------}
    { Accept the assessed value for a property.                        }
    {                                                                  }
    { IN           none                                                }
    {                                                                  }
    { OUT          worth:       assessed value of property             }
    {------------------------------------------------------------------}
```

```pascal
begin
  Write ('Enter assessed value of property: $');
  Readln (worth)
end;

procedure TaxDue (propvalue : real; var tax : real);
{-------------------------------------------------------------------------}
{ Calculate the tax due.                                                  }
{                                                                         }
{ IN            propvalue:    assessed value of property                  }
{                                                                         }
{ OUT           tax:          tax due                                     }
{-------------------------------------------------------------------------}
begin
  tax := propvalue * assessedpct * taxrate
end;

procedure DisplayTaxDue (tax : real);
{-------------------------------------------------------------------------}
{ Display the tax due.                                                    }
{                                                                         }
{ IN            tax:          tax due                                     }
{                                                                         }
{ OUT           none                                                      }
{-------------------------------------------------------------------------}
begin
  Writeln ('Tax due: $', tax:6:2)
end;

begin
  EnterAssessedValue (assessedvalue);
  TaxDue (assessedvalue, tax);
  DisplayTaxDue (tax)
end.
```

Output

```
Enter assessed value of property: $125000
Tax due: $2300.00
```

Store and Forward

System-defined procedures serve as good examples of procedures, since they follow the same syntax rules as programmer-defined procedures. In both cases, values are interchanged between the sending module and receiving modules.

The passing of values through parameters gives the sending and receiving modules a degree of independence, in that neither relies on the identifiers declared in the other. Parameters can be unidirectional, passing values only from the sending to the receiving module, or bidirectional, allowing the transfer of data to and from both modules.

Although global identifiers declared in the main program are considered defined in all procedures contained in that program, a procedure may also have its own private, or local, identifiers whose definitions are not legal outside that procedure. In addition, a procedure may contain statements that change the values of global identifiers and produce a side effect.

The debugging utilities in the Turbo Pascal IDE allow tracing the values of both global and local variables; they also assist in the top-down testing process.

Procedures aren't the only type of subprogram that can transfer data between program components; Pascal functions have similar capabilities. The next chapter focuses on how the use of functions complements the use of procedures in the creation of well-written, structured programs.

Snares and Pitfalls

- *Incorrectly ordering parameter lists:* The actual parameters and their corresponding formal parameters must occur in the same positions in the parameter lists.

- *Associating an actual parameter with a formal parameter of a different type:* An actual parameter must be of exactly the same data type as its corresponding formal parameter.

- *Using a value parameter instead of a variable parameter, or vice versa:* Value parameters can only send data to a procedure; a variable parameter must be used if data is sent from a procedure back to its call.

- *Not placing a procedure declaration before its call:* A procedure must be defined before it is called from another procedure or the main program.

- *Using a constant actual parameter that corresponds to a variable formal parameter:* The purpose of a variable formal parameter is to send data back to the calling statement; this is not possible if the corresponding actual parameter is a constant.

- *Failing to use a simple or programmer-defined data type for a parameter in a procedure heading:* A complex data type such as **string**[30] produces an error if used for a formal parameter. To pass a complex data type, you must create a new type for it in the main program.

- *Failing to precede variable parameters with the keyword* **var**: The inflence of **var** ends with the next occurrence of a semicolon. A parameter following that semicolon is considered a value parameter unless it also is preceded by **var**.

Exercises

1. Answer the following questions in paragraph form.
   a. Explain why value parameters are considered one-way parameters and variable parameters, two-way parameters.
   b. Are formal parameters considered global or local? Explain.
   c. Distinguish between actual and formal parameters.
   d. What is the scope of an identifier?
   e. What is a side effect? Give an example.

2. Classify each of the following Pascal statements as valid or invalid. If invalid, explain why. Unless otherwise stated, assume all identifiers have been properly declared.
   a. **procedure** A (x, y; **var** z);
   b. **procedure** B;
   c. **Insert** (sourcestring, 'destination', 3);
   d. **Delete** (sourcestring, 5, 3);
   e. **Val** ('1001A', number);

3. Write Pascal equivalents for each of the given descriptions.
   a. Convert the numeric value stored in the variable *total* to a string stored in the variable *stotal*.
   b. Change the contents of the string location *greet* containing the string *induce* to *introduce* by inserting the string constant *tro* in the correct position.
   c. Write a procedure heading that accepts values for the principal of a loan, the term of the loan, and an interest rate and returns the amount of the monthly payment.
   d. If an identifier called *place* contains the string *country*, use a procedure to remove the *r* from *place*, leaving *county*.
   e. Convert the string *341.87* to a real and store it in the location named *rnumber*.

4. Indicate whether the parameters used in each of the following system-defined procedures are value parameters or variable parameters.
   a. **Delete** (<source>, <index>, <count>);
   b. **Str** (<number>, <string>);
   c. **Val** (<string>, <number>, <code>);

5. Show the exact output produced by the following programs.

a.
```pascal
program PartA;
  type
    stringtype = string[20];
  var
    x : stringtype;

  procedure One (var z : stringtype);
    var
      y : stringtype;
  begin
    y := 'rwa';
    Writeln ('z before change: ', z);
    Insert (y, z, 3);
    Writeln ('z after change: ', z);
  end;

begin
  x := 'ford';
  Writeln ('x before call: ', x);
  One (x);
  Writeln ('x after call: ', x)
end.
```

b.
```pascal
program PartB;
  type
    stringtype = string[20];
  var
    x : stringtype;

  procedure Two (z : stringtype);
    var
      y : stringtype;
  begin
    y := 'rwa';
    Writeln ('z before change: ', z);
    Insert (y, z, 3);
    Writeln ('z after change: ', z);
  end;

begin
  x := 'ford';
  Writeln ('x before call: ', x);
  Two (x);
  Writeln ('x after call: ', x)
end.
```

c. **program** PartC;
   var
     i, j : **integer**;

   procedure Three (a : **integer**; **var** b : **integer**);
   begin
    Writeln ('a = ', a);
    b := 10 * a + a;
    Writeln ('b = ', b)
   end;

   procedure Four (c : **integer**; **var** d : **integer**);
   begin
    Writeln ('c = ', c);
    d := c **div** 4;
    Writeln ('d = ', d)
   end;

begin
  i := 3;
  Writeln ('i = ', i);
  Three (i, j);
  Writeln ('i = ', i);
  Writeln ('j = ', j);
  Four (j, i);
  Writeln ('i = ', i);
  Writeln ('j = ', j);
end.

d. **program** PartD;
   var
     i, j : **integer**;

   procedure Five (**var** a : **integer**; b : **integer**);
   begin
    Writeln ('a = ', a);
    b := 10 * a + a;
    Writeln ('b = ', b)
   end;

   procedure Six (**var** c : **integer**; d : **integer**);
   begin
    Writeln ('c = ', c);
    d := c **div** 4;
    Writeln ('d = ', d)
   end;

```
begin
  i := 3;
  Writeln ('i = ', i);
  Five (i, j);
  Writeln ('i = ', i);
  Writeln ('j = ', j);
  Six (j, i);
  Writeln ('i = ', i);
  Writeln ('j = ', j);
end.
```

6. Draw a structure chart and a module interface table for the solution to each of the following problems. Use parameters to pass values between modules.
   a. A 1985 census report indicated that there were 9,453,000 boys aged 5 and under in the United States. If the expected growth rate for this age group between 1985 and 1990 is 4% over the 5-year period, write a program that finds the expected population in 1990.
   b. Write a program that accepts the measure of an angle in degrees and outputs its measure in radians. (3.1416 radians = 180 degrees)
   c. A nurse taking the pulse of a patient counts the number of heartbeats in a 15-second period. Write a program that outputs the pulse rate per minute.
   d. The volume of a sphere, in cubic feet, is given by the product of 4.19 and the cube of the radius (in feet). A spherical ball of putty has a radius of 1.25 feet. Write a program to find the additional volume of putty needed to increase the radius to 2.10 feet. Use a separate procedure to find the cube of a number.

Programming Assignments

Some of the following assignments have appeared in previous exercises or programming assignments. Design and implement Pascal solutions for them using parameters to pass values between modules.

Elementary

1. A 1985 census report indicated that there were 9,453,000 boys aged 5 and under in the United States. If the expected growth rate for this age group between 1985 and 1990 is 4% over the 5-year period, find the expected population in 1990.

2. Determine the total cost of a purchase of video cassette tapes, given the cost of a single tape and the number of tapes purchased.

3. Lefty Romero hit 12, 8, 15, 20, and 17 home runs during his first 5 years in the major leagues. Find the average number of home runs hit by Lefty over that period.

4. Find the straight-line depreciation value for an item, given the purchase price, the salvage value, and the number of years the item is to be depreciated. The

straight-line value is the difference between the purchase price and the salvage value, divided by the number of years.

5. Write a program that accepts the measure of an angle in degrees and outputs its measure in radians. (3.1416 radians = 180 degrees)

6. Write a program that accepts a car salesperson's base weekly salary and the dollar value of the sales generated. Find and display the salesperson's total weekly salary (base salary + commission) if he or she receives a commission of 4.5% of the sales.

7. A company stores the current year as a string in several documents. Write a program that accepts the current year as a string, converts it into an integer, adds 1 to update it, and converts it back into a string. Display both the original year and the updated year.

8. In addition to a flat monthly fee of $25, a computer information service charges $1 for each minute a customer's computer is connected. Write a program that determines the monthly charge for a customer, given the total number of minutes a customer has used the service in a month.

9. A nurse taking the pulse of a patient counts the number of heartbeats in a 15-second period. Write a program that outputs the pulse rate per minute.

10. The energy E, in joules, possessed by a photon of light is related to its wavelength L, in meters, by the following formula:

$$E = \frac{hc}{L}$$

where h is a constant whose value is 6.63×10^{-34} joule-seconds and c is the speed of light with constant value 3.00×10^{8} meters/second. Write a program that accepts the wavelength of a beam of light and finds the energy of a photon of that light.

Challenging

11. A cord of wood occupies a volume of 128 ft³. Find the number of cords contained in a box-shaped pile of wood, given the length, width, and height of the pile.

12. It costs a company $850,000 a year to manufacture color monitors for computers. The selling price of a single monitor is $450. Determine the average number of monitors the company would have to sell every month in order to break even for the year.

13. A union has accepted a 6% increase in pay 4 months after its contract expired. The company must now reimburse all employees for the 4 months they worked under their previous salaries. As part of the agreement, this retroactive pay will be paid over the next 6 months. Given an employee's yearly salary before the increase, find his or her monthly salary for the 6 months following the settlement.

14. A distributor that rents movies to local theaters receives $195 each time a movie is shown and keeps for operating expenses 20% of all it receives. Of the remainder, the studio that produced the movie receives 80%, and the actors' guild 20%. Write a program that determines how much the distributor, the movie studio, and the actors' guild receive in a week, given the total number of showings for three different theaters during that week.

15. A manufacturer sells its computers to dealers at 250% of the cost of the materials needed to assemble them. The computer's selling price is determined by adding markups ranging from 25% to 60% of the computer's cost to the dealer. Write a program that accepts the materials cost for a computer and outputs the cost of that computer to the dealer, a range of selling prices for it based on which markup is used, and a range of profits based on the markup.

16. A measure of inflation involves comparing the prices of an item at different times and finding the percentage change between these prices (the difference between the two prices divided by the earlier one). Write a program that accepts the name of an item, its price in January of a given year, and its price in April of the same year. Use this data to determine and output the percentage change for these first 3 months, and percentage change for the entire year, assuming the price continues to climb at the same rate. The program should also use the yearly figure to predict the price of the item at the end of a year.

17. Write a program that accepts a length of time in hours, minutes, and seconds and converts it into a decimal figure representing that time in days.

18. The volume of a sphere, in cubic feet, is given by the product of 4.19 and the cube of the radius (in feet). A spherical ball of putty has a radius of 1.25 feet. Write a program to find the additional volume of putty needed to increase the radius to 2.10 feet. Use a separate procedure to find the cube of a number.

19. The combination of a post office mailbox is given by the string RnnLnnRnn, where R represents a turn to the right, L a turn to the left, and nn a two-digit integer. For example, a combination of R22L14R25 means turn the dial to the right until you reach 22, to the left to 14, and back to the right to 25. Write a program that creates and displays a new combination by inserting a new middle term into the old combination.

20. A bank has a system that accepts the amount for a cashier's check as a four-digit number without commas and prints out the amount with a comma inserted following the first digit. Write a program that accepts a check amount between 1000.00 and 9999.99, converts it into a string with a comma following the first digit, and displays the string.

CHAPTER 6

Functions

Objectives

- To introduce some Turbo Pascal system-defined functions as models for programmer-defined functions
- To show how to pass values between a function and a calling statement
- To compare procedures and functions
- To create programmer-defined functions and employ them in the problem-solving methodology

6.1 Introduction

A *subprogram*, or routine, is a set of instructions designed to perform a specific task. A procedure is a subprogram that accepts data from a calling statement and returns any number of values through variable parameters. A function is also a subprogram, but it differs from a procedure in its declaration statement, how it returns values, and how it is called.

Both procedures and functions have identifier names, use parameters, perform specific tasks, and must be declared before they are called. While a procedure can return any number of values to a calling statement, a function is designed to return only one value. In functions, values are returned through function names, whereas in procedures they are routed through variable parameters. Since the function name represents a value, it must be defined as a specific data type in the function header line.

A procedure call is, in itself, a complete Pascal statement, consisting of a procedure name followed by a list of actual parameters enclosed in parentheses. A function call must be part of an expression in the calling statement; it cannot stand by itself.

As with the procedure, the function acts like a black box: It accepts data from the calling statement, performs an action, and returns a single value. How that value is obtained need not be apparent.

Pascal contains a collection of functions, called a *library*, that can be accessed by referencing the unique name given to each function. Some of these functions are concerned with numeric quantities only, while others involve both numeric and string quantities. A discussion of some of them will provide you with a basis on which to create your own functions.

6.2 System-Defined Numeric Functions

Some of Turbo Pascal's built-in functions—such as absolute value, square, and square root—are routinely used in mathematical applications. Others—such as a rounding function and a random number generator—were designed to simplify the programming of other applications.

The Absolute Value Function

The **Abs** (absolute value) function accepts an integer or a real actual parameter and returns its absolute value, that is, the positive value of the parameter. For example, the absolute value of −45.7 is 45.7, and the absolute value of 91 is 91.

FORMAT: **Abs** (<number>)

If <number> is an integer, an integer value is returned; if <number> is real, a real value is returned.

Example

```
x := -6.31;
y := Abs(x) * 2;
```

In the second assignment statement, the absolute value of x (6.31) is multiplied by 2 and the result (12.62) stored in the real identifier y. In this example, the function call is part of an assignment statement.

The Square Function

Pascal does not have an exponentiation operator, but it does have a built-in **Sqr** function that calculates the square of an integer or real parameter. This function returns the value of the parameter multiplied by itself. For example, the square of 1.2 is 1.2 × 1.2, or 1.44, and the square of –25 is –25 × –25, or 625.

FORMAT: **Sqr (<number>)**

If **<number>** is an integer, **Sqr** returns an integer; if **<number>** is real, **Sqr** returns a real value.

Example

```
x := 2;
z := 3 * Sqr(x) + x - 4;
```

The right side of the second assignment statement is evaluated by finding the product of 3 and the square of *x*, adding *x* and subtracting 4. The result (10) is stored in the integer location *z*.

The Square Root Function

The **Sqrt** (square root) function returns the positive square root of a real non-negative value, that is, the number that when multiplied by itself yields the parameter. For example, the square root of 25.0 is 5.0, since 5.0 × 5.0 = 25.0.

FORMAT: **Sqrt (<nonnegative real>)**

The parameter must have nonnegative real value, and the function returns a nonnegative real value to the call. If the parameter has an integral value, it is converted to a real before the square root is returned. If the parameter has a negative value, an error message is displayed.

Examples

```
x := -1.44;
y := Sqrt(Abs(x));
```

Whenever one function is the parameter of another, the inner function is evaluated first. In this case, **Abs**(x) is a parameter of the **Sqrt** function, to ensure that its value is nonnegative. The absolute value of *x* is 1.44. As a result, the real identifier *y* stores the square root of 1.44, or 1.2.

```
a := 5;
b := 12;
c := Sqrt(Sqr(a)+Sqr(b));
```

The inner functions are evaluated first: **Sqr**(5) is 25, and **Sqr**(12) is 144. The square root of their sum (13) is stored in *c*.

The Pi Function

The **Pi** function returns the value of 3.1415926535897932385, the ratio of the circumference of a circle to its diameter.

FORMAT: **Pi**

This function returns the value of this mathematical constant and has no parameters.

Example

```
rad := 5;
area := Pi * Sqr(rad);
Writeln ('Area: ', area:6:2);
```

The product of **Pi** and the square of 5 is stored in the real location *area*. That value is displayed, rounded to two decimal places, as in the following:

```
Area: 78.54
```

The **Round** Function

The **Round** function rounds its real parameter to the nearest long integer value. For example, Round(-3.34) is –3 and Round(3.54) is 4.

FORMAT: **Round (<real number>)**

The parameter can be any real number. If the rounded value gives an integer outside the legal range for long integers, an error results.

Example

```
ans := Round(Sqrt(74.35));
```

The square root of 74.35 is approximately 8.6. Applying the **Round** function to that value returns a 9, and that value is stored in the integer location *ans*.

This function can also be used to round a value to any number of decimal places. For example, 135.694 can be rounded to two decimal places, yielding 135.69, or to a single decimal place, resulting in 135.7.

Example

```
r := 34.567;
s := Round(r*100)/100;
```

The expression in parentheses must be evaluated before **Round** is applied. *r* is multiplied by 100, yielding 3456.7, and the result rounded to the nearest integer (3457). That answer is divided by 100, giving 34.57. In effect, these statements store the value of *r*, rounded to two decimal places, in *s*. If a value is to be rounded to three decimal places, 1000 is substituted for 100 in the formula on the right side of the second assignment statement.

The Truncate Function   The **Trunc** (truncate) function removes the fractional part (all the digits to the right of the decimal point) from its real parameter and returns the remaining long-integer value. For example, **Trunc(3.34)** = 3, and **Trunc(-3.54)** = –3.

FORMAT: **Trunc(<real number>)**

The parameter can be any real number. If the rounded value gives an integer outside the legal range for long integers, an error results.

Example

`ans := Trunc(Sqrt(74.35));`

The square root of 74.35 is between 8 and 9. Applying the **Trunc** function to any value in that range returns the 8 that is stored in the integer location *ans*.

Random Number Generation   Computers sometimes recreate and test real-world environments. To introduce the measure of uncertainty and unpredictability that is inherent in such environments, numbers are chosen at random to closely approximate the probability, rather than the certainty, of certain events occurring.
    The **Random** function returns a random number in a specified range.

FORMAT: **Random [(<integer>)]**

The square brackets indicate that the integer parameter is optional. The **Random** function without a parameter returns a real number between 0 and 1, including 0 but not 1. If **Random** is followed by a positive integer in parentheses, the function produces a random integer between 0 and the designated integer, including 0 but not the integer. If the parameter is less than or equal to 0, 0 is returned.

Examples

`j := Trunc(Random);`

Since **Random** has no parameter, it returns a *real* value between 0 and 1, not including 1. The truncate function removes the fractional part, leaving 0 to be stored in the integer location *j*.

`i := Random(2);`

The parameter 2 indicates that an *integer* between 0 and 2, not including 2, is selected by the computer. Only 0 and 1 satisfy that description; therefore, one of them is stored in the integer location *i*.

Each time a program containing the **Random** function is executed, the same "random" numbers are produced in the same order. Although this makes it easy for you to check results, for most applications it is undesirable. To put the randomness back in **Random**, a **Randomize** procedure must be executed before random values are chosen.

FORMAT: **Randomize;**

Since **Randomize** is a procedure, it is a statement in itself. No parameters are needed.

Examples

```
program PartA;
  var
    j : integer;
begin
  j := Random(100);
  Writeln (j)
end.
```

Each time the program **PartA** is executed, Turbo Pascal chooses the same integer for *j*. If this program were run 100 times, that value would be displayed each time.

```
program PartB;
  var
    j : integer;
begin
  Randomize;
  j := Random(100);
  Writeln (j)
end.
```

In **PartB**, **Randomize** is executed before a random integer is chosen. When this program is run, there is a good chance that a different integer is displayed each time. There is always the possibility that, given enough runs, the same value might be chosen more than once.

Since it is a function, **Random** can be part of an expression that can generate a number in any range desirable. The expression

a + Random (b + 1 - a)

generates random integers between *a* and *b*, inclusive. If **Random** simulated the throw of a single die, *a* would be 1, *b* would be 6, and the generating expression would be:

1 + Random(6 + 1 - 1)   or   **1 + Random(6)**

6.3 System-Defined String-Related Functions

In addition to functions that are purely numeric, the Turbo Pascal library contains others that allow the manipulation of string data.

The **Length** Function

The **Length** function returns an integer that represents the number of characters, including spaces, in its string parameter. For example, the length of *Happy New Year* is 14 (spaces included).

FORMAT: **Length (<string>)**

The parameter may be a variable or a constant.

Example

```
s := 'Night and Day';
x := 2 + Length(s);
```

The length of the string *s*, 13, is added to the arbitrary value 2, and the result, 15, is stored in the integer location *x*.

The Position Function

The **Pos** (position) function returns the location of the first occurrence of a specified substring in a given string. If *def* is sought in the string *abcdefgh*, the function returns 4, since *def* starts at character position 4 in the string *abcdefgh*.

FORMAT: **Pos (<substring>, <string>)**

If **Pos** finds an exact copy of **<substring>** in the target string **<string>**, it returns the position of the first matching character in **<string>**. If the substring is not part of the target string, **Pos** returns 0. If the substring appears two or more times in the target string, **Pos** returns the starting location of the first occurrence only.

Example

```
s := 'about';
p := Pos('o', s);
Delete (s, p, 1);
```

p contains 3 after **Pos** finds the position of the letter *o* in *about*. The **Delete** procedure removes the single character *o* at position 3 and changes the string *s* to *abut*.

The **Copy** Function

The **Copy** function duplicates a portion of a given string. For example, the substring *and* can be copied from the string *handbook* by starting at the second character and reproducing the next three characters.

FORMAT: **Copy (<string>, <index>, <count>)**

The **<count>** characters starting at position **<index>** are copied from **<string>**. The index *and* count are integer parameters. If **<index>** is larger than the length of the string, an empty string is returned. If the count goes beyond the end of the string, whatever is present is copied. The original string does not change—a duplicate of a portion of it is made.

Example

```
s := 'processing';
t := Length(s);
dup := Copy(s, t-3, 4);
```

The length t of a string s is 10. Since the value of $t - 3$ is 7, the 4 characters starting at position 7 in s (*sing*) are stored in the string location *dup*.

The Concatenation Function

The **Concat** (concatenation) function attaches one or more strings to the end of another. For example, if *paper* is appended to *news*, the resulting string is *newspaper*.

FORMAT: **Concat (<string1> [, <string2>, . . . , <stringn>])**

<string2> is attached to the end of <string1>, <string3> to the end of <string2>, and so on. If the resulting string is longer than 255 characters, only the first 255 are stored.

Example

```
n := 'nation';
c := 'con';
t := 'cat';
ans := Concat(c, t, 'e', n);
```

The contents of the string variable t are appended to the contents of c, yielding *concat*. The string constant *e* and the contents of n are added in order, and the result, *concatenation*, is stored in the string variable *ans*.

If a concatenated string contains more characters than are declared for the variable containing that string, any excess characters are ignored. For example, if the identifier *ans* in the previous example had been declared to be of type **string**[10], only *concatenat*, the first ten characters of the concatenated string, would be stored in *ans*.

The ASCII Character Function

Every character on the keyboard is translated into a numeric code, called the ASCII code, before the computer can interpret that character. (A complete listing of this code is given in Appendix D.) For example, the decimal value of the code for the pound symbol, #, is 35.

FORMAT: **Chr (<decimal code>)**

The **Chr** (character) function returns the ASCII character associated with an integer decimal code value. An error occurs if the code is not entered as an integer. The returned character may be stored as a **char** type or **string** type identifier.

Example

```
st := Chr(97);
```

The ASCII character with the decimal code 97 is the lowercase letter *a*. It is stored in the location represented by the **char** or **string** identifier *st*.

The Ordinal Function

As you recall, an ordinal data type is one where, given a value, the next higher (or lower) value is uniquely determined. Of the data types previously defined, **integer**, **longint**, **char**, and **boolean** are ordinal data types. Integers are ordinal data types, since, given any integer, you can determine the next one. The integer 35 immediately follows 34. By definition, the Boolean value **TRUE** follows **FALSE**.

The **Ord** (ordinal) function returns the ordinal number associated with its parameter.

FORMAT: **Ord (<ordinal expression>)**

If the parameter is an integer, it returns that integer. If the parameter is a character, **Ord** returns the ASCII code for that character. The ordinal value for the Boolean FALSE is 0 and for TRUE is 1. If the parameter is not an ordinal type, an error message is displayed.

Examples

```
i := Ord(-546);
```

Since −546 is an integer, that value is stored in *i*.

```
c := 'h';
j := Ord(c) + 10;
c := Chr(j);
```

10 is added to the ASCII code for the lowercase *h* (104) and the result, 114, stored in *j*. The value of *c* then changes to the character whose ASCII code is 114 (the lowercase letter *r*).

6.4 Programmer-Defined Functions

You can create a function that accepts values from a calling statement and returns a single value through the function name. These programmer-defined functions are used the same way as a built-in function: The function call must be part of an expression in the calling statement, and the actual and formal parameters must match in order and in type.

Since a function is a subprogram, it has a declaration section for any local identifiers it needs, a body of instructions to perform a specific task, and a header describing the parameters it employs. Since a value is sent back to the call via the function name, the function header also must specify a data type for the function.

FORMAT: **function** <identifier> (<formal parameters>) : <type>;
    <local declarations>
begin
    <body of the function>
end;

    The function header consists of a unique identifier for that function; an optional list of parameters, with their data types, enclosed in parentheses; a colon; and a data type for the function itself. As in a procedure, any local identifiers are declared before the body of the function is written. The function name is considered a global variable identifier.

    Since procedures can return any number of values to a calling statement, any problem solution that can be written using programmer-defined functions also can be written with programmer-defined procedures.

STYLE TIP	Begin a programmer-defined function name with an uppercase letter. If the name consists of more than one word, the first letter of each word is also uppercase, with no spaces between words. With this convention it will be easier to spot function names when debugging a program.

Example

```
function X (a:real) : integer;
```

The function *X* accepts a real value *a* from the call and returns an integer through the function name *X*.

    Since a value is returned to the call through the function name, there must be at least one statement in the body of the function that assigns a value to the function name. If there is none, an arbitrary value is passed to the calling statement.

Example

```
function RndInteger : integer;
begin
  RndInteger := Random(5)
end;
```

call:
```
 i := RndInteger;
```

The function **RndInteger** chooses a random integer between 0 and 5, not including 5, and returns that value to the calling statement via the assignment statement in the function. Even though **RndInteger** has no parameters, its data type must be specified.

When the function name appears on the left side of an assignment statement in the body of a function, it behaves as an identifier, with only the function's name appearing. (No parameters in parentheses are written.) When that name is used to call a function, it *must* have its actual parameters enclosed in parentheses or an error results.

Example

```
function CylinderVol (radius, height : real) : real;
begin
   CylinderVol := Pi * Sqr(radius) * height
end;
```

call:
```
Write ('Enter radius: ');
Readln (rad);
Write ('Enter height: ');
Readln (hgt);
vol := CylinderVol(rad,hgt);
```

After real values have been entered for *rad* and *hgt*, these values are passed to the function's formal parameters, *radius* and *height,* respectively. The call is on the right side of an assignment statement, with the parameters enclosed in parentheses. The function calculates the volume of the cylinder and stores it in `CylinderVol`, which appears on the left of an assignment statement without parameters. The volume is returned to the calling statement, where it is stored in *vol.*

Some data types, such as strings, can be passed to a function if a data type has been established in a **type** declaration in the main program. For example, strings cannot be transferred unless a programmer-defined type has been declared for them.

Example

```
type
stringtype = string[30];

   .  .  .

function Acronym (name : stringtype) : stringtype;
  var
    first, second : stringtype;
     spacepos : integer;
begin
  first := Copy(name, 1, 1);
  spacepos := Pos(' ', name);
  second := Copy(name, spacepos + 1, 1);
  Acronym := Concat(first, second)
end;
```

call:
```
company := 'Acme Builders';
inits := Acronym(company);
```

The type *stringtype* is defined in the main program as **string**[30]. The string *Acme Builders* of that type is passed to the function **Acronym** and stored locally in the identifier called *name*. The function **Copy** makes a copy of *A*, the first letter in *name*, and stores it in *first*. The function **Pos** finds the position of the first space in *name* and stores it in *spacepos*. That value is used to locate the first letter in the second word of the company name, which is stored in *second*. The first letters in each word of the company name are concatenated, and the result, *AB*, is passed back to *inits* through **Acronym**.

6.5 Application Using Functions: Degrees Chirp

The air temperature on a warm day can be approximated by counting the number of chirps a cricket makes in a given period of time. The more chirps, the higher the temperature. This relationship is defined by the following equation:

$$\text{temperature} = (\text{number} + 160)/4$$

where *number* is a count of the chirps made in a minute and *temperature* is measured in degrees Fahrenheit. Write a program that accepts the number of chirps counted in a one-minute interval and displays the estimated temperature.

ANALYSIS OF THE PROBLEM

Figure 6.1 lists the input and output quantities.

MODULAR DESIGN OF
THE SOLUTION

The design of the solution and a description of the module interfaces is shown in Figure 6.2.

TEMPERATURE is a function, since it returns a single value. Procedures are used for ENTER COUNT and DISPLAY TEMPERATURE.

Since we are adopting the convention of starting the names of programmer-defined functions with a capital letter, the uppercase *T* in the Interface 2 Out column of the MIT indicates that the calculated value is returned through a function name. Identifiers in the Out column that

Figure 6.1
Temperature Estimation
Input/Output Chart

Input	Output
Number of chirps	Temperature

Figure 6.2
Temperature Estimation
Solution Design and
Module Interface Table

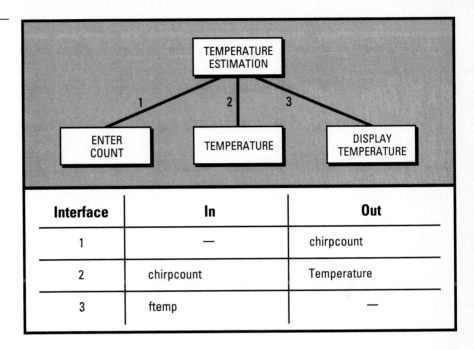

Interface	In	Out
1	—	chirpcount
2	chirpcount	Temperature
3	ftemp	—

consist of only lowercase characters are returned through procedure parameters rather than by a function name.

DESIGN OF THE STRUCTURE OF THE MODULES

TEMPERATURE ESTIMATION
   ENTER COUNT
   TEMPERATURE
   DISPLAY TEMPERATURE

ENTER COUNT
   enter number of chirps counted in a minute

TEMPERATURE
   determine the Fahrenheit temperature

DISPLAY TEMPERATURE
   output the temperature

PRODUCTION OF CODE AND VERIFICATION OF SOLUTION

```
program TemperatureEstimation;
  var
    chirpcount
      : integer;
    ftemp
      : real;
```

(continued)

171

```
procedure EnterCount (var count : integer);
begin
end;

function Temperature (count : integer) : real;
begin
end;

procedure DisplayTemperature (temp : real);
begin
end;

begin
  EnterCount (chirpcount);
  ftemp := Temperature (chirpcount);
  DisplayTemperature (ftemp)
end.
```

Use the **Trace into** option (F7) from the IDE to check that the actual parameters in the main program match their corresponding formal parameters in each of the subprograms. Any errors must be corrected before you add the **EnterCount** procedure to the solution.

```
procedure EnterCount (var count : integer);
begin
  Write ('Enter chirps counted in one minute: ');
  Readln (count)
end;
```

The actual parameter *chirpcount* corresponds to the formal parameter *count*. Use the IDE to verify this by placing both of these identifiers in the Watches window, installing a breakpoint at the *ftemp* assignment statement in the main program, and running the program. Once this module has been tested, the **Temperature** function can be added to the solution. Since **Temperature** is defined as a real number, real division should be used in the formula.

```
function Temperature (count : integer) : real;
  var
    temp : real;
begin
  temp := (count + 160) / 4;
  Temperature := temp
end;
```

The local variable temp contains the estimated temperature. Its value is then transferred to the function name **Temperature** in the last statement of the function.

STYLE TIP	To make it easier to debug large programs containing functions, define a local variable to temporarily contain the results to be returned to the calling statement. The last statement in the function should assign the value of the temporary variable to the function name through which it is returned.

Temperature is a global identifier and "belongs" to the main program. The identifier *ftemp* receives the value determined by and sent back through the function **Temperature**. Add *ftemp* to the Watches window, install a new breakpoint at the **DisplayTemperature** call in the main program, and rerun the program. Values for function names are not shown in the Watches window. If the hand-calculated value of *ftemp* does not correspond to its value in the Watches window, place a breakpoint at the last assignment statement in the **Temperature** function or use **Trace into** in that function to check if the value was properly determined. If the hand-calculated value matches its value in the Watchess window, the **DisplayTemperature** procedure is coded and added to the solution:

```
procedure DisplayTemperature (temp : real);
begin
  Writeln ('Estimated Fahrenheit temperature: ', temp:6:2)
end;
```

After a final run to check the validity and format of the output, documentation is added to the solution to produce the final version shown, along with sample output, in Figure 6.3.

Figure 6.3
TemperatureEstimation
Program Listing and
Sample Output

```pascal
program TemperatureEstimation;
{-------------------------------------------------------------------}
{ PROGRAM:        Estimating the Temperature                        }
{ PROGRAMMER:     J. Cricket                                        }
{ DATE:           June 2, 1990                                      }
{                                                                   }
{ This program estimates a Fahrenheit temperature by counting the  }
{ number of chirps a cricket makes in a one-minute time interval.  }
{                                                                   }
{ INPUT           number of chirps in one minute                   }
{                                                                   }
{ OUTPUT          Fahrenheit temperature                           }
{-------------------------------------------------------------------}
  var
    chirpcount                              { number of chirps per minute }
      : integer;
    ftemp                                   { Fahrenheit temperature }
      : real;

  procedure EnterCount (var count : integer);
  {-------------------------------------------------------------------}
  { Accept the number of chirps counted in a minute.                 }
  {                                                                   }
  { IN            none                                               }
  {                                                                   }
  { OUT           count: number of chips per minute                 }
  {-------------------------------------------------------------------}
  begin
    Write ('Enter chirps counted in one minute: ');
    Readln (count)
  end;
```

```pascal
function Temperature (count : integer) : real;
{-------------------------------------------------------------------------}
{ Calculate the estimated Fahrenheit temperature.                         }
{                                                                         }
{ IN              count: number of chirps per minute                      }
{                                                                         }
{ OUT             Temperature: estimated temperature                      }
{-------------------------------------------------------------------------}
  var
    temp                                    { estimated temperature }
      : real;
begin
  temp := (count + 160) / 4;
  Temperature := temp
end;

procedure DisplayTemperature (temp : real);
{-------------------------------------------------------------------------}
{ Display estimated temperature.                                          }
{                                                                         }
{ IN              temp: estimated temperature                             }
{                                                                         }
{ OUT             none                                                    }
{-------------------------------------------------------------------------}
begin
  Writeln ('Estimated Fahrenheit temperature: ', temp:6:2)
end;

begin
  EnterCount (chirpcount);
  ftemp := Temperature (chirpcount);
  DisplayTemperature (ftemp)
end.
```

```
─────────────────────────── Output ───────────────────────────
   Enter chirps counted in one minute: 74
   Estimated Fahrenheit temperature:  58.50
```

6.6 Applications Using Functions: Heavy Ice

Write a program that finds the difference in weight between two cubic blocks of ice, given the lengths of the sides of each. The density of ice is 57.3 pounds per cubic foot; that is, each cubic foot of ice weighs 57.3 pounds.

ANALYSIS OF THE PROBLEM   Figure 6.4 lists the input and output quantities.

MODULAR DESIGN OF
THE SOLUTION   The design of the solution and a description of the module interfaces are shown in Figure 6.5.

The code for the **CUBE VOLUME** module must precede the code for **DIFFERENCE**, since a called module must always appear before the module that calls it.

DESIGN OF THE
STRUCTURE OF THE
MODULES

WEIGHT DIFFERENCE
   ENTER SIDES
   DIFFERENCE
   DISPLAY DIFFERENCE

ENTER SIDES
   enter length of side of smaller cube
   enter length of side of larger cube

DIFFERENCE
   find weight of smaller cube (density × CUBE VOLUME)
   find weight of larger cube (density × CUBE VOLUME)
   find weight difference

CUBE VOLUME
   find volume of a cube

DISPLAY DIFFERENCE
   output weight difference

Figure 6.4
Weight Difference
Input/Output Chart

Input	Output
Side of smaller cube	Weight difference
Side of larger cube	

Figure 6.5
Weight Difference
Solution Design and
Module Interface Table

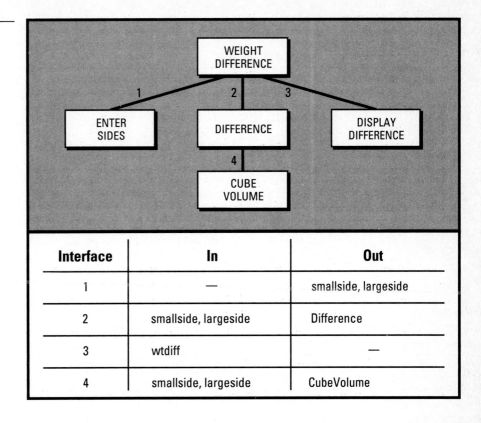

Interface	In	Out
1	—	smallside, largeside
2	smallside, largeside	Difference
3	wtdiff	—
4	smallside, largeside	CubeVolume

Although module code for **CUBE VOLUME** appears after its call in **DIF-FERENCE**, it must precede its call in the actual program.

PRODUCTION OF CODE
AND VERIFICATION OF
SOLUTION

```
program WeightDifference;
  var
    smallside,
    largeside,
    wtdiff
      : real;

  procedure EnterSides (var smallside, largeside : real);
  begin
  end;

  function CubeVolume (side : real) : real;
  begin
  end;
```

(continued)

```
function Difference (smallside, largeside : real) :real;
begin
end;

procedure DisplayDifference (wtdiff : real);
begin
end;

begin
  EnterSides (smallside, largeside);
  wtdiff := Difference (smallside, largeside);
  DisplayDifference (wtdiff)
end.
```

Use the **Trace into** option from the IDE to check that the actual parameters in subprogram calls match their corresponding formal parameters in the subprograms. In this case, the tracer never gets to the `CubeVolume` function, since no calls to that function are specified. Any errors must be corrected before you add the `EnterSides` procedure to the solution.

```
procedure EnterSides (var smallside, largeside : real);
begin
  Write ('Enter side of smaller cube in feet: ');
  Readln (smallside);
  Write ('Enter side of larger cube in feet: ');
  Readln (largeside)
end;
```

The actual parameters *smallside* and *largeside* correspond to the formal parameters with the same name. Although the same names appear in the calling procedure and the called procedure, one pair is local and the other global. The IDE does not distinguish between them. Use the IDE to test `EnterSides` by placing *smallside* and *largeside* in the Watches window, installing a breakpoint at the *wtdiff* assignment statement in the main program, and running the program. Once this module has been tested, the `Difference` function can be added to the solution:

```
function Difference (smallside, largeside : real) : real;
  const
    density = 57.3;
  var
    smallwt,
    largewt,
    diff
      : real;
```

```
begin
  smallwt := density * CubeVolume (smallside);
  largewt := density * CubeVolume (largeside);
  diff := largewt - smallwt;
  Difference := diff
end;
```

Since the density constant is needed only by this function, it is declared locally, as are the variables to temporarily store the smaller of the weights (*smallwt*), the larger of the weights (*largewt*), and their difference (*diff*). There are two calls to **CubeVolume**, one with *smallside* as the actual parameter and a second with *largeside*. The value of *diff* is transferred to the function name **Difference** in the last statement of the function.

The first two assignment statements use results determined by a function that is not yet written, **CubeVolume**. If you trace the execution path of the program, you find that the connection between **Difference** and **CubeVolume** is valid. The **CubeVolume** function can be inserted into the solution at this time:

```
function CubeVolume (side : real) : real;
  var
    volume : real;
begin
  volume := side * side * side;
  CubeVolume := volume
end;
```

Add the identifiers *volume, side, smallwt, largewt,* and *diff* to the Watches window. Set a breakpoint at the last statement in the **Difference** function and run the program. Choose 1 for the value of *smallside* and 2 for *largeside*, since these values are easy to check. If these values are chosen, *diff, largewt,* and *smallwt* should equal 401.1, 458.4, and 57.3, respectively. After errors have been corrected, the last component, the **DisplayDifference** procedure, is included in the solution:

```
procedure DisplayDifference (wtdiff : real);
begin
  Writeln ('Weight difference: ', wtdiff:7:2, ' lbs.')
end;
```

After a final run to test output format, internal documentation is added for the final product shown—along with sample output—in Figure 6.6.

Figure 6.6
WeightDifference
Program Listing and
Sample Output

```
program WeightDifference;
{-----------------------------------------------------------------}
{ PROGRAM:       Weight Difference                                }
{ PROGRAMMER:    I.C. Floe                                        }
{ DATE:          June 12, 1990                                    }
{                                                                 }
{ This program calculates and displays the weight difference      }
{ between two cubes of ice having sides with different lengths.   }
{                                                                 }
{ INPUT          length of side of small cube                     }
{                length of side of large cube                      }
{                                                                 }
{ OUTPUT         weight difference between cubes                   }
{-----------------------------------------------------------------}
  var
    smallside,                        { side length of smaller cube }
    largeside,                         { side length of larger cube }
    wtdiff                        { weight difference between cubes }
      : real;

  procedure EnterSides (var smallside, largeside : real);
  {-----------------------------------------------------------------}
  { Accept the lengths of the sides of the smaller and larger cubes. }
  {                                                                 }
  { IN           none                                              }
  {                                                                 }
  { OUT          smallside: length of side of small cube           }
  {              largeside: length of side of large cube           }
  {-----------------------------------------------------------------}
  begin
    Write ('Enter side of smaller cube in feet: ');
    Readln (smallside);
    Write ('Enter side of larger cube in feet: ');
    Readln (largeside)
  end;
```

```
function CubeVolume (side : real) : real;
{-------------------------------------------------------------------}
{ Find the volume of a cube given the length of its side.           }
{                                                                   }
{ IN           side: length of side of a cube                       }
{                                                                   }
{ OUT          CubeVolume: volume of cube                           }
{-------------------------------------------------------------------}
  var
    volume                                          { volume of cube }
      : real;
begin
  volume := side * side * side;
  Cubevolume := volume
end;


function Difference (smallside, largeside : real) : real;
{-------------------------------------------------------------------}
{ Calculate the difference in the weights of two cubes with sides   }
{ of given lengths.                                                 }
{                                                                   }
{ IN           smallside: length of side of smaller cube            }
{              largeside: length of side of larger cube             }
{                                                                   }
{ OUT          Difference: weight difference                        }
{-------------------------------------------------------------------}
  const
    density = 57.3;                                 { density of ice }
  var
    smallwt,                               { weight of smaller cube }
    largewt,                                { weight of larger cube }
    diff                                      { weight difference }
      : real;
begin
  smallwt := density * CubeVolume (smallside);
  largewt := density * CubeVolume (largeside);
  diff := largewt - smallwt;
  Difference := diff
end;
```

(continued)

```
procedure DisplayDifference (wtdiff : real);
{---------------------------------------------------------------------}
{ Display the weight difference between two cubes.                     }
{                                                                     }
{ IN             wtdiff: weight difference between cubes               }
{                                                                     }
{ OUT            none                                                  }
{---------------------------------------------------------------------}
begin
  Writeln ('Weight difference: ', wtdiff:7:2, ' lbs.')
end;

begin
  EnterSides (smallside, largeside);
  wtdiff := Difference (smallside, largeside);
  DisplayDifference (wtdiff)
end.
```

```
──────────────── Output ────────────────

  Enter side of smaller cube in feet: 1.25
  Enter side of larger cube in feet: 2.3
  Weight difference:  585.26 lbs.
```

Store and Forward

Turbo Pascal library functions and procedures provide valuable assistance when constructing well-written structured programs. Not only do they perform common operations on numeric and nonnumeric data, but they serve as models for the creation of programmer-defined functions and procedures. Although both subprogram types help to modularize problem solutions, they differ in their structure, how they are called, and how they return values to their calling statements. You must define a type in the header of each function you create, since a single value is returned through the function name. That name should appear on the left side of the last assignment statement in the function. No type is declared for a procedure, since it returns a value or values through its parameters. A function call must be part of another Pascal statement, whereas a procedure call is a statement in itself.

All the problems presented up to this point have been solved by an orderly sequence of processing steps or subprogram calls: You started at the beginning and proceeded to the end without deviating from this sequence. A computer is capable of much more than that. It can be used to make decisions or choose one of a series of paths to take. Our next step is to investigate these selection structures.

Snares and Pitfalls

- *Mismatching corresponding parameter types:* An actual parameter must be of the same type and in the same position in the parameter list as its corresponding formal parameter.

- *Failing to specify a function type:* Since values are returned through the function name, a function must have a type specified for it.

- *Neglecting to return a value through the function name:* If the function name does not appear at least once on the left side of an assignment statement in the function, an arbitrary value is returned to the calling statement.

- *Not including a function call in an expression:* A function call must be part of an expression in the calling statement. Unlike a procedure, it cannot stand by itself.

- *Failing to place a function declaration before its call:* As with procedures, the complete text defining a function should appear before its call.

Exercises

1. Answer the following questions in paragraph form.
   a. Explain why both functions and procedures are called subprograms.
   b. Distinguish between functions and procedures in how they are declared and how they are called.
   c. Why must the parameter for the **Ord** function be an ordinal data type?
   d. Why does a function have to assign at least one value to the function name before returning to the calling statement?
   e. Functions that choose random values are often called pseudo-random number generators, since they often do not spread random values throughout the specified interval; that is, more values may be chosen in one portion of a given range than in another. Describe a program that could be used to test the randomness of a particular random number generator.

2. Classify each of the following Pascal statements as valid or invalid. If invalid, explain why. Unless otherwise stated, assume all identifiers have been properly declared.
   a. **function PartA : real;**
   b. **Concat (st1, st2, st3);**
   c. **function PartC (a, b : real; c : char);**
   d. **x := Trunc (Sqrt(a+b));**
   e. **ans := Pos ('abc', sourcestring);**

3. Evaluate each of the following Pascal functions.
   a. **Chr(61)**
   b. **Abs(0)**
   c. **Sqr(1.3)**

    d. **Ord('m')**
    e. **Length('What a day!')**
    f. **Copy('lemonade', 3, 4)**
    g. **Pos('a', 'What a day!')**
    h. **Trunc(Random)**
    i. **Round(3.14159 * 1000 + 0.5) / 1000**

4. Write Pascal equivalents for each of the given descriptions.
    a. Attach the string stored in the location named *second* to the end of the string stored in the location named *last*, and store the result in *answ*.
    b. Choose a random integer between 0 and 36, inclusive.
    c. Write a function header that accepts the string passed to the formal parameter called *sentence* and returns a count of the number of words in the string.
    d. Write a function header that accepts three real values and returns the largest of the three.
    e. Find the first occurrence of letter *b* in the string stored in the location called *cipher*, and change it into the character whose ASCII code is 32 less than *b*'s.

5. Show the exact output produced by the following programs.
    a.
```
program PartA;
   var
     x, y : real;

   function One (x : real) : real;
   begin
     x := x + 10.2;
     Writeln ('x in One: ', x:6:2);
     One := x
   end;

begin
  x := 8.19;
  y := One(x);
  Writeln ('x in PartA: ', x:6:2);
  Writeln ('y in PartA: ', y:6:2)
end.
```

    b.
```
program PartB;
   var
     x, y : real;

   function Two (var x : real) : real;
   begin
     x := x + 10.2;
     Writeln ('x in Two: ', x:6:2);
     Two := x
   end;
```

```
begin
  x := 8.19;
  y := Two(x);
  Writeln ('x in PartB: ', x:6:2);
  Writeln ('y in PartB: ', y:6:2)
end.
```

c.
```
program PartC;
  var
    a, b : integer;

  function Three (a : integer) : integer;
    var
      c : integer;
  begin
    c := a div 3;
    Writeln ('c in Three: ', c);
    Three := c
  end;

  procedure Four (f : integer; var g : integer);
    var
      h : integer;
  begin
    h := f - 5;
    g := Three(h);
    Writeln ('g in Four: ', g)
  end;

begin
  a := 29;
  Four (a, b);
  Writeln ('a in PartC: ', a);
  Writeln ('b in PartC: ', b)
end.
```

d.
```
program PartD;
  type
    stringtype = string[20];
  var
    s, t : stringtype;

  procedure Five (s : stringtype; var a : integer);
  begin
    a := Pos ('f', s);
    Writeln ('a in Five: ', a)
  end;
```

(continued)

```
function Six (t : stringtype) : stringtype;
  var
    a : integer;
    b : stringtype;
begin
  Five (t, a);
  Writeln ('a in Six: ', a);
  b := Copy (t, a, 3);
  Writeln ('b in six: ', b);
  Six := b
end;

begin
  s := 'perforation';
  t := Six (s);
  Writeln ('s in PartD: ', s);
  Writeln ('t in PartD: ', t)
end.
```

6. Draw a structure chart and a module interface table (MIT) for the solution to each of the following problems. Use functions and parameters to pass values between modules.

   a. The braking distance for a car is directly proportional to the square of its speed and is given by the following formula:

   $$\text{distance} = 0.06 \times \text{speed}^2$$

   where *distance* is measured in feet and *speed* is measured in miles per hour. Write a program that uses a function to find the braking distance of a car, given its speed.

   b. Since astronomical distances are very large, they are measured in light years rather than miles. One light year is equivalent to 5.88×10^{12} miles. Write a program that uses a function to convert a distance in miles to light years.

   c. Two resistors R_1 and R_2 connected in series have an equivalent resistance given by the following formula:

   $$R_S = R_1 + R_2$$

   The same two resistors connected in parallel have an equivalent resistance given by:

   $$R_P = \frac{R_1 \times R_2}{R_1 + R_2}$$

   Write a program to find both these equivalent resistances, given values for R_1 and R_2.

   d. Write a program that (1) randomly generates three-letter codes by choosing three random integers between 65 and 90, inclusive; (2) converts each to its ASCII character equivalent; and (3) puts them together to form the code word.

e. Write a program that accepts a single string consisting of someone's first name, followed by a space and his or her last name. Use the program to create and display a string consisting of the last name, followed by a comma, a space, and then the first name.

Programming Assignments

Elementary

1. The braking distance for a car is directly proportional to the square of its speed and is given by the following formula:

    $$\text{distance} = 0.06 \times \text{speed}^2$$

    where *distance* is measured in feet and *speed* is measured in miles per hour. Write a program that uses a function to find the braking distance of a car, given its speed.

2. Since astronomical distances are very large, they are measured in light years rather than miles. One light year is equivalent to 5.88×10^{12} miles. Write a program that uses a function to convert a distance in miles into light years.

3. The money exchange rate between countries varies from day to day. Suppose 135 Japanese yen are equivalent to $1. Write a program using a function that accepts an amount in dollars and converts it into its Japanese equivalent, rounded to the nearest yen.

4. If the lengths of the sides of a triangle are known, its area is given by the following formula:

    $$\text{area} = \sqrt{s(s-a)(s-b)(s-c)}$$

    where a, b, and c are the lengths of the sides and s is one-half the sum of the sides. Write a program that accepts the lengths of the sides of a triangle and outputs its area.

5. Percentage difference is a measure used by scientists to determine how close two experimental values are. Its value is calculated by dividing the absolute value of the difference of two experimental values by their average.

    An experiment is performed in which 100 pellets are shot at a target. Write a program that uses a function to find the percentage difference between the number of bull's-eyes in each of two trials. Round your answer to two decimal places.

6. The economic order quantity Q is a measure of the most cost-efficient number of items to manufacture. It depends not only on the number of items manufactured at one time, but on the cost of storing those items until they are sold. Q is determined by:

    $$Q = \sqrt{\frac{2SN}{C}}$$

where S is the cost (in dollars) of setting up the machinery to make a run, N is the number of items manufactured in one run, and C is the cost (in dollars) of storage of a single unit between runs. Write a program that accepts values for N, S, and C and determines the economic order quantity, rounded to the nearest integer.

7. The reciprocal of a number is defined as 1 divided by that number. Write a program that accepts a real value and uses a function to find and display its reciprocal, rounded to three decimal places.

8. Write a program that accepts a sentence as a single string, stores the first word of that sentence in a separate variable, and displays it.

9. Two resistors R_1 and R_2 connected in series have an equivalent resistance given by the following formula:

$$R_S = R_1 + R_2$$

The same two resistors connected in parallel have an equivalent resistance given by:

$$R_P = \frac{R_1 \times R_2}{R_1 + R_2}$$

Write a program that finds both these equivalent resistances, given values for R_1 and R_2, where all resistances are measured in ohms.

10. In baseball, a pitcher's earned run average (ERA) is calculated by multiplying the number of earned runs allowed by 9 and dividing the result by the number of innings pitched.

    Write a program that uses a function to calculate a pitcher's ERA, rounded to the nearest hundredth.

Challenging

11. Write a program that (1) randomly generates three-letter codes by choosing three random integers between 65 and 90, inclusive; (2) converts each to its ASCII character equivalent; and (3) puts them together to form the code word.

12. Write a program that accepts a single string consisting of someone's first name, followed by a space and his or her last name. Use the program to create a string consisting of the last name, followed by a comma, a space, and then the first name.

13. Einstein's famous formula, $E = mc^2$, determines the amount of energy E, in joules, that can be produced if a certain mass m, in kilograms (kg), is converted entirely to energy. The c represents the speed of light and has a value of 3×10^8 meters per second. The average household consumes approximately 1×10^{10} joules of energy per year.

    Write a program that uses a function to determine the number of households that could be completely supplied with energy if an object with a mass of 0.10 kg (less than a quarter of a pound) were converted completely to energy.

14. A company estimates the cost to tile a floor by finding the area of the floor and estimating how many 1-foot by 1-foot tiles are needed to cover the area. The area of a rectangular floor is determined by finding its width and length and rounding them to *the next highest* integer before calculating their product. If tiles are only sold in boxes of 12, write a program that finds the number of boxes of tile and their cost if each tile costs 89 cents.

15. A binary number represents values by combinations of zeros and ones. A four-digit binary number can be converted to its decimal equivalent by adding the products of the left-most digit and 8, the second digit and 4, the third digit and 2, and the right-most digit and 1. For example, 12 is the decimal equivalent of 1100, since $12 = 1 \times 8 + 1 \times 4 + 0 \times 2 + 0 \times 1$. Write a program that accepts a four-digit binary number and determines its decimal equivalent.

16. In order to estimate the size of wildlife populations in certain areas, some are captured, tagged, and released. Subsequently, another sample is captured, and the ratio of the tagged to the total in this sample gives an estimate of the total wildlife in the area. If *initag* represents the number in the initial tagged group, *samptot* represents the total number in a sample, *samptag* represents the number in the sample that are tagged, and *total* represents the total wildlife population, their relationship is given by:

$$\frac{initag}{total} = \frac{samptag}{samptot}$$

Write a program that uses a function to estimate the total wildlife population in a given area.

17. Magazine publishers use a mailing label code for all subscribers. Given a subscriber's name (first name, followed by a space and the last name), street address (a number followed by a space and the street name), zip code, and expiration date (first three letters of the month, a space, and the last two digits in the year), write a program that creates a single string representing the mailing label code. The code is formed by attaching the following quantities, in the order given: the first three letters of the subscriber's last name, the first three letters of the street name, the last two digits in the zip code, two spaces, and the expiration date.

18. Forensic scientists often use the length of certain bones to determine the height of a person when that person was alive. For example, the height of a man is related to the length of his fibula (lower leg bone) by the following formula, where all measurements are given in centimeters (cm):

height = 69.089 + 2.238 × fibula length

The formula for a woman is:

height = 61.412 + 2.317 × fibula length

After 30 years of age, the height of a person decreases at a rate of 0.06 cm per year.

Write a program containing a function that calculates the height, in feet, of a man (or a woman) more than 30 years of age whose estimated age and fibula length are given. One foot is equivalent to 30.45 cm. The answer should be rounded to the nearest hundredth of a foot.

19. An assembly language program consists of instructions that determine, in more detail than is necessary in high-level languages such as Pascal, what the computer must do. An assembler is a translator that accepts an instruction, decodes it, and performs the indicated operation. Write a program that uses a function to read a single string that represents an addition operation, changes the operands to numeric values, and returns the sum. The instruction must be in the following form:

    ADD nn,mm

    where *ADD*, indicating the operation is addition, is followed by a space, one of the numbers to be added, a comma, and the second of the numbers to be added.

20. Pascal has no exponentiation operator, but the **Ln** and **Exp** Pascal functions can simulate one. The **Ln** function returns a real number that represents the natural logarithm of its real parameter. For example, **Ln(2.3)** returns the natural log of 2.3, or approximately 0.833. The **Exp** returns a real value representing the exponential (e^x) of its real argument (x). For example, if x is 3.7, **Exp(3.7)**, or $e^{3.7}$, is approximately 40.45. The value of a^b, where b is nonnegative, can be determined by **Exp(b * Ln(a))**.

    Create a function called **Power** that raises a number to a given exponent. Use **Power** in a program that calculates and displays the volume of a sphere by accepting its radius. The answer should be rounded to two decimal places. The volume of a sphere is the product of 4/3, pi, and the cube of the radius.

CHAPTER 7

Selection Structures

Key Terms

and	**in**
base type	logical operator
case	nesting
ClrScr	**not**
compound statement	**or**
conditional expression	relational operator
Crt	selector
decision structure	set
GotoXY	**Step over**
if . . . then . . . else	white-box testing

Objectives

- To present the fundamental concepts of nonsequential programming
- To introduce the **if . . . then . . . else** selection structure and apply it in the solution of problems
- To introduce and apply the **case** selection structure in the solution of problems
- To create menu-driven programs

7.1 Introduction

"The White Rabbit put on his spectacles. 'Where shall I begin, please your Majesty?' he asked. 'Begin at the beginning,' the King said, very gravely, 'And go on till you come to the end; then stop.'" This quotation from *Alice in Wonderland* by Lewis Carroll describes the general format of the programming solutions presented thus far: Each started with an input module, was followed by one or more processing modules, and concluded with an output module. All program statements were executed in sequence.

If problems with sequential solutions were the only kind computers could solve, a calculator would do as well. Two additional capabilities are incorporated into programming languages that expand the range of problems suitable for computer solution: (1) making a choice between two or more options, and (2) repeating a process. This chapter concentrates on the former, using a selection structure that permits a program to choose between alternatives.

Decisions can be as simple as whether to put sprinkles on ice cream or as complex as choosing the best move in a game of chess. One thing they all have in common is that each involves the selection of one action from among several actions. Also, each is based on a defined condition: For the ice cream the condition may include cost or calories; and for chess, the eventual loss or capture of a piece.

7.2 Altering the Flow of Control

Designing a solution that requires sequential coding is similar to driving along a road with no forks: Start at the beginning and drive until the end of the road is reached. Once decision structures are introduced, forks are put in the road and the driver has a choice of two or more alternative paths at one or more locations on the road. The selection can be determined by where the driver wants to go or by the condition of the roads. For example, if one of two roads is under repair, the other may be chosen. Once the decision is made, the driver selects one of the paths, makes a turn, and continues. There may be a choice of several paths, but only one is selected at each fork.

A *decision structure* is a programming construct that allows a deviation from sequential processing using a condition to assist in the selection of one or more possible execution paths. The condition generally is an expression that can be true or false: If its value is true, one path is taken and if false, another. See Figure 7.1.

Figure 7.1
Decision Structure with
Two Options

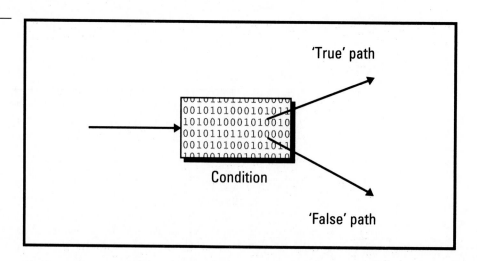

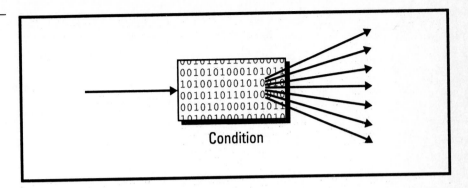

Figure 7.2
Decision Structure with
Multiple Options

Condition

The condition also may be an expression whose value is compared to a list of constants of the same type as the expression. The path taken is the one whose value matches the one in the constants list. See Figure 7.2.

7.3 Conditional Expressions

A *conditional expression* compares two quantities of the same type and returns a value of true if the relationship is valid and a value of false if it is not.

FORMAT: `<expression> <relational operator> <expression>`

The expressions are considered operands of the operator.

Relational Operators

A *relational operator* indicates how two expressions of the same data type are associated: One expression may be equal to, greater than, less than, greater than or equal to, less than or equal to, or not equal to another. For example, if $x = 5$, $y = 7$, and $z = 9$, then the expression $x + y > z$ is true, while the expression $y + z < x$ is false. Table 7.1 lists the Pascal symbols for the relational operators along with their algebraic counterparts.

Although the conditional operator `=` is similar in appearance to the assignment operator `:=`, they have entirely different meanings. The former compares two operands and returns a Boolean value indicating whether a conditional expression is true, while the latter assigns a value to a location.

Relational operators also can be used for string and character data by comparing the ASCII codes of the operands. (See Appendix D.) One character is considered "less than" a second if the ASCII code of the first is smaller than the ASCII code of the second. For example, the relational expression `'C' < 'R'` is true, since 67, the ASCII code for *C*, is smaller than 82, the code for *R*. There is, however, a distinction between upper-case and lowercase characters. All the uppercase letters precede all the lowercase ones, and so `'c' < 'R'` is false, since 99, the code for *c*, is larger than 67, the code for *R*.

Table 7.1
Relational Operators

Algebraic Symbol	Pascal Symbol	Meaning
=	=	Equal to
≠	<>	Not equal to
<	<	Less than
≤	<=	Less than or equal to
>	>	Greater than
≥	>=	Greater than or equal to

When the operands of a relational expression are strings, the ASCII codes for corresponding characters in both strings are compared. If the first characters in each operand are the same, the second characters are compared; if they are identical, the third characters are compared; and so on. The process continues until characters in the same place in each string differ. For example, even though the first two letters of *car* and *cat* are the same, `'car'` < `'cat'`, since the ASCII code for *r* is smaller than the ASCII code for *t*. As with character data, there is a distinction between uppercase and lowercase letters. Thus, *car* follows *Cat*, since the ASCII code for *c* is greater than that for *C*.

If the characters in two strings match, letter for letter, except one string contains additional letters not found in the other, the smaller string precedes, or is "less than," the larger. For example, even though the first three letters in the strings *car* and *cart* are identical, `'car'` < `'cart'`, since *cart* has an extra *t*.

Logical Operators

Simple relational expressions compare only two expressions and often are insufficient to handle more complex relational structures. One remedy is to use several simple relational expressions in succession. Another is to find a way to combine simple expressions into a single compound expression. The Pascal *logical operators* **not**, **and**, and **or** take the results of several simple relational expressions and combine them to produce a single Boolean value.

The **not** operator reverses the Boolean state of an expression; that is, if an expression is true, enclosing that expression in parentheses and preceding it with **not** makes the revised expression false. Since only a single operand is required, **not** is considered a unary operator. For example, 7 > 4 + 2 is true, while **not** (7 > 4 + 2) is false. Table 7.2 summarizes the use of the **not** operator on the relational expression *p*.

Table 7.2
The **not** Operator

p	**not** p
True	False
False	True

The other logical operators are binary operators, since both require two operands. The **and** logical operator combines two expressions and is true if and only if both expressions are true. For example, the expression

$$(5 = 4 + 1) \text{ and } (18 <= 6 * 4)$$

is true, since both operands of **and** are true. Parentheses should always enclose both operands separated by an **and**. If either operand were false, the entire logical expression would be false. Table 7.3 summarizes **and** operations on the relational expressions p and q.

The **or** logical operator is true if either of its two operands is true, and false if and only if both operands are false. For example, the expression

$$(\text{Sqr}(3) <= 3 * 2) \text{ or } (6 <> 7 - 3)$$

is true, since at least one of the **or**'s operands, the second, is true. Again, parentheses should enclose both operands that are separated by an **or**. Table 7.4 summarizes **or** operations on the relational expressions p and q.

Order of Operations

As with numeric operators, relational and logical operators are executed in an order predetermined by Pascal. A precedence table for all these operators is given in Table 7.5. High-precedence operators are executed before low-precedence operators. If two operators have the same precedence, they are executed from left to right. Expressions contained in parentheses are evaluated first; if more than one set of parentheses are present in an expression, inner ones are evaluated before outer ones and left ones before right ones.

Table 7.3
The **and** Operator

p	q	p **and** q
True	True	True
True	False	False
False	True	False
False	False	False

Table 7.4
The **or** Operator

p	q	p **or** q
True	True	True
True	False	True
False	True	True
False	False	False

Table 7.5
Order of Operations

Precedence	Operators	Class
High	**not**	Unary operator
↓	***, /, div, mod, and**	Multiplying operators
	+, −, or	Adding Operators
Low	**=, <, >, <=, >=, <>**	Relational Operators

You can evaluate the following complex expression according to the precedence rules summarized in Table 7.5. The value of x is 6, that of y is 13, and that of z is 4.2.

```
( (x <> y div 2) or (z <= y) )      and ( not (z = x/2) )
( (6 <> 13 div 2) or (4.2 <= 13) ) and ( not (4.2 = 6/2) )
     ( (6 <> 6) or (4.2 <= 13) ) and ( not (4.2 = 6/2) )
            (false or true)         and ( not (false) )
                  true              and        true
                                    true
```

> **STYLE TIP**
>
> If you are unsure whether to insert parentheses, put them in. Even though some parentheses are not needed, their inclusion can make expressions easier to read and understand.

7.4 The if . . . then . . . else Structure

Pascal's **if . . . then . . . else** statement contains a conditional expression for making decisions. Although this single statement can be employed for the

Ordinal subranges also can be used to describe a set, as they were in the declaration sections of programs.

Example

```
if category in [1..10]
  then
     commrate := 0.15
  else
     commrate := 0.095;
```

If *category* has an integer value in the range from 1 to 10, inclusive, *commrate* is assigned a value of 0.15. If the value of *category* is not in this range, the value assigned to *commrate* is 0.095. If *category* is not of type **integer**, an error results.

7.6 Application in Choosing Test Data: Pro Bonus

Supply City offers end-of-the-year salary bonuses for its salespersons. In addition to a commission, it pays each member of its sales force a base salary that increases every year an employee stays with the firm. At the end of each year, each salesperson receives a bonus that is based on his or her annual base salary and sales for the year. Those whose annual salaries are greater than $12,000 receive a bonus that is the sum of 0.5% of the sales plus 6% of their salary, with an upper limit of $5,000. All others receive a bonus that is the sum of 0.4% of the sales plus 10% of their salary, with a lower limit of $1,600. Write a program that accepts a salesperson's name, annual salary, and yearly sales and displays his or her bonus.

ANALYSIS OF THE PROBLEM   The input and output quantities are summarized in Figure 7.3.

MODULAR DESIGN
OF THE SOLUTION

The structure chart and its MIT for a possible solution are shown in Figure 7.4. In the structure chart, the module **ANNUAL BONUS**, which will be implemented as a function, accepts the base salary and annual sales for a salesperson and calls either the **BONUS FOR HIGHER PAY** module or the **BONUS FOR LOWER PAY** module to determine the amount of the annual bonus. To indicate that only one of these modules is called for each execution of the program, a selection "switch" is shown in the diagram. Since you

Figure 7.3
Salary Bonus
Input/Output Chart

Input	Output
Salesperson's name	Yearly bonus
Base salary	
Annual sales	

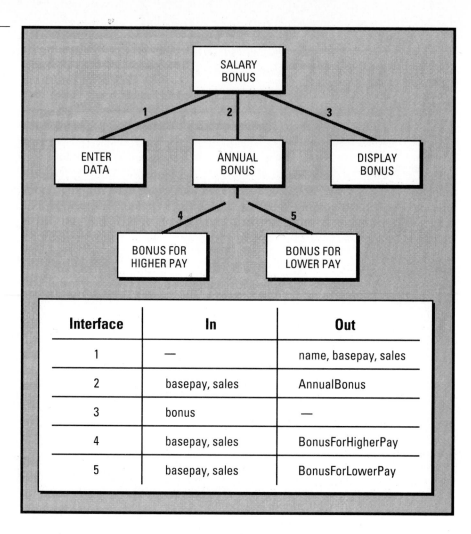

Figure 7.4
Salary-Bonus Solution
Design and Module
Interface Table

Interface	In	Out
1	—	name, basepay, sales
2	basepay, sales	AnnualBonus
3	bonus	—
4	basepay, sales	BonusForHigherPay
5	basepay, sales	BonusForLowerPay

do not know in advance which of the modules is actually executed, the switch is drawn in a neutral position. As illustrated in Figure 7.5, it can swing to the right or left depending on input values.

Figure 7.5
Selection "Switch"

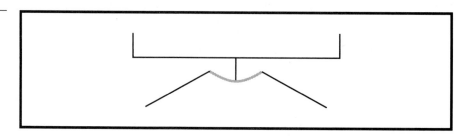

Both **BONUS FOR HIGHER PAY** and **BONUS FOR LOWER PAY** are implemented as functions, since each returns a single value to the function **ANNUAL BONUS**.

DESIGN OF THE
STRUCTURE OF THE
MODULES

SALARY BONUS
    ENTER DATA
    ANNUAL BONUS
    DISPLAY BONUS

ENTER DATA
    enter salesperson's name
    enter annual base salary
    enter annual sales

ANNUAL BONUS
    if annual base pay > $12,000
      then
        BONUS FOR HIGHER PAY
      else
        BONUS FOR LOWER PAY

BONUS FOR HIGHER PAY
    find bonus from salary
    find bonus from sales
    find total bonus
    if total bonus > $5,000
      then
        total bonus = $5,000

BONUS FOR LOWER PAY
    find bonus from salary
    find bonus from sales
    find total bonus
    if total bonus < $1,600
      then
        total bonus = $1,600

DISPLAY BONUS
    output annual bonus

If the total bonus extends beyond the high and low limits in the problem statement, the total bonus is raised (or lowered) to the appropriate value. Also, no **else** clauses were needed because no action is taken unless the calculated bonus falls outside the specified boundaries.

PRODUCTION OF CODE
AND VERIFICATION OF SOLUTION

```
program SalaryBonus;
  type
    nametype = string[20];
  var
    name
      : nametype;
    basepay,
    sales,
    bonus
      : real;

  procedure EnterData (var name : nametype; var basepay, sales : real);
  begin
  end;

  function BonusForHigherPay (basepay, sales : real) : real;
  begin
  end;

  function BonusForLowerPay (basepay, sales : real) : real;
  begin
  end;

  function AnnualBonus (basepay, sales : real) : real;
  begin
  end;

  procedure DisplayBonus (bonus : real);
  begin
  end;

begin
  EnterData (name, basepay, sales);
  bonus := AnnualBonus (basepay, sales);
  DisplayBonus (bonus)
end.
```

Since substitution of code in the **EnterData** procedure is the same as with previous problems, testing details are omitted here.

```
procedure EnterData (var name : nametype; var basepay, sales : real);
begin
  Write ('Enter name of salesperson: ');
  Readln (name);
  Write ('Enter annual base salary: $');
  Readln (basepay);
  Write ('Enter annual sales: $');
  Readln (sales)
end;
```

The next step is to replace the **AnnualBonus** stub with appropriate code that establishes calls to the **BonusForHigherPay** and **BonusForLowerPay** functions:

```
function AnnualBonus (basepay, sales : real) : real;
  var
    tempbonus
      : real;
begin
  if basepay > 12000
    then
      tempbonus := BonusForHigherPay (basepay, sales)
    else
      tempbonus := BonusForLowerPay (basepay, sales);
  AnnualBonus := tempbonus
end;
```

The values shown in the Watches window depend on the input data selected. If the value entered for *basepay* is greater than $12,000, a trace visits the **BonusForHigherPay** stub; if not, it visits the **BonusForLowerPay** stub. Since the bonus functions have not been coded and added to the solution yet, no value for the bonus is calculated or displayed. You should trace the execution path with one test value when *basepay* is less than $12,000 and another when *basepay* is greater than $12,000. The value that separates the two cases, in this case $12,000, also should be tested to verify that it calls the **BonusForLowerPay** function.

The structure for the **BonusForLowerPay** and **BonusForHigherPay** modules are similar and added to the solution at the same time:

```
function BonusForHigherPay (basepay, sales : real) : real;
  var
    bonusfromsales,
    bonusfromsalary,
    totalbonus
      : real;
begin
  bonusfromsales := 0.005 * sales;
  bonusfromsalary := 0.06 * basepay;
  totalbonus := bonusfromsales + bonusfromsalary;
  if totalbonus > 5000
    then
      totalbonus := 5000;
  BonusForHigherPay := totalbonus
end;

function BonusForLowerPay (basepay, sales : real) : real;
  var
    bonusfromsales,
    bonusfromsalary,
    totalbonus
      : real;
begin
  bonusfromsales := 0.004 * sales;
  bonusfromsalary := 0.10 * basepay;
  totalbonus := bonusfromsales + bonusfromsalary;
  if totalbonus < 1600
    then
      totalbonus := 1600;
  BonusForLowerPay := totalbonus
end;
```

You can use the **Step over** option from the **Run** menu or the **Trace into** utility to test the code in each function. The **Step over** option (F8) steps through one subprogram at a time rather than one statement at a time. If reasonably certain that your code for these two functions is accurate, you can use **Step over** by putting appropriate variables in the Watches window and checking the values of the variables upon leaving the function. If these values prove to be correct, there is no need to trace through each function line by line. If you need a more detailed examination of the execution path, the **Trace into** facility provides it.

The decision structure of this program is complex and therefore requires a more complete set of test data. Table 7.6 lists appropriate test values, the reasons for choosing these values, and the correct bonus for each set of inputs. These values are chosen to test the possible execution paths that the

Variable			Reason for Choosing
basepay	sales	bonus	
10000	0	1600	Below 1600 limit in BonusForLowerPay
10000	500000	3000	Above 1600 limit in BonusForLowerPay
12000	0	1600	At 12000 boundary, no sales
12000	500000	3200	At 12000 boundary, sales
20000	600000	4200	Below 5000 limit in BonusForHigherPay
20000	1000000	5000	Above 5000 limit in BonusForHigherPay

Table 7.6
Test Values for
SalaryBonus

program can take and any values that indicate the boundary between execution paths. When test values are chosen to test for the proper execution of all branches of a programming structure, the process is known as *white-box testing*, since the tester can read the code in the module that is undergoing testing.

When this section of the program is verified, the display procedure can be coded and added to the solution:

```
procedure DisplayBonus (bonus : real);
begin
   Writeln ('Annual bonus: $', bonus:7:2)
end;
```

After the program with this procedure added is verified, the fully documented final version of the solution can be produced, as shown, along with sample output from two test runs, in Figure 7.6.

Figure 7.6
SalaryBonus Program
Listing and Sample Output

```
program SalaryBonus;
{-------------------------------------------------------------------------}
{ PROGRAM:       Salary Bonuses                                           }
{ PROGRAMMER:    I.M. Generous                                            }
{ DATE:          July 2, 1990                                             }
{                                                                         }
{ This program finds the annual bonus given to Supply City               }
{ salespersons based on their annual base salary and sales for the       }
{ year. Those whose annual salary is greater than $12,000 receive a      }
{ bonus that is the sum of 0.5% of the sales plus 6% of their salary     }
{ with an upper limit of $5,000. All others receive a bonus that is      }
{ the sum of 0.4% of the sales plus 10% of their salary with a           }
{ lower limit of $1,600.                                                  }
{                                                                         }
{ INPUT          name of salesperson                                     }
{                annual base salary of salesperson                       }
{                annual sales                                            }
{                                                                         }
{ OUTPUT         annual bonus                                             }
{-------------------------------------------------------------------------}
  type
    nametype = string[20];                              { names }
  var
    name                                          { salesperson name }
      : nametype;
    basepay,                                    { annual base salary }
    sales,                                          { annual sales }
    bonus                                           { annual bonus }
      : real;
```

```
procedure EnterData (var name : nametype; var basepay, sales : real);
{--------------------------------------------------------------------}
{ Accept name of salesperson, annual base pay and annual sales.      }
{                                                                    }
{ IN            none                                                 }
{                                                                    }
{ OUT           name:       salesperson name                        }
{               basepay:    annual base salary                      }
{               sales:      annual sales                            }
{--------------------------------------------------------------------}
begin
  Write ('Enter name of salesperson: ');
  Readln (name);
  Write ('Enter annual base salary: $');
  Readln (basepay);
  Write ('Enter annual sales: $');
  Readln (sales)
end;


function BonusForHigherPay (basepay, sales : real) : real;
{--------------------------------------------------------------------}
{ Calculate bonus for salesperson with base salary exceeding $12,000 }
{ by finding the sum of 0.5% of the sales plus 6% of his or her      }
{ salary, with an upper limit of $5,000.                             }
{                                                                    }
{ IN            basepay:    annual base salary                      }
{               sales:      annual sales                            }
{                                                                    }
{ OUT           BonusForHigherPay:  annual bonus for this           }
{                                   class of salespersons           }
{--------------------------------------------------------------------}
var
  bonusfromsales,                            { bonus amount from sales }
  bonusfromsalary,                   { bonus amount from base salary }
  totalbonus                                    { total annual bonus }
     : real;
begin
  bonusfromsales := 0.005 * sales;
  bonusfromsalary := 0.06 * basepay;
  totalbonus := bonusfromsales + bonusfromsalary;
  if totalbonus > 5000
    then
      totalbonus := 5000;
  BonusForHigherPay := totalbonus
end;
```

(continued)

```
function BonusForLowerPay (basepay, sales : real) : real;
{--------------------------------------------------------------------}
{ Calculate bonus for salesperson with base salary less than or      }
{ equal to $12,000 by finding the sum of 0.4% of the sales plus      }
{ 10% of his or her salary, with a lower limit of $1,600.            }
{                                                                    }
{ IN            basepay:  annual base salary                         }
{               sales:    annual sales                               }
{                                                                    }
{ OUT           BonusForLowerPay:  annual bonus for this             }
{                                  class of salespersons             }
{--------------------------------------------------------------------}
var
  bonusfromsales,                        { bonus amount from sales }
  bonusfromsalary,              { bonus amount from base salary }
  totalbonus                          { total annual bonus }
    : real;
begin
  bonusfromsales := 0.004 * sales;
  bonusfromsalary := 0.10 * basepay;
  totalbonus := bonusfromsales + bonusfromsalary;
  if totalbonus < 1600
    then
      totalbonus := 1600;
  BonusForLowerPay := totalbonus
end;
```

```
function AnnualBonus (basepay, sales : real) : real;
{------------------------------------------------------------------}
{ Test annual salary and call either BonusForHigherPay or          }
{ BonusForLowerPay to calculate annual bonus.                      }
{                                                                  }
{ IN          basepay:  annual base salary                        }
{             sales:     annual sales                             }
{                                                                  }
{ OUT         AnnualBonus:  annual bonus for salesperson          }
{------------------------------------------------------------------}
var
  tempbonus                                      { annual bonus }
    : real;
begin
  if basepay > 12000
    then
      tempbonus := BonusForHigherPay (basepay, sales)
    else
      tempbonus := BonusForLowerPay (basepay, sales);
  AnnualBonus := tempbonus
end;

procedure DisplayBonus (bonus : real);
{------------------------------------------------------------------}
{ Display the annual bonus.                                        }
{                                                                  }
{ IN          bonus:  annual bonus                                }
{                                                                  }
{ OUT         none                                                }
{------------------------------------------------------------------}
begin
  Writeln ('Annual bonus: $', bonus:7:2)
end;

begin
  EnterData (name, basepay, sales);
  bonus := AnnualBonus (basepay, sales);
  DisplayBonus (bonus)
end.
```

(continued)

─────────── **Output 1** ───────────

```
Enter name of salesperson: Jones
Enter annual base salary: $10000
Enter annual sales: $500000
Annual bonus: $3000.00
```

─────────── **Output 2** ───────────

```
Enter name of salesperson: Smith
Enter annual base salary: $12000
Enter annual sales: $0
Annual bonus: $1600.00
```

7.7 Application in Accuracy: Pythagorean "Squares"

Write a program that determines whether three numbers form a Pythagorean triple, that is, whether they can represent the lengths of the sides of a right triangle. For three numbers to constitute a Pythagorean triple, they must satisfy the formula:

$$c^2 = a^2 + b^2 \quad \text{or} \quad c = \sqrt{a^2 + b^2}$$

where c represents the hypotenuse (longest side) of the triangle and a and b represent the lengths of the shorter sides (legs).

ANALYSIS OF THE PROBLEM   Figure 7.7 lists the input and output quantities required for the solution. Status indicates whether the three values satisfy the formula.

MODULAR DESIGN
OF THE SOLUTION   The structure chart outlining the solution and its supporting module interface table are shown in Figure 7.8. Specific details on how the modules are implemented are hidden at this stage.

Figure 7.7
Pythagorean Triples
Input/Output Chart

Input	Output
Leg 1	Status
Leg 2	
Hypotenuse	

Figure 7.8
Pythagorean Triples
Solution Design and
Module Interface Table

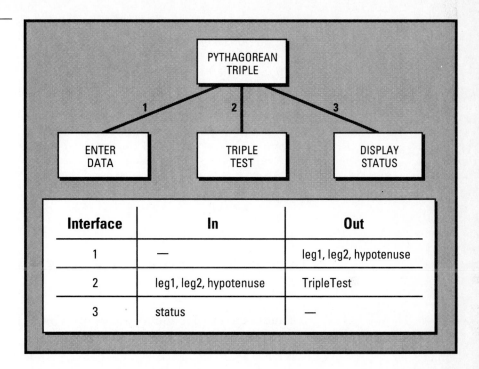

DESIGN OF THE
STRUCTURE OF THE
MODULES

The **ENTER DATA** and **DISPLAY STATUS** modules are similar to the ones in previous chapters. A decision is required in the **FIND STATUS** module. The outline of this module can be made using the words *if*, *then*, and *else* as in Pascal:

PYTHAGOREAN TRIPLE
    ENTER DATA
    TRIPLE TEST
    DISPLAY STATUS

    ENTER DATA
      enter length of leg 1
      enter length of leg 2
      enter length of hypotenuse

    TRIPLE TEST
      if $c = \sqrt{a^2 + b^2}$
        then
          status is "triple"
        else
          status is "not triple"

DISPLAY STATUS
  output status

PRODUCTION OF CODE
AND VERIFICATION OF
SOLUTION

The program skeleton with stubs replacing the actual subprograms follows.

```pascal
program PythagoreanTriple;
  type
    stringtype = string[20];
  var
    leg1,
    leg2,
    hypotenuse
      : real;
    status
      : stringtype;

  procedure EnterData (var a, b, c : real);
  begin
  end;

  function TripleTest (a, b, c : real) : stringtype;
  begin
  end;

  procedure DisplayStatus (status : stringtype);
  begin
  end;

begin
  EnterData (leg1, leg2, hypotenuse);
  status := TripleTest (leg1, leg2, hypotenuse);
  DisplayStatus (status)
end.
```

Although the solution can be written with procedures only, a function was chosen to return the status of the triple since only a single value is returned to the main program. The **EnterData** procedure is added to the solution first:

```pascal
procedure EnterData (var a, b, c : real);
begin
  Write ('Enter length of one leg: ');
  Readln (a);
  Write ('Enter length of other leg: ');
  Readln (b);
  Write ('Enter length of hypotenuse: ');
  Readln (c)
end;
```

Details for testing the **EnterData** procedure are straightforward and are omitted. The solution process is continued with the addition of the **TripleTest** function:

```
function TripleTest (a, b, c : real) : stringtype;
  var
    test
      : stringtype;
begin
  if c = Sqrt(Sqr(a) + Sqr(b))
    then
      test := 'a triple'
    else
      test := 'not a triple';
  TripleTest := test
end;
```

The local variable *test* temporarily stores the status message, passing it to **TripleTest** before the function returns to the main program.

When a program contains a decision structure, sample data should be selected that tests all possible outcomes of that structure and that are representative of the data expected in the normal execution of the program. This is necessary in order to have reasonable certainty of the correctness of the algorithm. In this problem, a set of "triple" and "nontriple" values should be chosen with real as well as integer values.

After making sure the variables *leg1*, *leg2*, *hypotenuse*, *a*, *b*, *c*, and *test* are in the Watches window, use the **Trace into** option (F7) to see which execution path in the **TripleTest** function the decision follows. If 3 is entered for *a*, 4 for *b*, and 5 for *c* in the **EnterData** procedure, the highlighted trace bar starts at the **if** statement in the **TripleTest** function, jumps to the assignment statement in the **then** clause, where it stores *a triple* in *test*, and skips over the **else** clause to the **TripleTest** assignment statement. The results check with those calculated by hand, proving that these three numbers constitute a Pythagorean triple.

Now use the trace facility to see if the **else** clause works by entering 1 for *a*, 2 for *b*, and 3 for *c* in the **EnterData** procedure. After evaluating the condition in the **if** statement of the function **TripleTest**, the trace bar skips to the *test* assignment statement in the **else** clause and then to the **TripleTest** assignment statement and then to the main program, where it returns a value *not a triple* for **TripleTest**. In this case, the hand-checking indicates that these three numbers do not form a triple, as was determined by the IDE.

The testing is not complete yet, since a representative set of test data should include real values with fractional parts. Suppose 0.5, 1.2, and 1.3 are entered for *a*, *b*, and *c*, respectively. After a trace is completed, the Watches window displays *not a triple* for the value of *status*. Checking the results with a calculator shows that the square root of $0.5^2 + 1.2^2$ does equal 1.3, contradicting the computer's answer. This set of data shows an inconsistency, but there is a reason for it.

To perform calculations, the computer must use binary numbers equivalent to the decimal values entered by a user. This poses some problems, since the conversion of the fractional parts of real numbers into fractional binary values is not exact. Whenever the binary value is involved in a calculation, the inaccuracy is compounded and may produce erroneous results when a significant number of decimal places is required. In this problem, the imprecision of the square root operation on the right side of the condition of the **if . . . then . . . else** statement was enough to throw off the equality.

Errors of this type can be corrected by substituting an expression that means "almost equal" rather than "equal." This is accomplished by determining if the absolute value of the difference of two values that are almost equal is small enough to be inconsequential, that is, less than a given value (the *tolerance*). The absolute value function is used because it is hard to determine whether the conversion between number systems raises or lowers a value. For example, if the absolute value of $(x - y)$ is less than 0.0001, it can be assumed that x is "almost equal" to y. If $x = 1.00000$, the absolute value expression is true for y values between 1.00001 and 0.99999, inclusive. The smaller the tolerance, the "more equal" the values are.

With that in mind, you can introduce a constant tolerance having a value of 0.0001 and replace the condition in the `TripleTest` module with `Abs(c - Sqrt(Sqr(a) + Sqr(b))) < tolerance`. The amended function is as follows:

```
function TripleTest (a, b, c : real) : stringtype;
  const
    tolerance = 0.0001;
  var
    test
      : stringtype;
begin
  if Abs(c - Sqrt(Sqr(a) + Sqr(b))) < tolerance
    then
      test := 'a triple'
    else
      test := 'not a triple';
  TripleTest := test
end;
```

After this function is substituted for the original one, the program must be retested using the values that produced incorrect results. This time the Watches window shows the correct value for *status*. The final procedure, `DisplayStatus`, is now added to the solution, and after a final run to test output format, the program is documented to produce the final version shown, along with output from two different program runs, in Figure 7.9.

Figure 7.9
PythagoreanTriple
Program Listing and
Sample Output

```
program PythagoreanTriple;
{-------------------------------------------------------------------}
{ PROGRAM:       Pythagorean Triples                                }
{ PROGRAMMER:    U. Clidd                                           }
{ DATE:          July 4, 1990                                       }
{                                                                   }
{ This program determines if three numeric values are a Pythagorean }
{ triple; that is, if they can represent the lengths of the sides of }
{ a right triangle. This can be done by determining if the length of }
{ the hypotenuse equals the square root of the sums of squares of   }
{ the lengths of the legs.                                          }
{                                                                   }
{ INPUT          three lengths                                      }
{                                                                   }
{ OUTPUT         message indicating whether the lengths are a       }
{                Pythagorean triple                                 }
{-------------------------------------------------------------------}
  type
    stringtype = string[20];                        { message types }
  var
    leg1,                                      { length of one leg }
    leg2,                                   { length of second leg }
    hypotenuse                             { length of hypotenuse }
      : real;
    status                            { message indicating triple or not }
      : stringtype;
```

(continued)

```
procedure EnterData (var a, b, c : real);
{-------------------------------------------------------------------}
{ Accept three lengths.                                             }
{                                                                   }
{ IN            none                                                }
{                                                                   }
{ OUT           a:  length of one leg                               }
{               b:  length of second leg                            }
{               c:  length of hypotenuse                            }
{-------------------------------------------------------------------}
begin
  Write ('Enter length of one leg: ');
  Readln (a);
  Write ('Enter length of other leg: ');
  Readln (b);
  Write ('Enter length of hypotenuse: ');
  Readln (c)
end;


function TripleTest (a, b, c : real) : stringtype;
{-------------------------------------------------------------------}
{ Test if three values are a Pythagorean triple.                    }
{                                                                   }
{ IN            a:  length of one leg                               }
{               b:  length of second leg                            }
{               c:  length of hypotenuse                            }
{                                                                   }
{ OUT           TripleTest: message indicating whether values form  }
{                              a triple or not                       }
{-------------------------------------------------------------------}
  const
    tolerance = 0.0001;                        { equality tolerance }
  var
    test                           { message indicating whether }
      : stringtype;                { or not values form a triple }
begin
  if Abs( c - Sqrt( Sqr(a) + Sqr(b) ) ) < tolerance
    then
      test := 'a triple'
    else
      test := 'not a triple';
  TripleTest := test
end;
```

```
procedure DisplayStatus (status : stringtype);
  {----------------------------------------------------------------}
  { Display status of three lengths.                               }
  {                                                                }
  { IN             status:  message indicating whether values form }
  {                                 triple or not                  }
  {                                                                }
  { OUT            none                                            }
  {----------------------------------------------------------------}
  begin
    Writeln ('These lengths are ',status)
  end;

begin
  EnterData (leg1, leg2, hypotenuse);
  status := TripleTest (leg1, leg2, hypotenuse);
  DisplayStatus (status)
end.
```

───────────────── **Output 1** ─────────────────

```
Enter length of one leg: 0.8
Enter length of other leg: 1.5
Enter length of hypotenuse: 1.7
These lengths are a triple
```

───────────────── **Output 2** ─────────────────

```
Enter length of one leg: 4
Enter length of other leg: 5
Enter length of hypotenuse: 6
These lengths are not a triple
```

219

7.8 The case Structure

The **case** structure uses an expression to transfer program control to any one of a collection of possible paths.

FORMAT:
```
case < selector > of
   < constants list > :
      < statements 1 >;
   < constants list > :
      < statements 2 >;
         ...
   < constants list > :
      < statements n >
   [else
      < default statement >]
end;
```

The reserved word **case** is followed by an ordinal expression called the *selector*; that is, the selector must be of type **integer**, **char**, or **boolean**. If the value of the selector matches a constant in any of the constants lists, the statement following that list is executed and control is transferred to the statement or compound statement following the **case** statement. A constants list may consist of a single value, a subrange of values, or many values separated by commas. A colon follows the constants list and precedes the statement triggered by the constant. Each statement must end with a semi-colon, with the exception of the one preceding **else**. An **end;** signals the end of the **case** structure. No constant can appear in more than one list.

If there is no match between the value of the expression and an element of a constants list, the default statement following **else** is executed. If the **else** clause is not present in this instance, the entire **case** structure is ignored.

Although not suitable for all decision structures, for many complex ones the **case** structure is easier to understand and code than an equivalent **if ... then ... else** structure.

STYLE TIP

It is good practice to include an **else** statement in most **case** structures, even if its only purpose is to display a message indicating no selector match was found.

Each constants list should be indented from the **case** statement and terminated with a colon. Its corresponding statement should be indented further, making it easier to spot the process executed for each set of constants. This is particularly useful when the options are compound statements. The **else** should align with the constants list, with its default statement indented.

Example

```
case year of
  1 :
    status := 'Freshman';
  2 :
    status := 'Sophomore';
  3 :
    status := 'Junior';
  4 :
    status := 'Senior'
  else
    status := 'Nonmatriculated'
end;
Writeln (status);
```

The defined **integer** *year* is the selector. If it has a value that matches any of the constants 1 through 4, the statement following that number is executed. For example, if *year* has the value 2, the word *Sophomore* is stored in the string variable *status* and the **Writeln** statement is executed. If no match occurs, program control jumps to the **else** clause, stores *Nonmatriculated* in *status*, and continues with the **Writeln** statement.

Any selection structure written using a **case** statement can also be written using **if ... then ... else** statements, but not all **if ... then ... else** structures can be written in **case** form. The following **if ... then ... else** structure is functionally identical to the **case** structure in the preceding example:

```
if year = 1
  then
    status := 'Freshman'
  else
    if year = 2
      then
        status := 'Sophomore'
      else
        if year = 3
          then
            status := 'Junior'
          else
            if year = 4
              then
                status := 'Senior'
              else
                status := 'Nonmatriculated';
Writeln (status);
```

Example

```
case letter of
  'A'..'C' :
    Writeln ('2');
  'D'..'F' :
    Writeln ('3');
  'G'..'I' :
    Writeln ('4');
  'J'..'L' :
    Writeln ('5');
  'M'..'O' :
    Writeln ('6');
  'P', 'R', 'S' :
    Writeln ('7');
  'T'..'V' :
    Writeln ('8');
  'W'..'Y' :
    Writeln ('9')
  else
    Writeln ('Illegal')
end;
```

This **case** structure converts letters on a telephone to their corresponding digits. The selector *letter* is of type **char**. In seven of the eight constants lists, a subrange is used. For example, if *letter* is in the range *'G'..'I'*, the digit 3 is displayed. There is no letter Q on a telephone, so a range was not used in the constants list producing 7, where the individual constants are listed separated by commas. If *letter* has a character value other than those in the lists, the **else** clause is executed and *Illegal* is displayed.

7.9 Program Menus

In most cases, programs are used by someone with little or no knowledge of programming. With this in mind, you should make ease of use a major consideration when designing a programming solution.

For the most part, design your programs so as to minimize the number of characters entered to produce the desired output. Explicit directions also should be provided on how to operate the program. This can be achieved by creating menus such as the following, where only a single character rather than an entire word signals a task to be performed:

```
              Areas of Polygons

Enter the number preceding your choice.

          <1> Rectangle
          <2> Square
          <3> Triangle
          <4> Other

Choice -->
```

A menu should be a snapshot of the screen and should appear on an uncluttered screen, to make the operating instructions more discernible.

A Turbo Pascal unit containing several system-defined procedures provides assistance in the creation of menus for the screen.

The Crt Unit

The **Crt** (*cathode ray tube*) unit includes procedures that control the use of the keyboard and display. This unit is not available until it is called by a **uses** statement. If the **Crt** unit is needed, place

uses
  Crt;

after the **program** header and before the **const** declaration.

Two of the procedures in the **Crt** unit can help to create a basic menu: one that clears the screen and another that positions the cursor at a specified location on the screen.

The Clear-Screen Procedure

Whenever it is called, the **ClrScr** (clear-screen) procedure removes all characters from the User screen and places the cursor in the upper left corner.

FORMAT: **ClrScr;**

This procedure has no parameters. The program in which it is called must contain the **uses Crt;** statement or an error message results.

The Cursor Positioning Procedure

The cursor positioning procedure **GotoXY** places the cursor at a column number and row number specified by its parameters. The numbering system for an 80-column, 25-row screen is illustrated in Figure 7.10, with specific

Figure 7.10
80-Column, 25-Row
Screen Grid

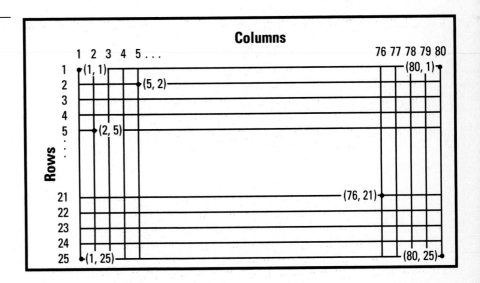

223

locations labeled. For each point, the first coordinate in parentheses represents a column number and the second, a row number.

FORMAT: **GotoXY (< column integer >, < row integer >);**

Column 1 is the left-most column on the screen and row 1, the top-most row. If the column or row value is not within the boundaries of the screen, this statement is ignored. As with **ClrScr**, a program with this procedure call must include **uses Crt**.

Example

```
ClrScr;
GotoXY (15,10);
Writeln ('Menu');
GotoXY (10,12);
Writeln ('Pick a number.');
GotoXY (12,14);
Writeln ('<1> One');
GotoXY (12,15);
Writeln ('<2> Two');
GotoXY (10,17);
Write ('Choice --> ');
Readln (choice);
```

The screen is cleared, the cursor placed at the intersection of column 15 and row 10, and *Menu* displayed there. Then the cursor is moved to column 10 and row 12, where *Pick a number.* is displayed. The menu choices are displayed in the 14th and 15th rows at column 12 and Choice --> at column 10, row 17. The final result is as follows:

```
            Menu

        Pick a number.

          <1> One
          <2> Two


        Choice --> _
```

The solution to the following application employs both menus and selection structures.

7.10 Application Using Menus: Have I Got a Car for You

The final purchase price of a new car at Corporal Motors is determined by the model, equipment packages, any rebates available, and sales tax. Write a program that produces an itemized price quotation containing the final cost to a buyer by making selections from a list of models and equipment packages, checking if any rebates are available, and adding the appropriate sales tax. Rebates are subtracted from the purchase price before the tax is added.

Corporal Motors sells three different models of its exclusive Flyer 555: the Sparrow, a two-door economy car with a base list price of $8,950; the Heron, a four-door sedan with a base list price of $11,950; and the Hawk, a two-door sports car with a base list price of $17,135. Two equipment packages are available for each of these models: The Works, which costs an additional $2,295; and The Extra, costing an additional $1,125. There is a $600 rebate on all Hawk purchases. The sales tax for the region is 4.5%.

ANALYSIS OF THE PROBLEM   Figure 7.11 lists the input and output quantities.

MODULAR DESIGN
OF THE SOLUTION   The solution design and its MIT are shown in Figure 7.12.

The model and equipment package menus are contained in the modules **MODEL CHOICE** and **PACKAGE CHOICE**, respectively, and are called by the **ENTER OPTIONS** module. Since only a single value is returned, both are implemented as functions. The **COST** module calls one module that looks up the cost of the selected model and the rebate if there is one, and another that looks up the chosen equipment package cost to calculate the total cost.

DESIGN OF THE
STRUCTURE OF
THE MODULES

AUTOMOBILE COST QUOTATION
    ENTER OPTIONS
    COST
    DISPLAY QUOTATION

ENTER OPTIONS
   MODEL CHOICE
   PACKAGE CHOICE

MODEL CHOICE
   clear screen
   display menu
   accept model choice

Figure 7.11
Automobile Cost Quotation
Input/Output Chart

Input	Output
Model	Model name
Equipment package	Model cost
	Equipment package
	Package cost
	Rebate
	Tax
	Total Cost

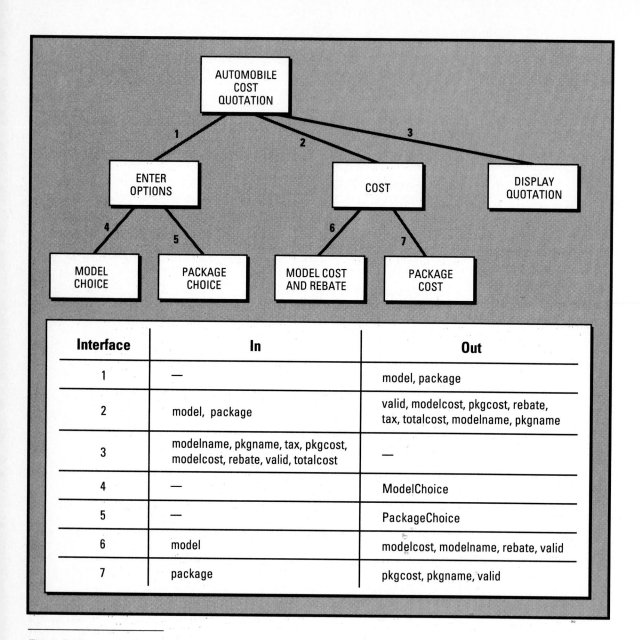

Interface	In	Out
1	—	model, package
2	model, package	valid, modelcost, pkgcost, rebate, tax, totalcost, modelname, pkgname
3	modelname, pkgname, tax, pkgcost, modelcost, rebate, valid, totalcost	—
4	—	ModelChoice
5	—	PackageChoice
6	model	modelcost, modelname, rebate, valid
7	package	pkgcost, pkgname, valid

Figure 7.12
Automobile Cost Quotation
Solution Design and
Module Interface Table

PACKAGE CHOICE
    clear screen
    display menu
    accept package choice

COST
    set valid to true
    MODEL COST AND REBATE
    PACKAGE COST
    calculate subtotal
    add tax
    determine total cost

MODEL COST AND REBATE
    case model is
      sparrow
        cost = 8950
        rebate = 0
      heron
        cost = 11950
        rebate = 0
      hawk
        cost = 17135
        rebate = 600
      else
        invalid input

PACKAGE COST
    case package is
    The Works
      cost = 2295
    The Extra
      cost = 1125
    No options
      cost = 0
    else
      invalid input

DISPLAY QUOTATION
    clear screen
    if valid input
      output model name and cost, equipment package
        and cost, rebate, tax, total cost
    else
      output message

The outline format for the **case** structure is similar to its corresponding Pascal implementation.

Case structures are appropriate for finding the model cost, rebate, and the equipment package cost. A single **case** structure can determine both the model cost and rebate, since each depends on the model. The **else** clauses in each of these **case** structures indicate that an improper menu choice was made. Before deciding to display either the price quotation or a message noting an error, the DISPLAY COST module checks whether the input was valid.

PRODUCTION OF CODE AND VERIFICATION OF SOLUTION

```pascal
program AutomobileCostQuotation;
  uses
    Crt;
  const
    taxrate = 0.045;
  type
    stringtype = string[20];
  var
    model,
    package
      : integer;
    modelname,
    pkgname
      : stringtype;
    tax,
    rebate,
    modelcost,
    pkgcost,
    totalcost
      : real;
    valid
      : boolean;

  function ModelChoice : integer;
  begin
  end;

  function PackageChoice : integer;
  begin
  end;

  procedure EnterOptions (var model, package : integer);
  begin
  end;
```

```
procedure ModelCostAndRebate (model : integer;
      var modelcost, rebate : real;
      var modelname : stringtype; var valid : boolean);
begin
end;

procedure PackageCost (package : integer; var pkgcost : real;
      var pkgname : stringtype; var valid : boolean);
begin
end;

procedure Cost (model, package : integer; var valid : boolean;
      var modelcost, pkgcost, rebate, tax, totalcost : real;
      var modelname, pkgname : stringtype);
begin
end;

procedure DisplayQuotation (valid : boolean; modelname, pkgname :
      stringtype; modelcost, pkgcost, rebate, tax, totalcost : real);
begin
end;

begin
  EnterOptions (model, package);
  Cost (model, package, valid, modelcost, pkgcost, rebate, tax,
      totalcost, modelname, pkgname);
  DisplayQuotation (valid, modelname, pkgname, modelcost, pkgcost,
      rebate, tax, totalcost)
end.
```

The **uses Crt;** statement is needed to create screen menus. Since strings cannot be selectors in **case** statements and because integers are easier to input than strings, integer identifiers called *model* and *package* represent a model number and an equipment package number in the menu modules. These integer values are converted to their corresponding string descriptions for the purposes of output. Whenever input is simplified for a user, code production becomes more time-consuming or more complex for you. The Boolean identifier *valid* determines whether choice from either of the two menus falls within acceptable ranges. If not, a message is displayed in the `DisplayCost` procedure.

Specific details of stub replacement and program testing at each stage are omitted and left as an exercise at the end of the chapter. The coding of each module is presented in the order of its implementation in the program.

`ModelChoice` and `PackageChoice` are functions that return integer values corresponding to selected options in their respective menus. Before each menu is displayed, the screen is cleared and text placed by positioning the cursor with **GotoXY** procedure calls. The code for each follows.

```
function ModelChoice : integer;
  var
    choice
      : integer;
begin
  ClrScr;
  GotoXY (20,9);
  Writeln ('Model Choices');
  GotoXY (10,11);
  Writeln ('Enter number preceding model choice.');
  GotoXY (15,13);
  Writeln ('<1> Sparrow');
  GotoXY (15,14);
  Writeln ('<2> Heron');
  GotoXY (15,15);
  Writeln ('<3> Hawk');
  GotoXY (10,17);
  Write ('Choice --> ');
  Readln (choice);
  ModelChoice := choice
end;

function PackageChoice : integer;
  var
    choice
      : integer;
begin
  ClrScr;
  GotoXY (10,9);
  Writeln ('Preferred Equipment Package Choices');
  GotoXY (10,11);
  Writeln ('Enter number preceding package choice.') ;
  GotoXY (15,13);
  Writeln ('<1> The Works');
  GotoXY (15,14);
  Writeln ('<2> The Extra');
  GotoXY (15,15);
  Writeln ('<3> No options');
  GotoXY (10,17);
  Write ('Choice --> ');
  Readln (choice);
  PackageChoice := choice
end;
```

The **EnterOptions** procedure simply calls each of these functions and returns the selections to the main program through the variable formal parameters *model* and *package:*

```
procedure EnterOptions (var model, package : integer);
begin
  model := ModelChoice;
  package := PackageChoice
end;
```

The `ModelCostAndRebate` procedure accepts the model number determined by the menu in the function `ModelChoice` and returns the model name and cost, the rebate, and whether the model number entered was correct (*valid* is true) or not (*valid* is false):

```
procedure ModelCostAndRebate (model : integer;
          var modelcost, rebate : real;
          var modelname : stringtype; var valid : boolean);
begin
  case model of
    1 :
      begin
        modelname := 'Sparrow';
        modelcost := 8950;
        rebate := 0.0
      end;
    2 :
      begin
        modelname := 'Heron';
        modelcost := 11950;
        rebate := 0.0
      end;
    3 :
      begin
        modelname := 'Hawk';
        modelcost := 17135;
        rebate := 600
      end
    else
      valid := false
  end
end;
```

The `PackageCost` procedure accepts the equipment package number determined by the menu in the function `PackageChoice` and returns the equipment package name and cost and whether the package number entered was correct (*valid* is true) or not (*valid* is false):

```
procedure PackageCost (package : integer; var pkgcost : real;
        var pkgname : stringtype; var valid : boolean);
begin
  case package of
    1 :
      begin
        pkgcost := 2295;
        pkgname := 'The Works'
      end;
    2 :
      begin
        pkgcost := 1125;
        pkgname := 'The Extra'
      end;
    3 :
      begin
        pkgcost := 0.0;
        pkgname := 'No options'
      end
    else
      valid := false
  end
end;
```

The **Cost** procedure is coded next. The Boolean parameter *valid* is initialized at true, and the procedures **ModelCostAndRebate** and **PackageCost** are called. If either of the input values is incorrect, *valid* is reset to false and returned through their parameters. A subtotal is determined by adding the model and package costs and subtracting the amount of the rebate. The tax determined on this subtotal is added to the subtotal to produce the total cost:

```
procedure Cost (model, package : integer; var valid : boolean;
        var modelcost, pkgcost, rebate, tax, totalcost : real;
        var modelname, pkgname : stringtype);
begin
  valid := true;
  ModelCostAndRebate (model, modelcost, rebate, modelname, valid);
  PackageCost (package, pkgcost, pkgname, valid);
  subtotal := modelcost + pkgcost - rebate;
  tax := subtotal * taxrate;
  totalcost := subtotal + tax
end;
```

Sample test data and expected results are given in Table 7.7.

Input		Output				
model	package	modelcost	pkgcost	rebate	tax	totalcost
1	1	8950	2295	0	506.02	11751.02
1	2	8950	1125	0	453.37	10528.37
1	3	8950	0	0	402.75	9352.75
2	1	11950	2295	0	641.02	14886.02
2	2	11950	1125	0	588.37	13663.37
2	3	11950	0	0	537.75	12487.75
3	1	17135	2295	600	847.35	19667.35
3	2	17135	1125	600	794.70	18454.70
3	3	17135	0	600	744.07	17279.07
1	4	Improper input				
4	1	Improper input				
4	4	Improper input				

Table 7.7
Test Values for
**AutomobileCost-
Quotation** Program

The **DisplayQuotation** procedure accepts all the required values, clears the screen, and displays a screen title. If the selections were valid, it displays sought-after information in a suitable format by using **GotoXY** procedures. If either of the selections was not valid, an appropriate message is shown:

```
procedure DisplayQuotation (valid : boolean;
        modelname, pkgname : stringtype;
        modelcost, pkgcost, rebate, tax, totalcost : real);
begin
  ClrScr;
  GotoXY (25,10);
  Writeln ('Automobile Quotation');
  if valid
    then
      begin
        GotoXY (10,12);
        Writeln ('Model: ', modelname);
        GotoXY (50,12);
        Writeln ('$', modelcost:8:2);
        GotoXY (10,13);
        Writeln ('Equipment Package: ', pkgname);
        GotoXY (50,13);
        Writeln ('$', pkgcost:8:2);
        GotoXY (10,14);
        Writeln ('Less rebate');
        GotoXY (48,14);
        Writeln ('- $', rebate:8:2);
        GotoXY (10,15);
        Writeln ('Sales tax');
        GotoXY (50,15);
        Writeln ('$', tax:8:2);
        GotoXY (50,16);
        Writeln ('---------');
        GotoXY (10,17);
        Writeln ('Total cost');
        GotoXY (50,17);
        Writeln ('$', totalcost:8:2)
      end
    else
      begin
        GotoXY (20,15);
        Writeln ('Improper input')
      end
end;
```

After verification, documentation is added for the final version shown, along with sample output from two runs, in Figure 7.13. Notice that comments are added after some of the **end** statements to clarify to which **begin** or **case** they belong.

Figure 7.13
AutomobileCost-
Quotation Program
Listing and Sample Output

```pascal
program AutomobileCostQuotation;
{------------------------------------------------------------------}
{ PROGRAM:        Automobile Price Quotations                      }
{ PROGRAMMER:     A. Carburetor                                    }
{ DATE:           July 20, 1990                                    }
{                                                                  }
{ This program produces an itemized price quotation for Corporal   }
{ Motors containing the final cost to a buyer by making selections }
{ from a list of models and equipment packages, checking if any    }
{ rebates are available, and adding the appropriate sales tax.     }
{ Rebates are subtracted from the purchase price. Corporal Motors  }
{ sells three different models of its exclusive Flyer 555: the     }
{ Sparrow, a two-door economy car with a base list price of $8,950;}
{ the Heron, a four-door sedan with a base list price of $11,950;  }
{ and the Hawk, a two-door sports car with a base list price of    }
{ $17,135. Two equipment packages are available for each of these  }
{ models: The Works, which costs an additional $2,295; and The     }
{ Extra, costing an additional $1,125. There is a $600 rebate on all}
{ Hawk purchases. The sales tax for the region is 4.5%.            }
{                                                                  }
{ INPUT           model                                            }
{                 equipment package                                }
{                                                                  }
{ OUTPUT          model name                                       }
{                 equipment package                                }
{                 rebate                                           }
{                 tax                                              }
{                 total cost                                       }
{------------------------------------------------------------------}
  uses
    Crt;                                  { screen utility procedures }
  const
    taxrate = 0.045;                           { sales tax rate }
  type
    stringtype = string[20];                     { descriptions }
  var
    model,                              { menu number for model }
    package                { menu number for equipment package }
      : integer;
```

(continued)

```
     modelname,                                    { model name }
     pkgname                                       { package name }
       : stringtype;
     tax,                                    { amount of sales tax }
     rebate,                                    { amount of rebate }
     modelcost,                              { base cost of model }
     pkgcost,                             { equipment package cost }
     totalcost                          { total cost of automobile }
       : real;
     valid                  { checks for correct input of data to menus }
       : boolean;

  function ModelChoice : integer;
  {------------------------------------------------------------------------}
  { Return number corresponding to model chosen.                           }
  {                                                                        }
  { IN              none                                                   }
  {                                                                        }
  { OUT             ModelChoice: number corresponding to model            }
  {------------------------------------------------------------------------}
     var
       choice                                       { menu selection }
         : integer;
  begin
    ClrScr;
    GotoXY (20,9);
    Writeln ('Model Choices');
    GotoXY (10,11);
    Writeln ('Enter number preceding model choice.');
    GotoXY (15,13);
    Writeln ('<1> Sparrow');
    GotoXY (15,14);
    Writeln ('<2> Heron');
    GotoXY (15,15);
    Writeln ('<3> Hawk');
    GotoXY (10,17);
    Write ('Choice --> ');
    Readln (choice);
    ModelChoice := choice
  end;
```

```
function PackageChoice : integer;
{-----------------------------------------------------------------------}
{ Return number corresponding to package equipment chosen.              }
{                                                                       }
{ IN            none                                                    }
{                                                                       }
{ OUT           PackageChoice: number corresponding to                  }
{                       equipment package                               }
{-----------------------------------------------------------------------}
  var
    choice                                      { menu selection }
       : integer;
begin
  ClrScr;
  GotoXY (10,9);
  Writeln ('Preferred Equipment Package Choices');
  GotoXY (10,11);
  Writeln ('Enter number preceding package choice.');
  GotoXY (15,13);
  Writeln ('<1> The Works');
  GotoXY (15,14);
  Writeln ('<2> The Extra');
  GotoXY (15,15);
  Writeln ('<3> No options');
  GotoXY (10,17);
  Write ('Choice --> ');
  Readln (choice);
  PackageChoice := choice
end;

procedure EnterOptions (var model, package : integer);
{-----------------------------------------------------------------------}
{ Determine model number and package number.                            }
{                                                                       }
{ IN            none                                                    }
{                                                                       }
{ OUT           model:    model number                                  }
{               package:  equipment package number                      }
{-----------------------------------------------------------------------}
begin
  model := ModelChoice;
  package := PackageChoice
end;
```

(continued)

```
procedure ModelCostAndRebate (model : integer;
                 var modelcost, rebate : real;
                 var modelname : stringtype; var valid : boolean);
{-------------------------------------------------------------------}
{ Look up model name, model cost and rebate amount.                 }
{                                                                   }
{ IN              model:        model number                        }
{                                                                   }
{ OUT             modelcost:    basic cost for model                }
{                 modelname:    name of model                       }
{                 rebate:       amount of rebate                    }
{                 valid:        indication of whether or not input  }
{                                  is correct                       }
{-------------------------------------------------------------------}
begin
  case model of
    1 :
      begin
        modelname := 'Sparrow';
        modelcost := 8950;
        rebate := 0.0
      end;
    2 :
      begin
        modelname := 'Heron';
        modelcost := 11950;
        rebate := 0.0
      end;
    3 :
      begin
        modelname := 'Hawk';
        modelcost := 17135;
        rebate := 600
      end
    else
      valid := false
  end { case model of }
end; { procedure }
```

```
procedure PackageCost (package : integer; var pkgcost : real;
               var pkgname : stringtype; var valid : boolean);
{------------------------------------------------------------------}
{ Look up package name and package cost.                           }
{                                                                  }
{ IN            package:  equipment package cost                   }
{                                                                  }
{ OUT           pkgcost:  cost for equipment package               }
{               pkgname:  name of equipment package                }
{               valid:    indication of whether or not input       }
{                              is correct                          }
{------------------------------------------------------------------}
begin
  case package of
    1 :
      begin
        pkgcost := 2295;
        pkgname := 'The Works'
      end;
    2 :
      begin
        pkgcost := 1125;
        pkgname := 'The Extra'
      end;
    3 :
      begin
        pkgcost := 0.0;
        pkgname := 'No options'
      end
    else
      valid := false
  end { case package of }
end; { procedure }
```

(continued)

```
procedure Cost (model, package : integer; var valid : boolean;
           var modelcost, pkgcost, rebate, tax, totalcost : real;
           var modelname, pkgname : stringtype);
{-------------------------------------------------------------------}
{ Determine total cost of automobile purchase by adding model cost  }
{ to equipment package cost, subtracting the amount of the          }
{ rebate and adding tax.                                            }
{                                                                   }
{  IN          model:       model number                            }
{              package:     equipment package number                }
{                                                                   }
{  OUT         valid:       indication of whether or not input      }
{                                 is correct                        }
{              modelcost:   basic cost for model                    }
{              pkgcost:     cost for equipment package              }
{              rebate:      amount of rebate                        }
{              tax:         amount of tax                           }
{              totalcost:   total cost to buyer                     }
{              modelname:   name of model                           }
{              pkgname:     name of equipment package               }
{-------------------------------------------------------------------}
  var
    subtotal                   { sum of model and equipment package costs }
       : real;
begin
  valid := true;
  ModelCostAndRebate (model, modelcost, rebate, modelname, valid);
  PackageCost (package, pkgcost, pkgname, valid);
  subtotal := modelcost + pkgcost - rebate;
  tax := subtotal * taxrate;
  totalcost := subtotal + tax
end;
```

```
procedure DisplayQuotation (valid : boolean;
       modelcost, pkgcost, rebate, tax, totalcost : real;
       modelname, pkgname : stringtype);
{-------------------------------------------------------------------}
{ Show price quotation on screen including model name and cost,     }
{ equipment package name and cost, rebate, sales tax, and total     }
{ cost of automobile.                                               }
{                                                                   }
{  IN           valid:      indication of whether or not input      }
{                               is correct                          }
{               modelcost:  basic cost for model                    }
{               pkgcost:    cost for equipment package              }
{               rebate:     amount of rebate                        }
{               tax:        amount of tax                           }
{               totalcost:  total cost to buyer                     }
{               modelname:  name of model                           }
{               pkgname:    name of equipment package               }
{                                                                   }
{  OUT          none                                                }
{-------------------------------------------------------------------}
begin
  ClrScr;
  GotoXY (25,10);
  Writeln ('Automobile Quotation');
  if valid
    then
      begin
        GotoXY (10,12);
        Writeln ('Model: ', modelname);
        GotoXY (50,12);
        Writeln ('$', modelcost:8:2);
        GotoXY (10,13);
        Writeln ('Equipment Package: ', pkgname);
        GotoXY (50,13);
        Writeln ('$', pkgcost:8:2);
        GotoXY (10,14);
        Writeln ('Less rebate');
        GotoXY (48,14);
        Writeln ('- $', rebate:8:2);
        GotoXY (10,15);
        Writeln ('Sales tax');
        GotoXY (50,15);
        Writeln ('$', tax:8:2);
        GotoXY (50,16);
        Writeln ('---------');
```

(continued)

241

```
          GotoXY (10,17);
          Writeln ('Total cost');
          GotoXY (50,17);
          Writeln ('$', totalcost:8:2)
        end
      else
        begin
          GotoXY (20,15);
          Writeln ('Improper input')
        end
  end;

begin
  EnterOptions (model, package);
  Cost (model, package, valid, modelcost, pkgcost, rebate, tax,
              totalcost, modelname, pkgname);
  DisplayQuotation (valid, modelcost, pkgcost, rebate, tax,
              totalcost, modelname, pkgname)
end.
```

Output 1

```
                    Automobile Quotation
  Model: Heron                                    $11950.00
  Equipment Package: The Extra                    $ 1125.00
  Less rebate                                    -$    0.00
  Sales tax                                       $  588.38
                                                  _____
  Total cost                                      $13663.37
```

Output 2

```
                    Automobile Quotation
  Model: Hawk                                     $17135.00
  Equipment Package: The Works                    $ 2295.00
  Less rebate                                    -$  600.00
  Sales tax                                       $  847.35
                                                  _____
  Total cost                                      $19677.35
```

Store and Forward

The ability to write a program to make decisions is an important tool to add to the techniques in our problem-solving toolkit. Decision structures may provide a single option or multiple options and be implemented by an **if . . . then . . . else** structure or a **case** structure.

With this capability comes the added complexity of testing programs with decision structures. Test data should be chosen to try to cover all possible execution paths—not always an easy thing to do.

Since computer users generally are not programmers, programs must be as easy as possible to use. One way this can be accomplished is by utilizing several Turbo Pascal screen procedures to create menu-driven programs.

But computers can do even more than make decisions—they can tirelessly perform tedious, repetitive tasks over and over again. Our next step is to investigate the several different types of available iteration (repetition) structures.

Snares and Pitfalls

- *Mismatching operands in relational expressions:* The expressions compared by relational operators must be the same type. This includes the operator **in**, where the value before **in** must be of the same type as the list in the set following **in**.

- *Failing to use necessary parentheses in a logical or a relational expression:* Relational and logical operators are included in the precedence order for all operators. Parentheses can override this predetermined order.

- *Failing to employ a default case:* The default case arises when none of the conditions in a selection structure have been satisfied. Unexpected results may be produced if no provision is made for it.

- *Improperly punctuating* **if . . . then . . . else** *structures:* Semicolons should terminate entire selection structures and not precede **else** clauses in **if . . . then . . . else** structures.

- *Improperly coding a compound statement:* The first statement in a compound statement must follow a **begin** statement and the last precede an **end** statement.

- *Confusing the assignment operator* (**:=**) *with the equal relational operator* (**=**)*:* The assignment operator places a value in a location, while the equal relational operator compares two quantities of the same type.

- *Duplicating elements in the constants lists of a* **case** *structure:* Any element in the constants list of a **case** structure cannot appear in another constants list of the same structure.

Exercises

1. Answer the following questions in paragraph form.
   a. Comment on the truth or falsity of the following statement: "Any **case** structure can be written as an **if . . . then . . . else** structure."
   b. Explain how one string data type is compared to another.
   c. What are nested structures?
   d. Are programs that are easier to use generally easier to design and code? Explain.
   e. Why shouldn't a semicolon precede the **else** clause in an **if . . . then . . . else** selection structure?

2. Classify each of the following Pascal statements as valid or invalid. If invalid, explain why. Unless otherwise stated, assume all identifiers have been properly declared.

   a. ```
      if name := 'last'
         then
            Writeln ('No additional data entry.');
      ```

   b. ```
      if a = 3.0
         then
            a := a * 2;
         else
            a := a / 2;
      ```

   c. ```
      if n in [1..25]
         then
            if n + x = 0
               then
                  Writeln ('Start')
               else
                  Writeln ('Middle')
         else
            Writeln ('End');
      ```

   d. ```
      case letter of
         'a', 'b' :
            Writeln ('Room 212');
         'c'..'m' :
            Writeln ('Room 300');
         'n'..'r' :
            begin
               Writeln ('Room 276');
               Writeln ('Bring pencil')
            end;
         else
            Writeln ('Check tomorrow.')
      end;
      ```

e. **case** digit **of**
   4, 5, 6 :
    begin
     digit := digit - 4;
     Writeln (digit)
    end;
   1, 2, 3, 4 :
    Writeln (digit)
 end;

3. Evaluate the following logical expressions if *p* is true, *q* is false, and *r* is true.
  a. **not** q
  b. **not** q **and** r
  c. **not** (q **and** r)
  d. p **or** q **and not** r
  e. (p **or** q) **and not** r

4. Write Pascal equivalents for each of the given descriptions.
  a. If the integer *hours* is greater than 40 but less than or equal to 60, then make *otpay* the product of the hours above 40 and 1.5 times *payrate*. If *hours* is greater than 60, make *otpay* the product of the hours above 40 and 2.0 times *payrate*.
  b. Display *positive* when *num* is positive, *negative* when *num* is negative, and *zero* in all other cases.
  c. When *lettergrade* is A, calculate *gradepoint* by multiplying 4 by *numcredits*; when *lettergrade* is B, find *gradepoint* by multiplying 3 by *numcredits*; for C, 2 times *numcredits*; for D, 1 times *numcredits*; and for F, 0 times *numcredits*. Use an **if . . . then . . . else** structure.
  d. Implement the description in part c with a **case** structure.
  e. Use a **case** structure to display the message *Register in January* if the first letter in the contents of *lastname* begins with a letter from A to H, inclusive; *Register in May* when the first letter is a letter falling in the range I through P, inclusive; and *Register in September* for any other first letter.

5. Complete the testing process in the **AutomobileCostQuotation** program (see page 235) with representative data.

6. **Readln** (x);
  if x **in** [1..4]
   then
    x := x + 2
   else
    if x <> 6
     then
      x := x - 2
     else
      x := x * 3;
  Writeln (x : 4);

Show the exact output of this program segment if the following values are entered for *x*.

a. 3
b. 4
c. 5
d. 6
e. 7

7.
```
class := 'oooo';
Readln (category);
case category of
   'a', 'b' :
      Insert ('z', class, 2);
   'c'..'h' :
     begin
        Delete (class, 1, 1);
        Insert ('a', class, 1)
     end;
   'i'..'p' :
      class := Concat (class, 'y')
   else
      Insert ('x', class, 1)
end;
Writeln (class);
```

Show the exact output of this program segment if the following characters are entered for *x*.

a. *a*
b. *d*
c. *h*
d. *p*
e. *z*

Programming Assignments

Elementary

1. One integer is a factor of a second if, when the second is divided by the first, the remainder is 0.

   Write a program that accepts two numbers and tells whether one is a factor of the other.

2. Write a program that accepts a time of day, on a 24-hour clock, in the format HH:MM and converts it to AM/PM format. Times between 0:00 and 11:59 are considered AM and those between 12:00 and 23:59, PM. For example, the program would change the 24-hour time 15:13 to 3:13 PM.

3. To become eligible for a driver's license, a prospect must pass a written examination with a grade of 70 or above and pass the driving test. Write a program that accepts an applicant's name, numeric grade on the written test,

and a P or an F on the driver's test and displays a message indicating whether a license should be issued or not.

4. Home owners often borrow money using their home as collateral. One bank determines the credit available to a home owner by taking 70% of the current market value of the home and subtracting the remaining principal on the current mortgage. The loan is approved if this value is at least $10,000.

   Write a program that accepts the current market value of a home and the remaining principal on a mortgage and determines the amount of the loan a home owner is eligible for, if any at all.

5. People often change American dollars into foreign currency when traveling abroad.

   Write a program that accepts a dollar amount, gives the user a choice of conversions to Japanese yen, German marks, British pounds, or French francs, and displays the desired equivalent. Use the following table for conversions:

Currency	Per $1 U.S.
British pound	0.55
French franc	6.04
Japanese yen	134.20
German mark	1.80

6. Television stations can be classified as commercial, news, sports, educational, or public access. Write a program that presents a menu of these choices and displays all the channels that can be classified in the selected category.

7. On the average, a woman's body needs 16 calories per pound on a daily basis while a man's body requires 18 calories per pound.

   Write a program that accepts a person's sex and weight and outputs his or her total calorie requirement for a day.

8. Write a menu-driven program that outputs the number of days in given month in a non-leap year.

9. Write a menu-driven program that accepts a person's weight on earth and outputs that person's weight on another planet. The following table lists the equivalent of 1 pound on other planets.

Planet	Equivalent of 1 lb
Mercury	0.38 lb
Venus	0.91 lb
Earth	1.00 lb
Mars	0.38 lb
Jupiter	2.53 lb
Saturn	1.06 lb
Uranus	0.92 lb
Neptune	1.20 lb
Pluto	0.57 lb

10. The general form for a system of linear equations with two unknowns x and y is:

$$ax + by = c$$
$$dx + ey = f$$

where a, b, c, d, e, and f are constants. If $ae - bd$ is not equal to zero, the values for x and y that satisfy both equations are:

$$x = (ce - bf)/(ae - bd)$$
$$y = (af - cd)/(ae - bd)$$

Write a program that accepts the constants and displays the solution if it exists, and a message if it doesn't exist.

Challenging

11. Charges for phone calls from Upper Eastborough County depend on the county in which the receiver is located, the length of the call, and when the call is made. Given these three data items, write a program that displays the cost of a call. The following table summarizes costs.

Receiving County	Cost per Minute	
	Day	Night
Lower Eastborough	$0.11	$0.07
Stoneburg	$0.16	$0.08

12. Write a menu-driven program that outputs the number of days in a given month in any given year. A leap year is one that is divisible by 4 except for "century" years, that is, those ending in 00. These century years must be divisible by 400 to be leap years. Therefore, the year 1700 is *not* a leap year, since it is not divisible by 400, while the year 2000 is.

13. The Torus Doughnut Store charges $0.40 per doughnut, but offers discounts of 12.5% if at least a half dozen are purchased, 20% if at least a dozen are purchased, and 25% if more than three dozen are purchased.
    Write a program that accepts the number of doughnuts purchased and outputs the cost.

14. Write a program that translates a dollar amount between $0.01 and $999.99 into its English equivalent. For example, if 325.56 were entered, the output would be *three hundred twenty-five dollars and fifty-six cents*.

15. Write a program that accepts the coordinates of a point on the Cartesian coordinate system and displays a message indicating whether the point lies in the first quadrant, in the second quadrant, in the third quadrant, in the fourth quadrant, on the positive x-axis, on the negative x-axis, on the positive y-axis, on the negative y-axis, or at the origin. This can be done with a **case** structure and a programmer-defined function called **Sign** that accepts a number and returns +1 for all positive arguments, −1 for all negative arguments, and 0 otherwise.

16. According to the United States Constitution, "No person shall be a Senator who shall not have attained to the age of thirty years, and have been nine years a citizen of the United States, and who shall not, when elected, be an inhabitant of that State for which he shall be chosen."

    Write a program that accepts a prospective senator's age, the number of years he or she has been a citizen, and the person's state of residence and outputs whether or not that person is eligible to be a senator.

17. A truth table indicates when a logical expression is true for all possible values of its Boolean components. For example, the truth table for *(p or not q) and p* might look as follows:

p	*q*	*(p or not q) and p*
TRUE	TRUE	TRUE
TRUE	FALSE	TRUE
FALSE	TRUE	FALSE
FALSE	FALSE	FALSE

    The first two columns show all of the four possible combinations of *p* and *q*, and the last column shows the truth values for each set of inputs. A logical expression that is always true (every combination of *p* and *q* yields *TRUE*) is called a tautology. A logical expression that is always false is said to be inconsistent.

    Write a program that produces a truth table for a logical expression containing two different Boolean components *p* and *q* and indicates whether that expression is a tautology, inconsistent, or neither.

18. An assembly language program consists of computer instructions that are more detailed than those of a higher-level language such as Pascal. An assembler is a translator that accepts an instruction and decodes it. Write a program that reads a single string that represents an addition, subtraction, multiplication, or division operation, changes the operands to numeric values, and returns the result of the given operations. In the instruction definitions that follow, a space separates the operation from the integer constant operands *nn* and *mm*, which are separated by a comma.

    ```
    ADD nn,mm    add mm to nn
    SUB nn,mm    subtract mm from nn
    MUL nn,mm    multiply nn by mm
    DIV nn,mm    divide nn by mm and return the integral quotient
    ```

19. A state university charges all students a $25 registration fee but bases its tuition charges on whether or not a student is a state resident and whether that student is full-time or part-time. A student is considered full-time if he or she takes 12 credits or more during a given term. Write a user-friendly, menu-driven program that accepts a student's name and residence status from one menu and full-time/part-time status from a second menu and produces a tuition receipt showing all relevant information and costs. Tuition charges are computed from the following table:

State Resident	**Out-of-State Resident**
full-time: $576 per term	full-time: $1080 per term
part-time: $53 per credit	part-time: $104 per credit

20. Wind speed often makes the air temperature feel colder than it is. The wind chill index (WCI) measures how cold it feels with a given air temperature and wind speed. Let WS represent the wind speed, in miles-per-hour (mph), and F represent the air temperature, in degrees Fahrenheit. For wind speeds less than or equal to 4 mph, the air temperature is unchanged. For speeds greater than 4 mph and less than or equal to 45 mph, the WCI is 91 − (WF × TF), where the wind factor WF is $11 + 6.7 \sqrt{\text{WS}} - 0.45 \times \text{WS}$, and the temperature factor TF is $(91 - F)/22$. For wind speeds greater than 45 mph, WCI is $1.6 \times F - 55$.

    Write a program that displays the wind chill index, in degrees Fahrenheit and in degrees Celsius, given the air temperature and wind speed on a given day. The Celsius equivalent C of a Fahrenheit temperature F is given by the following equation:

    $$C = 0.55 \times (F - 32)$$

CHAPTER 8

Iteration Structures

Key Terms

body of the loop
concatenation operator
downto
endcode
for . . . do
index
infinite loop
iteration structure

loop
loop control variable
repeat . . . until
sentinel
simulation
to
while . . . do

Objectives

- To introduce definite loop structures and apply them in the solution of problems
- To introduce indefinite loop structures and apply them in the solution of problems
- To present and utilize summing and counting statements
- To enhance the repetition capabilities of a program through the use of nested loops

8.1 Introduction

The third and final major programming structure, called the *iteration structure* or *loop*, permits a sequence of instructions to be repeated. For example, a client can instruct an investment counsellor to purchase 100 shares of stock, accumulate dividends for 5 consecutive days, and sell the shares at the end of the 5-day period. The client can also instruct the counsellor to purchase 100 shares and collect dividends as long as the price of the stock remains above the initial purchase price. In both cases, the client initiates the process with an original purchase of 100 shares of stock. The stock continues to accumulate dividends until a condition is met. In the first case, the process is stopped at the end of the 5-day period, in the second, when the stock price falls below the initial purchase price.

Pascal iteration structures are available to handle both types of situations. In a definite loop structure, the number of repetitions is known before the loop is executed, as when dividends are accumulated for 5 days. In an indefinite loop structure, the number of repetitions is governed by the value of a variable inside the loop; if that variable reaches a particular value, the loop terminates, as in the example where the loop ends when the price of the stock falls below the initial purchase price.

Iteration structures give you two other capabilities: the capability to count the number of times an action is performed, and the capability to keep a running total of the different values assigned to a variable. For example, these techniques can count the number of days that stock dividends are accumulated or can find the total value of a stock portfolio after a specified period of time.

Loops, along with sequential and selection structures, form the basic building blocks of any programming language. Any algorithm can be designed and coded using a combination of sequential, selection, and iteration structures.

8.2 Counting and Summing

Counting and summing statements are nothing more than customized assignment statements. In *counting* statements, a constant is added to the value of a variable identifier, with the result replacing the previous value of the identifier.

Example

```
count := count + 1;
```

Each time this statement is executed, 1 is added to the value of *count*, with the updated value replacing the initial value. If *count* had a value of 4 before this statement was executed, it would contain 5 after execution.

Similar statements can be formed with different constants and other operations.

Examples

```
down := down - 2;
```

2 is subtracted from the current value of *down* each time this statement is executed.

```
product := product * 2;
```

Each time this statement is executed, the value of *product* is doubled.

A *summing* statement keeps a running total of the value of a variable identifier.

Example

`sum := sum + item;`	The value of *item* is added to the current value of *sum*, and this total becomes the new value for *sum*. If this statement were repeated, it would keep a running total of all the values of *item*.

A similar statement can keep a running product of a series of values by replacing the addition operator with a multiplication operator.

The distinction between a counting and a summing assignment statement is that in a counting statement a variable identifier is changed by the same constant value each time it is executed, whereas in a summing statement, a variable identifier is changed by an alterable value each time it is executed.

8.3 The for . . . do Structure

The definite loop structure is implemented in Pascal by the **for . . . do** statement.

FORMAT:

```
for <index> := <initial value> to <final value> do
    < statement >;
```

The *index*, or *loop control variable*, must be a local variable identifier with an ordinal data type. The initial and final values are separated by the keyword **to**. They can be expressions or constants, but must be type-compatible with **<index>**. The *body of the loop*, **< statement >**, follows the reserved word **do**. If the body is a compound statement, it must be enclosed in a **begin-end** pair, with a semicolon following the **end** to separate it from the statement following the loop.

At execution time, **<initial value>** is stored in the variable **<index>**. If the value of the index is less than or equal to **<final value>**, the body of the loop is executed, the index incremented by one, and this new value tested against the final value. If the value of the loop control variable is greater than the final value, the body of the loop is ignored and control passes to the statement following the loop.

Example

`for i := 1 to 4 do`
`  Writeln ('Pass: ', i:2);`
`Writeln ('Out of loop');`
	The index *i* is a declared integer and is given the initial value 1. Since *i* is less than or equal to 4, the **Write** statement is executed, displaying the

current value of i, or 1. Control returns to the beginning of the loop, where the value of i becomes 2, the integer following 1. 2 is still not greater than 4, so the loop is executed again. When i becomes 5, the body of the loop is not executed and control passes to the **Writeln** statement that follows the loop. The output for this program segment is:

```
Pass: 1
Pass: 2
Pass: 3
Pass: 4
Out of loop
```

STYLE TIP

Place the body of a loop on the line following, and indented from, the **for** statement to make it stand out, as in the following:

```
for k := 1 to 10 do
    Writeln ('Body of loop');
```

If the body is a compound statement, indent the **begin** from the **for** statement and indent the statements in the body from the **begin**. The **end** statement that indicates the end of the loop should be aligned with its corresponding **begin**, as in the following:

```
for i := 8 to 12 do
    begin
        Writeln ('First statement in loop');
        Writeln ('Last statement in loop')
    end;
```

The following example calculates the grade point average for a student taking five courses. (Grade point average, a method for rating college students, is calculated by dividing the total number of grade points a student receives in all courses for a semester by the total number of course credits taken by the student that semester. In a 4-point system, a grade of A is a 4.0; B, 3.0; C, 2.0; D, 1.0; and F, 0.0.) Note that one summing statement is required to total the grade points and another to total the credits.

Example

```
sumgp := 0.0;
sumcred := 0.0;
for i := 1 to coursect do
  begin
    EnterData (gp, cred);
    sumgp := sumgp + gp;
    sumcred := sumcred + cred
  end;
gpa := sumgp / sumcred;
Writeln ('GPA: ', gpa:4:2);
```

The real variables *sumgp* and *sumcred* keep a running total of the grade points and credits, respectively. They *must* be initialized to 0.0 before the loop begins. This is similar to zeroing a scale before weighing an object. The variable *coursect* is declared as an integer and contains the number of courses taken by a student. If *coursect* is 5, each of the five times the loop is executed the values of *gp* and *cred* that are entered through the procedure **EnterData** are added to *sumgp* and *sumcred*. After the fifth pass through the loop, control passes to the assignment statement that calculates the grade point average displayed by the last statement.

The value of the index may be used in the body of the loop but should not be altered, since this produces unpredictable results, one of which may be an infinite loop. In an *infinite* (or never-ending) *loop*, the value of the condition that ends the loop is never reached, so, as a result, the body of the loop is continually executed.

Example

```
for j := 1 to 10 do
  begin
    j := j + 2;
    Writeln (j:4)
  end;
```

Here, an infinite loop produces an endless list of multiples of 3, because the loop control variable is changed in the body of the loop. The beginning of the output is:

```
   3
   6
   9
  12
 . . .
```

STYLE TIP   When the loop control variable (index of the loop) only controls the repetition of a process and is not a part of any of the calculations performed in the loop, choose a simple variable name for that index. The identifiers *i, j,* and *k* often serve this purpose.

The index of a loop can start at a higher initial value and proceed to a lower final value if you replace the reserved word **to** with **downto** in a **for ... do** statement. In this case, 1 is *subtracted* from the current index value each time the body of the loop is executed.

Example

```
for k := 5 downto 1 do
  Writeln (k:2);
Writeln ('Blastoff!');
```

The index *k* starts at 5 and goes down to 1, in decrements of 1, producing the following output:

```
         5
         4
         3
         2
         1
      Blastoff!
```

8.4 Application of Loop Tracing: Put It in Reverse

A palindrome is a word, phrase, or sentence that reads the same backward as forward. For example, "madam" and "noon" are one-word palindromes, while "Madam, I'm Adam" is a palindrome in sentence form. Punctuation marks, capitalization, and spaces are not counted in determining whether a string is a palindrome.

Write a program that accepts a word in lowercase letters and determines whether it is a palindrome.

ANALYSIS OF THE PROBLEM   Figure 8.1 lists the input and output quantities needed in the solution.

MODULAR DESIGN OF THE SOLUTION   The entry of a test word occurs in one module and the display of its status (whether it is a palindrome or not) in another. A third module determines the status of the word and calls a fourth module to reverse the letters in the word. Figure 8.2 represents the solution design.

Figure 8.1
Palindrome Input/Output Chart

Input	Output
Word	Status

Figure 8.2
Palindrome Solution
Design and Module
Interface Table

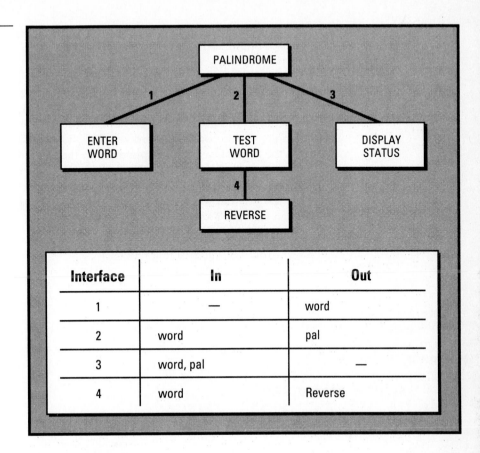

Interface	In	Out
1	—	word
2	word	pal
3	word, pal	—
4	word	Reverse

DESIGN OF THE
STRUCTURE OF THE
MODULES

PALINDROME
  ENTER WORD
  TEST WORD
  DISPLAY STATUS

ENTER WORD
  enter a word to be tested

TEST WORD
  if word equals REVERSE of word
    then
      word is palindrome
    else
      word not palindrome

REVERSE
  form reversed word from entered word

> DISPLAY STATUS
>> output whether palindrome or not

The **REVERSE** module needs additional detail, such as how to form the reverse of a word. One way is to start with the last letter in the given word and append to it the second-to-last letter. The process continues until the first letter in the given word is added to the end of the previous letters. For example, for the original word *cat*, the *t* is removed; then the *a* is copied from the original word and appended to the *t*, yielding *ta*; and finally, the *c* is copied and added to the end of the previous results, giving *tac*. Since the original word and its reverse are not equal, *cat* is not a palindrome. If *tot* were the original word, its reverse would also be *tot*, qualifying it as a palindrome. **REVERSE** can now be revised to read:

> REVERSE
>> from last letter to first letter
>>> isolate letter
>>> attach letter to end of letters previously removed

PRODUCTION OF CODE
AND VERIFICATION OF SOLUTION

```pascal
program Palindrome;
  type
    wordtype = string[20];
  var
    word : wordtype;
    pal : boolean;

  procedure EnterWord (var word : wordtype);
  begin
  end;

  function Reverse (word : wordtype) : wordtype;
  begin
  end;

  procedure TestWord (word : wordtype; var pal : boolean);
  begin
  end;

  procedure DisplayStatus (word : wordtype; pal : boolean);
  begin
  end;
```

```
begin
  EnterWord (word);
  TestWord (word, pal);
  DisplayStatus (word, pal)
end.
```

The coding and testing of the **EnterWord** procedure is straightforward:

```
procedure EnterWord (var word : wordtype);
begin
  Write ('Enter a word: ');
  Readln (word)
end;
```

The **TestWord** procedure is added to the program and its connection to the function **Reverse** tested with the **Trace into** option from the IDE:

```
procedure TestWord (word : wordtype; var pal : boolean);
begin
  if word = Reverse(word)
    then
      pal := true
    else
      pal := false
end;
```

The next step is to replace the **Reverse** stub with code that returns the original word with its letters in reverse order:

```
function Reverse (word : wordtype) : wordtype;
  var
    i : integer;
    tempword : wordtype;
begin
  tempword := '';
  for i := Length(word) downto 1 do
    tempword := tempword + Copy (word, i, 1);
  Reverse := tempword
end;
```

The plus sign (+) between *tempword* and the **Copy** function call is a *concatenation operator*. When it separates two strings, it appends the value of the second string to the end of the first.

Example

```
a := 'me';
b := 'ti';
c := b + a;
```

If *a* contains the string *me* and *b* contains the string *ti*, then the third assignment statement attaches the contents of *a* to the end of the contents of *b* and stores the result (*time*) in *c*.

The body of the loop is a summing statement for string characters. The summing variable *tempword* is initialized as a null string (a string with no characters) before the loop is entered. Each pass through the loop copies one letter at a time from the entered word, starting at the right, adds it to the end of the current contents of *tempword*, and stores the result back in *tempword*. When the loop is completed, the reverse of the entered word should be the final contents of *tempword*.

Test this updated version of the program using the **Trace into** option. Make sure *i* and *tempword* are in the Watches window before you start. After highlighting the statement **if word = Reverse(word)** in the **TestWord** procedure, program control jumps to the **begin** in the function **Reverse**. As you trace through the loop in **Reverse**, the values of *i* and *tempword* in the Watches window change. The index *i* starts at the length of the entered word and decreases by 1 with each pass through the loop, while the value of *tempword* starts as a null string and forms the reverse of the input word, one character at a time. You can actually see how the loop is processed.

Test runs should include some inputs that are palindromes, others that are not, and boundary cases such as the null string (a string with no characters) and a string with a single character. Once the testing is completed, the **DisplayStatus** procedure can be coded and tested:

```
procedure DisplayStatus (word : wordtype; pal : boolean);
begin
  Write ('The word ',word , ' is ');
  if not pal
    then
      Write ('not ');
  Writeln ('a palindrome.')
end;
```

The Boolean parameter *pal* determines whether the word *not* appears in the output. If a word is a palindrome (*pal* is true), then **not** pal is false and the **then** clause is skipped. If the word is not a palindrome (*pal* is false), then **not** pal is true and the word *not* is added to the output.

After a final test run to verify the output format, the final documented program is written, as shown, along with sample output, in Figure 8.3.

Figure 8.3
Palindome Program
Listing and Sample Output

```
program Palindrome;
{-----------------------------------------------------------------}
{ PROGRAM:        Palindromes                                     }
{ PROGRAMMER:     B. Cucuros                                      }
{ DATE:           August 19, 1990                                }
{                                                                 }
{ This program accepts one word in lowercase letters and determines }
{ whether it is a palindrome, that is, it is spelled the same     }
{ forward as backward.                                            }
{                                                                 }
{ INPUT           word                                            }
{                                                                 }
{ OUTPUT          whether the word is a palindrome or not         }
{-----------------------------------------------------------------}
  type
    wordtype = string[20];                        { word type }
  var
    word                                   { word to be tested }
      : wordtype;
    pal                        { indicates whether word is palindrome }
      : boolean;

  procedure EnterWord (var word : wordtype);
  {-----------------------------------------------------------------}
  { Accept a word to test.                                         }
  {                                                                 }
  { IN              none                                           }
  {                                                                 }
  { OUT             word:    word to be tested                     }
  {-----------------------------------------------------------------}
  begin
    Write ('Enter a word: ');
    Readln (word)
  end;
```

(continued)

```pascal
function Reverse (word : wordtype) : wordtype;
{----------------------------------------------------------------}
{ Reverse the letters of a word.                                 }
{                                                                }
{ IN            word:     word to be tested                      }
{                                                                }
{ OUT           Reverse: word written backwards                  }
{----------------------------------------------------------------}
  var
    i                                        { loop index }
      : integer;
    tempword                         { builds reverse of word }
      : wordtype;
begin
  tempword := '';
  for i := Length(word) downto 1 do
    tempword := tempword + Copy(word, i, 1);
  Reverse := tempword
end;

procedure TestWord (word : wordtype; var pal : boolean);
{----------------------------------------------------------------}
{ Test whether a word is a palindrome or not.                    }
{                                                                }
{ IN            word:     word to be tested                      }
{                                                                }
{ OUT           pal:      true if word is a palindrome;          }
{                         false if it is not                     }
{----------------------------------------------------------------}
begin
  if word = Reverse(word)
    then
      pal := true
    else
      pal := false
end;
```

```
procedure DisplayStatus (word : wordtype; pal : boolean);
{---------------------------------------------------------------}
{ Display a message indicating whether a word is a              }
{ palindrome or not.                                           }
{                                                              }
{ IN          word:    word to be tested                       }
{             pal:     true if word is a palindrome;           }
{                      false if it is not                      }
{                                                              }
{ OUT         none                                             }
{---------------------------------------------------------------}
begin
   Write ('The word ', word, ' is ');
   if not pal
     then
        Write ('not ');
   Writeln ('a palindrome.')
end;

begin
   EnterWord (word);
   TestWord (word, pal);
   DisplayStatus (word, pal)
end.
```

--------------------------------- Output ---------------------------------

```
Enter a word: madam
The word madam is a palindrome.
```

8.5 The while . . . do Structure

The first of two indefinite loop structures that are available in Pascal is **while . . . do.**

FORMAT: **while** < condition > **do**
             < statement >;

The condition is a relational or a logical expression with a Boolean value of true or false. If the body of the loop is a compound statement, its constituent statements must be enclosed in a **begin-end** pair. A semicolon ends the structure.

As long as the condition is true, the body of the loop is executed. When the condition becomes false, execution resumes with the statement following the **while** structure. The loop may not be executed at all, since the condition is evaluated *before* entry into the loop.

Example

```
pass := 1;
while pass <= 4 do
  begin
    Writeln ('Pass: ', pass:2);
    pass := pass + 1
  end;
Writeln ('Out of loop');
```

The variable *pass* is initialized and its value compared to 4. Since *pass* is less than or equal to 4, the body of the loop, which consists of a **Writeln** statement and an assignment statement enclosed in a **begin-end** pair, is executed. After the value of *pass* is increased by 1, control is transferred to the **while** test. The body is executed as long as *pass* is less than or equal to 4. When *pass* exceeds 4, control passes to the last **Writeln** statement. The output for this code is:

```
Pass: 1
Pass: 2
Pass: 3
Pass: 4
Out of loop
```

STYLE TIP

Place the body of the loop on the line following the **while** statement and indented from it. If the body is a compound statement, indent **begin** from **while** and indent the body from **begin**. Align the **end** statement terminating the body with its **begin**, as in the following:

```
x := 15;
while x > 10 do
  begin
    Writeln ('First statement in loop');
    x := x - 1;
    Writeln ('Last statement in loop')
  end;
```

The **while** loop often is used for repeated entry of data from the keyboard. This data entry loop is terminated when a *sentinel*, or *endcode*, value is entered for a particular variable. The sentinel value usually has no significance for the variable to which it is compared. For example, if the variable representing age were to be entered, any negative number could signal the end of a data entry loop.

In order for a loop to be entered for the first time, the loop must be primed; that is, the code asking for the initial piece of data must precede the loop. After this structure has been entered, an identical request for data is placed at the end of the body of the loop.

Example

```
count := 0;
sum := 0;
Writeln ('To end input,
  enter -1 for weight.');
Write ('Enter weight: ');
Readln (weight);
while weight <> -1 do
  begin
    count := count + 1;
    sum := sum + weight;
    Writeln ('To end input,
      enter -1 for weight.');
    Write ('Enter weight: ');
    Readln (weight)
  end;
avg := sum / count;
```

This code segment finds the average weight of a group of people. The variable *sum* keeps a running total of the weights, while *count* keeps track of the number of weights entered. The loop is primed by the three statements that indicate how to end the loop and ask for the first weight. These same three statements are repeated at the end of the body of the loop. The loop terminates when the sentinel, or endcode, −1 is entered for a weight. Control then passes out of the loop to a statement that calculates the average weight.

> **STYLE TIP**
>
> Since the **while** loop in the previous example continues until a particular value is entered, a message indicating how to end the loop should be included each time data entry is requested. If this is not done, the only way to end the loop may be to guess how to do it.

It is easier inadvertently to create an infinite loop with a **while** structure than with a **for** structure. If the terminating condition is never reached, the program continues to execute the body of the loop, tying up, or "hanging," the computer.

Example

```
n := 1;
sum := 0;
while sum <>10 do
  begin
    n := n + 1;
    sum := sum + n
  end;
Writeln (n, ' terms used.');
```

This loop adds consecutive integers, starting with 1, until their sum is 10. The variables *n* and *sum* are initialized at 1 and 0, respectively, and the **while** loop ends when *sum* is 10. Although there is no syntax error in the code for this series, *sum* has values of 2, 5, 9, 14, and so on. It never equals 10, and an infinite loop results.

8.6 The repeat . . . until Structure

The **repeat . . . until** structure is the second of the two indefinite loop structures in Pascal.

FORMAT:
```
repeat
   < statement >
until < condition >;
```

The reserved word **repeat** is followed by the statements in the body of the loop. A **begin-end** pair is *not* necessary to enclose a compound statement in a **repeat** structure. The **repeat** marks the beginning of the loop, and the **until**, the end. The reserved word **until** precedes a relational or a logical expression with a Boolean value of true or false, and a semicolon signals the end of the structure.

The body of the loop is repeated as long as the condition is false; that is, control is passed to the statement following the structure when the condition becomes true. Unlike the **while** structure, the condition in a **repeat** structure is tested *after* the body of the loop is executed at least once.

Example

```
pass := 1;
repeat
  Writeln ('Pass: ', pass:2);
  pass := pass + 1
until pass > 4;
Writeln ('Out of loop.');
```

The **Writeln** statement is executed during the first pass through the loop regardless of the value of *pass*. Then the value of *pass* is updated and tested against 4. Since the new value, 2, is still less than or equal to 4, the loop is repeated. When *pass* becomes 5, the loop terminates and the last **Writeln** statement is executed. The output for this code segment is identical to the output produced by the **for** and **while** structures in previous examples:

```
Pass: 1
Pass: 2
Pass: 3
Pass: 4
Out of loop
```

STYLE TIP

In a **repeat** structure, indent the body of the loop from **repeat**, with **until** aligned with **repeat**, as in the following:

```
repeat
   Writeln ('First statement of loop');
   x := x / 2;
   Writeln ('Last statement of loop')
until x < 1;
```

In most cases the **while . . . do** and **repeat . . . until** structures can produce identical results if conditions contain relational operators that have opposite meanings, such as = and <>. For example, if the condition in a **while** structure is

```
value <> endcode
```

then the condition in a **repeat** structure that produces the same result would be:

```
value = endcode
```

An important application of **repeat** is to reject any input data that is unsuitable or inappropriate. For example, if a variable identifier *testscore* is designed to accept integer test scores, any negative number or an integer greater than 100 may be inappropriate. One course of action is to define *testscore* as a subrange of integers:

```
type
   scoretype = 0..100;
var
   testscore : scoretype;
```

One disadvantage of this approach is that if an unsuitable value is entered for *testscore*, the program stops and displays an error message. If subranges are not used, unacceptable input data can be involved in calculations that produce incorrect results. The proper utilization of **repeat** prevents inappropriate values from filtering down to other parts of a program and getting involved in any other processes.

Example

```
repeat
  Write ('Continue? (y/n): ');
  Readln (ans)
until (ans='y') or (ans='Y')
  or (ans='n') or (ans='N');
```

Program control does not go beyond this loop until a *y, Y, n,* or *N* is entered for *ans.* If any other character is input, the prompt is repeated.

The **in** relational operator and sets can simplify this complex decision structure.

Example

```
repeat
  Write ('Continue? (y/n): ');
  Readln (ans)
until ans in ['y','Y','n','N'];
```

In this implementation, program control does not go beyond this loop until the value of *ans* matches one of the characters in the set that contains *y*, *Y*, *n*, or *N*. If any other character is input, the prompt is repeated.

As with both the **for** and **while** structures, infinite loops are always a possibility.

8.7 Application in Simulation: A Slice of Pi

An important application of computers is their ability to simulate real-world occurrences, that is, to create models of processes that are governed by specific sets of rules. The *simulation* may be as simple as mimicking a rudimentary calculator or as complex as imitating the traffic light switching sequence for all the streets in a large city. In addition to allowing for extensive testing of real-world situations, simulations can solve complex problems whose solutions might otherwise be unattainable, or they can be far more cost-effective than the construction of an expensive prototype.

Simulation techniques that involve an element of chance and the laws of probability are often known as Monte Carlo methods. A common example of this method approximates the value of pi, the ratio of the circumference of a circle to its diameter. The value of pi, rounded to eight decimal places, is 3.14159265.

Figure 8.4 shows a shaded quarter of a unit circle (one whose radius is 1) enclosed in a square with side of 1. In one experiment, imaginary pellets are shot at the square in a random fashion so that all the pellets hit

Figure 8.4
Monte Carlo
Estimation of Pi

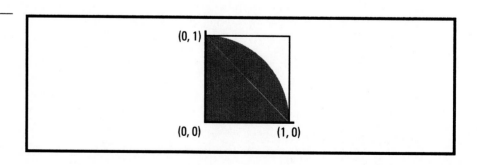

inside the square. The ratio of the number that hit inside the circle to the number fired is approximately pi/4.

Since each point is represented by a pair of coordinates, x and y, the computer chooses two random numbers between 0 and 1, one for the horizontal coordinate x and another for the vertical coordinate y. This point always falls inside the square and hits inside the circle if x and y satisfy the relational expression

$$x^2 + y^2 < 1$$

The more pellets that are shot at this target, the more accurate is the estimate of pi.

Write a program that accepts a margin of error, or tolerance—that is, how close the value of pi produced by this method is to the actual value of pi—and outputs the number of shots needed to find the estimated value of pi within the margin specified by the input value. Also display the estimated value of pi determined by this number of shots. Include the option of rerunning the simulation without having to reexecute the program.

ANALYSIS OF THE PROBLEM   Figure 8.5 summarizes the input and output quantities.

MODULAR DESIGN OF
THE SOLUTION

The structure chart and MIT for a solution are shown in Figure 8.6.

The **INTRODUCTION** module displays a brief introduction to simulation and the Monte Carlo method as it applies to this problem. It calls a module called **RUN SIMULATION** that asks the program user if he or she wishes to run the simulation. If the program is not terminated, the modules **RUN SIMULATION**, **ENTER MARGIN OF ERROR**, **CALCULATE PI**, and **DISPLAY ESTIMATE** are called until termination is indicated. The circular loop enclosing interfaces 2 through 5 signifies that the connecting module calls are in the body of a loop.

If the margin of error is small, it may require a large number of shots and a long period of time for the number of shots to closely approximate pi. To indicate that the shooting is in progress, the **WORKING** module is placed before the processing loop. This kind of output assures a user that processing is occurring and nothing is wrong with the program.

Figure 8.5
Input/Output Chart for
Monte Carlo Pi

Input	Output
Margin of error	Estimated value of pi
	Number of shots

269

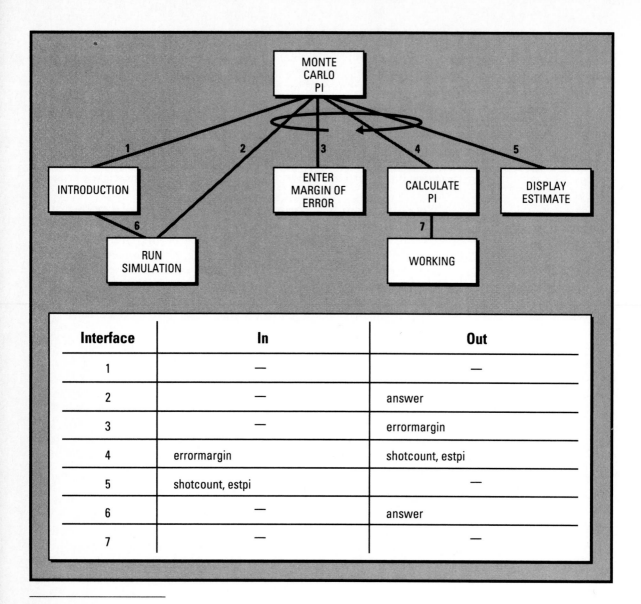

Interface	In	Out
1	—	—
2	—	answer
3	—	errormargin
4	errormargin	shotcount, estpi
5	shotcount, estpi	—
6	—	answer
7	—	—

Figure 8.6
Solution Design and
Module Interface Table for
Monte Carlo

DESIGN OF THE
STRUCTURE OF THE
MODULES

MONTE CARLO PI
  INTRODUCTION
  while want to continue do
    ENTER MARGIN OF ERROR
    CALCULATE PI
    DISPLAY ESTIMATE
    RUN SIMULATION

  INTRODUCTION
    describe simulation
    RUN SIMULATION

    RUN SIMULATION
      repeat
        want to continue?
      until correct answer

  ENTER MARGIN OF ERROR
    accept margin of error

  CALCULATE PI
    initialize shot count
    initialize hit count
    WORKING
    repeat
        select random x coordinate
        select random y coordinate
        increment shot count
        if point in circle
          then
            increment hit count
        find estimate of pi
    until estimate of pi within margin of error

    WORKING
      output working message

  DISPLAY ESTIMATE
    output shot count
    output estimate of pi

The **CALCULATE PI** module initializes both the shot and the hit counters before entering the loop. Once in the loop, the shot counter is updated and random values are chosen for the *x* and *y* coordinates of a point in the square. If the point is inside the circle, the hit counter is updated also. The value of pi is calculated and tested against the actual value determined by the built-in function to see whether the loop should continue or not.

PRODUCTION OF CODE
AND VERIFICATION
OF SOLUTION

The **EnterMarginOfError** procedure accepts the margin of error as a string called *strngmargin* and converts it to its numeric equivalent (*errormargin*) before returning that value to the calling statement:

```
procedure EnterMarginOfError (var errormargin : real);
  var
    code
      : integer;
    strngmargin
      : string[20];
begin
  repeat
    Write ('Enter margin of error: ');
    Readln (strngmargin);
    Val (strngmargin, errormargin, code);
    if code <> 0
      then
        Writeln ('Invalid numeric.')
  until code = 0
end;
```

This technique allows the program to continue if the user fails to type a 0 before the decimal point in the error margin, as is required in Pascal. The **Val** procedure accepts the margin as a string and converts it to the proper real value. If *strngmargin* contains an improper character, code gives the position of that character. If that code has any value other than 0, the program displays an error message and again asks for a margin of error.

The addition of each subprogram to the solution and its verification should be performed with the assistance of the IDE. When completed, the final documented solution can be produced, as shown, along with sample output of the result for a margin of error of 0.0001, in Figure 8.7.

Figure 8.7
MonteCarloPi Program
Listing and Sample Output

```pascal
program MonteCarloPi;
{-------------------------------------------------------------------}
{ PROGRAM:        Monte Carlo Estimate of Pi                        }
{ PROGRAMMER:     S. Lee                                            }
{ DATE:           August 26, 1990                                   }
{                                                                   }
{ The Monte Carlo method is a simulation technique whose results    }
{ are determined by chance and governed by the laws of probability. }
{ This method can be used to estimate the value of pi by shooting   }
{ imaginary pellets at a square on the Cartesian coordinate plane   }
{ with vertices (0,0), (0,1), (1,0) and (1,1). The shooting is done }
{ in a random fashion so that all the pellets hit inside the square.}
{ A quarter circle centered at the origin and having radius 1 is    }
{ inside the square. The ratio of the number of shots that fall     }
{ within the circle to the total number fired is approximately pi/4.}
{ This program accepts a margin of error, that is, how close the    }
{ value produced by this method is to the actual value of pi, and   }
{ outputs the number of shots needed to find the estimated value of pi }
{ within the margin specified by the input value. It also displays the }
{ estimated value of pi determined by this number of shots and      }
{ includes an option of rerunning the simulation without having     }
{ to re-execute the program.                                        }
{                                                                   }
{ INPUT           estimate of the margin of error                   }
{                                                                   }
{ OUTPUT          value of pi estimated by Monte Carlo method       }
{                 number of shots to produce this estimate          }
{-------------------------------------------------------------------}
  uses
    Crt;                            { screen formatting commands library }
  var
    answer                            { answer to "continue" question }
      : char;
    hitcount,                    { number of pellets hitting inside circle }
    shotcount                        { total number of pellets shot }
      : longint;
    errormargin,                               { margin of error }
    estpi                                 { estimated value of pi }
      : real;
```

```
procedure RunSimulation (var answer : char);
{-------------------------------------------------------------------}
{ Displays question on bottom of screen and accepts the response    }
{ to that question on whether to run the simulation.                }
{                                                                   }
{ IN            none                                                }
{                                                                   }
{ OUT           answer: response to the run simulation query        }
{-------------------------------------------------------------------}
begin
  repeat
    GotoXY (1,24);
    Writeln ('Do you want to run this simulation?');
    Write ('Enter y or n --> ');
    Readln (answer)
  until answer in ['n','N','y','Y'];
  ClrScr
end;
```

```
procedure Introduction (var answer : char);
{--------------------------------------------------------------------}
{ Briefly describes the Monte Carlo method for estimating pi and     }
{ asks if the user wants to run the simulation.                      }
{                                                                    }
{ IN            none                                                 }
{                                                                    }
{ OUT           answer:  response to the run simulation query        }
{--------------------------------------------------------------------}
begin
  GotoXY (11,1);
  Writeln ('MONTE CARLO ESTIMATE OF PI');
  GotoXY (1,3);
  Writeln ('The Monte Carlo method is a simulation technique');
  Writeln ('whose results are determined by chance and');
  Writeln ('governed by the laws of probability. This');
  Writeln ('method can be used to estimate the value of pi by');
  Writeln ('shooting imaginary pellets at a square on the');
  Writeln ('Cartesian coordinate plane with vertices (0,0),');
  Writeln ('(0,1), (1,0), and (1,1). The shooting is done in');
  Writeln ('a random fashion so that all the pellets hit');
  Writeln ('inside the square. A quarter circle centered at');
  Writeln ('the origin and having radius 1 is inside the');
  Writeln ('square. The ratio of the number of shots that');
  Writeln ('fall within the circle to the total number fired');
  Writeln ('is approximately pi/4. This program accepts a');
  Writeln ('margin of error, that is, how close the value');
  Writeln ('produced by this method is to the actual value');
  Writeln ('of pi, and outputs the number of shots needed to');
  Writeln ('find the estimated value of pi within the margin');
  Writeln ('specified by the input value. It also displays');
  Writeln ('the estimated value of pi found by this method.');
  RunSimulation (answer)
end;
```

(continued)

```
procedure EnterMarginOfError (var errormargin : real);
{-----------------------------------------------------------------------}
{ Accepts the margin of error for the estimate of pi.                    }
{                                                                        }
{ IN            none                                                     }
{                                                                        }
{ OUT           errormargin: margin of error                            }
{-----------------------------------------------------------------------}
  var
    code                        { position of first nonnumeric character }
      : integer;
    strngmargin                       { string value for error margin }
      : string[20];
begin
  repeat
    Write ('Enter margin of error: ');
    Readln (strngmargin);
    Val (strngmargin, errormargin, code);
    if code <> 0
      then
        Writeln ('Invalid numeric.')
  until code = 0
end;


procedure Working;
{-----------------------------------------------------------------------}
{ Displays a message while the estimate is determined.                   }
{                                                                        }
{ IN            none                                                     }
{                                                                        }
{ OUT           none                                                     }
{-----------------------------------------------------------------------}
begin
  ClrScr;
  GotoXY (36, 13);
  Writeln ('Working!')
end;
```

```pascal
procedure CalculatePi (errormargin : real; var shotcount :longint;
  var estpi : real);
{-----------------------------------------------------------------------}
{ Calculates the value of pi by randomly selecting points until the    }
{ value is within a specified margin of error of the actual value.     }
{                                                                       }
{ IN              errormargin:  margin of error                        }
{                                                                       }
{ OUT             shotcount:    number of shots to find pi             }
{                                within the margin of error            }
{                 estpi:        estimated value of pi                  }
{-----------------------------------------------------------------------}
  var
    hitcount                         { number of points within the circle }
      : longint;
    x,                        { x coordinate of randomly selected point }
    y                         { y coordinate of randomly selected point }
      : real;
begin
  shotcount := 0;
  hitcount := 0;
  Working;
  repeat
    x := Random;
    y := Random;
    shotcount := shotcount + 1;
    if Sqr(x) + Sqr(y) < 1
      then
        hitcount := hitcount + 1;
    estpi := 4 * hitcount / shotcount
  until Abs(Pi - estpi) < errormargin
end;
```

(continued)

```
  procedure DisplayEstimate (shotcount : longint; estpi : real);
  {----------------------------------------------------------------------}
  { Displays the estimate of pi established by a determined              }
  { number of shots.                                                    }
  {                                                                     }
  { IN           shotcount: number of shots to find pi                  }
  {                              within margin of error                 }
  {              estpi:    estimated value of pi                        }
  {                                                                     }
  { OUT          none                                                   }
  {----------------------------------------------------------------------}
  begin
    ClrScr;
    GotoXY (25,12);
    Writeln ('It took ', shotcount, ' shots to produce');
    GotoXY (26,14);
    Writeln ('an estimate of ', estpi:10:8 , '.')
  end;

begin
  Randomize;
  ClrScr;
  Introduction (answer);
  while answer in ['y','Y'] do
    begin
      EnterMarginOfError (errormargin);
      CalculatePi (errormargin, shotcount, estpi);
      DisplayEstimate (shotcount, estpi);
      RunSimulation (answer)
    end
end.
```

```
──────────────────────── Output ────────────────────────
            It took 13596 shots to produce

            an estimate of 3.14151221.
```

The **Randomize** procedure in the main program makes sure that the choice of values for x and y in **CalculatePi** are different each time the simulation is run. Both the *shotcount* and *hitcount* are of type **longint**, because for a reasonable margin of error both these variables will likely exceed the 32767 limit of the **integer** data type. If both are declared to be integers, unreasonable results may be produced.

8.8 Nested Looping Structures

When a loop structure is contained entirely within another, the first structure is "nested" in the second. The inner loop must begin and end execution for each iteration through the outer loop.

Example

```
Writeln ('Before loop');
for i := 1 to 3 do
  begin
    Writeln ('Outer ', i);
    for j := 8 downto 7 do
      Writeln ('  Inner ', j)
  end;
Writeln ('After loop');
```

Each time the body of the outer loop is repeated, a **Writeln** and an inner loop are executed. That is, when i is 1, j must cycle through the values from 8 down to 7; when i is 2, j restarts at 8 and goes down to 7; and when i is 3, j again starts at 8 and goes down to 7. The output for this code becomes:

```
Before loop
Outer 1
    Inner 8
    Inner 7
Outer 2
    Inner 8
    Inner 7
Outer 3
    Inner 8
    Inner 7
After loop
```

The *Inner* message is displayed six times, twice for each of the three executions of the outer loop.

In this example, one loop structure was explicitly contained within another; it was obvious, since the inner loop structure was indented from and "appeared" inside the outer one. Implicit nested structures may exist where the nesting is not as conspicuous. The program that calculated an estimate of pi with the Monte Carlo method contains an example of an implicit nested structure. The main program in the solution to that problem was:

```
begin
  Randomize;
  ClrScr;
  Introduction (answer);
  while answer in ['y','Y'] do
    begin
      EnterMarginOfError (errormargin);
      CalculatePi (errormargin, shotcount, estpi);
      DisplayEstimate (shotcount, estpi);
      RunSimulation (answer)
    end
end.
```

Although there seems to be a single **while** loop, both the `CalculatePi` and `RunSimulation` procedures themselves contain loop structures that are, in effect, both nested in this **while** loop. The code that follows shows the main program of `MonteCarloPi` with the code for the procedures `CalculatePi` and `RunSimulation` substituted for their procedure calls.

```
begin
  Randomize;
  ClrScr;
  Introduction (answer);
  while answer in ['y','Y'] do                        { Outer while loop }
    begin
      EnterMarginOfError (errormargin);
{ Start of CalculatePi }
      shotcount := 0;
      hitcount := 0;
      Working
      repeat                                           { Inner repeat loop }
        x := Random;
        y := Random;
        shotcount := shotcount + 1;
        if Sqr(x) + Sqr(y) < 1
          then
              hitcount := hitcount + 1;
        estpi := 4 * hitcount / shotcount
      until Abs(Pi - estpi) < errormargin;
{ End of Calculate Pi }
      DisplayEstimate (shotcount, estpi);
{ Start of RunSimulation }
      repeat                                           { Inner repeat loop }
        GotoXY (1,24);
        Writeln ('Do you want to run this simulation?');
        Write ('Enter y or n --> ');
        Readln (answer)
      until answer in ['n','N','y','Y'];
      ClrScr
{ End of RunSimulation }
    end
end.
```

The extra comments help to show how the **repeat . . . until** loops in each of the procedures are nested in the **while . . . do** loop of the main program.

An inner loop structure must be completely contained within an outer structure or an error results. To make sure loops in a program are properly nested, draw a box enclosing an entire loop structure, for each loop in the program. If none of the boxes overlap, the structure is correct; otherwise, the structure must be modified. Figure 8.8 shows examples of properly and improperly nested structures.

Figure 8.8
Nested Loop Structures

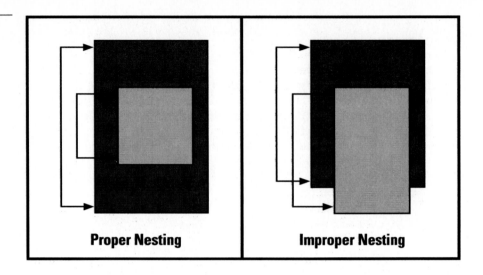

8.9 Application in Ending Loops: What a Guess!

High/Low is a game where the computer chooses a number between 1 and 100 and a player has six tries to guess the number. After each guess the program indicates whether it was correct or, if incorrect, displays a message indicating whether the guess was too low or too high.

Write a program that continues to play games of High/Low until prompted to end by a user.

ANALYSIS OF THE PROBLEM   Figure 8.9 lists the input and output quantities for the program.

MODULAR DESIGN OF   The structure chart and MIT of the solution are shown in Figure 8.10. The **PLAY**
THE SOLUTION   and **CONTINUE** modules are called from a loop inside the main program.

Figure 8.9
High/Low Input/Output
Chart

Input	Output
Player's guess	"High" or "low" message
	"Win" or "lose" message
	Number of attempts

Figure 8.10
High/Low Solution Design
and Module Interface Table

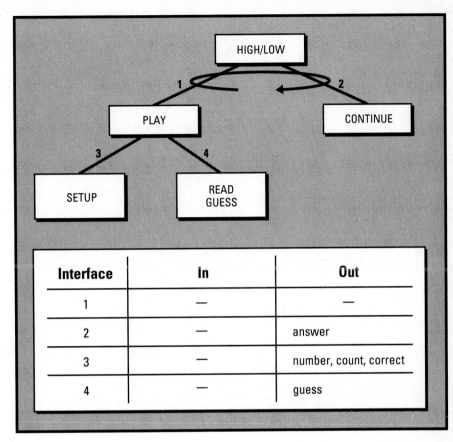

Interface	In	Out
1	—	—
2	—	answer
3	—	number, count, correct
4	—	guess

DESIGN OF THE
STRUCTURE OF THE
MODULES

HIGH/LOW
  repeat
    PLAY
    CONTINUE
  until not play again

```
PLAY
  SETUP
  repeat
    READ GUESS
    update guess count
    if guess = number
      then
        correct is true
      else
        if guess < number
          then
            display "too low"
          else
            display "too high"
  until correct or (reach maximum guesses)
  if correct
    then
      display win message and number of guesses
    else
      display loss message

SETUP
  initialize count of guesses
  initialize correct to false
  pick a number
  display start message

READ GUESS
  repeat
    enter guess
  until guess between 1 and 100

CONTINUE
  repeat
    enter play again response
  until proper response entered
```

The **repeat** structure in the **PLAY** module can end in two different ways. One action is taken if the answer is correct and another if the player runs out of guesses. A selection structure should follow a **repeat** or a **while** structure that can end in more than one way. An **if** structure determines which component of the condition ended the loop and takes the appropriate action. In the **SETUP** module, *correct* is initialized at false, since the guess must be assumed to be incorrect until a match is made, and *count* is initialized at 0.

PRODUCTION OF CODE
AND VERIFICATION OF
SOLUTION

The final documented solution after verification is shown, along with sample output, in Figure 8.11.

Figure 8.11
HighLow Program Listing
and Sample Output

```
program HighLow;
{---------------------------------------------------------------------}
{ PROGRAM:        Game of High/Low                                    }
{ PROGRAMMER:     J. Addams                                           }
{ DATE:           August 31, 1990                                     }
{                                                                     }
{ This program chooses a number between 1 and 100 and gives the       }
{ player 6 chances to guess it. To help the player, the program       }
{ indicates whether the guess is "too low" or "too high." The player  }
{ also has the option of replaying the game.                          }
{                                                                     }
{ IN              player's guess                                      }
{                                                                     }
{ OUT             high/low message                                    }
{                 win/lose message                                    }
{                 number of guesses                                   }
{---------------------------------------------------------------------}
  uses
    Crt;                                   { screen function library }
  const
    maxguesses = 6;                      { maximum number of guesses }
  var
    answer                     { y or n to continue playing or not }
      : char;
```

(continued)

```
procedure Setup (var target, count : integer; var correct : boolean);
{------------------------------------------------------------------}
{ Initializes quantities, chooses a number, and explains the game. }
{                                                                  }
{ IN          none                                                 }
{                                                                  }
{ OUT         target:   computer-chosen random number              }
{             count:    number of guess attempts                   }
{             correct:  true if guess is correct, false otherwise  }
{------------------------------------------------------------------}
begin
  ClrScr;
  count := 0;
  correct := false;
  target := Random(100) + 1;
  Writeln ('A number between 1 and 100 has been chosen.');
  Writeln ('You have ',maxguesses, ' tries to guess it.');
  Writeln
end;

procedure ReadGuess (var guess : integer);
{------------------------------------------------------------------}
{ Accepts a guess between 1 and 100 from the player.               }
{                                                                  }
{ IN          none                                                 }
{                                                                  }
{ OUT         guess: player's guess of the chosen number           }
{------------------------------------------------------------------}
begin
  repeat
    Write ('Enter your guess: ');
    Readln (guess)
  until guess in [1..100]
end;
```

```
procedure Play;
{-----------------------------------------------------------------}
{ Sets up the game and accepts guesses from a player until the    }
{ guess is correct or the maximum number of guesses has been      }
{ reached. An appropriate message is displayed in either case.    }
{                                                                 }
{ IN            none                                              }
{                                                                 }
{ OUT           none                                              }
{-----------------------------------------------------------------}
  var
    guess,                                      { player's guess }
    target,                     { target number chosen by computer }
    count                       { number of guesses made by player }
      : integer;
    correct                       { whether guess is correct or not }
      : boolean;
begin
  Setup (target, count, correct);
  repeat
    ReadGuess (guess);
    count := count + 1;
    if guess = target
      then
        correct := true
      else
        if guess < target
          then
            Writeln ('   Too low, try again.')
          else
            Writeln ('   Too high, try again.')
  until correct or (count = maxguesses);
  Writeln;
  if correct
    then
      Writeln ('You got it in ', count, ' guesses.')
    else
      Writeln ('Sorry, the correct number was ', target, '.')
 end;
```

```
procedure ContinuePlay (var answer : char);
{-------------------------------------------------------------------------}
{ Asks the player if he or she wants to play another game.                }
{                                                                         }
{ IN              none                                                    }
{                                                                         }
{ OUT             answer:   indicates whether to play again              }
{-------------------------------------------------------------------------}
begin
  repeat
    GotoXY (10, 23);
    Write ('Do you want to play again? (y/n): ');
    Readln (answer)
  until answer in ['n','N','y','Y']
end;

begin
  Randomize;
  repeat
    Play;
    ContinuePlay (answer)
  until answer in ['n','N'];
  ClrScr;
  GotoXY (30, 12);
  Writeln ('Thanks for playing!')
end.
```

──────────────────── **Output** ────────────────────

```
A number between 1 and 100 has been chosen.
You have 6 tries to guess it.

Enter your guess: 50
     Too low, try again.
Enter your guess: 75
     Too low, try again.
Enter your guess: 88
     Too high, try again.
Enter your guess: 81
     Too high, try again.
Enter your guess: 78

You got it in 5 guesses.
```

Store and Forward

Iteration, or looping, structures, along with sequential and selection structures, form the basic building blocks of all Pascal programs. You should employ a definite loop structure when the number of passes through the loop can be determined in advance of entry into the loop. Indefinite loop structures end when a variable that is part of an exiting condition changes in the body of the loop and causes the exit condition to change. Nesting loops, that is, placing one loop structure inside another, gives a program more potency, since an inner loop is completed for each pass through an outer loop.

We will next find a better way to store and manipulate data. For example, what if you want to store 1,000 values? Do you have to declare 1,000 different variables? What if you want to add a constant to each of these variables? Do you need 1,000 different assignment statements? Array and record structures were designed for the efficient storage and management of large amounts of data. Where does this efficiency come from? Iteration structures.

Snares and Pitfalls

- *Changing the index of a loop in the body of the loop:* The index of a loop should be altered only by the statements that are part of the looping structure, or the loop may not act as you expect.

- *Creating an infinite loop:* If a loop does not have a reachable terminating condition, the program gets caught in a never-ending cycle that must be stopped by outside intervention.

- *Failing to employ a* **begin-end** *pair to enclose a compound statement in a* **for** *or* **while** *loop structure:* If a compound statement is not enclosed in a **begin-end** pair, only the first statement in the body may be considered part of the loop. The remaining statements are executed when the loop is terminated.

- *Placing initialization statements in a loop:* Counting and summing statements must be given initial values *before* the loop begins and updated *in* the body of the loop.

- *Incorrectly nesting loops:* An inner loop structure must be contained entirely within an outer one. There should be no overlap of structures.

- *Placing a semicolon after* **do** *in a* **for** *or* **while** *statement:* A semicolon marks the end of a loop. If one is placed following **do**, the body of the loop is empty and no statements are repeated.

- *Failing to "prime" a* **while** *loop:* When entered data determines whether to continue a loop, the first such entry must occur prior to the loop and all others inside the loop.

- *Using incorrect index types in a* **for** *loop:* The index must be an ordinal data type (**integer**, **longint**, or **char**). Strings or reals are not allowed.

- *Declaring a global loop control variable:* The control variable for a loop should be a local variable, to avoid any possible side effects.

Exercises

1. Answer the following questions in paragraph form.
   a. Distinguish between definite and indefinite loop structures.
   b. Why are only ordinal data types such as **char** and **integer** allowed as the index of a **for** statement?
   c. Why is the initialization of summing and counting variables important?
   d. Explain what simulation is and give a suitable application other than the ones mentioned in the text.
   e. Why is tracing an important technique for error detection in looping structures?

2. Classify each of the following Pascal statements as valid or invalid. If invalid, explain why. Unless otherwise stated, assume all identifiers have been properly declared.

   a. ```
      for i := 8 to 7 do
         Writeln (i);
      ```

   b. ```
      while value <> 0
         begin
            Write ('Enter a value: ');
            Readln (value)
         end;
      ```

   c. ```
      repeat
      until y < 0;
      ```

   d. ```
      for letter := 'f' to 'p' do
         begin
            i := Ord(letter);
            Writeln (i)
         end;
      ```

   e. ```
      while not (answer in ['y','Y']) do
         Readln (answer);
      ```

3. Write Pascal equivalents for each of the given descriptions.
   a. Display the message "That's all folks!" eight times.
      ```

b. Start x with a value of -4 and continue to add 2 to x until the value of x exceeds 20.

c. Find the sum of input numbers by accepting values and keeping a running total until -1 is entered.

d. Enter and count the number of names and addresses of new subscribers to a magazine in a day. On some days, no new subscriptions may be received.

e. Display the even integers starting at 100 and ending at 0.

4. Find all the errors, both syntax and logical, in the following Pascal function designed to find the average of a set of input values entered through the ReadValue procedure.

```
function Average : real;
  var
    tempavg : real;
begin
  count := 1;
  ReadValue (value);
  while value <> -1 do
    count := count + 1;
    sum := sum + value;
    ReadValue (value)
  if count <> 0
    then
      tempavg := sum / count
    else
      tempavg := 0
end;
```

5. Show the exact output of the following programs.

a.
```
for k := 3 to 8 do
  Writeln (k:3);
```

b.
```
p := 3;
while p <= 8 do
  begin
    Writeln (p:3);
    p := p + 1
  end;
```

c.
```
x := 3;
repeat
  x := x * 3;
  Writeln (x:5)
until x > 200;
```

d.
```
last := 1;
repeat
  for i := 1 to last do
    Write (i);
  Writeln;
  last := last + 1
until not (last in [1..5]);
```

e.
```
base := 2;
power := 6;
answer := 1;
for i := 1 to power do
  begin
    answer := answer * base;
    Writeln (answer)
  end;
```

6. Consider the following code segment:
```
sum := 0;
for j := 12 downto 1 do
  begin
    sum := sum + j;
    Writeln ('Partial sum: ', sum:3)
  end;
Writeln ('Final sum: ', sum:3);
```

a. Write a similar segment using a **while . . . do** structure rather than a **for . . . do** one.

b. Write a similar segment using a **repeat . . . until** structure rather than a **for . . . do** one.

Programming Assignments

Elementary

1. Write a program that finds the sum of first n terms of the following series:

$$1 + 1/2 + 1/3 + 1/4 + 1/5 + \cdots$$

where n is input by the user.

2. Write a program that simulates the toss of a coin n times, where n is entered by the user. Output what percentage of the tosses results in a head and what percentage results in a tail. Provide an option to repeat the experiment.

3. Write a program that displays, in table form, a table of decimal ASCII codes ranging from 33 to 125 and their corresponding characters.

4. The factorial of an integer n, represented by $n!$, is the product of all the integers from n down to 1, including n and 1. Write a program that accepts a

value for *n* and displays its factorial. The answer should be of type **longint** since factorial values grow rapidly.

5. Businesses are very careful about how many copies of a product they produce at one time. If not enough are made, they may lose income due to buyer dissatisfaction. If too many are made, the added cost of storing extra quantities reduces the profit that can be realized from their sale.

   Suppose an ice cream manufacturer makes five different products. Write a program that determines the total value of storing all the products in a month, given the name of the product, the average number of boxes of each product made each month, the number sold each month, and the monthly cost of storing each box. Output the total storage cost as well as a table of all the input data.

6. Many cities have to depend on others to supply food for their growing populations. Suppose that every 10 years the population of a city doubles while the food supply is capable of feeding only 2,000 additional residents. Write a program that finds how many years it would take for the population to outgrow its food supply given a starting year, the population in that year, and the number of people the food supply could support in that year.

7. A state-run daily Pick-Four Lottery charges players $0.50 for each four-digit number they choose. If they match the number chosen by the lottery computer, they receive $3,000; otherwise, they lose their investment. If a player always plays the same number, simulate his or her winnings over a specified number of days by letting the computer choose a four-digit integer for each of the days and updating the player's account daily. Output the profit or loss at the end of the specified period.

8. Someone invests one cent and that investment doubles every five days. Write a program that determines how long it would take for that person to become a millionaire.

9. A prime number is an integer that is evenly divisible only by 1 and itself. To test if a number is a prime, the divisors from 2 up to the square root of the test number must be checked.

   Write a program that accepts an integer and determines whether it is a prime number or not. Provide an option to accept input until –1 is entered as a test value.

10. The break-even quantity is the number of units that must be manufactured for the cost of manufacture to be balanced by the income from the sale of the product. The break-even quantity depends on the fixed cost of setting up machinery for a manufacturing run, the variable cost (how much it costs to produce each item), and the unit selling price of the item. It is given by the following formula:

$$\text{break-even quantity} = \frac{\text{fixed cost}}{\text{selling price} - \text{variable cost}}$$

Write a program that creates a table of integral break-even quantities for the manufacture of an item whose unit selling price may vary from $8.00 to $14.00 in $0.50 increments while the fixed cost remains $3000 and variable cost stays at $2.50 per item.

Challenging

11. One of the application problems in the chapter was to determine if a word was a palindrome. Write a program that decides whether a phrase is a palindrome. All spaces and punctuation should be ignored. It is also of no consequence whether letters are in uppercase or lowercase form, that is, *M* and *m* are equivalent. (Hint: The Turbo Pascal library contains a built-in function **UpCase** that converts a lowercase character parameter to its uppercase equivalent. If the argument is not a lowercase letter, the function is ignored.)

12. In the game of Over/Under/Seven, a player bets on whether the throw of a pair of dice is 7, over 7, or under 7. If the wager is on 7 and it is thrown, twice the amount of the bet plus the original bet are returned to the player; a correct bet on either *over* or *under* returns the original bet and an amount equal to that bet.

    Write a program that simulates the play of Over/Under/Seven, starting a player with a bankroll of $100. The game should end if the player's bankroll falls to 0 or if the player wants to quit. The program should not allow a player to bet more than he has in his bankroll.

13. A computer must convert decimal values to their binary equivalents in order to perform calculations. One algorithm that converts decimal integers to their binary counterparts involves dividing the decimal integer by 2. The integer remainder becomes the low-order or right-most digit in the binary representation of the number. The quotient from the previous division is now divided by 2 again, with the remainder becoming the digit to the left of the first remainder. The process continues until the quotient becomes 0. The string that has been constructed is the binary equivalent of the original decimal integer. An example of the conversion of 41 to 101001 is shown in Figure 8.12.

    Write a program that accepts a decimal integer and displays a string representing the binary equivalent of the integer.

14. One method of encrypting a message shifts all the letters in the message a certain number of positions in the alphabet. For example, a *B* might become a *G* and a *D* might become an *I* if the key to the code is shifting each letter six positions toward the end of the alphabet. The alphabet is considered cyclic, meaning the letter following *Z* is *A*. To decode the message, the key is reversed. In this case that means shifting the letters in the decoded message six positions toward the beginning of the alphabet.

    Write a program that accepts a word in uppercase letters only and offers the user a choice of either encoding the word using a key value randomly chosen between 1 and 26 or decoding a word with a key entered by the user.

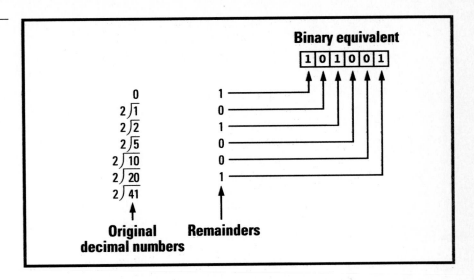

Figure 8.12
Decimal-to-Binary
Conversion

15. When a loan is made, a monthly payment schedule known as an amortization table is produced. The monthly payment is determined by the following formula:

$$\text{monthly payment} = p \times \frac{r}{1 - \dfrac{1}{(1 + r)^n}}$$

where p is the original principal, r is the monthly interest rate, in decimal form, and n is the term of the loan or the number of monthly interest payments. These monthly payments are not equally divided between the principal and the interest. Early payments are primarily interest and later ones predominantly principal. The formula for the interest portion of the monthly payment is

$$\text{interest} = \text{balance} \times \text{monthly interest rate}$$

where *balance* is the unpaid principal to date. The portion of the monthly payment applied to the principal is

$$\text{principal} = \text{monthly payment} - \text{interest}$$

This value of the principal is subtracted from the unpaid balance to determine the interest and principal portions for the next payment.

Write a program that accepts the amount of a loan, the annual interest rate, in percent, and the term of the loan; calculates the amount of each monthly payment; and outputs an amortization table for the loan.

The built-in Pascal functions **Ln** and **Exp** can be used to raise a number to a power.

$$a^b = \textbf{Exp} \ (b \ * \ \textbf{Ln(a)})$$

16. The number of different subcommittees of m people that can be chosen from a committee of n members is given by the following formula:

$$\frac{n!}{m!(n-m)!}$$

Write a program that determines this value, given the size of a committee and a subcommittee. (See Programming Assignment 4.)

17. Two logical expressions are equivalent if they produce the same truth value for all possible combinations of Boolean inputs. A truth table containing both the expression "**not** (p **and** q)" and the expression "(**not** p) **or** (**not** q)" follows:

p	q	**not** (p **and** q)	(**not** p) **or** (**not** q)
TRUE	TRUE	FALSE	FALSE
TRUE	FALSE	TRUE	TRUE
FALSE	TRUE	TRUE	TRUE
FALSE	FALSE	TRUE	TRUE

These expressions are logically equivalent, since they are both true in the same cases and false in the same cases.

Write a program that uses **for** loops to output a truth table for two logical expressions and indicates whether they are equivalent or not.

A **boolean** data type can be used as an index in a **for** statement, since the ordinal value of false precedes the ordinal value of true. If p is of type **boolean**, the loop

```
for p := false to true do
   Writeln (p);
```

displays **FALSE** on the first line of output and **TRUE** on the second.

18. Write a menu-driven program that produces the equation of a straight line for a different set of input quantities. The first screen should display a main menu that is similar to the following:

```
            EQUATION OF A STRAIGHT LINE
Enter the number preceding your choice of input data.

   <1> Two points on the line
   <2> The slope of a line and a point on that line
   <3> The slope of a line and its y-intercept
   <4> Quit
```

The program should continue to return to the main menu and accept choices until the Quit option is chosen.

19. A researcher would like to determine if there is any correlation between the height of a person and his or her weight. The correlation coefficient r is a statistical measure of how two quantities are related and is determined by

$$r^2 = \frac{(n\Sigma xy - \Sigma x \ \Sigma y)^2}{(n\Sigma x^2 - (\Sigma x)^2)\ (n\Sigma y^2 - (\Sigma y)^2)}$$

where x represents a person's height and y represents a person's weight. The symbol sigma (Σ) indicates a sum is to be calculated. For example, Σxy represents the sum of the products $x \times y$. The value of r is between -1 and 1. The closer its value is to 1 or -1, the better the association between the quantities; if r is close to 0, the quantities are not related. Write a program that accepts at least 10 pairs of data (heights and corresponding weights) and outputs their correlation coefficient.

20. A "perfect" number is a positive integer that equals the sum of all its factors (the integers that evenly divide it), not including the number itself. For example, 28 is a perfect number because all of its factors (1, 2, 4, 7, and 14) sum to 28.

Write a program that finds all the perfect numbers between 1 and 20,000.

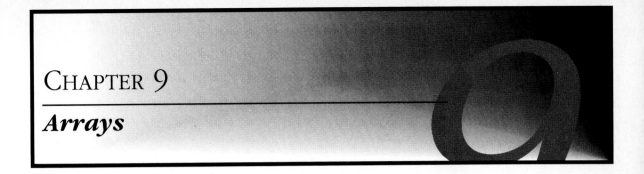

CHAPTER 9

Arrays

Key Terms

array	**ReadKey**
data structure	spreadsheet
index	structured data type
matrix	

Objectives

- To introduce the concept of a data structure
- To introduce one-dimensional and two-dimensional array data structures
- To use arrays in the solution of problems

9.1 Introduction

Imagine a board game with a set of playing pieces, cards, and a pair of dice but with no playing instructions. The game is virtually useless. The same would be true of a game with rules of play but no parts. Both parts and rules are needed to play the game. The same is true when a programming system defines a data structure to solve a problem. A *data structure* is a set of related data items and the operations that can be performed on those items. As with the board game, the set of items serves no purpose unless there are rules for its use, and the rules are meaningless unless items are defined.

The basic unit of information processed by a computer is called the *bit*. Bits are manipulated in different ways to represent the fundamental Pascal data types, such as integers, long integers, characters, reals, and strings. Each of these data types has a definition and a set of rules governing its use. For example, reals are numbers with fractional parts that can be operands for the operations +, −, *, and /. They also can be parameters for certain built-in functions and procedures. Reals cannot be operands for the **div** and **mod** operators or parameters for functions such as **Ord** and **Chr**.

As applications become more advanced, their solutions require more sophisticated data types, structures defining how these types are related, and operations that can be performed on these types. You can find the average of 100 real numbers with fundamental data types and programming structures, but it would be very difficult to store each one of the values for future reference. Pascal has built-in data structures, called *arrays* and *records,* to handle the storage and access of large amounts of related data. They are also called *structured data types,* since each is composed of two or more data types with a set of rules governing their use. The major difference is that the array is designed to store data of the same type in a single structure, whereas the record structure is designed to store data of different types in a single structure. This chapter will introduce arrays and show their application in the solution of problems.

9.2 The One-Dimensional Array Structure

An *array* is a collection of adjoining storage locations that can store data of the same type, and be accessed by specifying the name of the collection and a location in that collection. A member of the collection is termed an *element* of the array. For a one-dimensional array, the location of an element is determined by a single value. For instance, if a baseball card collector keeps all cards for the players on one team filed alphabetically in a drawer, to find a particular card, the drawer containing all the cards for a team (collection name) is located and that drawer searched until the correct card is found.

An array is considered a static data structure because its size must be established when it is declared and cannot be changed. For example, if an array is to contain the names of people in a business concern, an estimate would have to be made of how many locations might be needed. Extra locations could be added to allow for expansion. Once memory has been set aside for an array, these locations are reserved for only that purpose. If you overestimate the amount of memory needed for an array, it can lead to wasted memory, while underestimation can necessitate a program change.

In Pascal, a one-dimensional array element is represented by the following:

```
<identifier> [ <index> ]
```

where the choice of the identifier name follows the same rules as for any identifier and represents the name of the collection. The *index* of an array is a single constant or expression with an ordinal data type (such as an **integer** or **char,** but not the ordinal type **longint**) whose value specifies a particular element in the collection. The square brackets, [and], do *not* mean that the index is optional. These symbols *must* enclose the index. Figure 9.1 gives a physical representation of an array entitled *name.* The identifier *name[3]* refers to element number 3 in the collection of locations entitled *name.* Indices are positive integers in most applications.

Figure 9.1
The Array *name*

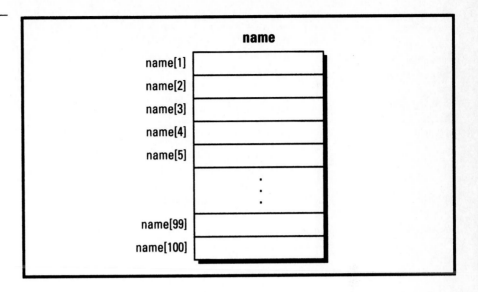

Arrays must be declared in a **var** or a **type** statement before they are used. Like strings, arrays are not simple data types and must be defined in a **type** statement if they are to be used as parameters in functions or procedures. This convention is adopted for the remainder of the text.

FORMAT: **type**
         <identifier> = array [<range>] of <item type>;

A type name must begin with a letter and cannot contain any spaces. The remainder of the name should consist of letters and digits. A range of legal indices is enclosed in square brackets and follows the reserved word **array.** The range can be a previously declared range type or consist of the first legal value in the range, two consecutive periods, and the last legal value for that range. For example, **1..10** indicates that the indices can take values from 1 through 10, inclusive. The type of data stored in the array is specified following the reserved word **of.**

STYLE TIP   End an identifier representing a data type with the letters *type.* This way, **type** identifiers are more easily distinguished from constants or variable identifiers.

Example

```
type
  digitype = 0..9;
  arraytype = array [digitype] of integer;
var
  alpha : arraytype;
```

These statements declare an array of integers called *alpha*. The legally defined elements of this array range from *alpha[0]* to *alpha[9]*, inclusive.

An array is initialized by storing a predetermined default value in each declared array element. Then, even if some of the elements are not referenced, their values are known. It is common to initialize numeric values to 0, or 0.0 when appropriate.

Example

```
type
  nametype = array[1..100] of string[20];
var
  name : nametype;

  . . .

for j := 1 to 100 do
  name[j] := '';
```

Each of the 100 elements in the string array *name* are initialized to the null string, the string containing no characters.

Putting Data in an Array

In general, the elements of an array are accessed with the assistance of iteration structures, where the index of the loop serves as the index of the array. One application is the entry of data from the keyboard into an array structure.

Example

```
count := 0;
Write ('Press y for more:');
Readln (ans);
while ans in ['y','Y'] do
  begin
    count := count + 1;
    Write ('Age: ');
    Readln (age[count]);
    Write ('Press y for more:');
    Readln (ans)
  end;
age[0] := count;
```

The **while** loop is primed by requesting a user to enter *y* for data entry and start the loop. If this is done, the loop is entered, *count* increased from 0 to 1, and a value entered for the integer array element *age[count]*, or in this case *age[1]*. If another age is to be entered, the value of *count* is increased from 1 to 2 and the next age stored in *age[2]*. This process continues until a character other than *y* or *Y* is entered for *ans*. At the end of the loop, *count* holds the number of ages entered in the array. This count is stored in array element *age[0]*.

> **STYLE TIP**
>
> The declared size of an array does not indicate how many elements contain significant data and how many are unused. For arrays storing numeric values, it is often worthwhile to store the index of the last "active" element of the array in the array itself. The element with index 0 is appropriate if it doesn't serve any other purpose. For example, if an array x is declared to have indices that range from 0 to 100 but the elements from 66 to 100 are not active, 65 should be stored in $x[0]$.

Using the Index to Fill an Array

The index of a loop structure also can be part of a formula that determines values for the elements of an array.

Example

```
for i := 1 to 10 do
  root[i] := Sqrt(i);
```

The **for** loop index serves as the actual parameter for the **Sqrt** function. If *root* is defined as an array of real numbers, this loop stores the square root of the values from 1 to 10 in *root[1]* to *root[10]*, respectively.

Manipulating Array Elements

When an array contains data, the index of a loop structure allows you to access significant elements with a minimum of code.

Example

```
last := gpa[0];
largest := gpa[1];
for k := 2 to last do
  if gpa[k] > largest
    then
      largest := gpa[k];
```

Assume that *gpa[0]* contains the index of the last significant element in the real array *gpa*. The first element of the array *gpa* is made the largest. The loop cycles through the array, starting at element 2 and ending at *last*. If any element has a value greater than *largest*, that value becomes *largest*. When the loop has been completed, *largest* contains the greatest value.

Outputting Array Elements

An entire array can be output with a loop structure by specifying the correct range of indices. The contents of a single element can be displayed by designating a specific index value.

Example

```
last := age[0];
Writeln ('Ages in Survey');
for i := 1 to last do
  Writeln (age[i]);
```

As the index *i* progresses from 1 to the last significant element in the array, each value in the real array *age* is displayed on a separate line.

9.3 Application in Counting: Random Eyes

The **Random** function generates values in a given range. If the values are to be truly random, the chosen values should be evenly distributed over the entire range. For example, if the function is designed to select randomly the integers 1, 2, 3, and 4, the chances for any one appearing should be identical: 1 in 4. Write a program that tests the randomness of **Random** by choosing an integer between 1 and 6, inclusive, for a specified number of trials, counting the number of trials that result in each possible value, and using this count to determine what percentage of the trials produces each outcome.

ANALYSIS OF THE PROBLEM   The input and output quantities are listed in Figure 9.2. There is no need to list the array elements individually.

MODULAR DESIGN OF THE SOLUTION   The structure chart and MIT outlining the solution are shown in Figure 9.3.

DESIGN OF THE STRUCTURE OF THE MODULES

    RANDOM TEST
      SETUP
      CHOOSE AND COUNT
      PERCENTAGES
      DISPLAY RESULTS

      SETUP
        describe program
        initialize counters for outcomes
        enter number of trials desired

Figure 9.2
Random Test
Input/Output Chart

Input	Output
Number of trials	Number of trials
	Array of counts
	Array of percentages

Figure 9.3
Random Test Solution
Design and Module
Interface Table

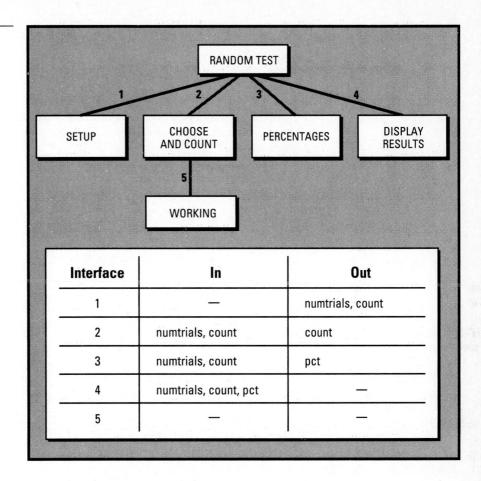

Interface	In	Out
1	—	numtrials, count
2	numtrials, count	count
3	numtrials, count	pct
4	numtrials, count, pct	—
5	—	—

CHOOSE AND COUNT
    WORKING
    for the number of trials indicated
        choose a number
        update the proper outcome counter

WORKING
    output working message

PERCENTAGES
    for all counters
        find percentage of total

DISPLAY RESULTS
    output number of trials, counts, and percentages

Consider the declaration portion of the main program:

```
program RandomTest;
  uses
    Crt;
  type
    countarraytype = array[1..6] of longint;
    pctarraytype = array[1..6] of real;
  var
    count : countarraytype;
    pct : pctarraytype;
    numtrials : longint;
```

The array *count* is of type *countarraytype,* where space is reserved for an array of six long integers. Similarly, the array *pct* is of type *pctarraytype* and reserves space for an array of six reals. Since the number of trials is not determined in advance, *numtrials* and the *count* array are long integers rather than integers.

The **Setup** procedure contains a loop that initializes the elements in the *count* array to 0. The elements in the array that determines the percentages of occurrence of each outcome do not have to be initialized, since they receive their values from a calculation that involves the *count* array and the number of trials.

```
procedure SetUp (var numtrials : longint; var count : countarraytype);
  var
    i : integer;
begin
  ClrScr;
  GotoXY (15,10);
  Writeln ('RANDOM NUMBER GENERATOR TEST');
  GotoXY (1,12);
  Writeln ('A random number generator chooses a specified');
  Writeln ('number of random integers between 1 and 6 and');
  Writeln ('determines what percentages of the trials');
  Writeln ('produce each of the possible outcomes.');
  for i := 1 to 6 do
    count[i] := 0;
  GotoXY (10,20);
  Write ('Enter number of trials desired: ');
  Readln (numtrials)
end;
```

In **ChooseAndCount**, a random number between 1 and 6 is chosen and an array element that keeps a running count of the number of times that particular integer has been chosen is updated. This can be done with a **case** structure:

```
num := Random(6) + 1;
case num of
  1 :
    count[1] := count[1] + 1;
  2 :
    count[2] := count[2] + 1;
  3 :
    count[3] := count[3] + 1;
  4 :
    count[4] := count[4] + 1;
  5 :
    count[5] := count[5] + 1;
  6 :
    count[6] := count[6] + 1
end;
```

This structure is correct but cumbersome, even though the random number generator produces only six possible outcomes. If the problem required 100 possible outcomes, this structure would become more unmanageable. The entire **case** structure can be replaced by a single assignment statement, since the selector in the **case** structure is identical to the index of the array counter. Thus, *num* is the index of the proper counter to update:

```
num := Random(6) + 1;
count[num] := count[num] + 1;
```

A call to the procedure `Working` indicating that processing is occurring precedes the loop containing the two assignment statements just shown:

```
procedure ChooseAndCount (numtrials : longint;
                          var count : countarraytype);
  var
    num : integer;
    i : longint;
begin
  Working;
  for i := 1 to numtrials do
    begin
      num := Random(6) + 1;
      count[num] := count[num] + 1
    end
end;
```

The trace utility in the Turbo Pascal IDE also details the activity of arrays. Put *count* and *num* in the IDE Watches window and use **Trace into** to follow these local variables. Since *count* is an array, it is represented in the Watches

Figure 9.4
The Trace of an Array

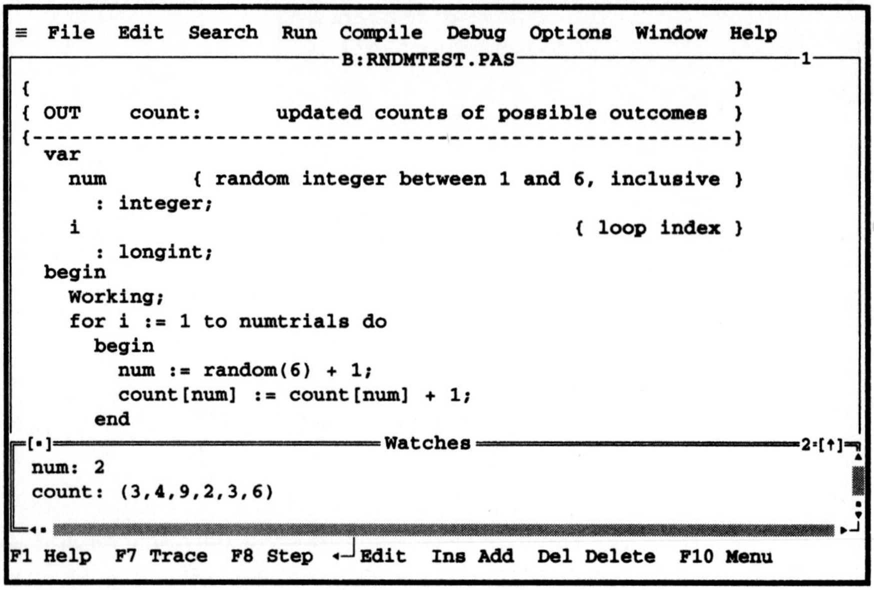

```
≡  File   Edit   Search   Run   Compile   Debug   Options   Window   Help
┌──────────────────────────────B:RNDMTEST.PAS──────────────────────────1─┐
│  {                                                                   }  │
│  { OUT     count:         updated counts of possible outcomes   }  │
│  {--------------------------------------------------------------}  │
│    var                                                                 │
│      num           { random integer between 1 and 6, inclusive }      │
│          : integer;                                                    │
│      i                                         { loop index }          │
│          : longint;                                                    │
│    begin                                                               │
│      Working;                                                          │
│      for i := 1 to numtrials do                                        │
│        begin                                                           │
│          num := random(6) + 1;                                         │
│          count[num] := count[num] + 1;                                 │
│        end                                                             │
┌─[•]════════════════════════ Watches ═══════════════════════════2·[↑]─┐
│  num: 2                                                                │
│  count: (3,4,9,2,3,6)                                                  │
│                                                                        │
└─◄·█████████████████████████████████████████████████████████████►─┘
 F1 Help  F7 Trace  F8 Step  ↵Edit  Ins Add  Del Delete  F10 Menu
```

window by six values enclosed in parentheses and separated by commas. Figure 9.4 shows a sample of what you might find in the middle of a trace.

The percentage of time each outcome occurs is determined by dividing a count by the number of trials and multiplying the result by 100:

```
procedure Percentages (numtrials : longint;
        count : countarraytype; var pct : pctarraytype);
  var
    i : integer;
begin
  for i := 1 to 6 do
    pct[i] := (count[i] / numtrials) * 100
end;
```

The **DisplayResult** procedure uses the **GotoXY** procedure to display a table of the counts and percentages centered on an 80-column screen. Figure 9.5 shows the final documented solution, after verification, along with sample output for the result screen.

Figure 9.5
RandomTest Program
Listing and Sample
Output

```
program RandomTest;
{-------------------------------------------------------------------}
{ PROGRAM:        Test for Randomness of Random Function            }
{ PROGRAMMER:     G. Browne                                         }
{ DATE:           September 1, 1990                                 }
{                                                                   }
{ This program tests the randomness of the random number generator }
{ by choosing an integer between 1 and 6, inclusive, for a specified}
{ number of trials, counting the number of trials that result in each}
{ possible value, and using this count to determine what percentage }
{ of the trials produces each outcome.                              }
{                                                                   }
{ INPUT           number of trials for the test                     }
{                                                                   }
{ OUTPUT          number of times each outcome occurs               }
{                 percentage of the time each outcome occurs        }
{-------------------------------------------------------------------}
  uses
    Crt;                            { screen formatting commands library }
  type
    countarraytype = array[1..6] of longint;
                                      { array of long integer counters }
    pctarraytype = array[1..6] of real;
                                        { array of real percentages }

  var
    count                           { array of counters of possible outcomes }
      : countarraytype;
    pct                             { array of percentages of possible outcomes }
      : pctarraytype;
    numtrials                                       { number of trials }
      : longint;
```

(continued)

```
procedure SetUp (var numtrials : longint; var count : countarraytype);
{-------------------------------------------------------------------}
{ Explains what the program does, initializes the array of          }
{ counters and accepts the number of trials.                        }
{                                                                   }
{ IN            none                                                 }
{                                                                   }
{ OUT           numtrials:  number of trials                        }
{               count:      array of counters of possible outcomes  }
{-------------------------------------------------------------------}
   var
    i                                              { loop index }
       : integer;
begin
  ClrScr;
  GotoXY (15,10);
  Writeln ('RANDOM NUMBER GENERATOR TEST');
  GotoXY (1,12);
  Writeln ('A random number generator chooses a specified');
  Writeln ('number of random integers between 1 and 6 and');
  Writeln ('determines what percentages of the trials');
  Writeln ('produce each of the possible outcomes.');
  for i := 1 to 6 do
    count[i] := 0;
  GotoXY (10,20);
  Write ('Enter number of trials desired: ');
  Readln (numtrials)
end;

procedure Working;
{-------------------------------------------------------------------}
{ Displays a message while the counts are determined.               }
{                                                                   }
{ IN            none                                                 }
{                                                                   }
{ OUT           none                                                 }
{-------------------------------------------------------------------}
begin
  ClrScr;
  GotoXY (36,13);
  Writeln ('Working!')
end;
```

```
procedure ChooseAndCount (numtrials : longint;
                          var count : countarraytype);
{--------------------------------------------------------------------}
{ Selects a random integer between 1 and 6, inclusive, and updates   }
{ an appropriate counter.                                            }
{                                                                    }
{ IN           numtrials: number of trials                          }
{              count:     initialized counts of possible outcomes    }
{                                                                    }
{ OUT          count:     updated counts of possible outcomes        }
{--------------------------------------------------------------------}
  var
    num                     { random integer between 1 and 6, inclusive }
      : integer;
    i                                               { loop index }
      : longint;
begin
  Working;
  for i := 1 to numtrials do
    begin
      num := Random(6) + 1;
      count[num] := count[num] + 1
    end
end;


procedure Percentages (numtrials : longint;
          count : countarraytype; var pct : pctarraytype);
{--------------------------------------------------------------------}
{ Determines the percentages of occurrence for all possible outcomes. }
{                                                                    }
{ IN           numtrials: number of trials                          }
{              count:     counts of possible outcomes                }
{                                                                    }
{ OUT          pct:       percentages of occurrence for all          }
{                         possible outcomes                          }
{--------------------------------------------------------------------}
  var
    i                                               { loop index }
      : integer;
begin
  for i := 1 to 6 do
  pct[i] := (count[i] / numtrials) * 100
end;
```

(continued)

```
  procedure DisplayResults (numtrials : longint;
          count : countarraytype; pct : pctarraytype);
  {------------------------------------------------------------------}
  { Displays the number of trials, the counts of the number of       }
  { occurrences of each outcome, and the percentage of occurrence of }
  { each outcome in table form.                                      }
  {                                                                  }
  { IN          numtrials:  number of trials                         }
  {             count:      count of possible outcomes               }
  {             pct:        percentages of occurrence for all        }
  {                            possible outcomes                      }
  {                                                                  }
  { OUT         none                                                 }
  {------------------------------------------------------------------}
    var
     i                                            { loop index }
         : integer;
  begin
    ClrScr;
    GotoXY (20,5);
    Writeln ('RANDOM NUMBER GENERATOR RESULTS');
    GotoXY (30,7);
    Writeln (numtrials, ' trials');
    GotoXY (1,10);
    Writeln ('VALUE':23, 'COUNT':10, 'PERCENTAGES':20);
    Writeln ('-----':23, '-----':10, '-----------':20);
    for i := 1 to 6 do
      Writeln (i:21, count[i]:12, pct[i]:17:2)
  end;

begin
  Randomize;
  SetUp (numtrials, count);
  ChooseAndCount (numtrials, count);
  Percentages (numtrials, count, pct);
  DisplayResults (numtrials, count, pct)
end.
```

```
 ──────────────── Output ────────────────
              RANDOM NUMBER GENERATOR RESULTS

                      1000 trials


              VALUE    COUNT      PERCENTAGES
              -----    -----      -----------
                1       153          15.30
                2       174          17.40
                3       174          17.40
                4       166          16.60
                5       167          16.70
```

Sample runs with as few as 10 trials may produce percentages that vary from 0% to 50%. If more trials are conducted, the percentage for each possible occurrence approaches the theoretical value of 16.67%. For example, a trial run with 1 million trials generated percentages that ranged from 16.62% to 16.71%.

9.4 Two-Dimensional Arrays

A two-dimensional array, also called a *matrix,* can be thought of as a collection of items of the same type stored in row-and-column form. An element is accessed by specifying the name of the collection and two indices, a row number and a column number. Either index can be any ordinal type except a long integer.

An apartment house can be thought of as a matrix: It is a collection of apartments that can be labeled by a floor number and a letter. For example, apartment 2J is apartment J on floor 2. But the building can also have an apartment J on floor 3 or an apartment K on floor 2. Thus, two values are needed to distinguish among the apartments; one is not enough.

In Pascal, a two-dimensional array element is represented by the following:

```
<identifier> [ <row index>, <column index> ]
```

where the choice of the identifier name follows the same rules as for any identifier and the indices are two constants or expressions that are ordinal data types. The first index represents a row number and the second represents a column number. Square brackets, [and], must enclose the indices, which are separated by a comma. Figure 9.6 shows a two-dimensional array *inventory,* with the names of several elements included. Each row represents

Figure 9.6
The Two-Dimensional
Array *inventory*

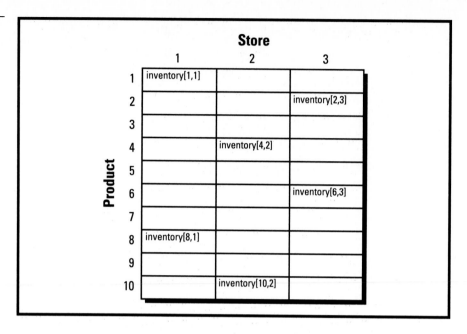

a different product, and each column represents a store selling that product. An element in this array contains the inventory (number of cases) of a particular product held by a particular store. The identifier *inventory[4,2]* refers to the inventory of product 4 held by store 2.

As with one-dimensional arrays, two-dimensional arrays must be defined in a **type** statement if they are to be used as parameters in functions or procedures.

FORMAT: **type**
**   <identifier> = array [<range1>,<range2>] of <item type>;**

For a two-dimensional array, two index ranges must be specified.

Example

```
type
  twodtype = array[1..6,-1..1] of real;
var
  matrix : twodtype;
```

The two-dimensional array *matrix* is of type *twodtype*, with six rows, numbered 1 through 6, and three columns, numbered –1 through 1.

As with one-dimensional arrays, the indices can be any ordinal data type.

Example

```
type
  aptype = array[1..16,'A'..'Z']
           of string[20];
var
  apt : aptype;
```

The array *apt* has 16 rows, numbered 1 to 16, and 26 columns, labeled *A* through *Z*.

Putting Data in a Two-Dimensional Array

Every element in a one-dimensional array can be accessed by enclosing the proper statement in one loop. In a two-dimensional array, however, nested loops are used to "visit" each element. For example, the index of the outer loop specifies a row, while the index of the inner loop cycles through all the columns in that row.

Example

```
for r := 1 to 10 do
  for c := 1 to 3 do
    inventory[r,c] := 0;
```

This segment of code initializes the elements in the previously defined two-dimensional array *inventory*. The outer loop index *r* chooses a row, while the inner loop index *c* cycles through columns 1 to 3, setting all those elements to 0. This process is repeated for all the rows as *r* moves from 1 to 10.

In order to put data into a two-dimensional array, the correct row number and column number of the entry should be part of a loop structure.

Example

```
Write ('Press y for more:');
Readln (ans);
while ans in ['y','Y'] do
  begin
    Write ('Product number: ');
    Readln (prod);
    Write ('Store Number: ');
    Readln (store);
    Write ('Inventory: ');
    Readln (inven [prod,store]);
    Write ('Press y for more:');
    Readln (ans)
  end;
```

The statements in the body of the loop ask for the product number (row) and store number (column). Inventory data is stored in the two-dimensional array element with row and column number *inven[prod,store]*.

Figure 9.7
The Array *a*

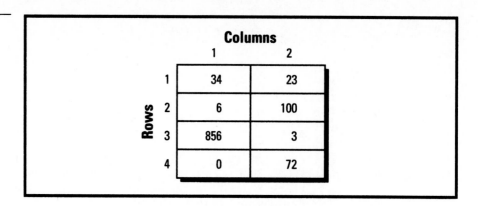

Outputting Two-
Dimensional Array
Elements

The display of a two-dimensional array in table form requires nested loops, screen formatting commands, and field descriptors. Consider the array *a* shown in Figure 9.7.

Example

```
ClrScr;
GotoXY (22,5);
Writeln ('NUMBERS');
GotoXY (22,7);
Writeln ('Columns');
GotoXY (1,8);
Writeln (1:20, 2:10);
GotoXY (1,9);
Writeln ('Rows':10);
GotoXY (1,10);
for r := 1 to 4 do
  begin
    Write (r:10);
    for c := 1 to 2 do
      Write (a[i,j]:10);
    Writeln
  end;
```

The **GotoXY** statements position the cursor in each screen row. Field descriptors simplify the aligning of the columns. In the loop, the **Write (r:10)** statement outputs the row number at the beginning of each line, while the inner loop outputs the values in that row. The **Writeln** statement after this loop moves the cursor to the next line for the display of the next row of data. Output for this code is:

```
                                       NUMBERS

                                       Columns
                             1                   2
                   Rows
                     1        34                 23
                     2         6                100
                     3       856                  3
                     4         0                 72
```

Row and Column
Operations

Operations can be performed on an entire row by keeping the row index constant while varying the column index, and on an entire column by keeping the column index constant while varying the row index.

Example

```
sum := 0;
for r := 1 to 4 do
  sum := sum + a[r,2];
Writeln ('Sum: ', sum);
```

This segment of code finds the sum of all the elements in column 2 of array *a* shown in Figure 9.7 by keeping the column index constant at 2 while placing a summing statement inside a loop that cycles through all the rows.

Although Turbo Pascal allows three or more dimensions for array structures, it is rare that more than three are used in practice. The discussion in this chapter is limited to one- and two-dimensional arrays.

9.5 Application in Spreadsheeting: Clarence Sales

A *spreadsheet* is a table of rows and columns that records data and performs fundamental numeric calculations. Budgeting, break-even analysis, and cash flow analysis are some of the many applications of spreadsheets. In recent years, electronic spreadsheets have played a more prominent role in many businesses. The row-and-column format of two-dimensional arrays makes them suitable for the same types of problems that electronic spreadsheets solve.

Suppose Clarence, Inc. sells three products and wishes to produce a summary of the quarterly and yearly income generated by sales. Assume the prices of the products do not change during the year. Write a program that accepts the quantity of each product sold for each of four quarters and the selling price for each of the products and finds the income from the sales, by product and by quarter. The program should also find the total number of products sold and income produced per quarter, the yearly total for each product, and the grand total from all products over the entire year. Display this data for the quantities and incomes in table form, where the rows represent products and the columns represent quarters, as shown in Figure 9.8.

Figure 9.8
Quantity and Income
Table Structure

Product	Quarter 1	2	3	4	Year Total
1					
2					
3					
Total					

	Input	Output

Figure 9.9
Quarterly Sales
Input/Output Chart

	Input	**Output**
	Selling prices	Quantity matrix
	Quantities	Income matrix

ANALYSIS OF THE PROBLEM   After the selling prices and quantities of products sold in each quarter have been entered, tables of the quantities and the income generated by these sales are output. See Figure 9.9.

MODULAR DESIGN OF THE SOLUTION   The structure chart and MIT for the solution appear in Figure 9.10. The **CONTINUE** module permits the quantity and income matrices to appear on the screen until the user signals for their removal.

DESIGN OF THE STRUCTURE OF THE MODULES

QUARTERLY SALES
   INITIALIZE
   FORM QUANTITY MATRIX
   ENTER PRICE LIST
   FORM INCOME MATRIX
   DISPLAY QUANTITY MATRIX
   DISPLAY INCOME MATRIX

INITIALIZE
   for each row
      for each column
         initialize quantity matrix
         initialize income matrix

FORM QUANTITY MATRIX
   ENTER QUANTITY DATA
   for each product
      for each quarter
         find yearly product sums
   for each quarter and yearly total
      for each product
         find quarterly and yearly total sums

ENTER QUANTITY DATA
    for each product
       for each quarter
          enter number sold

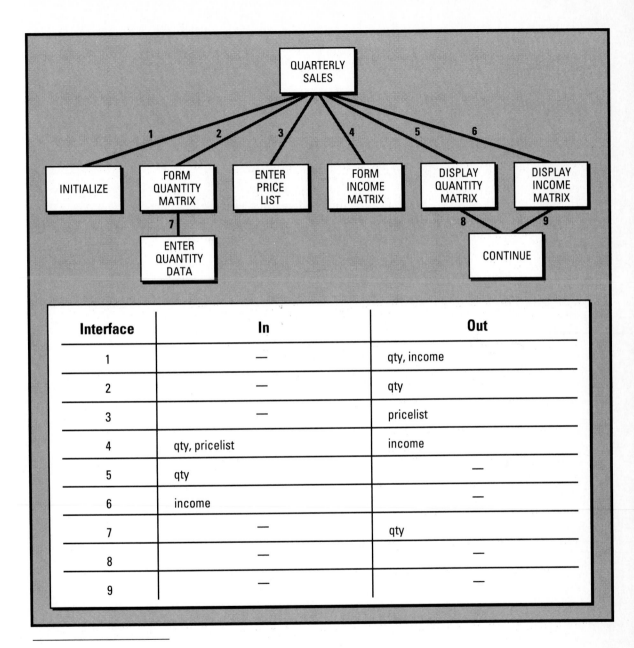

Interface	In	Out
1	—	qty, income
2	—	qty
3	—	pricelist
4	qty, pricelist	income
5	qty	—
6	income	—
7	—	qty
8	—	—
9	—	—

Figure 9.10
Quarterly Sales Solution
Design and Module
Interface Table

ENTER PRICE LIST
  for each product
    enter selling price

FORM INCOME MATRIX
  for each product
    for each quarter
      find income (quantity * selling price)
  for each product
    for each quarter
      find yearly income sums
  for each quarter and yearly total
    for each product
      find quarterly and yearly total sums

DISPLAY QUANTITY MATRIX
  display table headings
  for each product and total
    for each quarter and yearly total
      display quantity
  CONTINUE

DISPLAY INCOME MATRIX
  display table headings
  for each product and total
    for each quarter and yearly total
      display income
  CONTINUE

CONTINUE
  accept any keystroke

    Both the quantity and income matrices are initialized, since the fifth column and fourth row of each are summing variables. The fifth column keeps a running total of the quarterly figures for each product, and the fourth row keeps a running total of the product figures for each quarter and year.

PRODUCTION OF CODE
AND VERIFICATION OF
SOLUTION

The declaration section of the program defines constant identifiers for the number of rows in the table, the number of columns in the table, the number of products sold, and the number of quarters in a year:

```
const
  numrows = 4;
  numcols = 5;
  numprods = numrows - 1;
  numquars = numcols - 1;
type
  qtytype = array[1..numrows,1..numcols] of integer;
  incometype = array[1..numrows,1..numcols] of real;
  pricetype = array[1..numprods] of real;
```

These constant identifiers define array types and are used in the procedures of the program to make the solution easy to adapt to a change in program requirements, such as the addition of a product. For example, if a new product were added to the company's offerings, only the *numrows* declaration would have to be updated, since *numprods* depends on *numrows*.

Consider the procedure FormQuantityMatrix:

```
procedure FormQuantityMatrix (var qty : qtytype);
  var
    prod, quar : integer;
begin
  EnterQuantityData (qty);
  for prod := 1 to numprods do
    for quar := 1 to numquars do
      qty[prod,numcols] := qty[prod,numcols] + qty[prod,quar];
  for quar := 1 to numcols do
    for prod := 1 to numprods do
      qty[numquars,quar] := qty[numquars,quar] + qty[prod,quar]
end;
```

The *prod* loop chooses a product, and the *quar* loop keeps a running total of all quantity values for that product *(qty[prod,quar])* and stores this sum in column 5 *(numcols)* in the same row *(qty[prod,numcols])*. In this loop the column value in the summing variable remains constant at *numcols* while the row index varies from 1 to *numprods*. After the yearly product totals have been calculated and stored, the procedure chooses a quarter, or the yearly total, and keeps a running total of the quantity values for all the products in that column. The resulting sum is stored in the fourth row (row *numrows)* of the chosen column. In this case, the row index in the summing variable remains constant at *numquars* while the column index varies from 1 to *numcols*. The income matrix is constructed in a similar fashion.

321

The **ReadKey** Function
The **ReadKey** function in the `Continue` procedure accepts a character from the keyboard to continue processing. When Pascal encounters **ReadKey,** it stops and waits until any key, including the Enter key, is pressed before continuing. The Enter key does not have to be pressed following a character, and the character pressed is not echoed on the screen.

FORMAT: **ReadKey**

Since **ReadKey** is a function, it must be part of a Pascal statement, as in the `Continue` procedure:

```
procedure Continue;
  var
    ch : char;
begin
  GotoXY (10,23);
  Write ('Press any key to continue');
  ch := ReadKey
end;
```

The message *Press any key to continue* remains on the screen, since **ReadKey** appears in the following assignment statement. After the variable *ch* accepts the character, control returns to the calling statement.

After the verification process, the program is documented. The final version of the solution is shown in Figure 9.11, along with sample output for the quantity and income tables in a format similar to the one produced by the program.

Figure 9.11
QuarterlySales
Program Listing and
Sample Output

```
program QuarterlySales;
{-------------------------------------------------------------------}
{ PROGRAM:        Quarterly Sales for Clarence, Inc.                }
{ PROGRAMMER:     S. Chart                                          }
{ DATE:           September 9, 1990                                 }
{                                                                   }
{ This program produces an annual summary of the quarterly and yearly }
{ income generated by the sales of three products. The prices of the  }
{ products do not change during the year. It accepts the quantity of  }
{ each product sold for each of four quarters and the selling price   }
{ for each of the products, and finds the income from the sales by    }
{ product by quarter. It also calculates the total number of products }
{ sold and income produced per quarter, yearly totals for each        }
{ product and the grand total from all products over the entire       }
{ year. The output data are displayed in table form where the rows    }
{ represent products and the columns represent quarters.              }
{                                                                   }
{ INPUT          selling prices for products                        }
{                numbers of products sold by quarter                }
{                                                                   }
{ OUTPUT         quantity table with quarterly and product totals   }
{                income table with quarterly and product totals     }
{-------------------------------------------------------------------}
  uses
    Crt;                                 { screen formatting commands library }
  const
    numrows = 4;                                  { number of rows in table }
    numcols = 5;                                  { number of columns in table }
    numprods = numrows - 1;                       { number of products }
    numquars = numcols - 1;                       { number of selling quarters }
  type
    qtytype = array[1..numrows,1..numcols] of integer;
                                                        { table of integers }
    incometype = array[1..numrows,1..numcols] of real;
                                                        { table of reals }
    pricetype = array[1..numprods] of real;
                                                        { array of reals }
```

(continued)

```
var
  qty                              { table of quantities of products sold }
    : qtytype;
  income                               { table of income from sales }
    : incometype;
  pricelist                              { array of selling prices }
    : pricetype;

procedure Initialize (var qty : qtytype; var income : incometype);
{--------------------------------------------------------------------}
{ Initializes quantity and income matrices values to 0.              }
{                                                                    }
{ IN          none                                                   }
{                                                                    }
{ OUT         qty:    table of quantities of products sold           }
{             income: table of income from sales                     }
{--------------------------------------------------------------------}
  var
    prod,                                { product loop index }
    quar                                 { quarter loop index }
      : integer;
begin
  for prod := 1 to numrows do
    for quar := 1 to numcols do
      begin
        qty[prod,quar] := 0;
        income[prod,quar] := 0.0
      end
end;
```

```pascal
procedure EnterQuantityData (var qty : qtytype);
{------------------------------------------------------------------------}
{ Accepts quantity data for all products and quarters.                   }
{                                                                        }
{ IN             none                                                    }
{                                                                        }
{ OUT            qty:  table of quantities of products sold              }
{------------------------------------------------------------------------}
  var
    prod,                                          { prod loop index }
    quar                                       { quarter loop index }
      : integer;
begin
  ClrScr;
  GotoXY (10,1);
  Writeln ('ENTER QUANTITY SOLD');
  GotoXY (1,4);
  for prod := 1 to numprods do
    begin
      Writeln ('Product ',prod);
      for quar := 1 to numquars do
        begin
          Write ('  Enter number of units sold in');
          Write (' quarter ', quar, ': ');
          Readln (qty[prod,quar])
        end;
      Writeln
    end
end;
```

(continued)

```
procedure FormQuantityMatrix (var qty : qtytype);
{-------------------------------------------------------------------}
{ Accepts quantity data for products and quarters and calculates    }
{ quarterly and product totals.                                     }
{                                                                   }
{ IN            none                                                }
{                                                                   }
{ OUT           qty:  table of quantities of products sold          }
{-------------------------------------------------------------------}
  var
    prod,                                        { product loop index }
    quar                                         { quarter loop index }
      : integer;
begin
  EnterQuantityData (qty);
  for prod := 1 to numprods do
    for quar := 1 to numquars do
      qty[prod,numcols] := qty[prod,numcols] + qty[prod,quar];
  for quar := 1 to numcols do
    for prod := 1 to numprods do
      qty[numquars,quar] := qty[numquars,quar] + qty[prod,quar]
end;
```

```
procedure EnterPriceList (var pricelist : pricetype);
{----------------------------------------------------------------------}
{ Accepts selling prices for products.                                 }
{                                                                      }
{ IN            none                                                   }
{                                                                      }
{ OUT           pricelist:  selling prices for products               }
{----------------------------------------------------------------------}
  var
    strngunitprice                         { string value for unit price }
      : string[20];
    prod,                                           { product loop index }
    code                        { position of first nonnumeric character }
      : integer;
begin
  ClrScr;
  GotoXY (10,1);
  Writeln ('PRICE LIST DATA ENTRY');
  GotoXY (1,4);
  for prod := 1 to numprods do
    repeat
      Write ('Enter unit price for product ', prod:1, ': ');
      Readln (strngunitprice);
      Val (strngunitprice, pricelist[prod], code);
      if code <> 0
        then
          Writeln ('Invalid numeric.');
      Writeln
    until code = 0
end;
```

(continued)

```
procedure FormIncomeMatrix (pricelist : pricetype; qty : qtytype;
                            var income : incometype);
{--------------------------------------------------------------------}
{ Calculates the income matrix by finding the product of the         }
{ selling price and quantity sold for each product in each quarter.  }
{ Also, finds quarterly and product totals.                          }
{                                                                    }
{ IN            pricelist: selling prices for products               }
{               qty:       table of quantities of products sold      }
{                                                                    }
{ OUT           income:    table of income from sales                }
{--------------------------------------------------------------------}
  var
    prod,                                        { product loop index }
    quar                                         { quarter loop index }
      : integer;
begin
  for prod := 1 to numprods do
    for quar := 1 to numquars do
      income[prod,quar] := qty[prod,quar] * pricelist[prod];
  for prod := 1 to numprods do
    for quar := 1 to numquars do
      income[prod,numcols] := income[prod,numcols] +income[prod,quar];
  for quar := 1 to numcols do
    for prod := 1 to numprods do
      income[numrows,quar] := income[numrows,quar] +income[prod,quar]
end;

procedure Continue;
{--------------------------------------------------------------------}
{ Waits for user to press key to resume processing.                  }
{                                                                    }
{ IN            none                                                 }
{                                                                    }
{ OUT           none                                                 }
{--------------------------------------------------------------------}
  var
    ch                                         { continuation signal }
      : char;
begin
  GotoXY (10,23);
  Write ('Press any key to continue');
  ch := ReadKey
end;
```

```
procedure DisplayQuantityMatrix (qty : qtytype);
{-------------------------------------------------------------------------}
{ Displays the quantity matrix.                                           }
{                                                                         }
{ IN            qty:  table of quantities of products sold               }
{                                                                         }
{ OUT           none                                                      }
{-------------------------------------------------------------------------}
  var
    prod,                                        { product loop index }
    quar                                         { quarter loop index }
      : integer;
begin
  ClrScr;
  GotoXY (25,2);
  Writeln ('PRODUCT QUANTITIES SOLD');
  GotoXY (1,5);
  Writeln ('Quarter':38, 'Year':26);
  GotoXY (1,6);
  Writeln (1:17,2:12,3:12,4:12,'Totals':12);
  GotoXY (1,7);
  Writeln ('Products');
  GotoXY (1,8);
  for prod := 1 to numrows do
    begin
      if prod = 4
        then
          begin
            Writeln;
            Write ('Total':5)
          end
        else
          Write (prod:5);
      for quar := 1 to numcols do
        Write (qty[prod,quar]:12);
      Writeln
    end;
  Continue
end;
```

(continued)

```pascal
procedure DisplayIncomeMatrix (income : incometype);
{------------------------------------------------------------------------}
{ Displays table of income from sales.                                   }
{                                                                        }
{ IN            none                                                     }
{                                                                        }
{ OUT           income: table of income from sales                       }
{------------------------------------------------------------------------}
  var
    prod,                                          { product loop index }
    quar                                           { quarter loop index }
      : integer;
begin
  ClrScr;
  GotoXY (23,2);
  Writeln ('QUARTERLY INCOME IN DOLLARS');
  GotoXY (1,5);
  Writeln ('Quarter':38, 'Year':26);
  GotoXY (1,6);
  Writeln (1:17,2:12,3:12,4:12,'Totals':12);
  GotoXY (1,7);
  Writeln ('Products');
  GotoXY (1,8);
  for prod := 1 to numrows do
    begin
      if prod = 4
        then
          begin
            Writeln;
            Write ('Total':5)
          end
        else
          Write (prod:5);
      for quar := 1 to numcols do
        Write (income[prod,quar]:12:2);
      Writeln
    end;
  Continue
end;
```

```
begin
  Initialize (qty, income);
  FormQuantityMatrix (qty);
  EnterPriceList (pricelist);
  FormIncomeMatrix (pricelist, qty, income);
  DisplayQuantityMatrix (qty);
  DisplayIncomeMatrix (income);
  ClrScr
end.
```

─────── **Output** ───────

PRODUCT QUANTITIES SOLD

Products	Quarter 1	2	3	4	Year Totals
1	12	7	5	15	39
2	56	33	78	24	191
3	101	87	65	175	428
Total	169	127	148	214	658

─────── **Output** ───────

QUARTERLY INCOME IN DOLLARS

Products	Quarter 1	2	3	4	Year Totals
1	35.88	20.93	14.95	44.85	116.51
2	83.44	49.17	116.22	35.76	284.59
3	77.77	66.99	50.05	134.75	329.56
Total	197.09	137.09	181.22	215.36	730.76

Store and Forward

Many programming applications require the storage and management of large amounts of data. The array structure was developed with the intent of storing data of the same type in a single structure, where data is accessed by specifying a collection name and one or more indices.

Not all components of a collection of related data must be of the same type. For example, a collection of payroll data may contain string data (for names and addresses), integer data (for number of dependencies), and real data (for any money amounts). While this data can be stored in several related array structures, it is more suitable to store all these different types in one data structure that can accommodate them. The record data structure presented in the next chapter is such a structure.

Snares and Pitfalls

- *Defining an unsuitable range for the index of an array:* The range for indices in array declarations should be large (or small) enough to accommodate all realistic values for the index without wasting reserved memory.

- *Failing to enclose array indices in square brackets:* Array indices must be enclosed in [ ]; braces and parentheses are not permitted.

- *Failing to use a **type** statement to define an array structure that is a parameter in a procedure or function:* Since arrays and records are structured data types, these structures must be defined in the **type** declaration section of a program if they are parameters.

Exercises

1. Answer the following questions in paragraph form.
   a. What is a structured data type?
   b. Why is it inadvisable for the complete declaration of an array to appear in the **var** part of the declaration section of a program?
   c. In general, how many and what pieces of data must be specified to locate an element in an array structure?
   d. Why should elements of an array be given initial values?
   e. Explain what is meant by the statement "An array is a static data structure."

2. Classify each of the following Pascal statements as valid or invalid. If invalid, explain why. Unless otherwise stated, assume all identifiers have been properly declared.

   a. **type**
       ctype = **array**['e'..'j'] **of real**;

   b. **type**
       index1 = 1..10;
       index2 = 11..20;
       atype = **array**[index1] **of** index2;

c. `b[i] := a[c[i]];`

d.
```
if b[count[k]] > 0
   then
      Writeln ('OK')
   else
      Writeln ('Not OK');
```

e.
```
type
   etype = array[-2..2] of integer;
var
   e : etype;
   ...
for i := 1 to 5 do
   e[i] := i;
```

3. Evaluate each of the given expressions if $i = 3$, $j = 2$, and the one-dimensional array D has the following values:

D[1]	D[2]	D[3]	D[4]	D[5]	D[6]
0	-4	12	8	-3	1

   a. `D[2] / D[6]`
   b. `D[2*j]`
   c. `D[i] div D[i+j-1]`
   d. `D[i-j] + D[i+j] / D[i*j]`
   e. `D[D[i+3]]`

4. Evaluate each of the given expressions if $i = 3$, $j = 2$, and the two-dimensional array T has the following values:

   ```
   T[1,1] = 3    T[1,2] = 5    T[1,3] = 7
   T[2,1] = 8    T[2,2] = 6    T[2,3] = 4
   T[3,1] = 0    T[3,2] = 1    T[3,3] = 2
   ```

   a. `T[j,i] - T[i,j]`
   b. `T[i,i] mod T[j,j]`
   c. `3 * T[1,j] div T[i-1,i-1]`
   d. `(T[i,j] + T[j,i]) / T[j+1,i]`
   e. `T[T[1,2]-T[j,i],T[i,1]+T[i,i]]`

5. Write Pascal equivalents for each of the given descriptions.
   a. Define an array of characters whose indices range from 0 to 11.
   b. Load a 20-element integer array with indices ranging from 1 to 20, where each element contains twice its index.
   c. Count the number of elements whose value is 0 in a 7-row, 7-column array of integers.
   d. Find the smallest element of an array that consists of 100 real numbers.
   e. Find the sum of the integers in the third column of a 5-row, 6-column two-dimensional array.

6. Find all the errors, both syntax and logical, in the following Pascal procedure designed to sum and return the sum of the diagonal elements of a 5-row, 5-column array A.

```
procedure DiagonalSum (A : array[1..5,1..5] of real;
                              sum : real);
   var
      i : integer;
begin
   for i := 1 to 5 do
      sum := sum + A[i,i]
end;
```

7. Show the exact output for each of the following program segments.

a.
```
for k := 3 to 7 do
   begin
      A[k] := 3 * k - 2;
      Writeln (A[k]:5)
   end;
```

b.
```
i := 1
while i < 5 do
   begin
      B[i,i] := 2 * i - 1;
      Writeln (B[i,i]);
      i := i + 2
   end;
```

c.
```
for i := 1 to 6 do
   D[i] := i;
j := 1;
while j < 5 do
   begin
      D[j] := D[j] - 2;
      j := j + 1
   end;
k := 1;
repeat
   Writeln (D[k]:5)
until (D[k] > 2);
```

d.
```
for i := 1 to 3 do
   for j := 1 to 4 do
      E[i,j] := i + j * 2;
for k := 1 to 4 do
   begin
      for n := 1 to 3 do
         Write (E[n,k]:4);
      Writeln
   end;
```

Programming Assignments

Elementary

1. A small local theater can seat 120 people in 12 rows, labeled A through L. The seat numbers in each row are numbered 1 through 10. Write a program that initializes a two-dimensional character array with blanks, places an *X* into the appropriate row and seat number when a ticket is sold, and displays the seating plan when requested. Here is a sample display of the seating plan:

	1	2	3	4	5	6	7	8	9	10
A				X	X	X	X	X	X	
B		X	X			X	X		X	X
C	X	X		X	X					
D						X	X			
E				X	X					
F							X	X		
G										
H										
I										
J										
K										
L										

Since **char** is an ordinal data type, characters can be used as indices for arrays.

2. Write a program that uses a one-dimensional array to store the dollar values of an ounce of gold for 10 consecutive days and finds the number of days the daily value was above the average for that period and the number of days it was below the average.

3. In mathematics, a matrix is a rectangular array of elements. The *transpose* of a matrix is another matrix, one in which the rows of the original matrix are the columns of the transpose and the columns of the original are the rows of the transpose. For example, the transpose of the 3-row, 4-column matrix

$$\begin{pmatrix} 0 & 5 & -2 & 1 \\ -1 & 0 & 4 & 3 \\ 1 & 7 & 9 & 1 \end{pmatrix}$$

is the 4-row, 3-column matrix

$$\begin{pmatrix} 0 & -1 & 1 \\ 5 & 0 & 7 \\ -2 & 4 & 9 \\ 1 & 3 & 1 \end{pmatrix}$$

Write a program that accepts values for a matrix and displays that matrix and its transpose.

4. Write a program that determines and displays a table of values for the function $y = 0.4x + 5$. The *x*-coordinates should range from −10 to 10 and be stored in the first column of a two-dimensional array. The values of a *y*-coordinate should be stored in the second column of the same row containing its *x*-value.

5. A gas station is giving away $100 worth of free gas to one of its customers each day. Each customer purchasing gas on a particular day has his or her name entered into an array. At the end of the day, the computer chooses a random integer between 1 and the maximum number of customers for that day. The integer represents the index of the array element containing the name of the winning customer. Write a program that simulates this process and writes an appropriate letter to the winner using the name found in the array.

6. Each of seven judges in a diving contest scores a dive from 0.0 to 10.0 in steps of 0.5. To determine the final score, the highest and lowest scores are eliminated and the average of the remaining scores is multiplied by a difficulty factor ranging from 1.0 to 5.0. Write a program that accepts seven scores for a dive and its difficulty factor, and produces the final score.

7. The Hamming distance between two arrays of Booleans with the same number of active elements is defined as the number of locations in which corresponding elements differ. For example, for arrays *A* and *B* defined as follows:

A[1] = false	B[1] = false
A[2] = true	B[2] = false
A[3] = true	B[3] = true
A[4] = false	B[4] = false

the Hamming distance is 1, since the arrays differ only in position 2.
    Write a program that accepts two Boolean arrays of equal size and outputs their Hamming distance.

8. A town has four voting districts and three candidates running for mayor. Write a program that fills a two-dimensional array, similar to the one that follows, with the total number of votes received by each candidate from each voting district.

Candidate	Voting District			
	1	2	3	4
1	167	92	281	101
2	32	67	121	187
3	133	261	97	166

Calculate and store in the array the total number of votes received by each candidate as well as the voting turnout for each district. Display the entire array, in tabular form, and the number of the winning candidate.

9. Two theater critics have their own lists of the 10 best plays of the year. Write a program that creates a third list containing the plays that appear on both critics' lists and displays all three lists appropriately labeled.

10. A magic square is a two-dimensional table of consecutive integers with an equal number of rows and columns, where the sums of the values in each

Figure 9.12
3 × 3 Magic Square

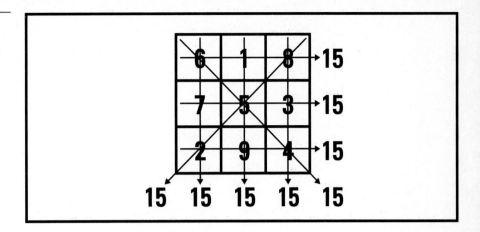

row, each column, and both diagonals are the same. For example, in the 3 × 3 magic square illustrated in Figure 9.12, the sums of the rows, columns, and diagonals are all 15.

Write a program that accepts values for a 4-row, 4-column table, outputs the table, and determines whether or not it is a magic square.

Challenging

11. In statistics, the coefficient of correlation r measures whether a relationship exists between two quantities. If those quantities are x and y, the correlation is based on several measurements of these two quantities, and is given by

$$r = \frac{(x_1 - x_{av})(y_1 - y_{av}) + \cdots + (x_n - x_{av})(y_n - y_{av})}{n s_x s_y}$$

where n is the number of measurements; the x_i's and the y_i's are the corresponding x and y measurements; x_{av} and y_{av} are the average of the x and y measurements, respectively; and s_x and s_y are the standard deviations for the x and y measurements, respectively. The standard deviation s for n values of x is given by

$$s = \sqrt{\frac{(x_1 - x_{av})^2 + \cdots + (x_n - x_{av})^2}{n}}$$

Calculated values for r range between –1 and +1. If r is close to –1, there is an inverse relationship between the measured quantities; if r is close to +1, there is a direct relationship; and if r is close to 0, there is no relationship.

Write a program that determines if there is a correlation between the heights of fathers and their sons by entering at least 20 pairs of heights into two arrays and outputting the resulting correlation coefficient.

12. One ciphering scheme takes a message and stores it in a two-dimensional array one row at a time. The coded message is read from the array one

column at a time. For example, Voltaire's message "The secret of being a bore is to tell everything." is stored row by row in a 5-row, 8-column array as

```
Thesecre
tofbeing
aboreist
otelleve
rything.
```

The decoded message is read from the array column by column, producing:
Ttaor hobty efoet sbrlh eeeli ciien rnsvg egte.
  Write a program that gives the option of either encoding or decoding input messages using this method.

13. The Catalan sequence can be used to determine the number of different ways an arithmetic expression can be parenthesized. The first term in this sequence, C_0, is by definition 1. Any other term C_i, where i is greater than or equal to 1, is given by

$$C_i = C_0 C_{i-1} + C_1 C_{i-2} + \cdots + C_{i-1} C_0$$

For example, $C_3 = C_0 C_2 + C_1 C_1 + C_2 C_0 = 1 \times 2 + 1 \times 1 + 2 \times 1 = 5$. The first six Catalan numbers, C_0 to C_5, are 1, 1, 2, 5, 14, and 42.
  Write a program that stores the first 15 Catalan numbers in an array and outputs a table of their values.

14. Hopper Computer International (HCI) manufactures three different computer models: the basic PV1, enhanced HS2, and powerful SD3. The unit selling prices of each to its three major markets are given in the following table:

Market	Model		
	PV1	HS2	SD3
Government	$1189	$1869	$3059
Education	979	1539	2519
Retail	1399	2199	3599

HCI can make a total of 2400 computers each year. The largest market is the retail market, where the HS2 model sells best. Most government buyers acquire SD3 models, while the majority of educational market purchases is for the PV1. HCI has come up with four different plans to estimate the number of each model to be manufactured for the coming year:

Model	Units Sold in Plan			
	1	2	3	4
PV1	400	600	800	1000
HS2	1200	1400	1000	800
SD3	800	400	600	600

Write a program that stores this data in two two-dimensional arrays and produces a third two-dimensional array, with each row representing a market

and each column representing the total income produced if that market purchased all the computers manufactured under each plan.

15. Pascal's triangle (part of which is shown here) is a pattern of numbers that can
be used to determine the probability of occurrence of certain events.

```
                    1
                 1     1
              1     2     1
           1     3     3     1
        1     4     6     4     1
     1     5    10    10     5     1
```

Each row begins and ends with 1. Each of the other terms is the sum of the
two numbers immediately above it. For example, 4 is the sum of 1 and 3, and
10 is the sum of 6 and 4.
    Write a program to create and display ten rows of Pascal's triangle.

16. A prime number is a positive integer whose only factors are 1 and itself. For
example, 13 is a prime number, since its only factors are 1 and 13; 12 is not,
since 2, 3, 4, and 6 are factors other than 1 and 12.
    One method for generating a list of prime numbers starts with a list of
positive integers from 2 to an arbitrary value *max*. The first step eliminates
all multiples of the first base value, 2, with the exception of 2. The process is
repeated by choosing the next remaining element in the list (in this case 3)
as the next base element. The process then removes all multiples of 3 and
continues until the base element is larger than the square root of *max*. This
method is called the Sieve of Eratosthenes.
    Write a program to simulate the Sieve of Eratosthenes, and output all the
prime numbers between 2 and a given input value *max*.

17. The manager of a corporation based in New York must make periodic visits to
regional offices in Chicago, Dallas, and Los Angeles. The following mileage
table gives the distances between these cities. Write a program that determines
the round trip that starts in New York, visits the other three cities, and covers
the least mileage.

	Chicago	Dallas	Los Angeles	New York
Chicago	—	917	2054	802
Dallas	917	—	1387	1552
Los Angeles	2054	1387	—	2786
New York	802	1552	2786	—

18. Square matrices (two-dimensional arrays with the same number of rows as
columns) have many properties that make them useful. A square matrix is
symmetric if the element in row i, column j of the matrix is identical to the
one in row j, column i, for all i and j. A square matrix is *diagonal* if all the

elements that are *not* on the main diagonal (the one from the upper left element of the matrix to the lower right element) are 0.

Write a program that accepts values for a 5-row, 5-column matrix and determines whether it is symmetric, diagonal, or neither.

19. Write a program that simulates a game in which a user determines the sequence of four unique colors randomly chosen by computer. The available colors are: red, orange, yellow, green, blue, and violet. To assist the user, after each incorrect guess, the following clues are given: the number of colors that are correct and are in the proper position, and the number of colors that are correct but are in the wrong position. Play should continue until the correct sequence is found or the player gives up, in which case the answer is revealed. At the end of the game, the number of attempts should be displayed.

20. The game of *Life* was developed by J. H. Conway, a British mathematician. A rectangular grid is drawn composed of cells. A cell can either be alive or dead. An initial configuration of live and dead cells is placed in the grid, and the life cycle of the grid, from generation to generation, is observed, using the following rules:

Each cell has eight neighbors that touch it: two horizontally, two vertically, and four on a diagonal. If a cell is alive in one generation but has no or one neighboring cell that is alive, that cell dies of loneliness in the next generation. If a cell is alive and has four or more neighbors in one generation, it dies of overcrowding in the next generation. If a cell has two or three neighbors in one generation, it remains alive for the next generation. If a cell is dead and has *exactly* three neighbors, it comes alive in the next generation; otherwise, it remains dead. An example with an initial configuration and three subsequent generations is illustrated in Figure 9.13.

Write a program simulating the game of *Life* with at least a 10-row, 10-column grid. The output should continue to show generations until signalled by the user.

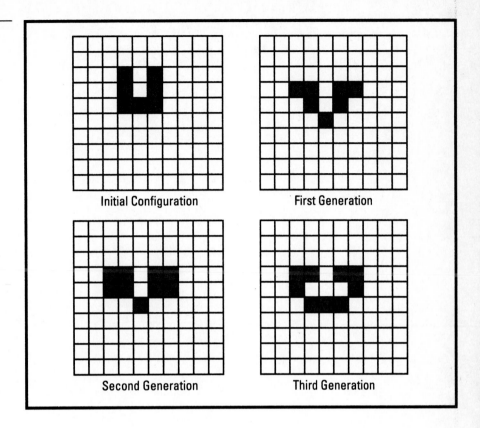

Figure 9.13
Example of *Life*
Generations

Initial Configuration

First Generation

Second Generation

Third Generation

CHAPTER 10

Records, Sorting, and Searching

Key Terms

bubble sort
field
key
record

searching
sorting
with

Objectives

- To present the record data structure and apply it in the solution of problems
- To introduce searching and sorting
- To employ data structures in algorithms for searching and sorting

10.1 Introduction

An array stores data of the same type in a single structure. What if you want strings, reals, and integers to be part of the same structure? Certainly, several arrays can be created, one for each different type of data, but the advantage of storing all relevant data in the same structure would be lost, since you would have to declare identifiers for more than one structure and use more than one identifier each time the structures are accessed. Fortunately, there is another way to handle this situation.

Records allow for the storage of different types of data in the same structure. A *record* is a collection of related data items, or *fields*. See Figure 10.1.

Figure 10.1
Record Structure

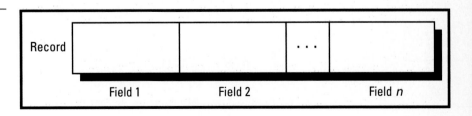

Record | Field 1 | Field 2 | ... | Field *n*

For example, a charitable organization may have donor records, with fields for the donor's name, donor's address, amount given, number of donation requests made, and date of last donation. This information—which consists of three pieces of string data (name, address, and date of last donation), an integer (number of donation requests made), and a real (amount given)—can be stored in a single record structure.

10.2 The Record Structure

As with the array data type, a record is declared in a **type** statement. The declaration must specify field names and types.

FORMAT:
```
type
  <type identifier> = record
    <field identifier> : <data type>;
    <field identifier> : <data type>;
          . . .
    <field identifier> : <data type>
  end;
```

The **type** identifier is followed by an equal sign and the reserved word **record.** A list of field identifiers with their corresponding data types precedes the **end** statement that terminates the declaration.

STYLE TIP

There are many different ways to indent the components of a record type. In one, the field identifiers are indented two spaces from **record,** with **end** lining up with **record,** as in:

```
type
  censustype = record
                 name : string[20];
                 age : integer
               end;
```

In another, the field identifiers are indented two spaces from the name of the record type, with **end** indented one space from the type name, as in:

```
type
  censustype = record
    name : string[20];
    age : integer
  end;
```

The remainder of the text adopts the second of these two conventions.

Example

```
type
  stringtype = string[20];
  cartype = record
    model : stringtype;
    mpg : real
  end;
var
  car : cartype;
```

The variable *car*, a record of type *cartype*, has two fields: a string representing a model of a car, and a real representing the miles-per-gallon rating of that model.

If two field names are of the same type, they can be separated by commas before specifying their common type.

Example

```
type
  temptype = record
    hightemp,
    lowtemp : real
  end;
```

Both the field identifiers *hightemp* and *lowtemp* are reals, so they can be included in the same field identifier list. They are listed on separate lines to make it easier to pick out the field names of the record *temptype*.

Once a record is declared, you must have access to each field of the record. Whereas subscripts distinguish among element components in array structures, to specify a particular field in a record requires a variable record identifier, followed by a period and the field name. Figure 10.2 illustrates the components of the *car* record defined in a previous example. The *model* field of the variable *car* is represented by *car.model* and the *mpg* field by *car.mpg*.

The use of records and their field identifiers is governed by the data type specified for that identifier; for example, a real field identifier is allowed in any statement that permits real identifiers.

Figure 10.2
Structure of Record *car*

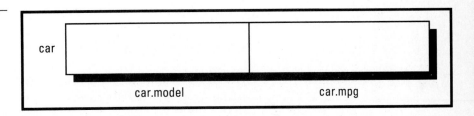

Examples

```
car.model := 'Hawk';

if car.mpg < 10
  then
    Writeln ('Lemon!')
  else
    Writeln ('OK!');

Writeln (car.model);
Writeln (car.mpg);
```

As these three examples show, field identifiers in the *car* record defined earlier can be part of an assignment statement, a selection structure, or an output statement.

If an attempt is made to reference a field without its record name, an error message may result.

One significant advantage of storing data in record format is that an entire record can be passed to a subprogram by just specifying the record name and its type.

Example

```
procedure Average (var grade : gradetype)
  var
     sum : integer;
begin
  sum := grade.test1 + grade.test2;
  grade.average := sum / 2
end;
```

call:
```
  Average (student1);
```

Suppose the global variable *student1* and the local variable *grade* are of **record** type *gradetype;* that is, each contains fields for a student's name, scores on two exams, and the average of the exam scores. All four fields of the record *student1* are passed to the procedure **Average** using a single parameter.

Figure 10.3
Record *invoice* Containing
an Array

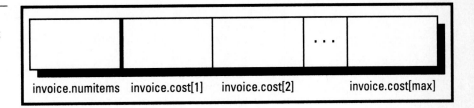

invoice.numitems   invoice.cost[1]   invoice.cost[2]   invoice.cost[max]

Records of Arrays

Record fields also may be arrays. One such structure is illustrated in Figure 10.3. The first field of the record *invoice* contains a count of the number of items in the second field (the array *cost)* that are active. The number of elements in that array is determined by a constant called *max*. A possible declaration for this structure is:

```
const
  max = 100;
type
  costtype = array[1..max] of real;
  invoicetype = record
    numitems : integer;
    cost : costtype
  end;
var
  invoice : invoicetype;
```

Example

```
total := 0;
for i := 1 to invoice.numitems do
  total := total + invoice.cost[i];
Writeln ('Total: $', total:6:2);
```

The *numitems* field determines the number of passes through a loop needed to find the sum of all the active array elements.

Records of Records

One record also may be a field of another record, as shown in Figure 10.4. The record *status* has two fields: date and time. Each one of these fields is also a record. *Date* has fields named *month, day,* and *year,* while *time* has fields named *hour, minute,* and *ampm*. A possible declaration for this structure is:

```
type
  daytype = 1..31;
  yeartype = 1900..2100;
  hourtype = 1..12;
  minutetype = 0..59;
  datetype = record
    month : string[10];
    day : daytype;
    year : yeartype
  end;
  timetype = record
    hour : hourtype;
    minute : minutetype;
    ampm : string[2]
  end
  statustype = record
    date : datetype;
    time : timetype
  end;
var
  status : statustype;
```

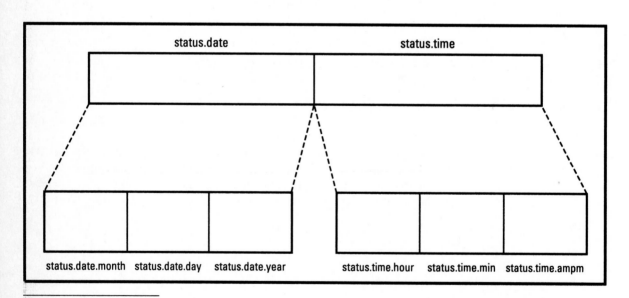

Figure 10.4
Record *status*
Containing Records

The *ampm* field in *timetype* consists of a string of two letters, *am* or *pm,* following the numeric value of the time.

Record types must be defined before they are referenced in a **type** declaration. In our example, the declarations for *datetype* and *timetype* must precede the declaration for *statustype,* or an error will result.

Example

```
Write ('Enter month: ');
Readln (status.date.month);
Write ('Enter day: ');
Readln (status.date.day);
Write ('Enter year: ');
Readln (status.date.year);
```

The identifier name for *month* must be preceded by its record name *(date)* and a period. Since *date* is also a field in a record, it must be preceded by the name of the record of which it is a part and a period.

The **with** Statement

Because it can be tedious to continually prefix each field name with a record variable and a period, you can utilize a **with** statement that allows access to field identifiers with a single reference to their common record name.

FORMAT: **with** \<record identifier> **do**
            \<statement>;

The record name, without the period, follows the reserved word **with** and is followed by **do.** All references to fields of that record name in **\<statement>** need only contain the field identifier name and do not have to be preceded by the record name and the period. A compound statement following **with** must be enclosed in a **begin-end** pair.

Examples

```
with car do
  model := 'Hawk';

with car do
  if mpg < 10
    then
      Writeln ('Lemon!')
    else
      Writeln ('OK!');

with car do
  begin
    Writeln (model);
    Writeln (mpg)
  end;
```

These three examples behave exactly the same as those in a previous set. Rather than prefacing each *model* or *mpg* with *car.,* the statements containing these field references are enclosed in a **with** structure.

With structures may be nested if records are fields of other records.

Example

```
with status do
  with date do
    begin
      Write ('Enter month: ');
      Readln (month);
      Write ('Enter day: ');
      Readln (day);
      Write ('Enter year: ');
      Readln (year)
    end;
```

The outer **with** statement automatically puts *status.* before any field reference within its structure. The prefix *date.* is implied for references contained in the inner **with** structure. Therefore, *month* in the first **Readln** statement is, in effect, *status.date.month*. *Day* and *year* are treated in a similar fashion.

Arrays of Records

Arrays were designed to store data of the same type, including records. Consider the array of records of blood donors shown in Figure 10.5. Each record contains fields for a name, bloodtype (A, B, AB, or O), and Rh factor (+ or −). The figure shows the names by which several locations are accessed; the subscript that selects one of the records is followed by a period and a field name. A declaration defining this array structure follows.

```
const
  max = 100;
type
  nametype = string[20];
  bloodtype = string[2];
  rhfactortype = char;
  donortype = record
    name : nametype;
    blood : bloodtype;
    rhfactor : rhfactortype
   end;
  listype = array[1..max] of donortype;
var
  donor : listype;
```

A sentinel value can be stored in the array location following the last element to signal the end of the active section of the array. When access to the data in the array is desired, a loop continues to read items until this sentinel value is reached.

Another method for determining the end of the active portion of an array is to initialize the field containing the sentinel value for the entire array. As proper values are entered for this field, they replace the sentinel value; thus, the first array element containing the sentinel value signals the end of the active elements. This method takes a lot of time if the array is large.

Figure 10.5
Array of Records

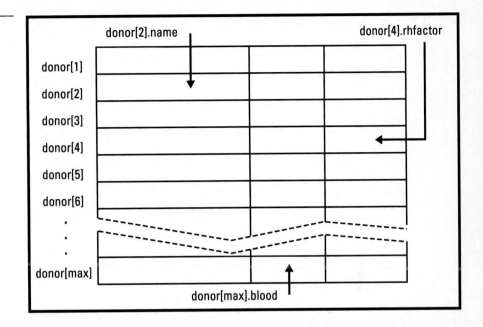

After a sentinel value for active array elements has been stored, a search through the array need only go as far as the array element containing this value rather than through the entire set of declared elements.

The **with** statement can contain an array name with a variable index, as in *donor[i]*, in many cases. If *i* is 1, then all references to field names are prefixed by *donor[1]*. If *i* changes, the prefix changes, and thus only a single **with** statement is required for an entire array of records. Avoid using **with** when entering data into an array of records; doing so produces unpredictable results.

Example

```
i := 1;
count := 0;
Write ('Enter type: ');
Readln (target);
with donor[i] do
  while name <> 'zzz' do
    begin
      if blood = target
        then
          count := count + 1;
      i := i + 1
    end;
Writeln (count);
```

This code counts the number of donors with a specific blood type *(target)* in the structure defined earlier. The **with** statement outside the loop means that only the field identifier has to be specified. The **while** loop continues to search the array until the *name* field contains *zzz*. If the *blood* field matches the *target* value, then *count* is updated; otherwise, the search continues with the next element in the array.

10.3 Application in Searching: It's Very Continental

Information retrieval is used in many data processing applications. In such applications, one of the fields of a record acts as a *key*—a data item identifying that record. Each record may have a unique key field (called the primary key), or that field value may be shared by many records. Also, a single record may have many keys. *Searching* is a process of looking for a certain record, one of whose key fields matches a specific, or target, value. For example, when information on someone's credit card record is desired, the key field contains the credit card number. The key fields of all the cardholder records are compared with an entered credit card number. When a match is found, all the information in the record is returned for processing.

The search method for a collection of data is determined by how that data is stored and whether the key field is unique or not. In the credit card example, the account number is a unique field. Once the search locates that number, there is no need to search further. A search also may be made for every cardholder whose unpaid balance is above $2000. In this case, the search cannot be terminated after the first record is found, since many cardholders may fall in this category. For the remainder of this chapter, it is assumed that the key field is unique.

Although in most cases it is not as efficient as other methods, the linear search can be used for any collection of data, regardless of how it is stored. After a target value is entered, the key field for the first record is compared with the target value. If there is a match, the processing stops and that record is returned for processing. Otherwise, the key field of the second record is compared to the target. The searching continues, record by record, until a match is found or the end of the collection of data is reached.

Table 10.1
Continent Information

Continent	Area (in 1,000 sq. mi.)	1985 Population (in thousands)	Percentage Growth 1980–1985
Africa	11,700	538,000	2.9%
Antarctica	5,400	0	0.0
Asia	17,250	2,946,200	1.8
Europe	3,800	673,900	0.3
North America	9,400	397,400	0.9
Oceania	3,300	24,200	1.5
South America	6,900	263,300	2.4

Table 10.1 gives the areas, 1985 populations, and population growth of the seven continents. Write a program that stores this information in an array of records with fields for the name, area, population, and growth. The *growth* field represents the percentage increase in population over the 5-year period from 1980 to 1985. Calculate and store the population and area for the entire world in an eighth record. The growth percentage for the world in the same time period is 1.7%; store that value in the proper field of the world record. A fifth field for the population density (population per square mile) should be calculated and stored as part of the array. The program then should search for and display all the information in the array for a selected continent or the world and project the population for a specified five-year period beyond 1985, assuming the growth rate remains constant over that period. The end of the array should be indicated by a sentinel value in the name field.

ANALYSIS OF THE PROBLEM   The input and output quantities are shown in Figure 10.6.

MODULAR DESIGN OF
THE SOLUTION
As shown in Figure 10.7, the filling of the continent arrays consists of entering data from the keyboard, calculating the data in the world record, and finding the population density. For each selection, the continent table is searched for the proper entry, the projected population calculated from that data, and the results displayed.

Figure 10.6
Continent Information
Input/Output Chart

Input	Output
Continent name	Continent or world name
Area	Area
1985 population	1985 population
Percent growth	Percent growth
Year for estimated population	Population density
	Future Population

DESIGN OF THE
STRUCTURE OF THE
MODULES

CONTINENT INFORMATION
   FILL TABLE
   GET INFORMATION

FILL TABLE
   ENTER DATA
   WORLD DATA
   POPULATION DENSITY

ENTER DATA
   initialize index to 1
   enter name
   while name not "end"
      enter area, population, growth
      update index
      enter name

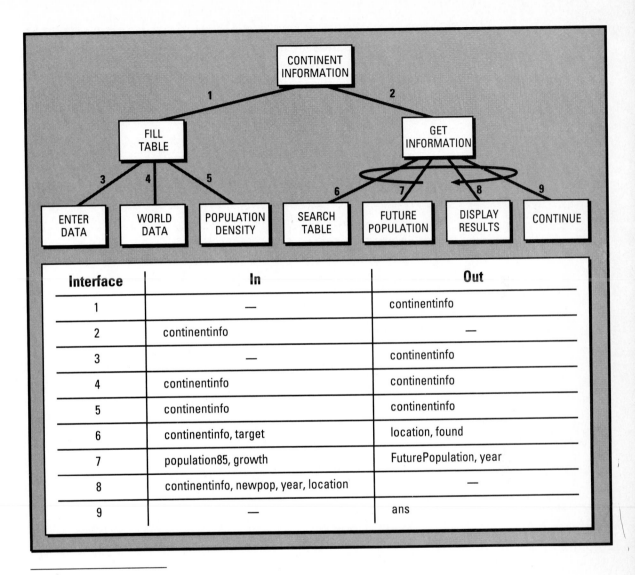

Interface	In	Out
1	—	continentinfo
2	continentinfo	—
3	—	continentinfo
4	continentinfo	continentinfo
5	continentinfo	continentinfo
6	continentinfo, target	location, found
7	population85, growth	FuturePopulation, year
8	continentinfo, newpop, year, location	—
9	—	ans

Figure 10.7
Continent Information
Solution Design and
Module Interface Table

WORLD DATA
  initialize areasum, popsum
  initialize index to 1
  repeat
    sum area
    sum population
    update index
  until no more continents
  store sums in proper fields of new record
  store "World" in name field of this record
  store 1.7 for growth field of this record
  store sentinel name in next record

POPULATION DENSITY
  initialize index to 1
  repeat
    find density (area/population)
    update index
  until sentinel reached

GET INFORMATION
  repeat
    accept target name
    SEARCH TABLE
    if found
      then
        FUTURE POPULATION
        DISPLAY RESULTS
      else
        display "not found" message
    CONTINUE
  until done

SEARCH TABLE
  initialize index to 1
  initialize found to false
  while additional continents and not found
    if target = name
      then
        location = counter
        found = true
      else
        update index
  if not found
    then
      location = 0

FUTURE POPULATION
    initialize tempop with population85
    repeat
        enter year for estimated population
    until proper year entered
    find number of growth periods
    for each of the growth periods
        update tempop (= tempop × (1 + growth))

DISPLAY RESULTS
    display continent information from array
    display newpop

CONTINUE
    accept "continue" or "exit" response

PRODUCTION OF CODE AND VERIFICATION OF SOLUTION

In the **EnterData** procedure, the name, area, 1985 population, and percent growth are put in appropriate fields in each record:

```
procedure EnterData (var continentinfo : tabletype);
  const
    sentinel = 'end';
  var
    index : integer;
begin
  index := 1;
  ClrScr;
  Writeln ('CONTINENT INFORMATION DATA ENTRY');
  Writeln;
  Writeln ('Type "end" for continent to stop entry: ');
  Write ('Continent name: ');
  Readln (continentinfo[index].name);
  while continentinfo[index].name <> sentinel do
    begin
      Write ('Area (in 1000 sq. mi.): ');
      Readln (continentinfo[index].area);
      Write ('1985 population in thousands: ');
      Readln (continentinfo[index].population85);
      Write ('Percent growth from 1980 to 1985: ');
      Readln (continentinfo[index].growth);
      index := index + 1;
      Writeln;
      Writeln ('Type "end" for continent to stop entry: ');
      Write ('Continent name: ');
      Readln (continentinfo[index].name)
    end
end;
```

The string *end* is stored in the *name* field of the record following the last continent. In future references to the array, records are processed until this sentinel is reached.

The area and population for the world are calculated in the procedure WorldData by summing those quantities for the continents:

```
procedure WorldData (var continentinfo : tabletype);
  const
    sentinel = 'end';
  var
    areasum,
    popsum
      : longint;
    index
      : integer;
begin
  areasum := 0;
  popsum := 0;
  index := 1;
  repeat
    with continentinfo[index] do
      begin
        areasum := areasum + area;
        popsum := popsum + population85;
        index := index + 1
      end
  until continentinfo[index].name = sentinel;
  with continentinfo[index] do
    begin
      name := 'World';
      area := areasum;
      population85 := popsum;
      growth := 1.7
    end;
  index := index + 1;
  continentinfo[index].name := sentinel
end;
```

This data, as well as the name "World" and a percent growth of 1.7, are stored in the record formerly occupied by the sentinel. The sentinel value is then moved to the name field of the record following the one containing the world data.

After the population density is calculated by dividing the population by the area, a prompt in the `GetInformation` procedure is issued requesting the name of a continent. Once that name is supplied, the `SearchTable` procedure is called and searched:

```
procedure SearchTable (continentinfo : tabletype; target : nametype;
         var location : integer; var found : boolean);
  const
    sentinel = 'end';
  var
    index
        : integer;
begin
  index := 1;
  found := false;
  while (continentinfo[index].name <> sentinel) and (not found) do
    if continentinfo[index].name = target
      then
        begin
          location := index;
          found := true
        end
      else
        index := index + 1;
  if not found
    then
      location := 0
end;
```

The loop that cycles through the records starting with the first terminates if the end of the data table has been reached or a match for the target value has been found. If the sought-after continent has not been found, a message is displayed and the user asked whether he or she wants to continue. If a match for the continent name has been found, the function `Future-Population` is called:

```
function FuturePopulation (population85 : longint; growth : real;
         var year : integer) : longint;
  var
    tempop
      : real;
    i,
    growthperiods
      : integer;
begin
  tempop := population85;
  repeat
    ClrScr;
    GotoXY (20,5);
    Writeln ('The current data gives the population in');
    GotoXY (20,6);
    Writeln ('1985. Enter the future year for which a');
    GotoXY (20,7);
    Writeln ('population projection is desired.');
    GotoXY (20,9);
    Writeln ('The year must be a multiple of 5.');
    GotoXY (25,12);
    Write ('Year: ');
    Readln (year)
  until (year >= 1985) and (year mod 5 = 0);
  growthperiods := (year - 1985) div 5;
  for i := 1 to growthperiods do
    tempop := tempop * (1 + growth/100);
  FuturePopulation := Round(tempop)
end;
```

The **repeat** loop only allows a future year that is a multiple of 5 (**year mod 5 = 0**) or is greater than 1985. The number of growth periods is determined by the difference between the input year and 1985, divided by 5. The percentage increase is added to the current population for each of the five-year periods, and this value is returned through the function name.

The identifier *tempop,* used to determine future populations, is declared as a **real,** since the growth formula produces a real result that cannot be stored in an **integer** identifier. After the final value of *tempop* is calculated, it is rounded before being returned to **FuturePopulation.**

Even though **FuturePopulation** is a function, *year* is returned to the calling procedure **GetInformation** through a variable parameter. This value is then passed to the **DisplayResults** procedure, where the desired information is displayed.

After the verification process, the final version of the solution is documented (Figure 10.8).

Figure 10.8
ContinentInformation
Program Listing

```pascal
program ContinentInformation;
{-------------------------------------------------------------------}
{ PROGRAM:        Information on the Continents                      }
{ PROGRAMMER:     G. O'Graphee                                       }
{ DATE:           September 11, 1990                                 }
{                                                                   }
{ This program stores the name, area, 1985 population, and percent  }
{ growth between 1980 and 1985 of the seven continents. It also     }
{ calculates and stores the population and area for the entire world }
{ (The growth percentage for the world in the same time period is   }
{ 1.7%). as well as the population density (population per square   }
{ mile) for the continents and the world. The program permits searches }
{ for and displays all the information for a selected continent or  }
{ the world, and projects the population for a specified five-year  }
{ period beyond 1985 assuming a constant growth rate over that period. }
{                                                                   }
{ INPUT           name of continent                                 }
{                 area of continent                                 }
{                 1985 population                                   }
{                 percent growth from 1980 to 1985                  }
{                 year for estimated population                     }
{                                                                   }
{ OUTPUT          name of continent                                 }
{                 area of continent                                 }
{                 1985 population                                   }
{                 percent growth from 1980 to 1985                  }
{                 population density                                }
{                 year for estimated population                     }
{                 estimated population                              }
{-------------------------------------------------------------------}
  uses
    Crt;                              { screen formatting commands library }
  type
    nametype = string[20];
    continentype = record                        { record of continents }
      name : nametype;
      area,
      population85 : longint;
      growth,
      popdensity : real
     end;
    tabletype = array[1..20] of continentype;
                                         { table of continent records }
```

(continued)

```
var
  continentinfo                                    { continent table }
    : tabletype;

procedure EnterData (var continentinfo : tabletype);
{---------------------------------------------------------------------}
{ Accepts name, area, 1985 population and percent growth for          }
{ seven continents.                                                   }
{                                                                     }
{ IN            none                                                  }
{                                                                     }
{ OUT           continentinfo:  table of continent records            }
{---------------------------------------------------------------------}
  const
    sentinel = 'end';                      { end of active array elements }
  var
    index                                        { array index }
      : integer;
begin
  ClrScr;
  index := 1;
  Writeln ('CONTINENT INFORMATION DATA ENTRY');
  Writeln;
  Writeln ('Type "end" for continent to stop entry: ');
  Write ('Continent name: ');
  Readln (continentinfo[index].name);
  while continentinfo[index].name <> sentinel do
    begin
      Write ('Area (in 1000 sq. mi.): ');
      Readln (continentinfo[index].area);
      Write ('1985 population in thousands: ');
      Readln (continentinfo[index].population85);
      Write ('Percent growth from 1980 to 1985: ');
      Readln (continentinfo[index].growth);
      index := index + 1;
      Writeln;
      Writeln ('Type "end" for continent to stop entry: ');
      Write ('Continent name: ');
      Readln (continentinfo[index].name)
    end
end;
```

```
procedure WorldData (var continentinfo : tabletype);
{-----------------------------------------------------------------}
{ Accepts name and growth percentage and calculates area and      }
{ 1985 population for world.                                       }
{                                                                 }
{ IN              continentinfo:  table of continent records      }
{                                                                 }
{ OUT             continentinfo:  table of continent records      }
{-----------------------------------------------------------------}
  const
    sentinel = 'end';                    { end of active array elements }
  var
    areasum,                                        { sum for areas }
    popsum                             { sum of 1985 populations }
      : longint;
    index                                           { array index }
      : integer;
begin
  areasum := 0;
  popsum := 0;
  index := 1;
  repeat
    with continentinfo[index] do
      begin
        areasum := areasum + area;
        popsum := popsum + population85;
        index := index + 1
      end
  until continentinfo[index].name = sentinel;
  with continentinfo[index] do
    begin
      name := 'World';
      area := areasum;
      population85 := popsum;
      growth := 1.7
    end;
  index := index + 1;
  continentinfo[index].name := sentinel
end;
```

(continued)

```
procedure PopulationDensity (var continentinfo : tabletype);
{-----------------------------------------------------------------------}
{ Calculates population density for seven continents and world by       }
{ dividing populations by areas.                                        }
{                                                                       }
{ IN            continentinfo:  table of continent records             }
{                                                                       }
{ OUT           continentinfo:  table of continent records             }
{-----------------------------------------------------------------------}
  const
    sentinel = 'end';                        { end of active array elements }
  var
    index                                              { array index }
      : integer;
begin
  index := 1;
  repeat
    with continentinfo[index] do
      begin
        popdensity := population85/area;
        index := index + 1
      end
  until continentinfo[index].name = sentinel
end;


procedure FillTable (var continentinfo : tabletype);
{-----------------------------------------------------------------------}
{ Accepts data for continents, accepts and calculates data for          }
{ world, and calculates population density for continents and world.    }
{                                                                       }
{ IN            none                                                    }
{                                                                       }
{ OUT           continentinfo:  table of continent records             }
{-----------------------------------------------------------------------}
begin
  EnterData (continentinfo);
  WorldData (continentinfo);
  PopulationDensity (continentinfo)
end;
```

```
procedure SearchTable (continentinfo : tabletype; target : nametype;
           var location : integer; var found : boolean);
{------------------------------------------------------------------}
{ Searches continent table for given continent and returns whether  }
{ it is found or not. If found, it returns the record number that   }
{ contains the information. A location value of 0 is returned if no  }
{ record is found.                                                  }
{                                                                   }
{ IN           continentinfo: table of continent records           }
{              target:        continent name sought                }
{                                                                   }
{ OUT          location:      index of continent sought            }
{              found:         indicates whether target was found   }
{------------------------------------------------------------------}
  const
    sentinel = 'end';                      { end of active array elements }
  var
    index                                           { array index }
       : integer;
begin
  index := 1;
  found := false;
  while (continentinfo[index].name <> sentinel) and (not found) do
    if continentinfo[index].name = target
      then
        begin
          location := index;
          found := true
        end
      else
        index := index + 1;
  if not found
    then
      location := 0
end;
```

(continued)

```
function FuturePopulation (population85 : longint; growth : real;
          var year : integer) : longint;
{------------------------------------------------------------------}
{ Calculates estimated population in a future year by using the    }
{ percent growth to find the new population for five-year          }
{ time periods.                                                    }
{                                                                  }
{ IN          population85: 1985 population                        }
{             growth:       percent growth for 1980 to 1985        }
{                                                                  }
{ OUT         FuturePopulation: estimated future population        }
{             year:         year for which population is estimated }
{------------------------------------------------------------------}
  var
    tempop                                  { population accumulator }
      : real;
    i,                                            { loop index }
    growthperiods                    { number of times growth applied }
      : integer;
begin
  tempop := population85;
  repeat
    ClrScr;
    GotoXY (20,5);
    Writeln ('The current data gives the population in');
    GotoXY (20,6);
    Writeln ('1985. Enter the future year for which a');
    GotoXY (20,7);
    Writeln ('population projection is desired.');
    GotoXY (20,9);
    Writeln ('The year must be a multiple of 5.');
    GotoXY (25,12);
    Write ('Year: ');
    Readln (year)
  until (year >= 1985) and (year mod 5 = 0);
  growthperiods := (year - 1985) div 5;
  for i := 1 to growthperiods do
    tempop := tempop * (1 + growth/100);
  FuturePopulation := Round(tempop)
end;
```

```
procedure DisplayResults (continentinfo : tabletype;
          year, location : integer; newpop : longint );
{----------------------------------------------------------------------}
{ Displays name, area, 1985 population, percent growth, and year       }
{ for which population is estimated, and the estimated population      }
{ for a given continent.                                              }
{                                                                     }
{ IN           continentinfo:  table of continent records            }
{              year:          year for which population estimate made }
{              location:      record number for continent data       }
{              newpop:        estimated population for future year    }
{                                                                     }
{ OUT          none                                                  }
{----------------------------------------------------------------------}
begin
  ClrScr;
  GotoXY (25,1);
  Writeln ('CONTINENT INFORMATION');
  with continentinfo[location] do
    begin
      GotoXY (15,5);
      Writeln ('CONTINENT: ', name);
      GotoXY (15,7);
      Writeln ('AREA (in 1000 sq. mi.): ',area:6);
      GotoXY (15,9);
      Writeln ('POPULATION (in 1000s): ',population85:7);
      GotoXY (15,11);
      Writeln ('GROWTH PERCENTAGE: ', growth:3:1, '%');
      GotoXY (15,13);
      Writeln ('POPULATION DENSITY: ', popdensity:6:2);
      GotoXY (15,15);
      Write ('POPULATION IN ', year:4, ': ', newpop:7);
      GotoXY (15,16);
      Writeln ('(estimated, in 1000s)')
    end
end;
```

(continued)

```
procedure Continue (var ans : char);
{------------------------------------------------------------------------}
{ Asks whether user wants to continue using the program.                 }
{                                                                        }
{ IN            none                                                     }
{                                                                        }
{ OUT           ans:  response to continue query                        }
{------------------------------------------------------------------------}
begin
  GotoXY (1,23);
  Write ('Press "x" to end, another key to continue -->');
  ans := ReadKey
end;


procedure GetInformation (continentinfo : tabletype);
{------------------------------------------------------------------------}
{ Accepts the name of a continent for an information search and          }
{ searches the table for a matching record. If the record is            }
{ found, the estimated future population is found and results           }
{ displayed; if the record is not found, a message is displayed.        }
{ An option to continue searching for information is provided.          }
{                                                                        }
{ IN            continentinfo: table of continent records               }
{                                                                        }
{ OUT           none                                                    }
{------------------------------------------------------------------------}
  var
    ans                            { response to continue query }
      : char;
    target              { name of continent whose record is sought }
      : nametype;
    oldpop,                             { 1985 population }
    newpop                    { estimated future population }
      : longint;
    chg                  { percent growth between 1980 and 1985 }
      : real;
    location,                  { record number of record sought }
    year            { year for which future population is estimated }
      : integer;
    found                { true if record found; false otherwise }
      : boolean;
```

```
begin
  repeat
    ClrScr;
    GotoXY (10,1);
    Writeln ('INFORMATION ON THE CONTINENTS');
    Writeln;
    Write ('Enter continent name: ');
    Readln (target);
    SearchTable (continentinfo, target, location, found);
    if found
      then
        begin
          oldpop := continentinfo[location].population85;
          chg := continentinfo[location].growth;
          newpop := FuturePopulation (oldpop, chg, year);
          DisplayResults (continentinfo, year, location, newpop)
        end
      else
        begin
          GotoXY (10,5);
          Writeln ('No information found for ',target)
        end;
    Continue (ans)
  until (ans = 'x')
end;

begin
  FillTable (continentinfo);
  GetInformation (continentinfo)
end.
```

10.4 Application in Sorting: Par for the Course

The ordering of a list of items (*sorting*) is a process that can be employed to improve the efficiency of searching or to produce a list arranged according to some criterion. It would be very difficult to find someone's phone number from an unalphabetized list of names or to produce student rankings from a list of unsorted grade point averages. In the case of the phone numbers, the name is the sorting key and records containing those names are sorted in ascending or alphabetical order, that is, from "lowest" to "highest." The grade point averages are the criterion in the latter case, where the records containing those averages are sorted in descending order, or from the highest value to the lowest.

One method of sorting data is called the *bubble sort*. It is not as efficient as other techniques, but it is relatively easy to understand. Figure 10.9 shows how the bubble sort arranges an initially unsorted list of five elements in ascending order.

This bubble sort starts by comparing the first and the second elements in the list, 35 and 47. They are already in the proper order, ascending in this case, so their positions are unchanged and the process continues by comparing the second and the third (25). Because 25 is less than 47, their positions are interchanged. The new third element, 47, is compared with the fourth (81), and no change takes place since these two values are in the proper order. Then 81 is compared to 15 and their positions are interchanged, because 15 is less than 81. This completes the first pass through the list, in which four comparisons and two interchanges were made. The smaller elements "floated," or "bubbled," toward the top of the list, while the largest one, 81, sunk to the bottom. Since 81 is in its final position, it need not be involved in future passes through the list.

The second pass restarts the process at the beginning of the new list. Since 25 is less than 35, their positions are interchanged. The 35 in position 2

Figure 10.9
Bubble Sort Example

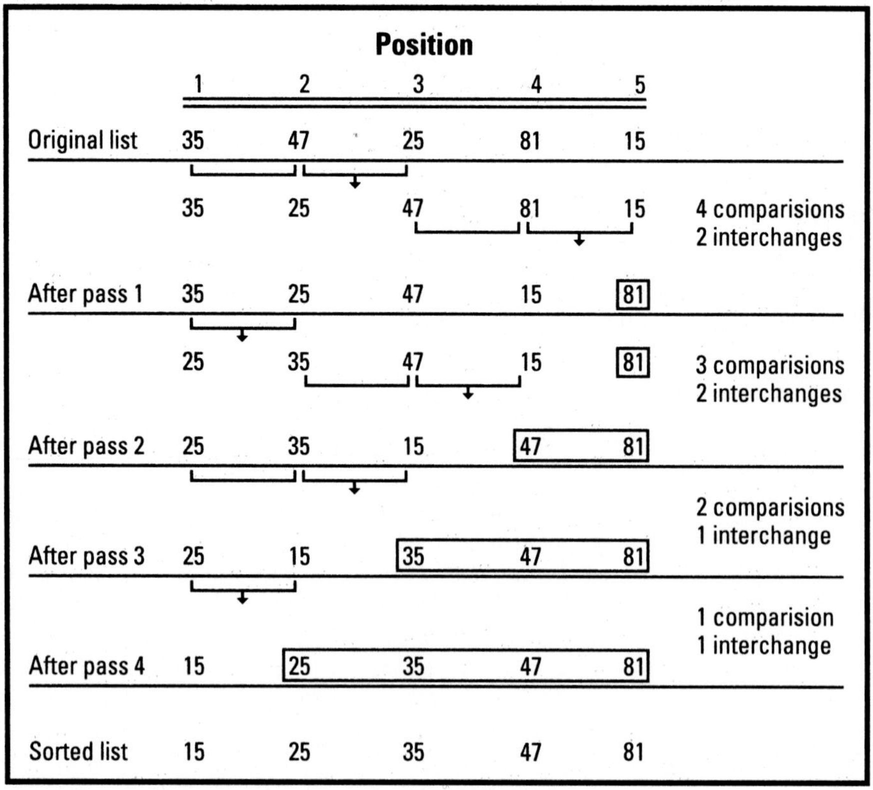

is compared to the 47 in position 3, with no change resulting. Since 15 is less than 47, 47 moves to position 4 and 15 to position 3. Three comparisons and two interchanges took place in this second pass. Now 47 has sunk to its final position, and the next pass concerns only the first three list elements.

During the third pass, 15 moves to position 2 and 35 moves to its final position. This pass requires two comparisons that result in one interchange. A fourth pass is needed to put the entire list in ascending order.

The number of comparisons in any pass through the list is always one less than the number of elements in the unsorted portion of the list. For example, after pass 2 is completed, only three elements are in the unsorted portion of the list, so only two comparisons have to be made.

Four passes, the maximum number, were required to put the list in order. Although the maximum number of passes needed to sort a list of n elements is $n - 1$, the process can be terminated earlier if a complete pass produces no interchanges. Consider the almost-sorted list in Figure 10.10. After the initial pass, which resulted in four comparisons and a single interchange, the list is ordered. Another pass produced no interchanges, which signals that the sorting process need not be continued.

In summary, the bubble sort for a list of n elements can stop if $n - 1$ passes have been completed, or if a single pass produces no interchanges.

Figure 10.10
Bubble sort with
Almost-Sorted List

		Position			
	1	2	3	4	5
Original list	23	34	41	77	52
					4 comparisions 1 interchange
After pass 1	23	34	41	52	77
					3 comparisions 0 interchanges
After pass 2					
Sorted list	23	34	41	52	77

Example

```
switch := true;
pass := 1;
while (pass <= max) and switch do
  begin
    switch := false;
    for i := 1 to max-pass do
      if a[i] > a[i+1]
        then
          begin
            switch := true;
            Interchange(a[i], a[i+1])
          end; { if...then }
    pass := pass + 1
  end { while }
```

This code sorts the elements of array *a* in ascending order. The Boolean *switch* is true if a position interchange has been made and false otherwise. The variable *pass* counts the number of passes. *Max* is an integer whose value is the number of elements in the list. **Interchange** is a procedure that interchanges the positions of its two parameters. *Switch* is initialized to true to enter the **while** loop. At the beginning of each pass it is set to false and the elements are compared. For example, when *i* is 1, *a[1]* is compared to *a[2]*, and if necessary the elements are interchanged and the Boolean *switch* updated. The process continues until the maximum number of passes is attained or a switch has not occurred. The terminating value for the **for** loop depends on the pass number: If the list has 10 elements and the pass number is 3, *i* initiates 10 − 3 = 7 comparisons, since after two passes the last two elements are in their proper positions.

Write a menu-driven program that provides up-to-date information for a golf tournament. Choices from the menu start the tournament by accepting the names of participating golfers and clearing the scoreboard; accepting the value of par for the golf course; entering the number of strokes for each golfer in a particular round and updating the scores for the tournament; allowing the scoreboard to be sorted by name or by score; and displaying the current scoreboard. Data for each golfer should be stored in a record containing the golfer's name, scores for each of four rounds (in number of strokes), and the cumulative score for the tournament, specifying the total number of strokes above or below par. For example, if 72 is par for the course and a golfer obtains scores of 69 and 78 for the first two rounds of the tournament, the cumulative score for this tournament is −3 + (+6), or +3. The field of golfers should be stored as an array of individual golfer records in another tournament scoreboard record that also contains the par value of the course as well as the number of participants.

ANALYSIS OF THE PROBLEM The input and output values are specified in Figure 10.11.

MODULAR DESIGN OF THE SOLUTION Figure 10.12a shows the solution design and Figure 10.12b, the module interface table outlining the solution.

The **START TOURNAMENT** module calls modules that accept the names of the participants and clears the score table. If the table is not initialized,

Figure 10.11
Golf Scores
Input/Output Chart

Input	Output
Golfer names	Golfer names
Par for course	Round scores
Scores for rounds	Tournament score

extraneous characters appear in the display of round scores not yet entered. The scores are entered one round at a time and update the cumulative scores for the entire tournament. A sort menu allows sorting by either name or score. Both the **SORT BY NAME** and **SORT BY SCORE** modules call **INTERCHANGE** for the swapping of records in the array. The **CONTINUE** module allows output to remain on the screen until the user presses a key.

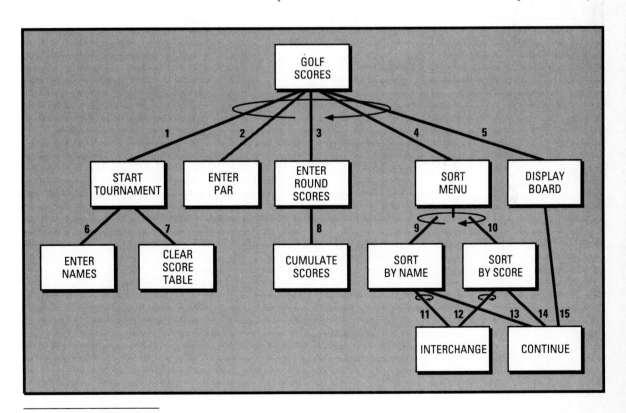

Figure 10.12a
Golf Scores Solution
Design

Figure 10.12b
Golf Scores Module
Interface Table

Interface	In	Out
1	—	board
2	—	board, par
3	board	board
4	board	board
5	board	—
6	board	board
7	board	board
8	board	board
9	board	board
10	board	board
11	golfer[i], golfer [i+1]	golfer[i], golfer[i+1]
12	golfer[i], golfer [i+1]	golfer[i], golfer[i+1]
13	—	—
14	—	—
15	—	—

DESIGN OF THE
STRUCTURE OF THE
MODULES

```
GOLF SCORES
   repeat
      display main menu
      case menu choice is
         start
            START TOURNAMENT
         par
            ENTER PAR
         round scores
            ENTER ROUND SCORES
         sort
            SORT MENU
         display
            DISPLAY BOARD
   until the exit choice is entered
```

START TOURNAMENT
  ENTER NAMES
  CLEAR SCORE TABLE

ENTER NAMES
    initialize count to 1
    enter name
    while name is not sentinel do
       update count
       enter name
    number of golfers is count − 1

CLEAR SCORE TABLE
    for each golfer
       for each round
          clear score location

ENTER PAR
  accept par value

ENTER ROUND SCORES
    accept round number
    for each golfer
       accept round score
    CUMULATE SCORES

CUMULATE SCORES
    for each golfer
       initialize total above or below par to 0
       for each round
          find difference between score and par
          update total
       store total in record

SORT MENU
  repeat
    display sort menu
    case choice is
       name
          SORT BY NAME
       score
          SORT BY SCORE
  until exit choice is entered

SORT BY NAME
  initialize switch flag to true
  initialize pass counter to 1
  while (pass counter equal to or less than number of golfers)
      and (switches have been made) do
    set switch to false
    for each unsorted item
      if "higher" golfer name follows
        "lower" golfer name in alphabetical order
      then
        set switch to true
        INTERCHANGE
    add 1 to pass counter
  CONTINUE

INTERCHANGE
  store first record in temporary location
  store second record in first record
  store temp contents in second record

CONTINUE
  accept any keystroke

SORT BY SCORE
  initialize switch flag to true
  initialize pass counter to 1
  while (pass counter equal to or less than number of golfers)
      and (switches have been made) do
    set switch to false
    for each unsorted item
      if "higher" golfer score > "lower" golfer score
      then
        set switch to true
        INTERCHANGE
    add 1 to pass counter
  CONTINUE

DISPLAY BOARD
  output table headings
  for each golfer
    output name
    output round scores
    output total score
  CONTINUE

PRODUCTION OF CODE
AND VERIFICATION
OF SOLUTION

Information for each golfer is kept in a record called *golfertype* that consists of the golfer's name, an array of scores for the four rounds of the tournament, and the total score:

```
nametype = string[20];
roundtype = array[1..4] of string[3];
golfertype = record
  name : nametype;
  roundscore : roundtype;
  totscore : integer
end;
```

The record of type *golfertype* is a field of a larger record called *boardtype* whose other fields store the par value of the course and the number of golfers in the tournament:

```
boardtype = record
  par,
  numgolfers : integer;
  golfer : array[1..100] of golfertype
end;
```

This arrangement facilitates the passing of data between the modules of the program by declaring *board* to be of type *boardtype.*

Even though the round scores are integers, they are stored as three-character strings and initialized to the null string so that blanks appear in the score column of the display board rather than a numerical value such as 0. These string values must be converted to their corresponding numeric values before total scores are calculated. The built-in Turbo Pascal procedure **Val** does the conversion in the **CumulateScores** procedure:

```
procedure CumulateScores (var board : boardtype);
  var
    i,
    j,
    total,
    score,
    code,
    diff
      : integer;
```

(continued)

```
begin
  for i := 1 to board.numgolfers do
    with board.golfer[i] do
      begin
        total := 0;
        for j := 1 to 4 do
          if roundscore[j] <> noscore
            then
              begin
                Val (roundscore[j], score, code);
                diff := score - board.par;
                total := total + diff
              end;
        totscore := total
      end
end;
```

A field in the record of type *golfertype* must be prefaced by the field name *golfer*, its index, and the variable name *board*. For example, in the procedure **ClearScoreTable** (which follows),

board.golfer[i].roundscore[j]

represents the score that golfer *i* achieved in round *j* of the tournament:

```
procedure ClearScoreTable (var board : boardtype);
  const
    noscore = '';
  var
    i,
    j
      : integer;
begin
  for i := 1 to board.numgolfers do
    for j := 1 to 4 do
      board.golfer[i].roundscore[j] := noscore
end;
```

Several procedures like **DisplayBoard** employ the **with** statement to avoid prefacing each field reference with a list of field names:

```
procedure DisplayBoard (board : boardtype);
  var
    i,
    j
      : integer;
begin
  ClrScr;
  GotoXY (13,1);
  Writeln ('GOLF TOURNAMENT LEADER BOARD');
  GotoXY (29,4);
  Write ('Round Score');
  GotoXY (1,5);
  Write ('Player');
  GotoXY (25,5);
  for i := 1 to 4 do
    Write (i:4);
  Writeln ('Total':10);
  for i := 1 to board.numgolfers do
    with board.golfer[i] do
      begin
        GotoXY (1,i+6);
        Write (name);
        GotoXY (25,i+6);
        for j := 1 to 4 do
          Write (roundscore[j]:4);
        Writeln (totscore:9)
      end;
  Continue
end;
```

When record positions are changed for the sort in the **Interchange** procedure, there is no need to switch each individual field. As long as the temporary variable *(temp)* is of the same type as the records that are interchanged, the contents of the entire record may be moved at one time:

```
procedure Interchange (var one, another : golfertype);
  var
    temp
      : golfertype;
begin
  temp := one;
  one := another;
  another := temp
end;
```

The final documented version of the solution after the verification process is shown in Figure 10.13.

Figure 10.13
GolfScores Program
Listing

```
program GolfScores;
{-----------------------------------------------------------------------}
{ PROGRAM:        Golf Tournament Tote Board                            }
{ PROGRAMMER:     S. Trapp                                              }
{ DATE:           September 19, 1990                                    }
{                                                                       }
{ This program provides up-to-date information for a golf tournament.   }
{ Choices from the main menu start the tournament by accepting the      }
{ names of participating golfers; accept the value of par for the       }
{ golf course; allow the entry of the number of strokes for each        }
{ golfer in a particular round and update the total number of strokes   }
{ above or below par for the tournament; allow the scoreboard to be     }
{ sorted by name or by score; and display the current scoreboard.       }
{                                                                       }
{ INPUT           names of golfers in tournament                        }
{                 par value for golf course                             }
{                 scores of each golfer in each round                   }
{                                                                       }
{ OUTPUT          names of golfers                                      }
{                 par value for golf course                             }
{                 scores of each golfer in each round                   }
{                 total score for each golfer                           }
{-----------------------------------------------------------------------}
  uses
    Crt;                              { screen formatting commands library }
  type
    nametype = string[20];                              { golfer name type }
    roundtype = array[1..4] of string[3];
                                   { scores in each of four rounds }
    golfertype = record                    { record for each golfer }
      name : nametype;
      roundscore : roundtype;
      totscore : integer
     end;
    boardtype = record                  { record for results scoreboard }
      par,
      numgolfers : integer;
      golfer : array[1..100] of golfertype
     end;
```

```
var
  choice                                    { main menu selection }
    : char;
  board                                     { results scoreboard }
    : boardtype;

procedure EnterNames (var board : boardtype);
{----------------------------------------------------------------------}
{ Accepts names of participating golfers.                              }
{                                                                      }
{ IN            board: results scoreboard                              }
{                                                                      }
{ OUT           board: results scoreboard                             }
{----------------------------------------------------------------------}
  const
    sentinel = 'xxx';                       { end of input signal }
  var
    count                           { number of participating golfers }
       : integer;
begin
  ClrScr;
  GotoXY (10,1);
  Writeln ('GOLFER NAME DATA ENTRY');
  count := 1;
  GotoXY (1,3);
  Writeln ('Enter last name, a comma, a space followed');
  Writeln ('by the first name of each participant.');
  Writeln ('Enter "xxx" for name to end input phase.');
  GotoXY (1,7);
  Write ('Name ("xxx" to end input): ');
  Readln (board.golfer[count].name);
  while board.golfer[count].name <> sentinel do
    begin
      count := count + 1;
      Write ('Name ("xxx" to end input): ');
      Readln (board.golfer[count].name)
    end;
  board.numgolfers := count - 1
end;
```

(continued)

```
procedure ClearScoreTable (var board : boardtype);
{------------------------------------------------------------------}
{ Clears scoreboard table by initializing all round scores to the  }
{ null string.                                                     }
{                                                                  }
{ IN            board: results scoreboard                          }
{                                                                  }
{ OUT           board: results scoreboard                          }
{------------------------------------------------------------------}
  const
    noscore = '';                    { initial value for round scores }
  var
    i,                        { loop index to cycle through golfers }
    j                         { loop index to cycle through rounds }
      : integer;
begin
  for i := 1 to board.numgolfers do
    for j := 1 to 4 do
      board.golfer[i].roundscore[j] := noscore
end;


procedure StartTournament (var board : boardtype);
{------------------------------------------------------------------}
{ Starts tournament by accepting names of participating golfers    }
{ and clearing the scoreboard.                                     }
{                                                                  }
{ IN            none                                               }
{                                                                  }
{ OUT           board:  results scoreboard                         }
{------------------------------------------------------------------}
begin
  EnterNames (board);
  ClearScoreTable (board)
end;
```

382

```
procedure EnterPar (var par : integer);
{-----------------------------------------------------------------}
{ Accepts par value for the golf course.                          }
{                                                                 }
{ IN             none                                             }
{                                                                 }
{ OUT            board: results scoreboard                        }
{                par:   par value for golf course                 }
{-----------------------------------------------------------------}
begin
  ClrScr;
  GotoXY (1,5);
  Write ('Par for this course: ');
  Readln (par)
end;

procedure CumulateScores (var board : boardtype);
{-----------------------------------------------------------------}
{ Determines and stores cumulative above par or below par scores  }
{ for tournament.                                                 }
{                                                                 }
{ IN             board: results scoreboard                        }
{                                                                 }
{ OUT            board: results scoreboard                        }
{-----------------------------------------------------------------}
  const
    noscore = '';                    { initial value for round scores }
  var
    i,                               { index to cycle through golfers }
    j,                               { index to cycle through rounds }
    total,                        { accumulates total tournament scores }
    score,                         { numeric value of score for a round }
    code,                          { code for string-to-number conversion }
    diff                      { difference between par and round score }
      : integer;
```

(continued)

```pascal
begin
  for i := 1 to board.numgolfers do
    with board.golfer[i] do
      begin
        total := 0;
        for j := 1 to 4 do
          if roundscore[j] <> noscore
            then
              begin
                Val (roundscore[j], score, code);
                diff := score - board.par;
                total := total + diff
              end;
        totscore := total
      end
end;

procedure EnterRoundScores (var board : boardtype);
{--------------------------------------------------------------------------}
{ Accepts golfers' scores for a round of the tournament.                   }
{                                                                          }
{ IN              board: results scoreboard                               }
{                                                                          }
{ OUT             board: results scoreboard                               }
{--------------------------------------------------------------------------}
  var
    i,                                    { index to cycle through golfers }
    roundnum                        { round number for which scores entered }
        : integer;
begin
  ClrScr;
  Write ('Enter round number: ');
  Readln (roundnum);
  ClrScr;
  GotoXY (20,1);
  Writeln ('SCORES FOR ROUND ', roundnum);
  GotoXY (1,4);
  for i := 1 to board.numgolfers do
    with board.golfer[i] do
      begin
        Write ('Enter score for ',name, ': ');
        Readln (roundscore[roundnum])
      end;
  CumulateScores (board)
end;
```

```
procedure Interchange (var one, another : golfertype);
{------------------------------------------------------------------}
{ Changes the positions of two records.                            }
{                                                                  }
{ IN          one:     one record whose position is interchanged   }
{             another: other record whose position is              }
{                      interchanged                                 }
{                                                                  }
{ OUT         one:     one record whose position is interchanged   }
{             another: other record whose position is              }
{                      interchanged                                 }
{------------------------------------------------------------------}
  var
    temp                   { temporary location for exchange of records }
      : golfertype;
begin
  temp := one;
  one := another;
  another := temp
end;


procedure Continue;
{------------------------------------------------------------------}
{ Waits for user to press key to resume processing.                }
{                                                                  }
{ IN          none                                                 }
{                                                                  }
{ OUT         none                                                 }
{------------------------------------------------------------------}
  var
    ch                                      { continue response }
      : char;
begin
  GotoXY (1,24);
  Write ('Press any key to continue.');
  ch := ReadKey
end;
```

(continued)

```
procedure SortByName (var board : boardtype);
{----------------------------------------------------------------}
{ Sorts scoreboard by player last names.                         }
{                                                                 }
{ IN            board: results scoreboard                         }
{                                                                 }
{ OUT           board: results scoreboard                         }
{----------------------------------------------------------------}
  var
    pass,                         { number of passes through the list }
    i                               { index to cycle through list }
      : integer;
    switch                  { indicates whether interchange made or not }
      : boolean;
begin
  switch := true;
  pass := 1;
  while (pass <= board.numgolfers) and (switch) do
    begin
      switch := false;
      for i := 1 to board.numgolfers - pass do
        with board do
          if golfer[i].name > golfer[i+1].name
            then
              begin
                switch := true;
                Interchange (golfer[i], golfer[i+1])
              end;
      pass := pass + 1
    end;
  Writeln ('Sort by name completed.');
  Continue
end;
```

```
procedure SortByScore (var board : boardtype);
{------------------------------------------------------------------}
{ Sorts scoreboard by player scores.                               }
{                                                                  }
{ IN              board: results scoreboard                        }
{                                                                  }
{ OUT             board: results scoreboard                        }
{------------------------------------------------------------------}
   var
     pass,                          { number of passes through the list }
     i                               { index to cycle through list }
       : integer;
     switch                  { indicates whether interchange made or not }
       : boolean;
begin
   switch := true;
   pass := 1;
   while (pass <= board.numgolfers) and (switch) do
     begin
       switch := false;
       for i := 1 to board.numgolfers - pass do
         with board do
           if golfer[i].totscore > golfer[i+1].totscore
             then
               begin
                 switch := true;
                 Interchange (golfer[i], golfer[i+1])
               end;
       pass := pass + 1
     end;
   Writeln ('Sort by score completed.');
   Continue
end;
```

(continued)

```
procedure SortMenu (var board : boardtype);
{------------------------------------------------------------------------}
{ Provides choice of whether to sort by name, sort by score or           }
{ return to main menu.                                                   }
{                                                                        }
{ IN              board: results scoreboard                             }
{                                                                        }
{ OUT             board: results scoreboard                             }
{------------------------------------------------------------------------}
  var
    choice                                          { menu choice }
        : char;
begin
  repeat
    ClrScr;
    GotoXY (20,5);
    Writeln ('SORT MENU');
    GotoXY (7,7);
    Writeln ('Press the number preceding your choice.');
    GotoXY (15,10);
    Writeln ('<1> Sort by name');
    GotoXY (15,12);
    Writeln ('<2> Sort by score');
    GotoXY (15,14);
    Writeln ('<3> Return to main menu');
    GotoXY (15,17);
    Write ('Choice --> ');
    choice := ReadKey;
    GotoXY (1,20);
    case choice of
      '1' :
        SortByName (board);
      '2' :
        SortByScore (board)
    end
  until choice = '3'
end;
```

```
procedure DisplayBoard (board : boardtype);
{-----------------------------------------------------------------------}
{ Displays scoreboard with player names, round scores, cumulative      }
{ scores, and par for the course.                                      }
{                                                                      }
{ IN            board:  results scoreboard                             }
{                                                                      }
{ OUT           none                                                   }
{-----------------------------------------------------------------------}
  var
    i,                                { index to cycle through golfers }
    j,                                { index to cycle through rounds  }
    k                                            { loop index }
      : integer;
begin
  ClrScr;
  GotoXY (13,1);
  Writeln ('GOLF TOURNAMENT LEADER BOARD');
  GotoXY (29,4);
  Write ('Round Score');
  GotoXY (1,5);
  Write ('Player');
  GotoXY (25,5);
  for k := 1 to 4 do
    Write (k:4);
  Writeln ('total':10);
  for i := 1 to board.numgolfers do
    with board.golfer[i] do
      begin
        GotoXY (1,i+6);
        Write (name);
        GotoXY (25,i+6);
        for j := 1 to 4 do
          Write (roundscore[j]:4);
        Writeln (totscore:9)
      end;
  Continue
end;
```

(continued)

```
begin
  repeat
    ClrScr;
    GotoXY (15,1);
    Writeln ('GOLF TOURNAMENT SCORING SYSTEM');
    GotoXY (10,3);
    Writeln ('Press the number preceding your choice.');
    GotoXY (15,6);
    Writeln ('<1> Enter participant names');
    GotoXY (15,8);
    Writeln ('<2> Enter par for golf course');
    GotoXY (15,10);
    Writeln ('<3> Enter scores for a round');
    GotoXY (15,12);
    Writeln ('<4> Sort player board');
    GotoXY (15,14);
    Writeln ('<5> Display player board');
    GotoXY (15,16);
    Writeln ('<6> Exit program');
    GotoXY (15,19);
    Write ('Choice --> ');
    choice := ReadKey;
    case choice of
      '1' :
        StartTournament (board);
      '2' :
        EnterPar (board.par);
      '3' :
        EnterRoundScores (board);
      '4' :
        SortMenu (board);
      '5' :
        DisplayBoard (board)
    end
  until choice = '6'
end.
```

Store and Forward

Many programming applications require the storage and management of large amounts of data. The record was designed for storing data of different types in the same structure. Record data is accessed by indicating the name of the record identifier and the field name containing the desired data.

Searching and sorting are two important applications for both arrays and records. Searching consists of inspecting each item in a structure to see if a component of that structure matches a key value. Sorting arranges the items in a structure in order, according to a given criterion.

You have seen that testing a program containing many data items can be very tedious. Each time the application programs in this chapter are executed, all the input data must be entered via the keyboard. It would be more efficient if the data could be entered from the keyboard once, stored in a disk file, and recalled when needed. Even if data is stored in a separate data file, it is easier to make changes in the file rather than retyping all the data. The Pascal file facilities that permit these operations are detailed in the next chapter.

Snares and Pitfalls

- *Using incomplete identifiers for fields of records:* The type for each field of a record must be specified.

- *Failing to use a* **type** *statement to define an array or record structure that is a parameter in a procedure or function:* Since arrays and records are structured data types, these structures must be defined in the **type** declaration section of a program if they are parameters.

- *Omitting an* **end** *statement in a record declaration:* An **end** statement must follow the last field declaration in the definition of a record.

Exercises

1. Answer the following questions in paragraph form.
   a. Compare the information required to access an element in an array to the information required to access a field in a record.
   b. Explain how a linear search algorithm would find *all* the records matching a key value rather than a unique record.
   c. How can a **with** structure simplify access to fields of a record?
   d. Give an example of a structure for which a record with two fields, rather than a two-dimensional array, must be declared.
   e. Explain how sorting a list can improve the efficiency of a linear search.

2. Classify each of the following Pascal statements as valid or invalid. If invalid, explain why. Unless otherwise stated, assume all identifiers have been properly declared.

a. **type**
```
     rtype = record
        a,
        b
          : real;
        c
          : integer;
```

b. **with r**
```
     field1 := field1 + 5;
```

c. `theater.event.cost := price[i];`

d. **while** j < max **do**
```
     if r.a[j] > 0
        then
           ct := ct + 1;
```

e. **while** i < 5 **do**
```
     begin
        with a[j] do
           begin
              Readln (fieldone);
              sum := sum + fieldone
           end
     end;
```

3. Evaluate each of the given expressions if $i = 1$, $j = 2$, and the record of arrays called R with fields one and two has the following values.

Record	Field	
	one	two
R[1]	alpha	32.0
R[2]	beta	1.6

a. `R[i].one`
b. `R[`**Round**`(R[2])].two`
c. **Concat** `(R[j].one, R[i].one)`
d. `R[j-i].two / R[2].two`
e. **Insert** `(R[1].one, R[2].one, 2)`

4. Write Pascal equivalents for each of the given descriptions.
   a. Define a record that keeps track of information on washing machine repairs. The first field stores the name of the model of a machine; the second, the total amount of money spent on repairs; and the third, the number of repairs.
   b. Define an array of 100 records for the washing machine repair records defined in part a.

c. Find the average cost per repair for all the washing machines in the array of 100 records defined in part b. Use the **with** statement in your answer.

d. Define a record with a car salesperson's name as the first field and, as the second field, an array of integers representing the number of cars sold during each month of a year.

e. Using the record defined in part d, find the number of months in which the salesperson sold more than four cars.

5. Find all the errors, both syntax and logical, in the following Pascal function, designed to count the number of male pandas in the zoos of the United States. A male panda is indicated when *panda* is stored in a string field called *name* and *M* is stored in a character field called *sex* in an array of records entitled *zoopop* of *populationtype*. The record containing the name *zzz* follows the last active element in the array.

```pascal
function MaleCount (zoopop : populationtype);
  var
     recnum, count : integer;
begin
  recnum := 1;
  while (name <> 'zzz') do
    begin
      Readln (zoopop.sex);
      if zoopop.sex = 'M'
        then
            count := count + 1;
      Readln (zoopop.name)
    end
end;
```

6. Show the exact output for each of the following program segments.

a.
```pascal
produce.name := 'potato';
produce.costperlb := 0.79;
produce.weight := 5;
with produce do
  begin
    total := weight * costperlb;
    Writeln (name, ' cost: $', total:5:2)
  end;
```

b.
```pascal
produce.name := 'tomato';
produce.costperlb := 1.29;
with produce do
  if costperlb > 1.09
    then
      Writeln (name, ' costs too much.')
    else
      Writeln ('I''ll buy a ', name);
```

```
  c.  animal.name := 'dog';
      animal.numlegs := 4;
      with animal do
        Writeln ('A ', name, ' has ', numlegs:1, ' legs.');

  d.  type
        stype = record
          first,
          second : integer;
          avg : real
         end;
        ctype = array[1..5] of stype;
      var
        c : ctype;
      ...
      for i := 1 to 5 do
        with c[i] do
          begin
            first := i;
            second := 2*i;
            avg := (first + second) / 2
          end;
      Writeln ('First':10, 'Second':10, 'Average':10);
      for j := 5 downto 1 do
        with c[j] do
          Writeln (first:10, second:10, avg:10:2);
```

7. Make the indicated changes in the specified application programs in the chapter.
   a. Change the program ContinentInformation (Figure 10.8) so it displays the entire continent table.
   b. Change the program ContinentInformation to display the information in the continent table of part (a) above in alphabetical order by continent name.
   c. Change the program GolfScores (Figure 10.13) to accept integer values, rather than strings, for the round scores; the DisplayBoard procedure should not display scores for rounds that have not been completed.
   d. Change the process for entering round scores for golfers in the program GolfScores so that you enter a golfer's name and score for a given round instead of having the program cycle through all the golfers' names and just entering that golfer's score when his or her name appears.

Programming Assignments

Elementary

1. Write a program that accepts baseball players' names, numbers of at-bats, and numbers of hits. Store these values in an array of records. From the data in each record, calculate a player's batting average, rounded to three decimal places, and store it in the player's record. Display the entire roster in tabular form, with columns for name, at-bats, hits, and batting average.

2. Write a program that stores the high and low temperatures for a 7-day period in an array of records. Display the average high temperature for the week, average low temperature for the week, the high temperature for the week, and the low temperature for the week.

3. Write a program that stores information on college faculty in an array of records. Each record should contain the faculty member's last name, first name, middle initial, rank (full professor, associate professor, assistant professor, or instructor), and annual salary. Create a menu-driven program that provides options to display the average salary for a given rank, the average salary for the entire faculty, the names of all faculty members, and the names of all those faculty with a given rank.

4. The Morse code was developed to send information over telegraph lines. Each letter is represented by a combination of short and long signals. Periods (.) represent the short signals and hyphens (-) the long signals. The following table shows the Morse code for letters, digits, and some punctuation marks.

Character	Code	Character	Code	Character	Code
A	.-	O	---	2	..---
B	-...	P	.--.	3	...--
C	-.-.	Q	--.-	4	....-
D	-..	R	.-.	5	.....
E	.	S	...	6	-....
F	..-.	T	-	7	--...
G	--.	U	..-	8	---..
H	....	V	...-	9	----.
I	..	W	.--	.	.-.-.-
J	.---	X	-..-	,	--..--
K	-.-	Y	-.--	?	..--..
L	.-..	Z	--..	:	---...
M	--	0	-----	;	-.-.-.
N	-.	1	.----	"	.-..-.

Write a program that stores the Morse code in an array of records and uses it to translate a string to its Morse code equivalent. Leave a space after each coded character.

5. The following table lists the masses and volumes of the planets in the solar system relative to the earth, which is given a value of 1.0 in each category.

Planet	Mass	Volume
Mercury	0.0553	0.0559
Venus	0.8150	0.8541
Earth	1.0000	1.0000
Mars	0.1074	0.1506
Jupiter	317.83	1403
Saturn	95.16	832
Uranus	14.50	63
Neptune	17.20	55
Pluto	0.0025	0.01

Write a program that stores this information in an array of records. Each record should contain fields for the name of the planet, its relative mass, its relative volume, and its density (mass/volume). After calculating the density of each planet, sort and output the records in descending order, using density as the key field.

6. Twenty players are to be selected for four basketball teams in a recreational league. Write a program that randomly selects the rosters for each of the teams from a master list (array of records) consisting of a player's name and a unique number from 1 to 20. If the random number chosen by the program matches the player's number, that player is chosen. Make sure to incorporate safeguards against choosing the same player more than once.

7. Write a program that accepts presidential election information and stores it in an array of records with fields representing the name of a state, the number of votes for the Democratic candidate, the number of votes for the Republican candidate, and the number of votes for the Independent candidate. Create a fifth field for the total number of votes cast in the state. Display election results, by state, in tabular form, including the total number of votes received by each candidate.

8. A linear search becomes more effective if sought-after items appear closer to the beginning of a list. Write a program for an inquiry system designed to locate and output the age of a famous person, given that person's name. The names and ages should be stored in an array of records. Since searches for certain famous people are more likely, each time a name is selected, switch the record containing that name with the record immediately preceding it. This transposition process allows the more popular records to work their way to the beginning of the list, increasing the efficiency of the linear search.

9. Three measures of central tendency for a collection of numeric values are the mean, the median, and the mode. The *mean* is the sum of the values divided by the number of values. The *median* is middle value when an odd number of values is placed in order, or the average of the middle two values when an

even number of values is ordered. The *mode* is the value or values that occur most frequently.

Write a program that stores the number of occupants in each car, truck, or bus that passes through a toll booth in an hour and outputs the mean, the median, and the mode of the number of occupants. Store all data in an array of records with fields indicating the type of vehicle (car, truck, or bus) and number of occupants.

10. Each city in the United States has at least one area code preceding every local phone number. Write a program that creates an array of records with fields for a city, its state, and its area code(s). Assume a city has no more than three area codes within its boundaries. The program should offer options to display the area code(s) for a particular city and state, to display all cities with a specified area code, or to terminate processing.

Challenging

11. Linear regression analysis uses statistical methods to describe a linear relationship between two quantities. A farmer would like a formula that describes the relationship between the amount of fertilizer used on a plot of land and the production of wheat on that land. He has acquired the following data through experimentation:

Fertilizer amount	0.5	1.0	1.5	2.0	2.5	3.0	3.5	4.0
Wheat produced	20	30	60	75	50	60	100	90

This relationship can be estimated by the equation $y = mx + b$, where

$$m = \frac{\Sigma x \Sigma y - n \Sigma xy}{(\Sigma x)^2 - n \Sigma x^2}$$

$$b = \frac{\Sigma y \Sigma x^2 - \Sigma x \Sigma xy}{n \Sigma x^2 - (\Sigma x)^2}$$

The symbol sigma (Σ) indicates a sum is to be calculated. Let the amount of fertilizer be represented by the independent variable x, and the wheat produced by the dependent variable y. Write a program that accepts the data in the table and stores it in an array of records. Calculate and output the linear equation that approximates the relationship between the amount of fertilizer used and the amount of wheat produced, in the form $y = mx + b$, where m and b are determined by the given equations.

12. Write a program that stores the names of all United States presidents and the month, day, and year of birth for each in an array of records. Display the entire array sorted by birthday, that is, in increasing calendar order. Also, determine and output the number of presidents born in each month.

13. Write a program that creates a menu-driven electronic address book that stores names, addresses (including city, state, and zip code), and phone numbers. Menu options should consist of changing an address or phone number given a name, displaying a phone number given a name or address, displaying the names and phone numbers of all those with a specified zip code, and displaying, in alphabetical order, complete data for all those in the address book.

14. Write a menu-driven program that stores and displays information on available real estate. Each record should contain the name of a seller, the complete address of a home, its asking price, and the local tax rate. Create another field that stores the calculated annual taxes, based on the asking price and tax rate. Menu options should include changing any field in a record given a specified address, displaying a list of all houses in a given zip code, displaying a list of all houses at or below a specified asking price, and displaying all data for a house at a specified address.

15. Write a program that deals a bridge hand to each of four players (designated as North, East, South, and West). One random number generator chooses the suit and another chooses the value of a playing card. The chosen card is stored in an array of records for each of the four players, with one field for the suit and another for the value. Make sure no duplicate cards are chosen.

16. A firm that specializes in mail order sales has a master mailing list sorted alphabetically by customer name. The list also contains each customer's complete mailing address. The company periodically receives lists of additional prospective customers. Write a program that loads a master mailing list and a list of new customers into two different arrays of records, sorts both lists, and merges them both into a single alphabetized master list.

17. Magazine publishers store subscriber data such as name, address, title(s) of magazine(s), and expiration date(s). Write a program that creates an array of records that allows fields for three magazines per subscriber and provides for adding new subscriber records to the file, deleting records from the file, and changing the address of a subscriber, as well as adding or removing a magazine from a subscriber's list and changing the expiration date of a magazine.

18. Write a program that stores information on the scheduling of television programs by creating an array of records with fields representing the name of the show, the network on which it is shown, the day and time it is shown, and the show's rating. The program should be capable of updating any of the fields in the record as well as producing reports that display all the programs in a given time slot, the complete schedule for any particular network, and a list of the shows rated in decreasing order.

19. In a linear search, you start at the beginning of a list and compare each element, one at a time, to a target value. If there is a match, the search is halted and the address of the target element is saved. The search also terminates if you reach the end of the list without finding a match. In other methods, the speed of the search process can be increased if the list is initially

sorted. One of these methods is the *binary search,* in which a list is repeatedly cut in half until the target value is found. If the list contains 1000 elements, a linear search may take 1000 comparisons to find the target, whereas a binary search will need no more than 10.

A binary search compares the pivot, or middle, element in a list to the target value. If there is a match, the process stops. If not, you test whether the target value is less or greater than the middle element. If it is greater, you search the upper half of the list; if less, the lower half. (Since the list is sorted, there is no need to search the wrong half of the list.) The process is repeated on the chosen half: finding the middle, testing it for a match to the target value. If there is a match, the search ends; if not, the correct half of the list is chosen and the process repeated until a single element remains. At this point, either you have found the proper element or it isn't in the list.

Write a program that creates an interactive business phone book by loading an array of records with a collection of names of companies and their phone numbers. Sort the list in ascending order by company names by any method you choose, and construct a subprogram that uses a binary search to display a company's phone number. The pivot of a list with an even number of elements can be either of the two elements in the middle of the list.

20. A list of integer test grades is to be sorted in ascending order using a *straight selection sort.* By this method, the largest grade in the list of n elements is found and placed in the last position, position n. The largest element in the remaining $n - 1$ grades is found and placed in position $n - 1$. This process continues until the remaining list consists of a single element, at which point the full list has been sorted. For example, consider the following list of grades:

78   62   95   81   88

After the largest grade (95) is found, its value is interchanged with the grade in the last (fifth) position, yielding

78   62   88   81   95

The 95 is now in its proper position. The largest grade in the remaining list of four grades (88) is found and its value interchanged with the grade in the fourth position (81), giving

78   62   81   88   95

The process is repeated until the list is sorted as shown here:

78   62   81   88   95
62   78   81   88   95

If there are n elements in a list, the process of finding the largest value and moving it to the end of the active list must be performed $n - 1$ times to ensure a sorted list.

Write a program that stores grades from a test in an array, displays that list as entered, sorts the list using the straight selection sort, and displays the sorted list.

CHAPTER 11

Data File Techniques

Key Terms

Assign	**FilePos**
binary file	internal file structure
Close	**Read**
data file	**Reset**
Eof	**Rewrite**
Erase	**Seek**
external file	text file
file of	**Write**
file pointer	

Objectives

- To introduce the concept of a binary data file of records
- To learn how to create and read a binary file
- To discover how to add records to an existing binary file
- To understand how to update a record in a binary file

11.1 Introduction

Suppose you must write a program to manage a list of the occupants of a motel. The program would allow a user to change the name of the occupant of a given room, update the costs charged to an occupant, or display a list of currently occupied rooms. There may be a problem: Do you want to enter all the data each time the program is executed, make the data part of the program, or simply leave the computer on all the time so you don't have to reenter the data? Or perhaps it would be easier to separate the data used by a program from the program itself and just have the program call that data when it is needed. This way you can use the same program with a set of data items for another motel, or the same data file with another program.

Programming languages allow you to store program instructions in one file and the data accessed by those instructions in another file—a *data file*.

Figure 11.1
Coin File Records Structure

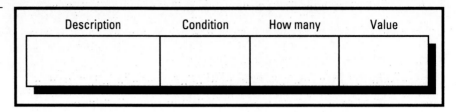

Description	Condition	How many	Value

Once a data file is created, it can be written to, read from, or changed without affecting instructions in the program file.

Chapter 3 introduced *text files*—files composed of keyboard characters arranged line by line. Although text files are easy to create and read, non-character data must be converted to characters when the file is created and changed back to their original form when read from a file. This conversion takes time. In *binary* (nontext) *files,* real values are stored as reals, integer values as integers, and so on. Since there is no conversion, the process is less time-consuming. This chapter introduces the fundamental concepts in the use of binary data files.

In general, a file is a collection of related data items, or records. Each of these records is composed of one or more fields, each representing a unique part of the record. For example, a numismatist (coin collector) can create a file of all the coins of a given country in her collection, where each record contains fields for a description of the coin (year, mint, and face value), its condition (G for good, F for fine, VF for very fine, and U for uncirculated), the number of coins in the collection with this description and condition, and the current market value. Figure 11.1 shows the structure of a record in the *coin* file. The fields contain different data types. Thus, *description* and *condition* are string data, while *value* is real. The record data structure defined in Chapter 10 formed the basis for an array of records. Here, the record structure forms the basis for a file of records. Although similar, a file of records offers one major advantage—it is a dynamic structure. An upper limit to the number of records in a file need not be declared before the file is created (as is the case in an array of records), and the size of the file is limited only by the medium on which it is stored.

In the event you have not covered text files in Chapter 3, this chapter repeats some of the details on the creation and use of files and introduces others as they apply to a file of records. These repetitions are presented for completeness and convenience.

11.2 Preparing to Use Files

Pascal file operations require communication between data in an *internal file structure* stored in main memory and a corresponding *external file* stored on disk. The internal file structure must be defined by a program and is represented by an identifier. A name for the disk file must be associated with this identifier before the data can transferred.

A file identifier that specifies the structure of the internal file can be completely declared in a **var** statement. It can also be declared as a file type in a **type** statement, with a variable identifier for that type defined in a **var** statement. The latter method is widely employed, since it produces programs that are easier to understand and more adaptable to change. When defining an internal file structure in a **type** statement, the reserved words **file of** must be followed by the type of data contained in the file.

Example

```
type
  descriptype = string[20];
  condtype = string[2];
  cointype = record
    description : descriptype;
    condition : condtype;
    howmany : integer;
    value : real
  end;
  coinfiletype = file of cointype;
  extfilenametype = string[14];

var
  coinrecord : cointype;
  coins : coinfiletype;
  filename : extfilenametype;
```

A record in the *coins* file has two different string fields (*descriptype* for the coin's description and *condtype* for its condition), an integer field for the number of coins with the same description and condition, and a real field for the market value of the coin. The identifier *coinrecord* is declared a single record with these four fields, while *coins* is defined as a file of records of type *cointype*. The variable identifier *filename* stores the external file name of the *coins* file.

The Assign Procedure   The **Assign** procedure establishes a link between an internal file structure and an external file.

FORMAT: **Assign (<file identifier>, <external file name>);**

The file identifier for the internal file structure must have been declared as a file type before appearing in **Assign.** The external file name is a string that can consist of the disk drive designation and a colon, a back-slash, and, if necessary, a path to the subdirectory that is to contain the file.

Example

```
Assign (coins, 'a:\USA');
```

The internal file structure defined in the previous example is associated with the file called *USA* stored in the root directory of the disk in drive a. Since the external file name is a string constant, it must be enclosed in single quotation marks.

If the collector has coin collections from several countries, she can define a variable identifier to store the external file name associated with each collection. That identifier can be used as the second parameter in the **Assign** statement.

Example

```
procedure GetExtFileName (var extfilename : extfilenametype);
begin
  Write ('Enter name for external file: ');
  Readln (extfilename)
end;
```

```
GetExtFileName (coinfile);
Assign (coins, coinfile);
   . . .
```

Assume that *coinfile* and *extfilename* are strings of type *extfilenametype* and that the identifier *coins* is defined by the internal file structure in the previous examples. A call to the procedure **GetExtFileName** passes the complete file name (including the drive designation and the complete path name) to the identifier *coinfile,* and that string becomes the external file name in the **Assign** statement.

The **Assign** statement is the only Pascal procedure that contains the external file name. After the connection between the internal file structure and an external file is made, the program need only refer to the internal identifier. Pascal takes care of the transfer of data to and from the external file at the appropriate times.

11.3 Creating a File of Records

Once the connection between an internal file structure and its external counterpart is established, data is sent either from the internal structure to the external file or vice versa. The **Assign** procedure establishes the link, but it does not determine the direction of the data flow.

The **Rewrite**
Procedure

The **Rewrite** procedure prepares the system for sending data from the internal structure to the external file by creating and opening a new file to receive output from the computer.

FORMAT: **Rewrite (<file identifier>);**

When this statement is executed, the external file associated with the internal file identifier is created and a *file pointer* is set to the beginning of the file. The file pointer indicates where the next data written to the file is to be placed. If an external file with that name already exists, the old file is deleted, with the new, empty file replacing it. **Rewrite** establishes a one-way path from the internal file structure to the external file.

Example

```
Assign (coins, coinfile);
Rewrite (coins);
```

A file pointer is set to the beginning of the defined internal file structure *coins,* which is now ready to receive data from the program. It will store that data in the external file *coinfile* linked to it by the **Assign** statement.

The **Write** Procedure for Files

While **Rewrite** establishes the data path direction, it is the **Write** procedure for files that actually stores data in the internal file structure.

FORMAT: **Write (<file identifier>, <output identifier>);**

If the first parameter in a **Write** procedure is a file identifier, then the output identifier must be a variable identifier. Output data is stored in the internal file structure, and the file pointer is advanced to prepare for any subsequent data transfer. If the output data in this statement is not of the same type as expected by the internal file, an error results.

Example

```
Assign (coins, coinfile);
Rewrite (coins);
Write (coins, coin1);
Write (coins, coin2);
Write (coin1);
Write (coin2);
  . . .
```

The internal structure *coins* is linked to the file *coinfile* in the **Assign** statement. The **Rewrite** statement prepares the file to receive output and sets the file pointer at the beginning of the file. The record *coin1* is written to *coins* and the file pointer advanced so that the data for the second record, *coin2,* follows the data for *coin1* in the file. Since the last two **Write** statements do not contain file identifiers, their output is sent to the screen.

Because data must be stored in a variable identifier before being transferred to the internal file structure, you cannot use a constant or constant identifier for the output parameter in a **Write** statement for files.

Example

`Write (intfile, 35);`	If *intfile* is a file identifier, this statement produces an error message since a variable identifier, not 35, is required for the output parameter.

Once a file is opened for receiving output data with a **Rewrite** statement, it must be closed before data can be read from that file.

The **Close** Procedure   The **Close** procedure removes access to an open file. Once the file is closed, no processing can be done on it until it is reopened.

FORMAT: **Close (<file identifier>);**

When a **Close** statement is encountered, the external file associated with the file identifier is updated, and access to that external file is ended. All the steps involved in the creation of a file must be enclosed between a **Rewrite** statement and a **Close** statement.

Example

```
procedure CreateFile (extfile : extfilenametype);
  var
    coinrecord : cointype;
    intfile : intfiletype;
begin
  Assign (intfile, extfile);
  Rewrite (intfile);
  EnterRecordData (coinrecord);
  while coinrecord.description <> '' do
    begin
      Write (intfile, coinrecord);
      EnterRecordData (coinrecord)
    end;
  Close (intfile)
end;
```

`CreateFile (coinfile);`

After the procedure `CreateFile` is called, the **Assign** statement links the internal file structure *intfile* with the external file *extfile*. Then **Rewrite** opens *intfile* to accept data that is eventually transferred to an external file. The procedure `EnterRecordData` accepts data for a coin record and returns it to `CreateFile.` The **while** loop continues to accept data and put it in the internal file structure until a blank description field is returned. At that point, the internal file is closed and the entered data transferred to the external file.

STYLE TIP   To avoid errors, include the **Assign, Rewrite,** and **Close** statements in the same procedure, enclosing all output file operations.

The Turbo Pascal system signifies the end of all data files by storing an end-of-file (eof) marker after the last record. This marker comes in handy when data is read from an existing file. An example of the structure of the external file *coinfile,* containing two records, is shown in Figure 11.2.

11.4 Reading from a File of Records

Once data is stored in an external file, there must be a method to access that data. The **Assign** statement establishes a link, and the **Rewrite** indicates that data can be moved only from the internal structure to the external file. Another procedure is needed to transfer data from the external file into an internal file structure.

The **Reset** Procedure

The **Reset** procedure uses the link established by **Assign** to open an existing file for the purpose of transferring data from the external file to its corresponding internal file structure.

FORMAT: **Reset (<file identifier>);**

When this statement is executed, the external file associated with the internal file identifier is opened and a file pointer set to the first record of the file. (The first record in a file is labeled record 0.) If there is no external file with the given name, an error results. This statement establishes a one-way path from the external file to the internal file structure.

Figure 11.2
Sample *Coin* File

1939D NICKEL	VF	2	6.00	1921 DIME	F	1	50.00	EOF

Example

```
Assign (coins, coinfile);
Reset (coins);
```

A file pointer is set to the beginning of the defined internal file structure *coins* and is now ready to receive data from the external file *coinfile*. The incoming data is stored in the internal file structure defined by the identifier *coins*.

The **Read** Procedure for Files

The **Reset** procedure serves only to establish the direction of the data flow. The **Read** procedure accepts data from an external file for storage in the internal file structure.

FORMAT: **Read (<file identifier>, <input identifier>);**

If the first parameter in a **Read** statement is an internal file identifier, the record at the current file pointer position is transferred to the location represented by the second parameter, the input identifier. The file pointer is then advanced to the next record in the file. The second parameter must be a variable identifier, and the structure of the record in the file must match the structure for the internal file variable declared in the main program.

Example

```
Assign (coins, coinfile);
Reset (coins);
Read (coins, coin1);
Read (coins, coin2);
    . . .
```

The internal structure *coins* is linked to *coinfile* in the **Assign** statement. The **Reset** statement prepares the system to receive input from *coinfile* and sets the file pointer at the beginning of that file. If the file has at least two records, the first record is read into the variable *coin1* and the file pointer advanced so that the next **Read** accepts the second record's data for the variable *coin2*.

If the file in the **Read** statement is not open, or an attempt is made to read beyond the end of the file, errors result. The first error can be corrected by inserting a **Reset** in the appropriate place in the program. But then how do you determine the number of records contained in a file? One method would be to store the number of records within the file itself. Each time a record is added or removed from the file, however, this value would have to be updated. Another method uses the end-of-file marker.

The End-of-File Function

The **Eof** (end-of-file) function returns a Boolean value (true or false) that indicates whether the file pointer is at the end of a file.

FORMAT: **Eof (<file identifier>)**

This function returns *true* if the file pointer is beyond the last record in the file, or it returns *false* if it is not.

Example

```
while not Eof(coins) do
  begin
   . . .
  end;
```

The statements in the **while** loop continue to be executed until the end of the file is reached, or as long as **not Eof(coins)** remains true.

As with the **Rewrite** statement, any file input operation opened by **Reset** must conclude with a **Close** statement.

Example

```
procedure ReadFile (extfile : extfilenametype);
  var
    coinrecord : cointype;
    intfile : intfiletype;
begin
  Assign (intfile, extfile);
  Reset (intfile);
  while not Eof(intfile) do
    begin
      Read (intfile, coinrecord);
      ProcessRecord (coinrecord)
    end;
  Close (intfile)
end;
```

```
ReadFile (coinfile);
```

The **Assign** statement in the procedure **Read-File** links the internal file structure *intfile* with the external file *extfile*. After **Reset** opens *intfile* for receiving data, the **while** loop continues to accept data, put it in the internal file structure, and advance the file pointer until the end of the file is reached. The **Close** statement then removes read access to *intfile*.

STYLE TIP   To avoid errors, include an **Assign** statement and a **Reset-Close** statement pair enclosing all input file operations in the same procedure.

11.5 Adding to a File of Records

Suppose our coin collector finds some old coins in a cigar box in her attic and would like to add records to her file. Since data is to be output to the file, it would seem that a **Rewrite** statement could be employed. To do this, however, would erase the existing file and place the file pointer at the beginning of the new file—and erasing the original file is something you don't want to do.

One way to add records to an existing file is to create a separate temporary file of the new entries and then unite or combine that file with the original or master file. To avoid cluttering the disk, the contents of the temporary external file should be erased after it is united with the master file.

The **Erase** Procedure

The **Erase** procedure erases the external file associated with the internal file specified by its parameter.

FORMAT: **Erase (<file identifier>);**

The external file linked to the file identifier by an **Assign** statement is erased from the disk containing it. The **Erase** procedure must be executed after the internal file is closed.

Example

```
Assign (intfile, extfile);
    . . .
Close (intfile);
Erase (intfile);
```

The external file name stored in the location *extfile* is linked to *intfile* by the **Assign** statement and removed from a disk by the **Erase** statement.

The process of uniting two files is not complicated; much of the groundwork has already been laid.

Example

```
procedure Unite (extfile1, extfile2 : extfilenametype);
  var
    coinrecord : cointype;
    intfile1, intfile2, intunitedfile : intfiletype;
begin
  Assign (intfile1, extfile1);
  Reset (intfile1);
  Assign (intfile2, extfile2);
  Reset (intfile2);
  Assign (intunitedfile, 'united');
  Rewrite (intunitedfile);
  while not Eof(intfile1) do
    begin
      Read (intfile1, coinrecord);
      Write (intunitedfile, coinrecord)
    end;
  while not Eof(intfile2) do
    begin
      Read (intfile2, coinrecord);
      Write (intunitedfile, coinrecord)
    end;
  Close (intfile2);
  Erase (intfile2);
  Reset (intunitedfile);
  Rewrite (intfile1);
  while not Eof(intunitedfile) do
    begin
      Read (intunitedfile, coinrecord);
      Write (intfile1, coinrecord)
    end;
  Close (intfile1);
  Close (intunitedfile);
  Erase (intunitedfile)
end;
```

```
Writeln ('Master File');
GetExtFileName (coinfile);
Writeln;
Writeln ('New Coin File');
GetExtFileName (newcoinfile);
Unite (coinfile, newcoinfile);
```

The external file names for the master file and the new-coins file are entered using the **GetExt-FileName** procedure defined earlier in the chapter and are stored in the variables *coinfile* and *newcoinfile*, respectively. These names are passed to the **Unite** procedure and linked with corresponding internal file names. A third internal file, *intunitedfile*, designed to hold the united file, is also linked to the temporary external file *united*. Records from the master file and then the new-coins file are read and written to the united file one at a time. See Figure 11.3. After the new-coins file is closed and erased, the *intunitedfile* file, now of a combination of both files, is opened for reading

Figure 11.3
Unite File Transfers

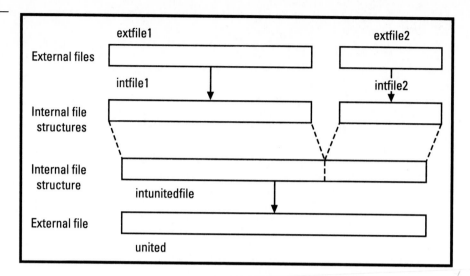

and the original master file (*intfile1*) is opened for writing. The contents of *intunitedfile* are copied to the original master file *intfile1*, the remaining internal files are closed, and the temporary external file *united* erased.

11.6 Changing Records in a File of Records

Adding records to an existing file is only one common file operation; changing the contents of an individual record is another. Suppose our coin collector acquires another coin with the same description and condition as one in the existing file, or that the market value of one of her coins triples. Is it necessary to create a new record? Or can she change one or more fields in an existing record? Basically, if you can find a record in a file and remember its location in the file, you can alter any or all fields of that record and place the updated record back in the file in its original location. But first, you must be able to find the record.

The File Position Function

The **FilePos** (file position) function accepts a file identifier and returns a long integer representing the record number that corresponds to the current position of the file pointer in that file. The first record in a file is record 0.

FORMAT: **FilePos (<file identifier>)**

The internal file identifier must have been previously defined. If the file pointer is at the beginning of a file, 0 is returned; this function does not change the position of the file pointer.

Example

```
recnum := FilePos (coins);
Read (coins, coinrecord);
```

The identifier *recnum* stores the number of the record in *coins* pointed to by its file pointer. Then the record in this position is stored in *coinrecord* and the pointer moved to the next record. Using the file shown in Figure 11.4, 3 is stored in *recnum,* the **Read** statement is executed, and the file pointer is advanced to the next record (record 4) in the *coins* file.

The updated record cannot be written back to the file at this point, since the file pointer has moved beyond the original record. Pascal provides a procedure, however, that moves the file pointer to the proper record in a file.

The **Seek** Procedure

The **Seek** procedure moves a pointer from its current position in a file to a specified record number represented by a long integer.

FORMAT: **Seek (<file identifier>, <record number>);**

This procedure can be used to place a record at the record number position in a file defined by the file identifier.

Example

```
recnum := FilePos (coins);
Read (coins, coinrecord);
    . . .
UpdateRecord (coinrecord);
Seek (coins, recnum);
Write (coins, coinrecord);
```

After one or more fields in *coinrecord* are changed by **UpdateRecord**, the **Seek** procedure places the file pointer at its position previous to the **Read** file statement, and the **Write** file statement replaces the old copy of *coinrecord* with an updated one. Figure 11.5 is a revised version of Figure 11.4, showing the file after **Seek** is executed.

Figure 11.4
FilePos Example

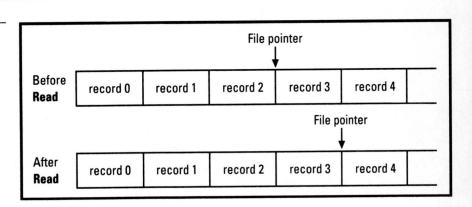

413

Figure 11.5
Seek Example

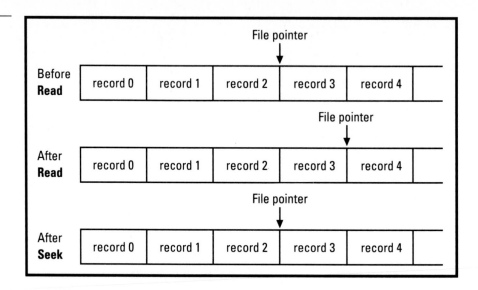

The update process (searching for the record to be altered, changing the appropriate fields, and writing that record back into the file) can occur only if a file has been opened by **Reset.** Remember that if you open an existing file using **Rewrite,** the file is erased. Be cautious in your use of **Rewrite.**

Example

```
procedure UpdateRecord (var extfile : extfilenametype);
  var
    coinrecord : cointype;
    found : boolean;
    location : longint;
    intfile : intfiletype;
begin
  Assign (intfile, extfile);
  Reset (intfile);
  SearchForRecord (extfile, coinrecord, location, found);
  if found
    then
      begin
        EnterChange (coinrecord);
        Seek (intfile, location - 1);
        Write (intfile, coinrecord)
      end
    else
      Writeln ('No match found.');
  Close (intfile)
end;
```

(continued)

```
UpdateRecord (coinfile);
```

After the file is opened for reading, **SearchFor-Record** is called to find the record matching a particular target value. If the sought-after item is found, the procedure **EnterChange** is called to change any or all fields of the record, the file pointer is restationed at the proper position in the file by **Seek,** and the updated record is written to the file. If a value of false is returned through *found,* a message is displayed. The file is closed before leaving the procedure.

11.7 Application: Numismatic Drill

To restate the original coin problem, a coin collector wants to create a file of records to keep track of her collection. Each record contains a separate field for a description of the coin (year minted, mint designation, and face value), its condition (good, fine, very fine, or uncirculated), the number of coins with this description and condition, and the coin's market value. She should be able to create a file, add to the file, or change any record in the file.

The solution design and corresponding module interface table are shown in Figure 11.6.

The complete, documented solution in Figure 11.7 reflects the techniques developed in the chapter.

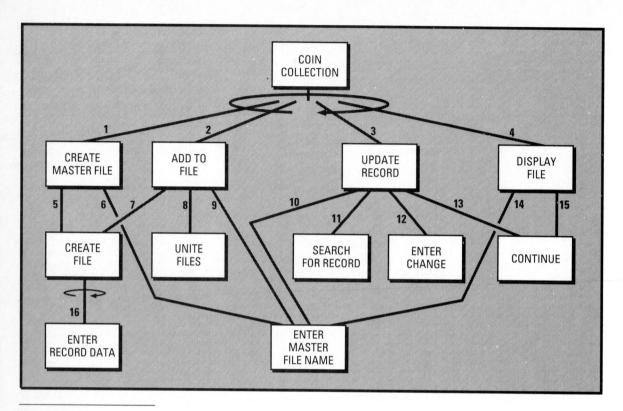

Figure 11.6a
CoinCollection
Structure Chart

```pascal
procedure EnterChange (var coinrecord : cointype);
{----------------------------------------------------------------------}
{ Accepts changes to number of coins of a given type and market        }
{ value of a coin in a record.                                         }
{                                                                      }
{ IN             coinrecord: record of coin information                }
{                                                                      }
{ OUT            coinrecord: record of coin information                }
{----------------------------------------------------------------------}
begin
  GotoXY (15,13);
  Writeln ('Update Record in Master File');
  Writeln;
  with coinrecord do
    begin
      Writeln ('Description: ', description);
      Writeln ('Condition: ', condition);
      Writeln;
      Writeln ('Current number of this type: ',howmany);
      Write ('Enter new number of coins of this type: ');
      Readln (howmany);
      Writeln;
      Writeln ('Current market value: $', value:8:2);
      Write ('Enter new market value: $');
      Readln (value)
    end
end;
```

(continued)

```
procedure UpdateRecord;
{-----------------------------------------------------------------------}
{ Changes contents of coin record.                                      }
{                                                                       }
{ IN            none                                                    }
{                                                                       }
{ OUT           none                                                    }
{-----------------------------------------------------------------------}
  var
   coinrecord                              { record of coin information }
      : cointype;
   found                      { indicates whether record found in file }
      : boolean;
   location                      { number of found record in file }
      : longint;
   intfile                   { internal master coin file structure }
      : intfiletype;
   masterfile                      { external master coin file }
      : extfilenametype;
begin
  ClrScr;
  GotoXY (15,3);
  Writeln ('Update Record in Master File');
  GotoXY (10,5);
  GetMasterFileName (masterfile);
  Assign (intfile, masterfile);
  Reset (intfile);
  SearchForRecord (masterfile, coinrecord, location, found);
  if found
    then
      begin
        EnterChange (coinrecord);
        Seek (intfile, location - 1);
        Write (intfile, coinrecord)
      end
    else
      begin
        Writeln ('No match found.');
        Continue
      end;
  Close (intfile)
end;
```

```pascal
procedure DisplayFile;
{-------------------------------------------------------------------}
{ Displays contents of master coin file in tabular form.            }
{                                                                   }
{ IN              none                                              }
{                                                                   }
{ OUT             none                                              }
{-------------------------------------------------------------------}
  var
    coinrecord                             { record of coin information }
      : cointype;
    intfile                          { internal master coin file structure }
      : intfiletype;
    masterfile                             { external master coin file }
      : extfilenametype;
begin
  ClrScr;
  GotoXY (15,1);
  Writeln ('COIN COLLECTION FILE');
  GotoXY (10,3);
  GetMasterFileName (masterfile);
  GotoXY (1,5);
  Writeln ('Description':20, 'Condition':15, 'Quantity':15,
           'Value in $':15);
  Writeln ('-----------':20, '---------':15, '--------':15,
           '----------':15);
  Assign (intfile, masterfile);
  Reset (intfile);
  while not Eof(intfile) do
    begin
      Read (intfile, coinrecord);
      with coinrecord do
        Writeln (description:20, condition:15, howmany:15, value:15:2)
    end;
  Continue
end;
```

(continued)

```
begin
  repeat
    ClrScr;
    GotoXY (15,1);
    Writeln ('COIN COLLECTION FILE SYSTEM');
    GotoXY (10,3);
    Writeln ('Press the number preceding your choice.');
    GotoXY (15,6);
    Writeln ('<1> Create Master File');
    GotoXY (15,8);
    Writeln ('<2> Add Records to File');
    GotoXY (15,10);
    Writeln ('<3> Update Record in File');
    GotoXY (15,12);
    Writeln ('<4> Display Coin File');
    GotoXY (15,14);
    Writeln ('<5> Exit Program');
    GotoXY (15,17);
    Write ('Choice --> ');
    choice := ReadKey;
    case choice of
      '1' :
        CreateMasterFile;
      '2' :
        AddToFile;
      '3' :
        UpdateRecord;
      '4' :
        DisplayFile
    end
  until choice = '5'
end.
```

The **type** declaration defines a record called *cointype* to include fields for a description of the coin, its condition, the number of coins in the collection with this description and condition, and the market value of the coin. The internal file is defined as a file of records, while the external file name is a string specifying where the file is stored on the disk.

The main program uses a menu to call four modules and to make selecting among the basic operations as easy as possible. Each of the called modules calls a **GetMasterFileName** module to accept the name of the external (disk) file whose data is to be processed. **GetMasterFileName** simply prompts the user to enter an external file name for the coin file.

The **CreateMasterFile** procedure clears the screen, gets a name for a new master coin file, and calls **CreateFile** to create this new file. **CreateFile** employs a **while** loop calling an **EnterRecordData** procedure to accept input for each of the four fields in the *coinrecord*. Values for the number of coins and their market values are entered as strings, and they are converted to numbers in order to avoid any input errors. Input ends when no coin description is entered.

The **AddToFile** procedure calls **GetMasterFileName** to accept the name of the file to which data is added. This procedure also asks for the drive that is to contain the temporary file with the records to be appended to the master file. It calls **CreateFile** to create a file on that drive with the name *temp*. That file is passed to the **UniteFiles** procedure and combined with the old master file to produce an updated master file.

The **UpdateRecord** procedure initially accepts the name of the external file that contains the record to be changed. After linking the internal file structure with the master file, the external file name is passed to the procedure **SearchForRecord**. The coin's description and condition are entered, and the file is read, one record at a time. If a match for both the description and the condition occurs, the location (number) and contents of the record are returned to **UpdateRecord**, along with a *true* value for the parameter found. The **then** clause of the condition statement in **Update-Record** is executed, and the record data is passed to the **EnterChange** procedure to make the necessary changes. The current quantity and market value are displayed, and the user is asked to enter new or the same values for each. If no record in the master file matches both the description and the condition, then a *false* value is returned to **UpdateRecord**, the **else** clause in the condition is executed, a message is displayed, and the **Continue** procedure is called. **Continue** allows the message to remain on the screen until a key is pressed.

The **DisplayFile** procedure asks for an external file and displays the contents of the file in tabular form.

Store and Forward

Storing a program and its data in separate files gives program designers and users increased flexibility, allowing a data file to be used with several programs and a program to operate on several data files. Program and data files thus enjoy a certain measure of independence, since a change in one does not necessarily dictate a change in the other.

Creating a data file of records involves defining an internal data structure to hold the data temporarily while the program works on it, and an external data file that stores the final copy of this internal structure on a disk. Turbo Pascal provides a means of associating an internal file structure with its external counterpart, opening a file for input or output, reading or writing to the file, closing it, and erasing an external file. These instructions also are capable of adding records to, or changing existing records in, a file.

The basic components of programming languages presented in this and the previous chapters are just that: basics. Turbo Pascal has additional capabilities that include the capability to define data types and objects, dynamic memory allocation with pointer variables, and subprograms that call themselves. The next chapter introduces some of these more sophisticated concepts.

Snares and Pitfalls

- *Using **Rewrite** to open an existing file:* All the data in an existing file opened by **Rewrite** is erased.

- *Incorrectly positioning the file pointer:* If the file pointer is not pointing to the correct record, incorrect data may be read from or written to a file.

- *Attempting to access data from an unopened file:* A file of records must be opened by a **Rewrite** or a **Reset** statement before the program can have access to the file's contents.

- *Reading beyond the end of a file:* Unpredictable results occur from attempting to read beyond the end-of-file marker. This can be avoided by using the **Eof** function.

- *Trying to write to a file prepared for reading or to read from a file prepared for writing:* A **Read** statement for files must be preceded by a **Reset** statement indicating which file is to be read; a **Write** statement for files follows a **Rewrite** statement if a new file is to be created, or follows a **Reset** and a **Seek** statement if a record in a file is to be changed.

- *Failing to close an open file:* An error message may result if an attempt is made to read from a file opened for writing, unless that file is closed and reopened with **Reset**.

Exercises

1. Answer the following questions in paragraph form.
   a. Why is a file a dynamic structure?
   b. Explain how records can be added to the end of an existing file.
   c. Distinguish between an internal file structure and an external file.
   d. Discuss the validity of the following statement: The end-of-file function is not really necessary, but it makes working with files easier.
   e. Both files and arrays can store large quantities of data. What system limitations would dictate the choice of one over the other?

2. Classify each of the following as valid or invalid. If invalid, explain why. Unless otherwise stated, assume all identifiers have been properly declared.

a. **Assign** (intfile);

b. **Reset** (intfile);
   Write (intfile, name);

c. **repeat**
      Read (intfile, age)
   until Eof(intfile);

d. **Seek** (intfile, **FilePos**(intfile) + 1);

e. **Close;**

3. Write Pascal equivalents for each of the given descriptions.
   a. Link an internal file structure called *repairs* with the external file *b:\rprfile.*
   b. Open the internal file structure *employee* and read the 10th record into a variable identifier called *emprecord.*
   c. Remove the external file *b:\cars* (associated with the internal file structure *carfile*) from a disk.
   d. The variable identifier *nameage* is a record containing a person's name in a field called *name,* and his or her age in a field called *age.* Create an internal file structure *intfile* containing exactly 10 of these records.
   e. Add one year to the age field of each of the records in the file created in part d.

4. Make the following changes to the **CoinCollection** file program developed in Section 11.7.
   a. Change the structure of the record *cointype* by replacing the description field with separate fields for the year the coin was minted, the mint designation, and the name of the coin. Make all appropriate changes in the program to conform to this record change.
   b. The Turbo Pascal function **FileSize** returns a long integer that indicates the size of a file. For example, **FileSize (intfile)** returns the number of records in the file *intfile.* Replace the **AddToFile** module in the original **CoinCollection** program with one that uses the **Seek** procedure and **FileSize** to add records to an existing file.

5. Write a Pascal procedure to perform each of the following processes.
   a. Make a copy of an external file of characters called *original.* Name the copy with the external file name *dupe.*
   b. Read a file of real numbers and create a second file consisting of all those numbers whose values are greater than 30,000.

6. Find all errors in the following program. It is designed to read the real numbers in an external file called *oldlist,* double them, create another file called *newlist* containing the doubled values, and display the list of doubles.

```
program Double;
  type
    intfiletype = file of real;
  var
    r : real;
begin
  Assign (intfile1, 'oldlist');
  Rewrite (intfile1);
  Assign (intfile2, 'newlist');
  Reset (intfile2);
  while not Eof(intfile1) do
    begin
      Read (intfile1, r);
      Write (intfile2, r);
      r := 2 * r
    end;
  Close (intfile1);
  Close (intfile2);
  Reset (intfile2);
  while not Eof(intfile2) do
    begin
      Read (r);
      Write (r:8:2)
    end;
  Writeln;
  Close (intfile2)
end.
```

7. Show the exact output for the given program using the following input data, in the order given: 34, 19, 2, 8, 10, 25.

```
program Walkthrough;
  type
    intfiletype = file of integer;
  var
    value, i : integer;
    intfile : intfiletype;
begin
  Assign (intfile, 'a:extfile1');
  Rewrite (intfile);
  for i := 1 to 5 do
    begin
      Write ('Enter integer: ');
      Readln (value);
      Write (intfile, value)
    end;
  Close (intfile);
  Reset (intfile);
  Seek (intfile, 3);
```

(continued)

```
      Write ('Enter integer: ');
      Readln (value);
      Write (intfile, value);
      Seek (intfile, 0);
      while not Eof(intfile) do
        begin
          Read (intfile, value);
          Write (value:5)
        end;
      Writeln;
      Close (intfile)
  end.
```

Programming Assignments

Programming assignments involving files can be tailored to any level of sophistication by incorporating one or more of the following file operations into the program: creating a file, deleting a file, adding records to a file, searching for a particular record, changing part of an existing record, inserting a record, and deleting a record.

Elementary

1. Write a program to manage a personal phone directory by creating a file containing a person's name, address, and phone number. In addition to creating the file, the program should be capable of adding records to the file and searching the file for a phone number, given a person's last name.

2. Write a program to manage a file of blood donor information. Each record should contain the donor's name, address, telephone number, blood type (A, B, AB, or O), and Rh factor (+ or –). The program should be capable of adding new donor records to the file and of producing a report of all the donors in the file who match a specified type and Rh factor.

3. A television chef would like to create a file of all his recipes. Each record should include a recipe category (soup, fish, meat, vegetable, dessert), a list of ingredients, and instructions. Write a program that can create a recipe file, add records to it, and display the recipes in a given category one at a time.

4. A small library would like to keep track of its holdings and make that information available on demand. Write a program to create a file of records with fields representing the classification number, author, and title of each book in the library. The program also should be capable of adding new book information to the file.

5. After years of accumulating programs, a programmer decides to create a file of information on all of them. Each record should include a software category (entertainment, spreadsheet, word processing, database, communication, graphics, other), title, and software publisher. Write a program that allows him to add records to the file and to generate reports of all packages in a given category.

6. To determine how much the length of a certain material changes during a variation in temperature, a physicist must know the coefficient of linear expansion for the material. A product of this coefficient, the original length, and the change in temperature gives the change in the length. If the length is given in meters and the temperature in degrees Celsius, the change in length is also in meters. Write a program that creates a file of records with fields for the material name and its coefficient and uses this file to determine the length change, given the material and a temperature change.

7. Important information in the periodic table of elements can be placed in a file for easy access. Each record should contain the name of the element and its symbol, atomic mass, and atomic number. Write a program that stores all the elements in the periodic table in a file and, given the symbol, allows access to the information in the record.

8. Write a game program in which a player is given the names of 10 states in the United States and asked to supply the names of their capitals. The states and their capitals should be stored in a file, and state names should be chosen at random. (A random number generator can be designed to choose a record number in the file.) The program should indicate whether the player's response is correct or incorrect, and notify the player of the percentage of his or her correct answers.

9. Write a program that drills students in learning the vocabulary of a foreign language by creating a file of records in which one field is an English word and a second is its foreign-language equivalent. For example, an English–Spanish file might contain a record with *goodbye* as the first field and *adios* as the second. The program should offer a choice of translating from English to the foreign language or vice versa. Records from the file should be chosen at random and the appropriate word displayed. After a student types in the equivalent word, the program indicates whether the response is correct. At the end of a session, the percentage of correct answers should be displayed. The program should also include an option to increase the file's vocabulary. Make the program as general as possible so that it executes properly with vocabulary files for many languages.

10. A movie buff would like to keep track of all the movies she has on videotape. Each record should consist of the year the movie was made, title, lead actress, lead actor, and director. Write a program that creates a file, provides the capability of adding to that file, and allows searches for all movies that were made in a particular year, that have the same lead actress and lead actor, or that were directed by the same person.

Challenging

11. A thesaurus is a book of synonyms, i.e., words with the same or nearly the same meaning. Write a program that simulates a thesaurus by allowing a user to enter a word and then displaying synonyms for that word. Each record should contain a list of words with the same or nearly the same meaning, the part of speech of the word (noun, verb, etc.), and the number of synonyms in a given list. The program should be capable of adding a new list as well as adding a new word to an existing list.

12. In order to process customer checkout more quickly, many supermarkets now have scanning devices connected to their cash registers. These scanners read a universal product code (UPC) printed on the item sold, search a file for that item, and record the current price. Write a program that creates an item file whose records include the name of the item, its UPC, and the current price. Simulate the action of the register by accepting a UPC code for several items and printing the names of those items, their prices, a subtotal, applicable tax, and grand total. The program also should have the ability to add an item to the file and change the price of an existing item.

13. A small local theater can seat 120 people in its 12 rows, labeled A through L. Each row contains 10 seats, numbered 1 through 10. Write a program that keeps a file of available seats for events in the theater. Each record should contain the name of the event, its date, and a two-dimensional array of characters, with blanks indicating available seats and X's indicating unavailable ones. A sample display of the seating plan is shown below.

	1	2	3	4	5	6	7	8	9	10
A				X	X	X	X	X	X	
B		X	X			X	X		X	X
C	X	X		X	X					
D						X	X			
E					X	X				
F							X	X		
G										
H										
I										
J										
K										
L										

The program also should update the seating plan matrix when a ticket is purchased, add events to the file, change the date of a event, and remove events from the file.

14. Magazine publishers store subscriber data such as name, address, title(s) of magazine(s), and expiration date(s). Write a program that creates a file of records that allows fields for three magazines per subscriber and provides for adding new subscriber records to the file, deleting records from the file, and changing the address of a subscriber, as well as adding or removing a magazine from a subscriber's list and changing the expiration date of a magazine.

15. Write a program that stores information on the scheduling of television programs by creating records with fields representing the name of the show, the network on which it is shown, the day and time it is shown, and the show's rating. The program should be capable of updating any of the fields in the record as well as producing reports that display all the programs in a given time slot, the complete schedule for any particular network, and a list of the shows rated in decreasing order.

16. A charity wishes to keep a file of its donors. Each record should contain the name and address of the donor, the date of the last donation, the amount of that donation, and the total contribution for the year. Write a program that creates this file, updates its fields if necessary, and produces reports showing an entire donor list or a list of donors whose total contributions are more than a specified amount. The program also should be capable of setting all the contribution amounts to 0 at the end of a year.

17. A mail-order software firm monitors its inventory very closely so that customers can find out immediately whether an item is in stock. A record of each software package contains the item number, the title of the package, the number currently in stock, and the unit price. Write a program that creates a software inventory file with the capability of deleting a record, changing the number of items in stock or the unit price of an item, determining the value of all the items in stock, and producing a report that displays all the items whose totals fall below a specified level.

18. Write a program that helps a small real estate office keep track of all the houses it lists for sale. Each record should contain the name and address of the seller, the location of the house and its asking price, and the name of the agent handling the transaction. The program also should be capable of removing a listing from the file, changing the asking price or the name of the agent, and producing reports detailing all the houses assigned to a particular agent or all the houses whose asking prices are below a given value.

19. A computerized dating firm has a file for each client, containing the client's name, address and telephone number, sex, and yes or no responses to 15 questions. Whenever a client wishes to use the service, the service compares the clients' responses to the 15 questions with those of the opposite sex. The name of the person with the most matches is sent to the client. If there is more than one person with the same number of matches, all those names are sent. Write a program that creates a file to fit the needs of this service and is capable of removing client records from the file.

20. A college student's record contains a student identification number, his or her name, the number of credits accumulated, the grade points accumulated, and the grade point average (total credits divided by total grade points). Values for the grade point average are determined by the program and should be real numbers between 0.0 and 4.0, inclusive. Write a program that creates a student file and is capable of updating the three numeric fields by accepting the grade points and credits accumulated in a semester, adding these figures to the amounts in the file, and storing the new totals in the file. The new grade point average should be calculated from the updated totals and also stored in the file. At the end of all the processing, recreate the file, with the records sorted in descending order by the revised grade point averages. At the completion of the update process, the program should have the capability of outputting an ordered listing of student identification numbers, names, and grade point averages as well as a listing of all students whose grade point averages are 3.8 or above, greater than or equal to 3.6 but less than 3.8, and greater than or equal to 3.4 but less than 3.6.

An Introduction to Advanced Pas
and Object-Oriented Programmi

constant identifier list	**object**
Dispose	object field
encapsulation	object-oriented programming
enumerated data type	(OOP)
heap	pointer
linked list	**Pred**
method	recursion
New	**Succ**
nil	traversal
node	

Objectives

- To introduce enumerated data types and show how they can improve the readability of programs
- To define pointer data types
- To show how pointers can be used to create linked lists
- To compare linked lists with array storage of a collection of data items
- To define recursion and show how it can be applied in the solution of certain classes of problems
- To understand the advantages and disadvantages of using recursion rather than iteration in the solution of problems containing repetitive structures
- To introduce basic concepts in object-oriented programming

12.1 Introduction

Among the many features of Turbo Pascal are some that allow you to write programs that are easier to understand or that make more efficient use of memory and time. One feature gives you the power to define your own data type, another allows you to create a dynamic memory structure that uses only the memory it needs, and a third lets you construct a subprogram that calls itself.

Although Pascal programs certainly can be written without using any of these features, such features perform tasks in a way that takes advantage of different capabilities of a computer system. As you work through this chapter, think about how these enhancements are implemented, how they differ from more standard methods, and what the advantages and disadvantages are of using one rather than the other.

12.2 Enumerated Data Types

In the preceding chapters, you've been introduced to and learned to use fundamental data types, such as integer, real, character, string, and Boolean, for both constants and variables. All but reals were considered ordinal data types. Pascal also enables you to define your own ordinal data type by listing the allowable values for that type. Although it is not necessary to use them, these *enumerated data types* can make your program easier to understand.

Enumerated data types are defined in a **type** statement.

FORMAT: **type**
      `<identifier> = ( <constant-identifier list> );`

A list of legal values for any variable of type `<identifier>` (called a *constant-identifier list)* is enclosed in parentheses. The items in the list are separated by commas and arranged in order from the lowest to the highest. In other words, even though none of the items in the list are numbers, characters, or strings, the first item is less than the second, the second less than the third, and so on. The valid constants are not case-sensitive; that is, you can express them with either uppercase or lowercase letters. Remember, these values are not string constants; attempting to treat them as such results in an error.

Example

```
type
  answertype = (yes, no);
var
  answer : answertype;
```

The only legal constants for the variable identifier *answer* are the values *yes* and *no,* with *yes* preceding *no.* They are *not* equivalent to the string values 'yes' and 'no'.

The same identifier may not appear in constants lists for two different enumerated data types.

Example

```
type
  handtype = (right, left);
  answertype = (right, wrong);
```

This **type** declaration produces an error, since the constant identifier *right* is in both enumerated data type lists.

Values from the constant-identifier list can be compared to others of the same type. In the previous example, *yes* is the first item in the parentheses in the **type** statement, making the relational expression *yes* < *no* true. Since the items in the constant-identifier list are ordered, they can define a subrange for another defined type.

Example

```
type
  daytype = (M, Tu, W, Th, F, Sa, Su);
  weekdaytype = M..Sa;
var
  workday : weekdaytype;
  playday : daytype;
```

The legal values for the variable *playday* are those in the parentheses in the *daytype* definition. The legal values for *workday* are a subrange of those defined for *daytype* and include *M, Tu, W, Th, F,* and *Sa*. The declaration for *daytype* must precede the one for *weekdaytype*. No parentheses are used for *weekdaytype*, since the constant identifiers *M* through *Sa* have already been defined in *daytype*.

Values from the constant-identifier list can be assigned to variable identifiers of the proper type or compared with other variable identifiers of the same type.

Example

```
if playday <= F
  then
    workday = Sa;
```

Assume *workday* and *playday* have been declared in the previous example. If the variable identifier *playday* has a value in the range from *M* to *F*, inclusive, *workday* is assigned the constant identifier value *Sa. Sa* is not enclosed in single quotation marks, since it is not a string constant.

Enumerated data types and integers are both ordinal data types. This means that if you are given one value for either of these types, you can determine the next higher or lower value. For integers, you can add 1 to get to the next higher value and subtract 1 for the next lower value. If the value of *workday* is *Tu,* how do you go to *W?* You can't add 1. There are several Turbo Pascal functions that work with all classes of ordinal data types.

The Successor Function   The **Succ** (successor) function returns the next higher value for its ordinal data type parameter. For example, the successor of 23 is 24 and the successor of *W* in the *workday-playday* example is *Th*.

FORMAT: **Succ (< ordinal constant>)**

The value returned by **Succ** is of the same type as the ordinal constant, and follows it in the order defined by the ordinal constant's type. If the constant has no successor *(Su* for a value of *playday),* an error results.

Example

```
playday := M;
while Succ(playday) <= Su do
  begin
    . . .
    playday := Succ(playday)
  end;
```

This section of code cycles through the constant values for *playday* and terminates when the successor of the current *playday* follows *Su* in the constants list. Because *Su* is the last item in the list, no error results from attempting to access an element after the last one.

The Predecessor   The **Pred** (predecessor) function returns the next lower value for its ordinal
Function   data type parameter. For example, the predecessor of the character *f* is the character *e,* and the predecessor of *W* in the *workday-playday* example is *Tu*.

FORMAT: **Pred (< ordinal constant>)**

The value returned by **Pred** is of the same type as the ordinal constant, and precedes it in the order defined by the type of the ordinal constant. If the constant has no predecessor *(M* for a value of *playday),* an error results.

Example

```
playday := Su;
repeat
  . . .
  playday := Pred(playday)
until playday = M;
```

This section of code also cycles through the constant values for *playday,* from the last *(Su)* back to the first *(M),* and terminates when the current value of *playday* is *M* in the constants list. Again, since *M* is the first item in the list, no error results from attempting to access an element before the first one.

The **Ord** (ordinal) function presented in Chapter 6 gives the ordinal value associated with its parameter. It also can be applied to enumerated data types. Since a character is an ordinal data type, **Ord** returns the ASCII code associated with that character (see Appendix D). For example, **Ord('b')** is 98, because the ASCII decimal code for a lowercase *b* is 98. The **Ord** function applied to the value in an enumerated data type gives its position in the declaration list, where the first item in a list is number 0.

Example

```
for playday := M to Su do
  begin
    i := Ord(playday);
    Write (i:3)
  end;
Writeln;
```

The variable identifier *playday* serves as a loop control variable in the **for** structure. The body of the loop displays the ordinal values, or position numbers, of each value in the enumerated data type *daytype*, from *M* to *Su*. Since the first element is number 0, the output appears as:

0   1   2   3   4   5   6

Although members of the constant-identifier list can be used in many of the same statements as other constant identifiers, a program cannot directly read or write variables whose values are enumerated data types. You can, however, construct procedures with decision structures to perform these tasks.

Example

```
type
  seasontype = (spring, summer, fall, winter);
var
  valid : boolean;
  season : seasontype;

procedure ReadSeason (var season : seasontype; var valid : boolean);
  var
    seasonstr : string[6];
```

(continued)

```
begin
  Write ('Enter a season (spring, summer, fall, winter): ');
  Readln (seasonstr);
  if seasonstr = 'spring'
    then
      season := spring
    else
      if seasonstr = 'summer'
        then
          season := summer
        else
          if seasonstr = 'fall'
            then
              season := fall
            else
              if seasonstr = 'winter'
                then
                  season := winter
                else
                  valid := false
end;
```

```
repeat
  ReadSeason (season, valid)
until valid;
```

The procedure **ReadSeason** accepts a string representing one of the seasons, and nested **if . . . then . . . else** structures convert that string to the correct constant in the enumerated list for *seasontype*. If an improper value is entered for *seasonstr, false* is returned to the calling program through the Boolean *valid.* The **repeat** loop continues to ask for values for *season* until a valid one is entered.

Since the index or subscript of an array must be an ordinal data type, enumerated data types also can serve in this capacity.

Example

```
type
  seasontype = (spring, summer, fall, winter);
  countype = array[seasontype] of integer;
var
  season : seasontype;
  valid : boolean;
  count : countype;
```

```
ReadSeason (season, valid);
while valid do
  begin
    count[season] := count[season] + 1;
    ReadSeason (season, valid)
  end;
```

An array of type *countype* has only four possible subscripts—the enumerated data types of *season-type*. After values have been entered and converted through **ReadSeason**, the count for a chosen season is updated. This process continues until an invalid entry is made for *season*.

Programs with enumerated data types often are longer and more tedious to code than those without them. The major advantage in their use is that they increase the understandability of program structures.

12.3 Application: Any Questions?

The creator of a trivia game wants to assess the difficulty of the questions by determining the percentage of the questions in a given category that were answered correctly. The game poses questions in four different categories: media, literature, history, and science. Write a program that accepts data (a category and whether the response to that question is correct) for one question at a time and produces a table summarizing the results for each category.

The declaration section defines an enumerated data type to act as the subscript for the array of records representing question data in each category:

```
type
  categorytype = (media, literature, history, science);
  nametype = string[10];
  questiontype = record
    name : nametype;
    asked,
    correct : integer;
    pctcorrect : real
  end;
  questionsetype = array[categorytype] of questiontype;
var
  questionset
    : questionsetype;
```

This record structure (illustrated in Figure 12.1) defines *questionset* as an array containing four records, each with four fields. The enumerated data type *categorytype* defines the range for the subscripts of *questionsetype*.

The solution design and corresponding module interface table are shown in Figure 12.2.

The main program contains a menu offering the choices of adding data to the question set data, displaying a table of the results, or exiting.

Figure 12.1
Question Set Record
Structure

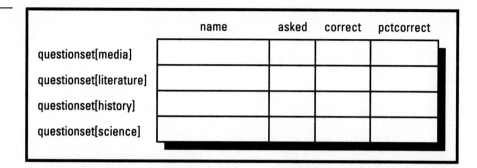

Figure 12.2
Question Analysis
Structure Chart and
Module Interface Table

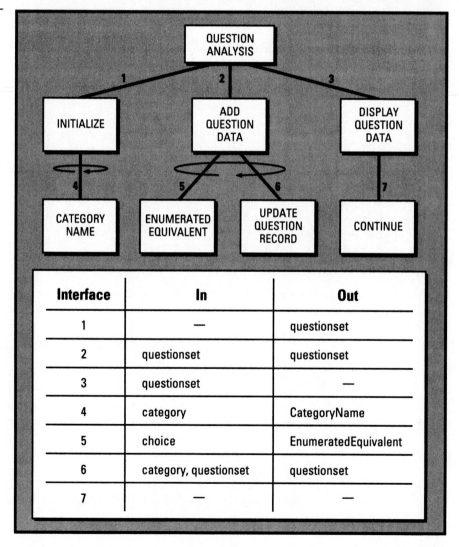

Interface	In	Out
1	—	questionset
2	questionset	questionset
3	questionset	—
4	category	CategoryName
5	choice	EnumeratedEquivalent
6	category, questionset	questionset
7	—	—

```
begin
  Initialize (questionset);
  repeat
    ClrScr;
    GotoXY (18,3);
    Writeln ('QUESTION SET ANALYSIS');
    GotoXY (10,5);
    Writeln ('Press the number preceding your choice.');
    GotoXY (15,8);
    Writeln ('<1>  Add Question to Set Data');
    GotoXY (15,10);
    Writeln ('<2>  Display Question Data');
    GotoXY (15,12);
    Writeln ('<3>  Exit Program');
    GotoXY (15,15);
    Write ('Choice --> ');
    choice := ReadKey;
    case choice of
      '1' :
        AddQuestionData (questionset);
      '2' :
        DisplayQuestionData (questionset);
      '3' :
        repeat
          GotoXY (10,22);
          Write ('Are you sure you want to exit (y/n)? ');
          sure := ReadKey
        until sure in ['y','Y','n','N']
    end
  until (choice = '3') and (sure in ['y','Y'])
end.
```

The **repeat** structure in the **case** structure is an extra safeguard against entering the wrong choice, exiting the program, and losing all the data. The program doesn't end until *Exit Program* is chosen and a *y* value is entered for *sure*.

The **Initialize** procedure is called immediately after the program is executed and gives all the fields for the four records' starting values:

```
procedure Initialize (var questionset : questionsetype);
  var
    category
      : categorytype;
begin
  ClrScr;
  for category := media to science do
    with questionset[category] do
      begin
        name := CategoryName (category);
        asked := 0;
        correct := 0;
        pctcorrect := 0.0
      end
end;
```

This procedure sends the enumerated constant representing a category name to the **CategoryName** function, which converts it to a string and stores it in the name field of the appropriate record:

```
function CategoryName (category : categorytype) : nametype;
begin
  if category = media
    then
      CategoryName := 'media'
    else
      if category = literature
        then
          CategoryName := 'literature'
        else
          if category = history
            then
              CategoryName := 'history'
            else
              CategoryName := 'science'
end;
```

This process enables the program to read the category name more easily in the form of a string, rather than converting category names from enumerated to string form each time they are output.

The **AddQuestionData** procedure displays a secondary menu that requires a single character entry to select a category:

```
procedure AddQuestionData (var questionset : questionsetype);
  var
    category
      : categorytype;
    choice
      : char;
begin
  repeat
    ClrScr;
    GotoXY (15,1);
    Writeln ('ADD QUESTIONNAIRE DATA');
    GotoXY (5,3);
    Writeln ('Enter number preceding your choice.');
    GotoXY (5,6);
    Writeln ('<1>  Media');
    GotoXY (5,8);
    Writeln ('<2>  Literature');
    GotoXY (5,10);
    Writeln ('<3>  History');
    GotoXY (5,12);
    Writeln ('<4>  Science');
    GotoXY (5,14);
    Writeln ('<5>  Return to main menu');
    repeat
      GotoXY (5,17);
      Write ('Choice --> ');
      choice := ReadKey
    until choice in ['1'..'5'];
    if choice <> '5'
      then
        begin
          category := EnumeratedEquivalent (choice);
          UpdateQuestionRecord (category, questionset)
        end
  until choice = '5'
end;
```

For any of the category choices, the program passes the string value of that choice to the **EnumeratedEquivalent** function and receives its enumerated equivalent for the subscript of the record array:

(continued)

```
function EnumeratedEquivalent (choice : char) : categorytype;
  var
    category
      : categorytype;
begin
  case choice of
    '1' :
      category := media;
    '2' :
      category := literature;
    '3' :
      category := history;
    '4' :
      category := science
  end;
  EnumeratedEquivalent := category
end;
```

That enumerated category type is then passed to the **Update-QuestionRecord** procedure, which adds 1 to the number of questions asked, determines if the question was answered correctly, updates the correct count if necessary, and calculates a new percentage:

```
procedure UpdateQuestionRecord (category : categorytype;
                           var questionset : questionsetype);
  var
    ans
      : char;
begin
  ClrScr;
  GotoXY (15,3);
  Writeln ('UPDATE QUESTION RECORD');
  GotoXY (5,6);
  with questionset[category] do
    begin
      asked := asked + 1;
      Writeln ('One question added to the ', name, ' total');
      repeat
        GotoXY (5,8);
        Write ('Was this question answered correctly (y/n): ');
        ans := ReadKey
      until ans in ['y','Y','n','N'];
      if ans in ['y','Y']
        then
          correct := correct + 1;
      pctcorrect := 100 * correct / asked
    end
end;
```

The `DisplayQuestionData` procedure shows the results in table form and calls a **Continue** procedure to keep the table on the screen until a key is pressed:

```
procedure DisplayQuestionData (questionset : questionsetype);
  var
    category
      : categorytype;
begin
  ClrScr;
  GotoXY (15,3);
  Writeln ('QUESTION DATA ANALYSIS');
  GotoXY (1,6);
  Writeln;
  Writeln ('Questions':30, 'Correctly':15, 'Percentage':15);
  Writeln ('Category':15, 'Asked':13, 'Answered':17, 'Correct':13);
  Writeln ('--------':15, '---------':15, '---------':15,
    '----------':15);
  for category := media to science do
    with questionset[category] do
      Writeln (name:15, asked:15, correct:15, pctcorrect:15:2);
  Continue
end;
```

The complete, documented solution is shown in Figure 12.3.

Figure 12.3
QuestionAnalysis
Program Listing

```pascal
program QuestionAnalysis;
{--------------------------------------------------------------------------}
{ PROGRAM:      Analysis of Question Difficulty                            }
{ PROGRAMMER:   P. Morales                                                 }
{ DATE:         November 2, 1990                                           }
{                                                                          }
{ This program analyzes the difficulty of trivia questions by             }
{ determining what percentage of the questions asked in a given           }
{ category were answered correctly. The game poses questions in four      }
{ different categories: media, literature, history, and science.          }
{ The program accepts data (a category and whether the response to        }
{ that question was correct) for one question at a time and produces      }
{ a table summarizing the results for each category.                      }
{                                                                          }
{ INPUT         question category                                         }
{               whether question was answered correctly                   }
{                                                                          }
{ OUTPUT        category                                                   }
{               number of questions asked in a category                   }
{               number of questions correctly answered in a category      }
{               percentage of correct answers in a category               }
{--------------------------------------------------------------------------}
  uses
    Crt;                              { screen formatting commands library }
  type
    categorytype = (media, literature, history, science);
                                      { question category type }
    nametype = string[10];                      { category name type }
    questiontype = record                       { question record type }
      name : nametype;
      asked,
      correct : integer;
      pctcorrect : real
     end;
    questionsetype = array[categorytype] of questiontype;
                                      { record collection type }
  var
    choice,                                          { menu selection }
    sure                              { exit confirmation response }
     : char;
    questionset                       { collection of question records }
     : questionsetype;
```

```
procedure Continue;
{---------------------------------------------------------------------}
{ Keeps output on screen until key is pressed.                        }
{                                                                     }
{ IN            none                                                  }
{                                                                     }
{ OUT           none                                                  }
{---------------------------------------------------------------------}
  var
    ch                                              { continue response }
      : char;
begin
  GotoXY (1,24);
  Write ('Press any key to continue.');
  ch := ReadKey
end;

function CategoryName (category : categorytype) : nametype;
{---------------------------------------------------------------------}
{ Converts enumerated category type to its string equivalent.         }
{                                                                     }
{ IN            category:  enumerated category type                   }
{                                                                     }
{ OUT           CategoryName:  string category name                   }
{---------------------------------------------------------------------}
begin
  if category = media
    then
      CategoryName := 'media'
    else
      if category = literature
        then
          CategoryName := 'literature'
        else
          if category = history
            then
              CategoryName := 'history'
            else
              CategoryName := 'science'
  end;
```

(continued)

451

```
procedure Initialize (var questionset : questionsetype);
{-----------------------------------------------------------------}
{ Sets all fields of question record to starting values.          }
{                                                                 }
{ IN            none                                              }
{                                                                 }
{ OUT           questionset:  array of question records           }
{-----------------------------------------------------------------}
  var
    category                                        { loop index }
      : categorytype;
begin
  ClrScr;
  for category := media to science do
    with questionset[category] do
      begin
        name := CategoryName (category);
        asked := 0;
        correct := 0;
        pctcorrect := 0.0
      end
end;


function EnumeratedEquivalent (choice : char) : categorytype;
{-----------------------------------------------------------------}
{ Converts choice character into its enumerated constant equivalent. }
{                                                                 }
{ IN            choice:  question choice character                }
{                                                                 }
{ OUT           EnumeratedEquivalent:  enumerated equivalent of    }
{                  choice character                               }
{-----------------------------------------------------------------}
  var
    category                    { temporary enumerated category choice }
      : categorytype;
begin
  case choice of
    '1' :
      category := media;
    '2' :
      category := literature;
    '3' :
      category := history;
    '4' :
      category := science
  end;
  EnumeratedEquivalent := category
end;
```

```
procedure UpdateQuestionRecord (category : categorytype;
                         var questionset : questionsetype);
{------------------------------------------------------------------}
{ Adds 1 to question count, updates number of correct answers if   }
{ necessary, and recalculates the percentage of correct answers.   }
{                                                                  }
{ IN            category:  category choice                         }
{               questionset:  array of question records            }
{                                                                  }
{ OUT           questionset:  array of question records            }
{------------------------------------------------------------------}
  var
    ans                   { indicates whether question answered correctly }
      : char;
begin
  ClrScr;
  GotoXY (15,3);
  Writeln ('UPDATE QUESTION RECORD');
  GotoXY (5,6);
  with questionset[category] do
    begin
      asked := asked + 1;
      Writeln ('One question added to the ', name, ' total');
      repeat
        GotoXY (5,8);
        Write ('Was this question answered correctly (y/n): ');
        ans := ReadKey
      until ans in ['y','Y','n','N'];
      if ans in ['y','Y']
        then
           correct := correct + 1;
      pctcorrect := 100 * correct / asked
    end
end;
```

(continued)

```
procedure AddQuestionData (var questionset : questionsetype);
{--------------------------------------------------------------------}
{ Allows selection of question category and update of                }
{ corresponding record.                                              }
{                                                                    }
{ IN              questionset:   array of question records           }
{                                                                    }
{ OUT             questionset:   array of question records           }
{--------------------------------------------------------------------}
  var
    category                              { enumerated category choice }
      : categorytype;
    choice                                    { category menu choice }
      : char;
begin
  repeat
    ClrScr;
    GotoXY (15,1);
    Writeln ('ADD QUESTIONNAIRE DATA');
    GotoXY (5,3);
    Writeln ('Enter number preceding your choice.');
    GotoXY (5,6);
    Writeln ('<1>  Media');
    GotoXY (5,8);
    Writeln ('<2>  Literature');
    GotoXY (5,10);
    Writeln ('<3>  History');
    GotoXY (5,12);
    Writeln ('<4>  Science');
    GotoXY (5,14);
    Writeln ('<5>  Return to main menu');
    repeat
      GotoXY (5,17);
      Write ('Choice --> ');
      choice := ReadKey
    until choice in ['1'..'5'];
    if choice <> '5'
      then
        begin
          category := EnumeratedEquivalent (choice);
          UpdateQuestionRecord (category, questionset)
        end
  until choice = '5'
end;
```

```
procedure DisplayQuestionData (questionset : questionsetype);
{-------------------------------------------------------------------}
{ Displays a table of question data, including name of category,    }
{ number of questions asked, number answered correctly, and         }
{ percentage of correct answers.                                    }
{                                                                   }
{ IN             questionset:  array of question records            }
{                                                                   }
{ OUT            none                                               }
{-------------------------------------------------------------------}
  var
    category                                        { loop index }
      : categorytype;
begin
  ClrScr;
  GotoXY (25,3);
  Writeln ('QUESTION DATA ANALYSIS');
  GotoXY (1,6);
  Writeln;
  Writeln ('Questions':30, 'Correctly':15, 'Percentage':15);
  Writeln ('Category':15, 'Asked':13, 'Answered':17, 'Correct':13);
  Writeln ('--------':15, '---------':15, '---------':15,
     '----------':15);
  for category := media to science do
    with questionset[category] do
      Writeln (name:15, asked:15, correct:15, pctcorrect:15:2);
  Continue
end;
```

(continued)

```
begin
  Initialize (questionset);
  repeat
    ClrScr;
    GotoXY (18,3);
    Writeln ('QUESTION SET ANALYSIS');
    GotoXY (10,5);
    Writeln ('Press the number preceding your choice.');
    GotoXY (15,8);
    Writeln ('<1>  Add Question to Set Data');
    GotoXY (15,10);
    Writeln ('<2>  Display Question Data');
    GotoXY (15,12);
    Writeln ('<3>  Exit Program');
    GotoXY (15,15);
    Write ('Choice --> ');
    choice := ReadKey;
    case choice of
      '1' :
        AddQuestionData (questionset);
      '2' :
        DisplayQuestionData (questionset);
      '3' :
        repeat
          GotoXY (10,22);
          Write ('Are you sure you want to exit (y/n)? ');
          sure := ReadKey
        until sure in ['y','Y','n','N']
    end
  until (choice = '3') and (sure in ['y','Y'])
end.
```

12.4 Pointer Data Types

Collections of related data items have been stored as either arrays or files. Because the size of the array data structure has to be declared and is fixed prior to its application, it is static. Main memory can be wasted if too many locations are reserved in advance. On the other hand, errors result if too few are reserved and an attempt is made to access locations outside the declared range. Files are dynamic structures, in that the size of a file does not have to be declared in advance and is restricted only by how much data the secondary storage media can hold.

Pointer data types allow the creation of dynamic data structures in main memory, since they acquire locations only when needed. No memory locations have to be reserved before they are referenced. When a location is needed, it is pulled from a pool of all the available locations in main memory (called the *heap*). When it is no longer required, the location can be returned to the heap for use in other applications.

Array and pointer structures also differ in the manner in which they reference a main memory location. The name given to an array element represents the location in which a data item is stored, while the name given to a pointer represents the location that contains the address of the location with the desired data.

A **type** statement defines a pointer data type.

FORMAT: **type**
<identifier> = ^<definition>;

The caret symbol ^ preceding the definition indicates that the identifier represents a pointer data type and stores the address of a memory location containing the data type in its definition.

Example

```
type
  pointertype = ^integer;
var
  p : pointertype;
```

The variable *p* represents a location that can contain the address of another location that stores an integer. You never know the address of the location containing the integer; *p* finds it for you.

You cannot assign any value to a pointer location or output the contents of a pointer location, but you can treat the location that the pointer references like any other variable. To avoid possible confusion, a pointer variable followed by a caret (^) references the location to which the variable points.

Example

```
p^ := 7;
Writeln (p^);
```

If *p* is defined as a pointer to an integer location, the first statement stores 7 in the location pointed to by *p*. The location *p* contains the address of the location that contains 7, as shown in Figure 12.4. The **Writeln** statement then displays the contents of the location that *p* points to.

When array locations are used for counting or summing, they are initialized, generally to 0. You can also initialize the address in a pointer location by storing the reserved word **nil** there to indicate that the pointer does not currently refer to any other location.

Figure 12.4
Example of Pointer
Data Type

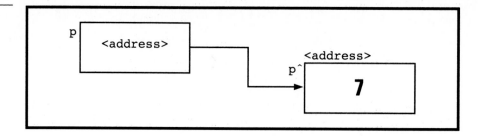

Example

p := nil;   Since **nil** is an address value and is stored in loca-
                                             tion *p, p* need not be followed by a caret.

Now all that remains is the capability of taking a memory location from the heap when you need one, and returning a location there when you no longer need it.

The **New** Procedure   The **New** procedure takes an available location from the heap and assigns a pointer variable to it.

FORMAT: **New (<pointer variable>);**

The address of the location selected from the heap is stored in the location represented by **<pointer variable>.** Every time **New** is called, a new memory location is selected and assigned.

Example

```
type
  pointertype = ^real;
var
  p, q : pointertype
  . . .

New (q);  { Step 1 }
New (q);  { Step 2 }
New (p);  { Step 3 }
```

Figure 12.5 illustrates the action of this section of Pascal code. In Step 1, the pointer variable *q* is assigned the address of a location that stores reals. The pointer *q* is reassigned to point to a new location taken from the memory pool in Step 2. All reference to the first location is lost and it becomes a wasted location. The last call to **New** grabs another memory location and stores its address in pointer location *p* (Step 3).

Figure 12.5
Example of the Use of
the **New** Procedure

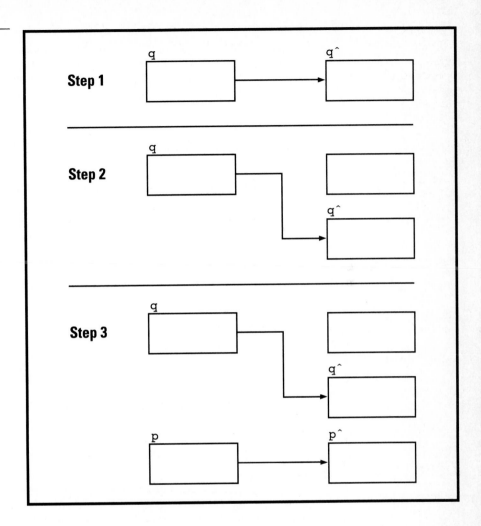

The **Dispose**
Procedure

The **Dispose** procedure returns a location to the memory pool.

FORMAT: **Dispose (<pointer variable>);**

The location whose address is stored in **<pointer variable>** is returned to the heap. The contents of the returned location must be removed or copied before **Dispose** is executed, or that data is permanently lost. If a pointer does not point to a memory location when **Dispose** is invoked, an error results.

Example

```
type
  stringtype := string[3];
  stringptrtype = ^stringtype;
var
  p, q, r : stringptrtype;
  . . .

New (p);              { 1 }
p^ := 'd';            { 2 }
q := p;               { 3 }
New (p);              { 4 }
p^ := 'c';            { 5 }
New (r);              { 6 }
r^ := Concat(p^,q^);  { 7 }
Dispose (p);          { 8 }
Dispose (q);          { 9 }
Dispose (r);          { 10 }
```

The numbers in the comment braces refer to the steps in this process shown in Figure 12.6. In step 1, a memory location is taken from the heap and its address stored in *p*. The letter *d* is stored in that location in the next step. The address in pointer *q* is copied into pointer *q*, with both *p* and *q* referencing the same main memory location. The **New** procedure in step 4 gets a new location, stores its address in *p* (*p* and *q* reference different locations), and puts the letter *c* in it (step 5). In step 6, a new location is taken from the heap and its address stored in *r*. It is filled with a concatenation of the contents of the locations pointed to by *p* and *q*, that is, *cd*. In the remaining three steps, each of these locations is returned to the heap.

12.5 Linked Lists

An array is a related collection of memory locations. You know how to get from one element in the array to the others by specifying a subscript. If pointers are to save memory when collections are involved, there also has to be a way to get from one item in the collection of pointers to another; that is, you must be able to link all related memory locations into a single structure, a *linked list*.

In a linked list, an item in the collection, called a *node*, has two components: one that contains the data the item was designed to hold, and another that points to the next item in the list. In general, the information component is a record data type and the next-item component is a pointer data type. Figure 12.7 illustrates a typical node structure for a linked list; the information component is a record with four fields, and the next component is a pointer.

Suppose a teacher wanted to call on class members in alphabetical order without changing students' seats. He could remember all the names and sort them mentally to produce the correct order, or he could remember the student whose last name is first in alphabetical order, have that student remember the student whose last name came next, and so on. The last student need only remember that no one follows. To go through the class in alphabetical order, the teacher would call on the first student in the list, ask that student for the next name, and continue until a student indicates that he or she is last.

Figure 12.6
Example of the Use of
New and **Dispose**

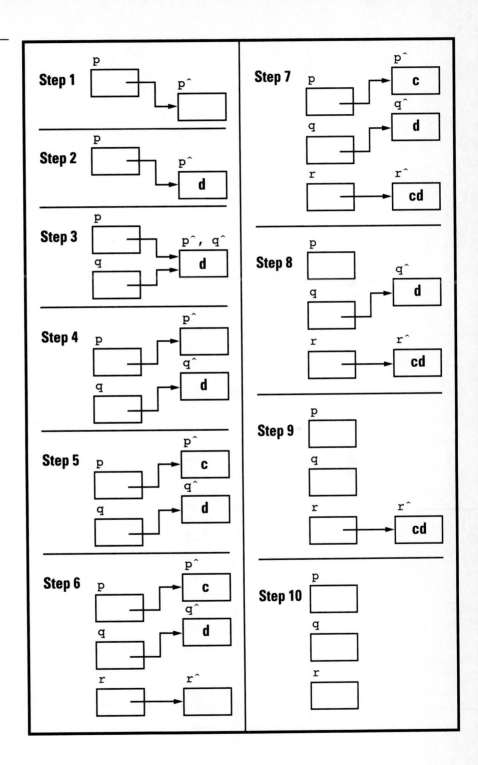

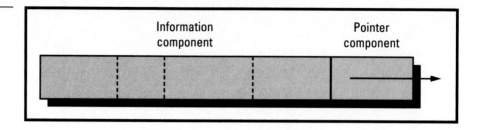

A simple linked list is a collection of nodes with the pointers providing a similar one-way trip through the list. To visit each node in the list, you have to know where the first node is and use the information in its pointer field to find the next. In Figure 12.8, the pointer variable *first* contains the address of the first item in the linked list. The pointer field of the first item gives the address of the second item, and the second gives the address of the third. The slash in the next field of the third node indicates that it is the last node in the list. In practice, the next field of this node would contain the pointer value **nil.** When visiting all the nodes in a list, it is important not to change the value of the pointer to the first node in the list. If you change its value, you won't be able to find the beginning of the list—and for all practical purposes you have just erased it.

Among the standard operations performed on linked lists are adding a node to a list and visiting each node in the list. (A trip through the entire list is called a *traversal*.) In either case, there must be a pointer that gives the address of the first node in the list. In the following examples, assume *start* points to the first node and that each node is a record defined by:

```
type
   pointertype = ^nodetype;
   infotype = record

      . . .

    end;
   nodetype = record
     info : infotype
     next : pointertype
   end;
var
   start
     : pointertype;
```

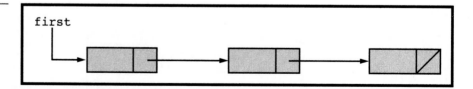

first

A pointer of type *pointertype* points to (stores the address of) a node of type *nodetype*. The specific definition of *infotype* would depend on the particular application. Each node has an information field of type *infotype* and a next field of type *pointertype* so you can reference the next node in the list.

If the order in which elements are added to a linked list is not important, it is easiest to add a node to the front of the list. The three steps needed to perform an insertion are to get a node, load data into its information component, and connect it to the existing list.

Example

```
procedure InsertNode (var start : listptr);
  var
    p : listptr;
begin
  New (p);
  LoadInformation (p);
  if start = nil
    then                      { add to an empty list }
      p^.next := nil
    else                    { add to a nonempty list }
      p^.next := start;
  start := p
end;
```

InsertNode (start);

The **New** procedure takes a *nodetype* location from the heap and stores its address in *p*. A call to **LoadInformation** fills the information field of the node. If the list is initially empty (see Figure 12.9), the next field of the new node is set to **nil,** indicating it is also the last node in the list. If the list is not empty (see Figure 12.10), the next field of the new node points to the former first element in the list, the one pointed to by *start*. In any case, the address of the new node stored in *p* is copied into *start* so it can become the new first element in the list.

To visit the nodes in a linked list, you have to start at the first node and use its *next* field to go to the next node. This process continues until the next field of a node is **nil.**

Figure 12.9
Inserting a Node into an
Initially Empty Linked List

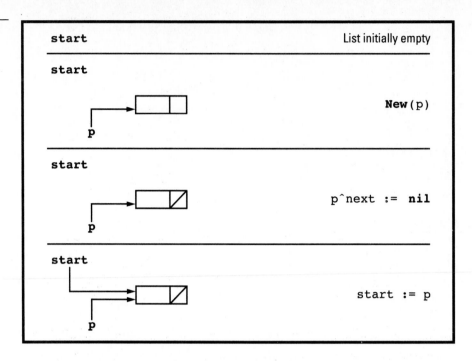

Figure 12.10
Inserting a Node into a
Nonempty Linked List

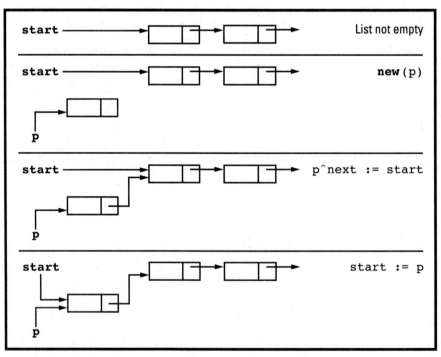

Example

```
procedure TraverseList (start : listptr);
  var
    visitor : listptr;
begin
  visitor := start;
  while visitor <> nil do
    begin
      ...
      visitor := visitor^.next
    end
end;
```

`TraverseList (start);`

The address of the first node in the list is copied from *start* into the local variable *visitor*. If it is **nil,** the list is empty and the traversal stops. If it is not **nil,** some operation is performed on the information in the node and the address that is stored in the current node pointed to by *visitor* is copied into *visitor,* in effect moving that pointer to the next node. The traversal continues until *visitor* reaches the end of the list. Figure 12.11 illustrates this process for a list with three nodes.

12.6 Application: The Write Stuff

One method of analyzing writing is to determine how often the same words appear in a writing sample. You can expect the common words *the* and *is* to occur frequently, but if forms of words such as *use* do, then it may be better to rewrite or rephrase the sample.

The task, then, is to write a program that displays a frequency count of all the words in a writing sample after accepting the words in the sample one at a time. As the words are entered, form a linked list whose nodes store both the word and a count of the number of times it appears in the sample passage.

The declaration section defines *wordcountype* as a record with two information fields and a next field: a text word, a count of the number of times that word occurs, and a pointer indicating the address of the next node in the list. A variable of type *nodeptr* is defined to point to this record.

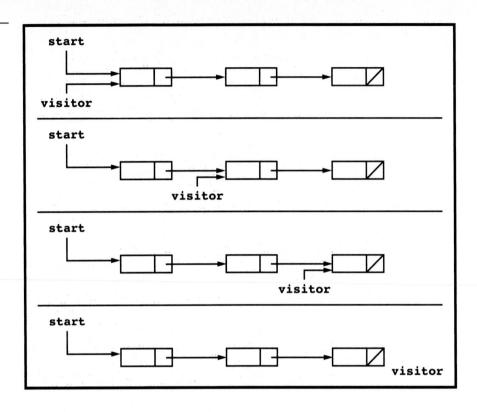

```
type
  wordtype = string[20];
  nodeptr = ^wordcounttype;
  wordcounttype = record
    textword : wordtype;
    count : integer;
    next : nodeptr
  end;
var
  start
    : nodeptr;
```

Only a single pointer, *start*, is needed to perform any operations on the list.

The solution design and corresponding module interface table are shown in Figure 12.12.

The main program initializes *start* to **nil** and calls procedures to create a linked list containing the word counts and to display the data in the list:

```
begin
  start := nil;
  FormWordList (start);
  DisplayWordList (start)
end.
```

FormWordList has a variable parameter that contains the address of the beginning of the linked list:

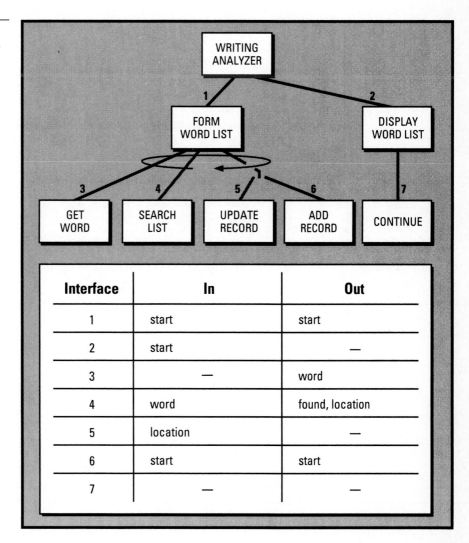

Figure 12.12
Writing Analyzer Structure Chart and Module Interface Table

Interface	In	Out
1	start	start
2	start	—
3	—	word
4	word	found, location
5	location	—
6	start	start
7	—	—

```
procedure FormWordList (var start : nodeptr);
  var
    word
      : wordtype;
    found
      : boolean;
    location
      : nodeptr;
    ans
      : char;
begin
  repeat
    GetWord (word);
    SearchList (word, start, found, location);
    if found
      then
        UpdateRecord (location)
      else
        AddRecord (start, word);
    repeat
      GotoXY (15,10);
      Write ('Another word (y/n)? ');
      Readln (ans)
    until ans in ['n','N','y','Y']
  until ans in ['n','N']
end;
```

The **repeat** structure continues to accept words, using the procedure GetWord, and adds them to the linked list until there are no additional words to enter:

```
procedure GetWord (var word : wordtype);
begin
  ClrScr;
  GotoXY (15,3);
  Writeln ('TEXT WORD ENTRY');
  GotoXY (15,6);
  Write ('Enter word: ');
  Readln (word)
end;
```

After a word is entered, the linked list is searched to determine whether the word currently appears in the list:

```
procedure SearchList (word : wordtype; start : nodeptr;
          var found : boolean; var location : nodeptr);
begin
  found := false;
  location := start;
  while (not found) and (location <> nil) do
    if location^.textword = word
      then
        found := true
      else
        location := location^.next
end;
```

The pointer *location* starts at the beginning of the list. If the word is already in the list (the *textword* field of the node that *location* points to equals the input word), then the **while** loop ends, *found* returns *true,* and the pointer *location* returns the address of the node containing the word. The **while** loop also terminates if location equals **nil** (i.e., no match for the input word has been found). In this case, a *false* value for *found* is returned to FormWordList.

If a word is already in the list, its count field is increased by 1 in the UpdateRecord procedure:

```
procedure UpdateRecord (location : nodeptr);
begin
  location^.count := location^.count + 1
end;
```

If a word is not in the list, then a node is taken from the heap, its information fields are initialized, and its next field is adjusted to place it at the beginning of the new linked list:

```
procedure AddRecord (var start : nodeptr; word : wordtype);
  var
    p
      : nodeptr;
begin
  New (p);
  p^.textword := word;
  p^.count := 1;
  if start = nil
    then
      p^.next := nil
    else
      p^.next := start;
  start := p
end;
```

Once the completed list has been formed, the information it contains is output by **DisplayWordList** in tabular form by going through the list from beginning to end and displaying the contents of each node visited:

```
procedure DisplayWordList (start : nodeptr);
  var
    p
      : nodeptr;
begin
  ClrScr;
  GotoXY (12,1);
  Writeln ('WORD FREQUENCY LIST');
  GotoXY (1,5);
  Writeln ('word':15, 'frequency':15);
  Writeln ('----':15, '---------':15);
  p := start;
  while p <> nil do
    begin
      Writeln (p^.textword:15, p^.count:12);
      p := p^.next
    end;
  Continue
end;
```

The **Continue** call allows the output to remain on the screen until a key is pressed.

The complete, documented solution for this writing analyzer is given in Figure 12.13.

Figure 12.13
Writing Analyzer
Program Listing

```pascal
program WritingAnalyzer;
{----------------------------------------------------------------------------}
{ PROGRAM:        Writing Analyzer                                           }
{ PROGRAMMER:     J. Conrad                                                  }
{ DATE:           November 11, 1990                                          }
{                                                                            }
{ This program displays a frequency count of all the words in a             }
{ writing sample after accepting the words in the sample one at a            }
{ time. As the words are entered, a linked list is formed whose nodes        }
{ store a word and a count of the number of times it appears in the          }
{ sample passage.                                                            }
{                                                                            }
{ INPUT          words from a writing sample                                 }
{                                                                            }
{ OUTPUT         words from the sample                                       }
{                frequency of occurrence of words in sample                  }
{----------------------------------------------------------------------------}
  uses
    Crt;                                  { screen formatting commands library }
  type
    wordtype = string[20];
    nodeptr = ^wordcounttype;                     { pointer to word count node }
    wordcounttype = record                           { record of word counts }
      textword : wordtype;
      count : integer;
      next : nodeptr
     end;
  var
    start                                        { beginning of linked list }
      : nodeptr;
```

(continued)

```
procedure GetWord (var word : wordtype);
{-------------------------------------------------------------------}
{ Accepts word from writing sample.                                 }
{                                                                   }
{ IN            none                                                }
{                                                                   }
{ OUT           word:  word from writing sample                     }
{-------------------------------------------------------------------}
begin
  ClrScr;
  GotoXY (15,3);
  Writeln ('TEXT WORD ENTRY');
  GotoXY (15,6);
  Write ('Enter word: ');
  Readln (word)
end;

procedure SearchList (word : wordtype; start : nodeptr;
          var found : boolean; var location : nodeptr);
{-------------------------------------------------------------------}
{ Searches linked list for input word and returns whether it was    }
{ found. If the word is found, its location is also returned.        }
{                                                                   }
{ IN            word:       word to search for                      }
{               start:      beginning of linked list                }
{                                                                   }
{ OUT           found:      determines whether word is currently     }
{                           in list or not                          }
{               location:   points to node containing match         }
{                           for entered word                        }
{-------------------------------------------------------------------}
begin
  found := false;
  location := start;
  while (not found) and (location <> nil) do
    if location^.textword = word
      then
        found := true
      else
        location := location^.next
  end;
```

```
procedure UpdateRecord (location : nodeptr);
{-------------------------------------------------------------------}
{ Adds 1 to count of a word already in the list.                    }
{                                                                   }
{ IN            location:  points to node containing word           }
{                                                                   }
{ OUT           none                                                }
{-------------------------------------------------------------------}
begin
  location^.count := location^.count + 1
end;


procedure AddRecord (var start : nodeptr; word : wordtype);
{-------------------------------------------------------------------}
{ Creates a new node for the linked list of words, initializes      }
{ fields of the record stored in the node, and makes it the first   }
{ node in the list.                                                 }
{                                                                   }
{ IN            start:  beginning of linked list                    }
{                                                                   }
{ OUT           start:  beginning of linked list                    }
{-------------------------------------------------------------------}
  var
    p                                        { pointer to new node }
      : nodeptr;
begin
  New (p);
  p^.textword := word;
  p^.count := 1;
  if start = nil
    then
      p^.next := nil
    else
      p^.next := start;
  start := p
end;
```

(continued)

```pascal
procedure FormWordList (var start : nodeptr);
{------------------------------------------------------------------------}
{ Creates list of words accepted from a writing sample.                  }
{                                                                        }
{ IN            start:  beginning of linked list                         }
{                                                                        }
{ OUT           start:  beginning of linked list                         }
{------------------------------------------------------------------------}
  var
    word                                   { word from writing sample }
      : wordtype;
    found                          { determines if word in list or not }
      : boolean;
    location                          { points to node containing word }
      : nodeptr;
    ans                                { response to continue query }
      : char;
begin
  repeat
    GetWord (word);
    SearchList (word, start, found, location);
    if found
      then
        UpdateRecord (location)
      else
        AddRecord (start, word);
    repeat
      GotoXY (15,10);
      Write ('Another word (y/n)? ');
      Readln (ans)
    until ans in ['n','N','y','Y']
  until ans in ['n','N']
end;
```

```
procedure Continue;
{---------------------------------------------------------------------}
{ Keeps output on screen until key is pressed.                        }
{                                                                     }
{ IN            none                                                  }
{                                                                     }
{ OUT           none                                                  }
{---------------------------------------------------------------------}
  var
    ch                                   { response to continue directive }
      : char;
begin
  GotoXY (10,24);
  Write ('Press any key to continue.');
  ch := ReadKey
end;

procedure DisplayWordList (start : nodeptr);
{---------------------------------------------------------------------}
{ Displays table of words and their frequency counts.                 }
{                                                                     }
{ IN            start:  beginning of linked list                      }
{                                                                     }
{ OUT           none                                                  }
{---------------------------------------------------------------------}
  var
    p                                    { pointer for traversing list }
      : nodeptr;
begin
  ClrScr;
  GotoXY (12,1);
  Writeln ('WORD FREQUENCY LIST');
  GotoXY (1,5);
  Writeln ('word':15, 'frequency':15);
  Writeln ('----':15, '---------':15);
  p := start;
  while p <> nil do
    begin
      Writeln (p^.textword:15, p^.count:12);
      p := p^.next
    end;
  Continue
end;
```

(continued)

```
begin
  start := nil;
  FormWordList (start);
  DisplayWordList (start)
end.
```

12.7 Recursion

In addition to one subprogram having the capability of calling another, a Pascal subprogram can also call itself. Subprograms that call themselves are termed *recursive* and the process is called *recursion.*

As with iteration, recursion is a process of repetition, but unlike iteration, the repetition in recursion is implied: There are no statements in a recursive subprogram that explicitly indicate repetition. In the explicit iterative structures **while, repeat,** and **for,** one or more variables are involved in a terminating condition that determines when the loop stops. Recursive solutions also must have terminating conditions.

The general form for any recursive definition designed to calculate the value of a given parameter is as follows:

> if a terminating condition is met
> > then
> > > parameter has a constant value
> > else
> > > value of parameter is changed and the same
> > > subprogram is called with this new value

If the terminating condition is never satisfied, the equivalent of an infinite loop is produced. Recursion is possible only if the solution can be expressed in a form that allows the termination condition to be reached in a finite number of steps.

The most common example of a recursive solution to a problem is finding the factorial of an integer value. The factorial of a positive integer is a product of that integer with all the positive integers less than it. By definition, 0 factorial (written 0!) = 1. For example, 5 factorial (5!) is $5 \times 4 \times 3 \times 2 \times 1$, or 120. A nonrecursive, iterative function can be written to calculate $n!$:

```
function IterativeFactorial (n : integer) : longint;
  var
    i : integer;
    prod : longint;
begin
  prod := 1;
  for i := n downto 1 do
    prod := prod * i;
  IterativeFactorial := prod
end;
```

The loop index *i* selects the integers from *n* down to 1, while the body of the loop keeps a running product. Since factorial values grow very rapidly, they are defined as long integers.

A recursive definition for determining *n*! is:

if *n* = 0
    then
        n! = 1
    else
        find the product of *n* and (*n* − 1)!

In general, *n*! equals $n \times (n-1) \times (n-2) \times \cdots \times 3 \times 2 \times 1$, which is equivalent to $n \times (n-1)!$, since $(n-1)!$ is the product of the positive integers from *n* − 1 down to 1. In other words, in order to find *n*!, first find $(n-1)!$ and then multiply it by *n*. Suppose, for example, that you want to find 4! Here, *n* is 4, so 4! is $4 \times (4-1)!$, or $4 \times 3!$. But what is 3!? 3! is $3 \times 2!$, and 2! is $2 \times 1!$. 1! equals $1 \times 0!$, but 0! is 1 (according to the definition, the recursion stops when *n* is 0). After breaking the problem down into easier and easier problems, you finally reach a constant value for an answer. When that occurs, 1 is substituted for 0!, so 1! becomes 1×1, or 1; 2!, which was $2 \times 1!$, becomes 2×1, or 2; and so on A summary of the process follows:

$$4! = 4 \times 3!$$
$$3! = 3 \times 2!$$
$$2! = 2 \times 1!$$
$$1! = 1 \times 0!$$
$$0! = 1$$
$$1! = 1 \times 1, \text{ or } 1$$
$$2! = 2 \times 1, \text{ or } 2$$
$$3! = 3 \times 2, \text{ or } 6$$
$$4! = 4 \times 6, \text{ or } 24$$

The code for the recursive solution to the factorial problem closely imitates the recursive definition.

Example

```pascal
function Factorial (n : integer) : longint;
  var
     ntemp : integer;
     factemp : longint;
begin
  if n = 0
    then
      Factorial := 1
    else
      begin
        ntemp := n - 1;
        factemp := Factorial (ntemp);
        Factorial := n * factemp
      end
end;
```

```pascal
ans := Factorial(3);
```

3 becomes the first value of the parameter n in the function header, and an initial level of memory locations is allocated (see Figure 12.14a). Since n is not 0, the **else** part of the conditional is executed. After *ntemp* becomes 2, the right side of the next statement places another call to *Factorial* but uses 2 as the parameter. Since this is a different call, a different level of local variable locations is stacked on the first level (Figure 12.14b). This process continues (Figure 12.14c and d) until 0 is passed to *Factorial*. Since 0! is 1, the top level of memory is removed and 1 is passed back to its call (the second statement in the **else** clause) on level 3 and stored in *factemp* on that level (Figure 12.14e). The product of n and *factemp* on that level gives the next value of *Factorial*. After level 3 is removed, 1 is passed to *factemp* on level 2 (Figure 12.14f). The return process continues until all the levels are removed and the answer is returned to the original call and stored in *ans* (Figure 12.14g and h).

Calls to Factorial			
Level 1	3	2	
	n	ntemp	factemp

(a)

Level 2	2	1	
Level 1	3	2	
	n	ntemp	factemp

(b)

Level 3	1	0	
Level 2	2	1	
Level 1	3	2	
	n	ntemp	factemp

(c)

Level 4	0		
Level 3	1	0	
Level 2	2	1	
Level 1	3	2	
	n	ntemp	factemp

(d)

Returns from Factorial			
Level 4	0		
Level 3	1	0	1
Level 2	2	1	
Level 1	3	2	
	n	ntemp	factemp

(e)

Level 3	1	0	1
Level 2	2	1	1
Level 1	3	2	
	n	ntemp	factemp

(f)

Level 2	2	1	1
Level 1	3	2	2
	n	ntemp	factemp

(g)

Level 1	3	2	2
	n	ntemp	factemp

(h)

Factorial(3) = 6

Figure 12.14
Recursive Factorial Memory
Allocation

The **else** clause in this example was written with three statements, to make the memory allocation process easier to understand. The variables *ntemp* and *factemp* are not needed. The statements of which they are a part could have been replaced by the following single assignment statement:

```
Factorial := n * Factorial (n-1);
```

This implementation more closely mirrors the original recursive definition of factorial.

To better visualize how memory is allocated and released for recursive calls and returns from calls, put the local variables *n, ntemp,* and *factemp* in the Watches window, and trace the program using function key F7 while comparing the values in the Watches window with those in Figure 12.14.

Not all problem solutions requiring repetition structures can be written recursively. Many can be written only with iterative structures, while others offer a choice between the two methods. All recursive solutions, however, can be expressed iteratively. In general, a recursive solution is possible if the same operation can be performed on a set of variables where the value change in one of the variables eventually leads to a limiting value.

The major advantage of using recursion is that you can solve complex problems with very few lines of code. The price you pay for this economy in code is that a recursive program takes more time to execute and requires both extra memory and a more complex memory management policy. Each time a recursive subprogram is called, a new set of memory locations for local variables is stacked on top of the previous set. When data items are returned to these calls, levels of memory locations must be removed in the reverse order in which they were stacked.

12.8 Application: Scrabble Scramble

In the game of Scrabble, each player is given a rack of seven letters from which to form words. Although there are many permutations of the letters on the rack, only a few of these may form legitimate words. The number of permutations of *k* objects taken from a set of *n* objects is given by:

$$\frac{n!}{(n-k)!}$$

Write a program that produces a table that gives the number of possible permutations of letters, choosing one at a time, two at a time, and so on.

The structure chart and module interface table outlining a solution to this problem is shown in Figure 12.15.

The declaration section defines a constant for the size of the letter rack and a two-dimensional array that stores both the sizes of the groups of letters chosen at one time and their respective permutation values:

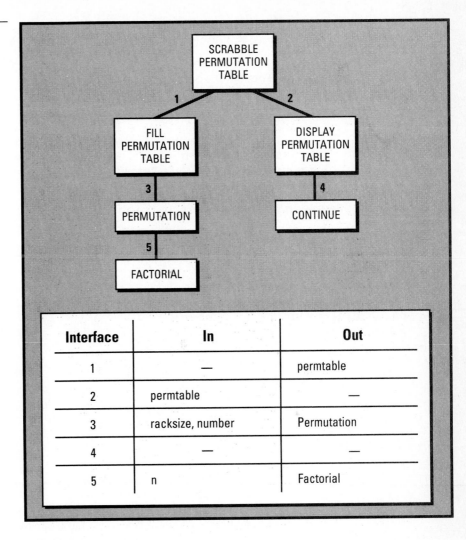

Interface	In	Out
1	—	permtable
2	permtable	—
3	racksize, number	Permutation
4	—	—
5	n	Factorial

```
const
   racksize = 7;
type
   tabletype = array[1..7,1..2] of longint;
var
   permtable
      : tabletype;
```

Long integers are chosen for the array so as to avoid any errors that might be caused by the rapid growth of factorial values and the limits imposed on the maximum-value **integer** data types.

The main program consists of calls to procedures that fill the permutation array and display it:

```
begin
  FillPermutationTable (permtable);
  DisplayPermutationTable (permtable)
end.
```

The `FillPermutationTable` procedure uses the size of the group of letters chosen in the first column of the two-dimensional array as a loop control variable, and calls **Permutation** to calculate the number of permutations for a group of that size:

```
procedure FillPermutationTable (var permtable : tabletype);
  var
    groupsize
      : integer;
begin
  for groupsize := 1 to racksize do
    begin
      permtable[number,1] := number;
      permtable[number,2] := Permutation (racksize, groupsize)
    end
end;
```

`Permutation` accepts the *racksize* and *groupsize,* and calls Factorial twice to determine the factorial values of the numerator and denominator in the given formula:

```
function Permutation (n, k : integer) : longint;
begin
  Permutation := Factorial(n) div Factorial(n-k)
end;
```

The integer division operator **div** is used to find the quotient of the results of two recursive calls to the **Factorial** function. (The **Factorial** function here is identical to that in the previous example):

```
function Factorial (n : integer) : longint;
  var
    ntemp
      : integer;
    factemp
      : longint;
begin
  if n = 0
    then
      Factorial := 1
    else
      begin
        ntemp := n - 1;
        factemp := Factorial (ntemp);
        Factorial := n * factemp
      end
end;
```

Finally, the `DisplayPermutationTable` procedure shows the results in tabular form:

```
procedure DisplayPermutationTable (permtable : tabletype);
  var
    i : integer;
begin
  ClrScr;
  GotoXY (10,1);
  Writeln ('SCRABBLE PERMUTATION TABLE');
  GotoXY (15,2);
  Writeln ('(Rack size: ',racksize, ')');
  GotoXY (1,5);
  Writeln ('Letters':15, 'Permutations':20);
  Writeln ('-------':15, '------------':20);
  for i := 1 to racksize do
    Writeln (permtable[i,1]:12, permtable[i,2]:20);
  Continue
end;
```

The final, documented solution is shown in Figure 12.16.

Figure 12.16
ScrabblePermutation-
Table Program Listing

```pascal
program ScrabblePermutationTable;
{-------------------------------------------------------------------}
{ PROGRAM:        Permutation Table for Scrabble Letter Rack        }
{ PROGRAMMER:     N. Webster                                        }
{ DATE:           November 22, 1990                                 }
{                                                                   }
{ This program produces a table that gives the number of possible   }
{ permutations of letters chosen one at a time, two at a time, and so }
{ on from a group of seven. The number of permutations of k objects }
{ taken from a set of n objects is given by:                        }
{                                                                   }
{                              n!                                   }
{                          --------                                 }
{                          (n - k)!                                 }
{                                                                   }
{ INPUT           none                                              }
{                                                                   }
{ OUTPUT          table of permutation values                      }
{-------------------------------------------------------------------}
  uses
    Crt;                            { screen formatting commands library }
  const
    racksize = 7;                                   { size of letter rack }
  type
    tabletype = array[1..7,1..2] of longint;              { table type }
  var
    permtable                          { letter permutation table }
      : tabletype;
```

```
function Factorial (n : integer) : longint;
{-------------------------------------------------------------------------}
{ Determines the factorial value of its parameter.                        }
{                                                                         }
{ IN              n:  integer value                                       }
{                                                                         }
{ OUT             Factorial:  n!                                          }
{-------------------------------------------------------------------------}
  var
    ntemp                                   { copy of current value of n }
      : integer;
    factemp                                 { copy of current value of n! }
      : longint;
begin
  if n = 0
    then
      Factorial := 1
    else
      begin
        ntemp := n - 1;
        factemp := Factorial (ntemp);
        Factorial := n * factemp
      end
end;


function Permutation (n, k : integer) : longint;
{-------------------------------------------------------------------------}
{ Determines the number of permutations taken from a population of        }
{ n items k at a time.                                                    }
{                                                                         }
{ IN              n:  size of population                                  }
{                 k:  size of group taken from population                 }
{                                                                         }
{ OUT             Permutation:  number of permutations                    }
{-------------------------------------------------------------------------}
begin
  Permutation := Factorial(n) div Factorial(n-k)
end;
```

(continued)

```
procedure FillPermutationTable (var permtable : tabletype);
{------------------------------------------------------------------}
{ Loads table with size of group of letters taken from the rack and }
{ the number of permutations possible with a group of that size.    }
{                                                                   }
{ IN            none                                                }
{                                                                   }
{ OUT           permtable:  table of permutations                   }
{------------------------------------------------------------------}
  var
    groupsize                                     { size of letter group }
      : integer;
begin
  for groupsize := 1 to racksize do
    begin
      permtable[groupsize,1] := groupsize;
      permtable[groupsize,2] := Permutation (racksize, groupsize)
    end
end;


procedure Continue;
{------------------------------------------------------------------}
{ Keeps output on screen until key is pressed.                      }
{                                                                   }
{ IN            none                                                }
{                                                                   }
{ OUT           none                                                }
{------------------------------------------------------------------}
  var
    ch                                  { response to continue directive }
      : char;
begin
  GotoXY (10,24);
  Write ('Press any key to continue.');
  ch := ReadKey
end;
```

```
procedure DisplayPermutationTable (permtable : tabletype);
{----------------------------------------------------------------}
{ Displays table of permutation values on screen.               }
{                                                               }
{ IN          permtable:  table of permutations                 }
{                                                               }
{ OUT         none                                              }
{----------------------------------------------------------------}
  var
    i                                      { loop control variable }
      : integer;
begin
  ClrScr;
  GotoXY (10,1);
  Writeln ('SCRABBLE PERMUTATION TABLE');
  GotoXY (15,2);
  Writeln ('(Rack size: ',racksize, ')');
  GotoXY (1,5);
  Writeln ('Letters':15, 'Permutations':20);
  Writeln ('-------':15, '------------':20);
  for i := 1 to racksize do
    Writeln (permtable[i,1]:12, permtable[i,2]:20);
  Continue
end;

begin
  FillPermutationTable (permtable);
  DisplayPermutationTable (permtable)
end.
```

12.9 Object-Oriented Programming

We've been stressing the importance of modularity in the design of the problem solutions, with modules implemented by procedure and functions forming the basic building blocks. While modules were presented to break a problem into smaller, more manageable components, parameters were introduced to pass data between modules, minimizing the dependence of one module on another. Even though these techniques simplify program maintenance, they don't go far enough. Turbo Pascal 6.0 has the capability of defining data and a collection of procedures and/or functions (called *methods)* that operate on that data as a single *object*. The process of treating related data types *and* methods as a single entity is called *encapsulation*.

Just as with a procedure or function, an object can be a part of many different programs without having to change any of its components. The idea is to create a "toolbox" of useful objects and have programs consist primarily of collections of these objects that are adapted to a particular application, thus minimizing any duplication of effort while improving the usability of existing code. A programming process that makes efficient use of these data structures and methods is called *object-oriented programming (OOP)*.

Objects are defined in **type** statements and implemented like records. The object declaration includes method headers, as well as variable identifiers defined in object fields.

FORMAT:
```
type
  <class identifier> = object
    <variable identifier> : <data type>;
    <variable identifier> : <data type>;
                    . . .
    procedure <identifier> [(<parameter list>)];
    procedure <identifier> [(<parameter list>)];
                    . . .
    function <identifier> [(<parameter list>)]
                      : <function type>;
    function <identifier> [(<parameter list>)]
                      : <function type>;
                    . . .
  end;
```

In the **type** declaration for an object, an identifier for the object class is followed by the equal sign and the reserved word **object.** This line is followed by fields that assign appropriate data types to variable identifiers in the object. The headers for any methods (procedures and/or functions) that operate on the variable identifiers are specified next. Only the headers are listed; the complete code for these methods follows the **type** declaration. Unlike other structures, this structure requires a semicolon to follow the last method header—the one preceding the **end;** that signifies the end of the object's definition.

Example

```
type
  accountype = object
    balance : real;
    function NewBalance (transaction : real)
                : real;
  end;
```

The object called *accountype* has a field that defines the variable *balance* and one method, a real function NewBalance with a local variable called *transaction*.

The object is not complete until the methods listed in the object declaration are defined. To identify a method as belonging to a defined object, the method identifier that heads the body of the method must be preceded by both the class identifier for the object and a period, similar to the way in which a field of a record is specified. All object field identifiers used by this method are assumed to be of the same class as the object type preceding the method name.

Example

```
function accountype.NewBalance
      (transaction : real) : real;
begin
  balance := balance + transaction;
  NewBalance := balance
end;
```

The function name **NewBalance** in the header must be preceded by the class identifier, *accountype*. The *accountype* preface is assumed for the identifier *balance* since it is part of the object's definition. In all other aspects, the function behaves like functions that are not object methods.

The **type** statement and the code for each of the methods declared in the **type** statement completely describe the object. Now that the object is defined, how can we use it in a particular application program? First, the application must know how the object is constructed and must request to use it by declaring a variable to be of that object type after the object's declaration in a **type** statement. The variable declaration in a program containing the object defined in the two previous examples might be:

```
var
   account
     : accountype;
```

Any component of an object of type *accountype* is accessed through the variable *account*.

Second, each reference to a field or method of an object must be prefaced by the variable identifier of that object type (*account*, in this case) and a period, in the same way a field of a record is referenced by preceding it with a record identifier and a period. Consider the following example, in which the object *accountype* is used in a program to accept a transaction and update the balance in a checking account.

Example

```
type
  accountype = object
    balance : real;
    function NewBalance (transaction : real) : real;
  end;

function accountype.NewBalance (transaction : real) : real;
begin
  balance := balance + transaction;
  NewBalance := balance
end;
```

```
var
  account
    : accountype;
  startbalance,
  endbalance,
  transaction
    : real;

    . . .

begin
  EnterStartBalance (startbalance);
  account.balance := startbalance;
  EnterTransaction (transaction);
  endbalance := account.NewBalance (transaction);
    . . .
```

The **EnterStartBalance** procedure accepts a value for the opening balance of checking account and returns it through *startbalance*. That value is stored in *account.balance,* the *balance* field of the object called *account* that is defined as type *accountype.* A value for *transaction* is returned by the **EnterTransaction** procedure and is passed to the object method **NewBalance**, returning the updated account balance, which is finally stored in *endbalance.*

STYLE TIP Keep the code for all the components of an object together at the beginning of the program, and use comments, spacing, and blank lines to document the object and make its code easily distinguishable from the remainder of the program, as in the following program segment:

(continued)

```
{========================= ACCOUNTYPE OBJECT ========================= }
{ Updates the balance in a checking account.                          }
{-------------------------------------------------------------------- }
  type
    accountype = object
      balance                                 { checking account balance }
        : real;
      function NewBalance (transaction : real) : real;
    end;

  function accountype.NewBalance (transaction : real) : real;
  {-------------------------------------------------------------------- }
  { Updates checking account balance.                                   }
  {                                                                     }
  { IN            transaction:  deposit or withdrawal amount           }
  {                                                                     }
  { OUT           accountype.NewBalance:  update account balance       }
  {-------------------------------------------------------------------- }
  begin
    balance := balance + transaction;
    NewBalance := balance
  end;

{===================== END OF ACCOUNTYPE OBJECT ==================== }
```

12.10 Application Using Objects: OOPsy Daisy

A marketing firm would like to determine the popularity of flowers by asking participants whether or not they like particular types of flowers. Write a program that (a) asks participants whether they like daisies and (b) determines the number of respondents who do and the number who do not. Create an object that stores responses in an array, tabulates the results, and displays those results.

The **type** statement that defines the structure of the object declares an array field called *responses* that stores replies and three integer counters whose values range from 0 to the maximum number of possible responses. The responses are stored as Booleans to conserve memory, since each Boolean requires a single bit for storage as opposed to the 8 bits required for each character. The object also includes five methods—all procedures—that perform various operations on the data field items.

```
const
  maxresponses = 100;
type
  responsetype = array[1..maxresponses] of boolean;
  surveytype = object
    responses
      : responsetype;
    responsecount,
    yesresponsecount,
    noresponsecount
      : 0..maxresponses;
    procedure ZeroResponseCount;
    procedure ZeroYesAndNoCounts;
    procedure AddResponse (answer : boolean);
    procedure TabulateResults;
    procedure DisplayResults;
  end;
```

The `ZeroResponseCount` and `ZeroYesAndNoCounts` procedures initialize the *responsecount, yesresponsecount,* and *noresponsecount* variables to 0. In defining both these methods, the procedure identifier must be preceded by the class identifier for object, *surveytype,* linking them with an object of this type.

```
procedure surveytype.ZeroResponseCount;
begin
  responsecount := 0
end;


procedure surveytype.ZeroYesAndNoCounts;
begin
  yesresponsecount := 0;
  noresponsecount := 0
end;
```

The `AddResponse` procedure updates the response count and stores the reply in an array element whose index is the response count.

```
procedure surveytype.AddResponse (answer : boolean);
begin
  responsecount := responsecount + 1;
  responses[responsecount] := answer
end;
```

The `TabulateResults` procedure calls the `ZeroYesAndNoCounts` procedure in the same object to initialize the counters of the yes and no responses. It then goes through the array, from the first to the last active element, and counts the number of yes and no responses.

```
procedure surveytype.TabulateResults;
  var
    i
      : integer;
begin
  ZeroYesAndNoCounts;
  for i := 1 to responsecount do
    if responses[i]
      then
        yesresponsecount := yesresponsecount + 1
      else
        noresponsecount := noresponsecount + 1
end;
```

The `DisplayResults` procedure calls `TabulateResults` and displays the contents of two of the object's data fields determined by that procedure. There is no need to pass identifiers defined in object fields via parameters, since both procedures are methods of the same object structure.

```
procedure surveytype.DisplayResults;
begin
  TabulateResults;
  Writeln;
  Writeln ('SURVEY RESULTS');
  Writeln;
  Writeln ('Number of yes responses: ', yesresponsecount);
  Writeln ('Number of no responses: ', noresponsecount)
end;
```

The menu-driven main program calls procedures, some of which are in the object structure and others of which are not. Complete and proper documentation of all objects is of great importance since a programmer must know something about the structure of the object in order to use it in a program.

Figure 12.17 presents the complete, documented solution.

Figure 12.17
MarketSurvey
Program Listing

```pascal
program MarketSurvey;
{------------------------------------------------------------------------}
{ PROGRAM:        Market Survey of Flowers                               }
{ PROGRAMMER:     D. M. Killian                                          }
{ DATE:           December 2, 1990                                       }
{                                                                        }
{ This program asks participants whether or not they like daisies,       }
{ and determines the number of respondents who do and the number         }
{ who do not.                                                            }
{                                                                        }
{ INPUT           responses to query                                     }
{                                                                        }
{ OUTPUT          number of positive responses                           }
{                 number of negative responses                           }
{------------------------------------------------------------------------}
  uses
    Crt;                                  { screen formatting commands library }

{======================= SURVEYTYPE OBJECT =========================== }
{ Tabulates and displays responses to flower survey                     }
{---------------------------------------------------------------------- }
  const
    maxresponses = 100;                        { maximum number of responses }
  type
    responsetype = array[1..maxresponses] of boolean;
    surveytype = object
      responses
        : responsetype;                               { survey responses }
      responsecount,                              { number of respondents }
      yesresponsecount,                       { number of positive responses }
      noresponsecount                         { number of negative responses }
        : 0..maxresponses;
      procedure ZeroResponseCount;
      procedure ZeroYesAndNoCounts;
      procedure AddResponse (answer : boolean);
      procedure TabulateResults;
      procedure DisplayResults;
    end;
```

```
procedure surveytype.ZeroResponseCount;
{-------------------------------------------------------------------}
{ Initializes number of replies to 0.                               }
{                                                                   }
{ IN              responsecount:  number of replies                 }
{                                                                   }
{ OUT             responsecount:  number of replies                 }
{-------------------------------------------------------------------}
begin
  responsecount := 0
end;


procedure surveytype.ZeroYesAndNoCounts;
{-------------------------------------------------------------------}
{ Initializes number of positive and negative replies.              }
{                                                                   }
{ IN              yesresponsecount:  number of 'yes' responses      }
{                 noresponsecount:   number of 'no' responses       }
{                                                                   }
{ OUT             yesresponsecount:  number of 'yes' responses      }
{                 noresponsecount:   number of 'no' responses       }
{-------------------------------------------------------------------}
begin
  yesresponsecount := 0;
  noresponsecount := 0
end;


procedure surveytype.AddResponse (answer : boolean);
{-------------------------------------------------------------------}
{ Adds response to array of replies.                                }
{                                                                   }
{ IN              answer:  reply to question; true means 'yes',     }
{                          false means 'no'                         }
{                 responsecount:  number of replies                 }
{                 responses:  array of replies                      }
{                                                                   }
{ OUT             responsecount:  number of replies                 }
{                 responses:  array of replies                      }
{-------------------------------------------------------------------}
begin
  responsecount := responsecount + 1;
  responses[responsecount] := answer
end;
```

(continued)

```
procedure surveytype.TabulateResults;
{------------------------------------------------------------------------}
{ Counts number of positive and negative responses.                      }
{                                                                        }
{ IN         responsecount:      number of replies                       }
{            responses:          array of replies                        }
{            yesresponsecount:   number of 'yes' responses               }
{            noresponsecount:    number of 'no' responses                }
{                                                                        }
{ OUT        yesresponsecount:   number of 'yes' responses               }
{            noresponsecount:    number of 'no' responses                }
{------------------------------------------------------------------------}
  var
    i                                                  { loop index }
      : integer;
begin
  ZeroYesAndNoCounts;
  for i := 1 to responsecount do
    if responses[i]
      then
        yesresponsecount := yesresponsecount + 1
      else
        noresponsecount := noresponsecount + 1
end;


procedure surveytype.DisplayResults;
{------------------------------------------------------------------------}
{ Displays number of positive and negative responses.                    }
{                                                                        }
{ IN         yesresponsecount:   number of 'yes' responses               }
{            noresonsecount:     number of 'no' responses                }
{                                                                        }
{ OUT        none                                                        }
{------------------------------------------------------------------------}
begin
  TabulateResults;
  Writeln;
  Writeln ('SURVEY RESULTS');
  Writeln;
  Writeln ('Number of yes responses: ', yesresponsecount);
  Writeln ('Number of no responses: ', noresponsecount)
end;


{===================== END OF SURVEYTYPE OBJECT ===================== }
```

```
var
  survey                                    { survey fields and methods }
    : surveytype;
  choice                                        { menu selection }
    : char;
  response                                    { reply to question }
    : boolean;

procedure GetAnswer (var response : boolean);
{-------------------------------------------------------------------------}
{ Accepts response to question as a character and converts it             }
{ to a Boolean.                                                           }
{                                                                         }
{ IN            none                                                      }
{                                                                         }
{ OUT           response:  reply to question as Boolean                   }
{-------------------------------------------------------------------------}
  var
    answer                              { reply to question as character }
      : char;
begin
  ClrScr;
  repeat
    GotoXY (10,5);
    Write ('Do you like daisies (Y/N)? ');
    answer := ReadKey
  until answer in ['Y','y','N','n'];
  if answer in ['Y','y']
    then
      response := true
    else
      response := false
end;
```

(continued)

```pascal
procedure Continue;
{-------------------------------------------------------------------}
{ Keeps output on screen until key is pressed.                      }
{                                                                   }
{ IN            none                                                }
{                                                                   }
{ OUT           none                                                }
{-------------------------------------------------------------------}
  var
    ch                                     { response to continue directive }
      : char;
begin
  GotoXY (1,24);
  Write ('Press any key to continue.');
  ch := ReadKey
end;

procedure ShowResults;
{-------------------------------------------------------------------}
{ Displays questionnaire results.                                   }
{                                                                   }
{ IN            survey.DisplayResults:  number of yes and no        }
{                  responses from object surveytype                 }
{                                                                   }
{ OUT           none                                                }
{-------------------------------------------------------------------}
begin
  ClrScr;
  GotoXY (10,5);
  survey.DisplayResults;
  Continue
end;
```

```
begin
  survey.ZeroResponseCount;
  repeat
    ClrScr;
    GotoXY (20,1);
    Writeln ('MARKETING SURVEY');
    GotoXY (10,3);
    Writeln ('Press the number preceding your choice.');
    GotoXY (15,6);
    Writeln ('<1>  Add Response');
    GotoXY (15,8);
    Writeln ('<2>  Tabulate and Display Results');
    GotoXY (15,10);
    Writeln ('<3>  Exit Program');
    GotoXY (15,13);
    Write ('Choice --> ');
    choice := ReadKey;
    case choice of
      '1' :
        begin
          GetAnswer (response);
          survey.AddResponse (response)
        end;
      '2' :
        ShowResults;
    end
  until choice = '3'
end.
```

Store and Forward

Enumerated data types allow you to define your own data type, making programs more readable—but at the possible expense of having to write more code than would otherwise be necessary.

The pointer data type is the key component of dynamic data structures such as linked lists. These structures obtain memory only when it is needed and release it when it is no longer needed.

Certain classes of problems involving repetition are more easily solved with recursive techniques than with iterative ones. In these cases, a difficult solution may be expressed by few lines of code if a subprogram is allowed to call itself. Recursion, however, uses more main memory than do equivalent iterative methods.

Object-oriented programming allows you to define an object that consists of fields (data types) and the methods (procedures and functions) that operate on those fields. With this capability, you can improve the modularization of programs and reusability of program segments by minimizing the dependence of one segment of a program on another.

This text by no means exhausts the capabilities of Turbo Pascal. It does not include features such as the ability to define and work with sets of data objects and to produce graphic images. Even with the capabilities presented in the text, other applications are possible—you can construct data structures such as stacks, queues, and trees. You can even use these data structures to construct different algorithms for sorting a collection of items or for searching for an item in an existing collection.

This text provides you with basic tools, but it is only a stepping-off point. This is not the end; it is the beginning.

Snares and Pitfalls

- *Not employing parentheses to define an enumerated data type:* The constant-identifier list in the definition of an enumerated data type must be enclosed in parentheses.

- *Treating a constant from an enumerated data list as a string value or a variable:* A constant from an enumerated data type list can be stored in or compared to only a variable that is of the same type. It is not a string constant or a variable name.

- *Failing to take a location from the heap before using it:* You can fill the information and next fields of a location only after the **New** procedure takes an available location from the memory pool.

- *Changing the address of a node stored in a pointer before removing data from that node:* The data in the information field of a node must be removed before the pointer to that node is released by **Dispose** or assigned to a different location. The pointer to a node is the only way to access the data stored in that node.

- *Writing a recursive algorithm without a terminal condition:* Every recursive subprogram must have a condition that is capable of ending the looping process. A recursive parameter that does not eventually attain a constant value causes an infinite loop.

- *Not preceding a reference to an object's method with an object identifier:* All calls to methods must be prefaced by both the identifier associated with the object and a period.

Exercises

1. Answer the following questions in paragraph form.
   a. How is the ordinal value of a constant identifier in an enumerated data type list determined?
   b. What is meant by *encapsulation*?
   c. Why is it important not to lose the pointer to the first node in a linked list?
   d. Compare linked lists and arrays with regard to how each structure is traversed.
   e. Why is the following formula unsuitable for a recursive solution to finding *n*!?

$$n! = \frac{(n + 1)!}{n + 1}$$

2. Classify each of the following as valid or invalid. If invalid, explain why. The following declaration applies to parts a, b, and c:

   ```
   type
      cardsuitype = (clubs, diamonds, hearts, spades);
   var
      cardsuit, i : cardsuitype;
   ```

   a.
   ```
   if cardsuit = hearts
      then
         Writeln ('Spades wins.');
   ```

   b.
   ```
   for i := clubs to spades do
      Writeln (i:20);
   ```

   c.
   ```
   cardsuit := Pred(diamonds);
   ```

   The following declaration applies to parts d and e:

   ```
   type
      nametype = string[20];
      ptrtype = ^membertype;
      membertype = record
        name : nametype;
        next : ptrtype
      end;
   var
      p, q : ptrtype;
   ```

   d.
   ```
   Readln (p.name);
   ```

   e.
   ```
   if p^.next = nil
      then
         p^.next := q;
   ```

3. Write Pascal equivalents for each of the given descriptions.
   a. Define an enumerated data type called *flavortype* that contains the following list of constant identifiers: vanilla, chocolate, and strawberry.
   b. Define an enumerated data type called *cointype* that contains the following list of constant identifiers: quarter, nickel, cent, and dime. Make sure the list is ordered so coins that are worth less precede those that are worth more.
   c. Define a pointer *p* to a record that contains fields for a person's name, age, and a pointer to another record of the same type.
   d. Store the successor to *nickel* of type *cointype* (defined in part 3b) in a variable called *change*.
   e. Store the predecessor to *nickel* of type *cointype* (defined in part 3b) in a variable called *change*.

4. Find all the errors in the following Pascal recursive function, which is designed to find the sum of the integers from its parameter down to 1. The parameter *n* must be a positive integer.

```
function Sum (n : integer) : integer;
   var
      ntemp : integer;
begin
   if n = 1
      then
         Sum := 0
      else
         ntemp := n - 1;
         Sum := Sum (ntemp) + n
   end;
```

5. Show the exact output for each of the following programs.

a.
```
program A;
  type
    intptr = ^integer;
  var
    p, q, r : intptr;
begin
  New(q);
  q^ := 9;
  p := q;
  New(r);
  r^ := 8;
  Writeln (p^:5, q^:5, r^:5);
  New(p);
  p^ := 7;
  Writeln (p^:5, q^:5, r^:5);
  q^ := p^ + r^;
  Writeln (p^:5, q^:5, r^:5);
  Dispose(p);
  Dispose(q);
  Dispose(r)
end.
```

b.
```
program B;
  type
    nodeptr = ^valuetype;
    valuetype = record
      value : integer;
      next : nodeptr
    end;
  var
    i : integer;
    start : nodeptr;
```

```
procedure F (var start : nodeptr);
  var
    p, q : nodeptr;
begin
  New(p);
  q := p;
  p^.value := 10;
  p^.next := nil;
  start := p;
  for i := 1 to 3 do
    begin
      New(p);
      p^.value := 10 - i;
      p^.next := nil;
      q^.next := p;
      q := p
    end
end;

procedure D (start : nodeptr);
  var
    p : nodeptr;
begin
  p := start;
  while p <> nil do
    begin
      Writeln (p^.value:5);
      p := p^.next
    end
end;

begin
  start := nil;
  F (start);
  D (start)
end.
```

c.
```
program C;
  var
    l, s : integer;
```

```
          procedure One (a, b : integer);
          begin
            if a <> b
              then
                begin
                  Writeln (a:5, b:5);
                  if a < b
                    then
                      One (a, b-a)
                    else
                      One (a-b, b)
                end
              else
                Writeln ('Answer: ', a:5)
          end;

      begin
        l := 66;
        s := 30;
        One (l, s)
      end.
```

d. **program** D;
    var
       l, s : **integer**;

```
      procedure One (a, b : integer);
        begin
          if a <> b
            then
              begin
                Writeln (a:5, b:5);
                if a < b
                  then
                    One (a, b-a)
                  else
                    One (a-b, b)
              end
            else
              Writeln ('Answer: ', a:5)
        end;

  begin
    l := 13;
    s := 2;
    One (l, s)
  end.
```

6. Write a Pascal procedure for each of the following.
   a. Display each constant value in the enumerated data type defined by:

   ```
   type
     flagcolortype = (red, white, blue);
   var
     flagcolor : flagcolortype;
   ```

   b. Remove the first element in a linked list pointed to by *start*. Consider the case where the list is empty.

7. Define an object class for information on squares. It should have a field for the length of the side of a square and methods that determine the perimeter and area of the square.

Programming Assignments

Elementary

1. Write a program that creates a linked list containing 20 random integers from 1 through 100. Display the integers by traversing the list, and output their average.

2. The movie industry would like to determine the income produced by movies in each of the following rating categories: G, PG, PG13, R, and NC17. Write a program that creates an array of records that keeps a running total of the income of the films and the average income per film in each category. Define an enumerated data type for the five different ratings, and use those constants as subscripts for the array. Each record should contain the following information on the movies in a category: rating, the number of movies, the total income they produce, and the average income per film.

3. Write a program that displays the hours a library is open by creating an enumerated data type whose constants list contains the days of the week. The program should have the option of displaying the weekly schedule or the hours for a particular day.

4. Write a program that fills an array with the dollar values of an ounce of gold for 10 consecutive days. Define an object that finds the number of days the daily value was above the average for a given period and the number days it was below the average. The program should output the number of days the dollar value was above and below the average for the 10-day period.

5. The Hamming distance between two linked lists of Booleans with the same number of active elements is defined as the number of locations in which corresponding elements differ. For example, for the following defined lists

> node 1 = false   node 1 = false
> node 2 = true   node 2 = false
> node 3 = true   node 3 = true
> node 4 = false   node 4 = false

the Hamming distance is 1, since only node 2 contains values that are different.

Write a program that creates two linked lists of equal size with Boolean information fields and outputs their Hamming distance.

6. Twenty players are to be selected to make up four basketball teams in a recreational league. Write a program that randomly selects the rosters for each of the teams from a master linked list of records consisting of a player's name and a unique number from 1 to 20. If the random number chosen by the program matches the player number, that player is chosen. Be sure to incorporate safeguards against choosing the same player more than once.

7. A palindrome is a word or phrase that reads the same forward and backward. A linked list can be used to determine whether a word is a palindrome by adding the letters of the word, one at a time, to the beginning of a linked list. After the list is completed, the reverse of the word can be created by copying the letters from the list one at a time, starting at the beginning. If the original word and its reverse are identical, a word is a palindrome. Write a program that uses this method to determine whether a word is a palindrome.

8. A bird watcher would like to keep track of all sightings by storing the name of the species and the time of day when it was seen (morning, afternoon, evening). Each record should contain the date of the observation, the species observed, and when it was observed. Write a program that creates a linked list in which each node stores the information for a single sighting. For the time of day, define an enumerated data type. Provide options to display the following:

> The entire linked list in tabular form
> The date and time of day when a particular type of bird was observed
> A summary indicating the total number of observations for each species in the list for each time of day

9. A recursive definition that finds the product of two integers m and n is:

> if $n = 1$
>   then
>   product $= m$
>   else
>   product $= m \times (n - 1) + m$

Write a program that uses a recursive function to find the product of two integers.

10. The contents of an array with n elements can be displayed backward with the recursive definition:

if $n = 1$
  then
    output the first element
  else
    output the last element
    output the first $n - 1$ elements in reverse order

Write a program that loads a 20-element one-dimensional array where the content of each element is its subscript. Display the contents of the array in reverse order using the recursive procedure based on the definition just given.

Challenging

11. An advertising firm wants to monitor how much income five major television networks (ABC, CBS, Fox, NBC, and CNN) receive from the advertisements in each show they air. Write a program that creates an array of pointers to the beginning of five linked lists whose nodes contain records with fields for the name of a program, the amount of income generated from ad sales, and a pointer to the next node in the linked list. Use an enumerated data type to define the subscripts for the array of pointers. Figure 12.18 illustrates the structure. The program should allow for the creation and placement of a node in the structure. It should generate a report that lists all programs shown on all networks, their ad revenues, and the total incomes; a similar report for a specific network; and a list of programs whose ad revenues fall below an entered value for a given network or all networks.

12. A firm that specializes in mail order sales has a master mailing list sorted alphabetically by customer name. Each record in the list contains the customer's name and complete mailing address. The company periodically receives lists of additional prospective customers.

    Write a program that loads a master linked list and alphabetizes it as new records are entered. (You must find the correct position for each record—and

Figure 12.18
Network Income Structure

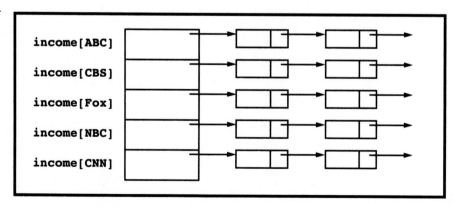

508

you may have to insert a node in the middle of the list rather than at the beginning.) The program should have the capability of merging a supplementary list with the master list (while maintaining the alphabetization), displaying the contents of the entire list, or displaying the names and addresses for a particular state. (Hint: in order to insert a node in the middle of a linked list, you have to know the address of the previous node. Create a pointer that follows the pointer traversing the list.)

13. A doubly linked list has an information field and two pointers: one pointing to the following node, and another pointing to the preceding node. A graphic representation of the doubly linked list and its node format is shown in Figure 12.19.

    Write a solution to Programming Assignment 12, the mail-order sales problem, using a doubly linked list rather than a simple linked list.

14. The mail-order firm described in Programming Assignment 12 frequently changes the address of a customer or removes a customer's name and address from its mailing list. The company also finds that it often has identical records for the same customer. Write a program using a simple linked list that adds the following options to the ones presented in Programming Assignment 12:

    Change the address of a customer
    Remove a node containing a customer's record
    Eliminate all duplicates from the list by traversing the list and determining
       whether two records have identical fields

Figure 12.19
Doubly Linked List and
Its Node Format

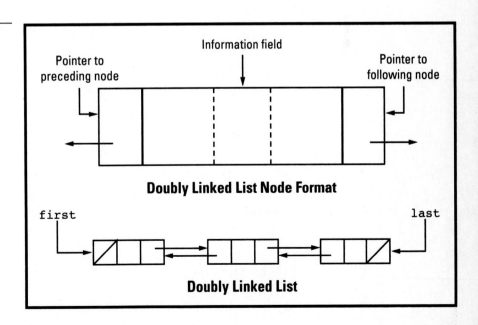

Doubly Linked List Node Format

Doubly Linked List

15. Define an object that calculates the mean, median, and mode of a set of, at most, 1000 real values stored in an array. The *mean* of a set of values is the sum of the values divided by the number of values; the *median* is the middle score after the values are arranged in numerical order (If there are an even number of values, the median is the average of the two middle values.); and the *mode* is the value that occurs most frequently. Use that object in a program that determines and outputs the mean, median, and mode of shoe sizes sold by a store in a one-week period.

16. The first 10 terms of the Fibonacci sequence are 1, 1, 2, 3, 5, 8, 13, 21, 34, and 55. Each term, with the exception of the first two (1 and 1), is formed by adding the previous two terms. For example, 21 is the sum of 8 and 13.

    Write a program that employs a recursive function called **Fibonacci** to determine and output the first 25 terms of the Fibonacci sequence.

17. Pascal does not have an exponentiation operator, but you can create a function to raise a real value to an integral power, for example, to find 1.2^3.

    Write a program that uses a recursive function to raise a real value to an integral power. Make sure your solution includes negative exponents such as x^{-n}, which is equivalent to $1/x^n$.

18. A *stack* is a last-in first-out (LIFO) data structure similar to a tidy pile of dishes: All action takes place at the top of the stack. To add a dish, simply place it on the top of the existing stack; to remove a dish, take the one on the top of the stack. Sample activity with a stack storing integers follows.

start	top →
add 5	top → 5
add 7	top → 7 5
add 9	top → 9 7 5
remove	top → 7 5
add 3	top → 3 7 5
remove	top → 7 5
remove	top → 5
remove	top →

    You must specify a value when placing an element on the stack. Since only the top element of a stack can be removed, however, no value need be designated for a removal.

    Write a program that simulates a stack with a linked list of words, where the beginning of the list represents the top of the stack. The program should give the user the option of adding or removing an element, and show the words in the stack, with the top labeled, after each operation. Create a procedure called **Push** to add an element to the stack and one called **Pop** to remove an element. Make sure you handle the case in which an attempt is made to remove an element from an empty stack.

19. In a linear search, you start at the beginning of a list and compare each element, one at a time, to a target value. If there is a match, the search is halted and the address of the target element is saved. The search also terminates if

you reach the end of the list without finding a match. In other methods, the speed of the search process can be increased if the list is initially sorted. One of these methods is the *binary search,* in which a list is repeatedly cut in half until the target value is found. If the list contains 1000 elements, a linear search may take 1000 comparisons to find the target, whereas a binary search will take no more than 10.

A binary search compares the pivot or middle element in a list to the target value. If there is a match, the process stops. If not, you test whether the target value is less or greater than the middle element. If it is greater, you search the upper half of the list; if less, the lower half. (Since the list is sorted, there is no need to search the wrong half of the list.) The process is repeated on the chosen half: finding the middle, testing it for a match to the target value. If there is a match, the search ends; if not, the correct half of the list is chosen and the process repeated until a single element remains. At this point, either you have found the proper element or it isn't in the list. Because the same steps are repeated on smaller and smaller portions of the list, the search algorithm can be written recursively.

Write a program that creates an interactive business phone book by loading an array of records with a collection of names of companies and their phone numbers. Sort the list in ascending order by company names by any method you choose, and construct a recursive subprogram that searches for and displays a company's phone number. The pivot of a list with an even number of elements can be either of the two elements in the middle of the list.

20. To sort a list of elements using the quicksort, take the first element in the list as a pivot element. Rearrange the list by moving those elements whose values are less than the pivot to its left and those that are greater to its right, leaving the pivot element in its correct place in the sorted list. You now have two smaller unsorted lists, one on each side of the pivot. Choose the first element in each of these lists as the pivot and continue to rearrange the list until there is a single element in each of the smaller lists. The list is now sorted. Figure 12.20 shows the quicksort applied to a list of integers. (The box enclosing a list value indicates that the value has found its proper position in the sorted list and should not be moved.) Since the same set of rules is applied to successively smaller lists of numbers, the quicksort algorithm can be written recursively, with the most difficult part consisting of rearranging the list.

Write a program that loads an array of records with a student's name and grade point average (GPA). Sort the list in descending order, by GPA, using the quicksort, and display the sorted list in tabular form.

Figure 12.20
Quicksort Example

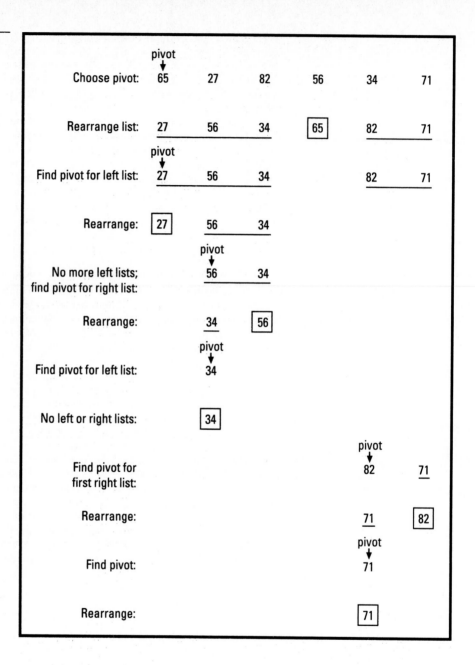

APPENDIX A

Turbo Pascal 6.0 Hot Keys

The hot keys in this listing can be shortcuts to certain menu selections and can be used from any place in the integrated development environment.

Hot Key	Menu Equivalent	Function
F1	Help	Displays a Help screen
F2	File/Save	Saves active editor file
F3	File/Open	Opens file
F4	Run/Go to cursor	Executes to cursor location
F5	Window/Zoom	Zooms the active window
F6	Window/Next	Cycles through open windows
F7	Run/Trace into	Traces into subroutines
F8	Run/Step over	Steps over subroutine calls
F10		Activates main menu bar
Alt-F1	Help/Previous topic	Displays previous Help screen
Alt-F3	Window/Close	Closes active window
Alt-F5	Window/User screen	Displays User screen
Alt-F9	Compile/Compile	Compiles active program
Alt-Spacebar	≡ menu	Goes to ≡ (System) menu
Alt-C	Compile menu	Goes to **Compile** menu
Alt-D	Debug menu	Goes to **Debug** menu
Alt-E	Edit menu	Goes to **Edit** menu
Alt-F	File menu	Goes to **File** menu
Alt-H	Help menu	Goes to **Help** menu
Alt-O	Options menu	Goes to **Options** menu
Alt-R	Run menu	Goes to **Run** menu
Alt-S	Search menu	Goes to **Search** menu
Alt-W	Window menu	Goes to **Window** menu
Alt-X	File/Exit	Exits Turbo Pascal to DOS
Ctrl-F1	Help/Topic search	Gives language-specific help while in editor
Ctrl-F2	Run/Program reset	Resets running program
Ctrl-F7	Debug/Add watch	Adds a watch expression
Ctrl-F8	Debug/Toggle breakpoint	Clears or sets conditional breakpoint
Ctrl-F9	Run/Run	Executes active program

Appendix B

Turbo Pascal 6.0 Editor Commands

This appendix gives a summary of selected Turbo Pascal 6.0 editor commands. In some cases different keystroke combinations or menu selections can be used to activate the command. Notation such as Ctrl-Q/S means: Hold down the Ctrl key while pressing Q, and then, after releasing both keys, press S.

Function	Keystroke
Movement Commands	
Character left	Ctrl-S or left arrow
Character right	Ctrl-D or right arrow
Word left	Ctrl-A or Ctrl-left arrow
Word right	Ctrl-F or Ctrl-right arrow
Line up	Ctrl-E or up arrow
Line down	Ctrl-X or down arrow
Page up	Ctrl-R or PgUp
Page down	Ctrl-C or PgDn
Beginning of line	Ctrl-Q/S or Home
End of line	Ctrl-Q/D or End
Top of window	Ctrl-Q/E or Ctrl-Home
Bottom of window	Ctrl-Q/X or Ctrl-End
Beginning of program	Ctrl-Q/R or Ctrl-PgUp
End of program	Ctrl-Q/C or Ctrl-PgDn
Insert and Delete Commands	
Delete line	Ctrl-Y
Delete block	Ctrl-K/Y
Delete to end of line	Ctrl-Q/Y
Delete character left of cursor	Ctrl-H or Backspace
Delete character under cursor	Ctrl-G or Delete
Insert line	Ctrl-N

Function	Keystroke
Block Commands	
Copy block to edit file	Ctrl-K/C
Copy block to Clipboard	Edit/Copy or Ctrl-Ins
Delete block (not saving to Clipboard)	Edit/Clear or Ctrl-Del
Delete block (saving to Clipboard)	Edit/Cut or Shift-Del
Hide/display block	Ctrl-K/H
Mark block begin	Ctrl-K/B
Mark block end	Ctrl-K/K
Mark single word	Ctrl-K/T
Move block from Clipboard	Edit/Paste or Shift-Ins
Move block to edit file	Ctrl-K/V
Read block from disk	Ctrl-K/R
Write block to disk	Ctrl-K/W
Miscellaneous	
Find	Ctrl-Q/F or Search/Find
Find and replace	Ctrl-Q/A or Search/Replace
Invoke main menu	F10
Language help	Ctrl-F1
Open file	F3 or File/Open
Save file	Ctrl-K/S or F2 or File/Save

APPENDIX C

Turbo Pascal 6.0 Reserved Words

In this text, reserved words appear in lowercase **boldface**. Turbo Pascal also allows uppercase representations of these words.

absolute	**goto**	**repeat**
and	**if**	**set**
array	**implementation**	**shl**
begin	**in**	**shr**
case	**inline**	**string**
const	**interface**	**then**
constructor	**interrupt**	**to**
destructor	**label**	**type**
div	**mod**	**unit**
do	**nil**	**until**
downto	**not**	**uses**
else	**object**	**var**
end	**of**	**virtual**
external	**or**	**while**
file	**packed**	**with**
for	**procedure**	**xor**
forward	**program**	
function	**record**	

APPENDIX D

ASCII Code

DEC CODE	CHAR	DEC CODE	CHAR	DEC CODE	CHAR	DEC CODE	CHAR
0	NUL	32	SP	64	@	96	`
1	SOH	33	!	65	A	97	a
2	STX	34	"	66	B	98	b
3	ETX	35	#	67	C	99	c
4	EOT	36	$	68	D	100	d
5	ENQ	37	%	69	E	101	e
6	ACK	38	&	70	F	102	f
7	BEL	39	'	71	G	103	g
8	BS	40	(	72	H	104	h
9	HT	41	)	73	I	105	i
10	LF	42	*	74	J	106	j
11	VT	43	+	75	K	107	k
12	FF	44	,	76	L	108	l
13	CR	45	-	77	M	109	m
14	SO	46	.	78	N	110	n
15	SI	47	/	79	O	111	o
16	DLE	48	0	80	P	112	p
17	DC1	49	1	81	Q	113	q
18	DC2	50	2	82	R	114	r
19	DC3	51	3	83	S	115	s
20	DC4	52	4	84	T	116	t
21	NAK	53	5	85	U	117	u
22	SYN	54	6	86	V	118	v
23	ETB	55	7	87	W	119	w
24	CAN	56	8	88	X	120	x
25	EM	57	9	89	Y	121	y
26	SUB	58	:	90	Z	122	z
27	ESC	59	;	91	[	123	{
28	FS	60	<	92	\	124		
29	GS	61	=	93	]	125	}
30	RS	62	>	94	^	126	~
31	US	63	?	95	—	127	DEL

Summary of Turbo Pascal 6.0 Instructions

This appendix lists, in alphabetical order, the instructions presented in the text. Each entry contains a flow diagram, a format, and an example.

array Declaration

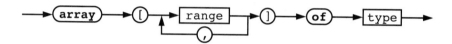

FORMAT: **array** [<range>] of <item type>

Example: **type**
listype = **array** [1..10] **of** valuetype;

Assignment Statement

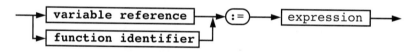

FORMAT: <identifier> := <expression>;

Example: areatriangle := 0.5 * base * altitude;

case Structure

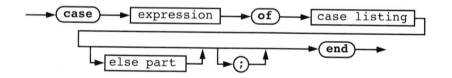

FORMAT:
```
case <selector> of
    <constant list> :
        <statement 1>;
    <constant list> :
        <statement 2>;

        . . .

    <constant list> :
        <statement n>
 [else
        <default statement>]
end;
```

Example:
```
case letter of
  'p', 'P' :
    Writeln ('Pass');
  'f', 'F' :
    Writeln ('Fail')
  else
    Writeln ('Illegal entry')
end;
```

Compound Statement

FORMAT:
```
begin
    <statement>;
    <statement>;

        . . .

end
```

Example:
```
while name <> '' do
    begin
        Write ('Enter name: ');
        Readln (name);

            . . .

    end;
```

const Declaration

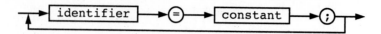

FORMAT: **const**
              `<identifier> = <value>;`

Example: **const**
              `overhead = 170.00;`

Enumerated Data Type Declaration

FORMAT: `<identifier> = ( <constant identifier list> );`

Example: **type**
              `colortype = (red, white, blue);`

file Declaration

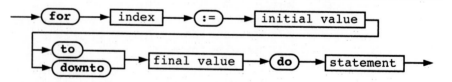

FORMAT: **file** **of** `<file data type>`

Example: **type**
              `namefiletype = `**file of** ` nametype;`

for . . . do Structure

FORMAT: **for** `<index> :=` `<initial value>` **to** `<final value>` **do**
              `<statement>;`

Example: **for** `count := 1` **to** `10` **do**
              Writeln `(count:5);`

function Declaration

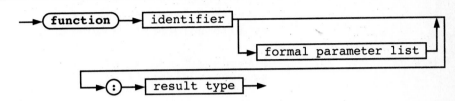

FORMAT: **function** <identifier> (<formal parameters>) : <type>;

Example: **function** Average (a, b : **real**) : **real**;

if ... then ... else Structure

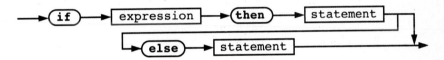

FORMAT: **if** <condition>
     then
       <statement>
     else
       <statement>;

Example: **if** num > 0
     then
       Writeln ('Positive')
     else
       Writeln ('Not positive');

object Declaration

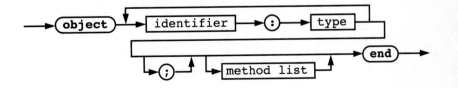

```
FORMAT:  type
           <class identifier> = object
             <variable identifier> : <data type>;
             <variable identifier> : <data type>;
                            . . .
             procedure <identifier> [(<parameter list>)];
             procedure <identifier> [(<parameter list>)];
                            . . .
             function <identifier> [(<parameter list>)]
                                      : <function type>;
             function <identifier> [(<parameter list>)]
                                      : <function type>;
                            . . .
           end;

Example:  type
           accountype = object
             balance : real;
             function NewBalance (transaction : real) : real;
           end;
```

Pointer Data Type

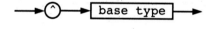

```
FORMAT:  <identifier> = ^<base type>;

Example:  type
           nodeptr = ^nodetype;
```

procedure Declaration

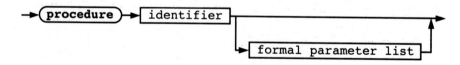

```
FORMAT:  procedure <identifier> (<formal parameter list>);

Example:  procedure (var double : real; number : real);
```

program Statement

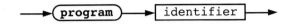

FORMAT: **program** <identifier>;

Example: **program** TestCase;

record Declaration

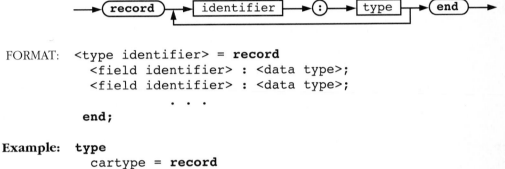

FORMAT: <type identifier> = **record**
    <field identifier> : <data type>;
    <field identifier> : <data type>;
         . . .
   end;

Example: **type**
    cartype = **record**
     model : modeltype;
     year : **integer;**
     value : **real**
     end;

repeat . . . until Structure

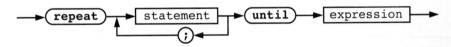

FORMAT: **repeat**
    <statement>
   until <condition>;

Example: **repeat**
    sum := sum + 1/num;
    num := num + 1
   until sum > 0.67;

string Declaration

FORMAT: **string**[<string length>]

Example: **type**
    nametype = **string**[20];

Subrange Declaration

FORMAT: <constant>..<constant>

Example: **type**
    digitype = 0..9;

type Declaration

FORMAT: **type**
    <identifier> = <definition>;
    <identifier> = <definition>;
        . . .

Example: **type**
    stringtype = **string**[30];
    listype = **array**[1..100] **of real**;

uses Statement

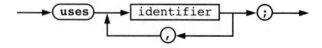

FORMAT: **uses** <library name list>;

Example: **uses**
    Crt;

var Declaration

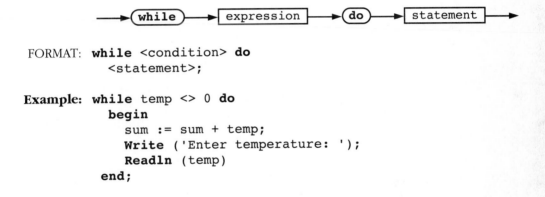

FORMAT: **var**
    <identifier list> : <type>;
    <identifier list> : <type>;
         . . .

Example: **var**
    count : **integer**;
    letter : **char**;

while . . . do Structure

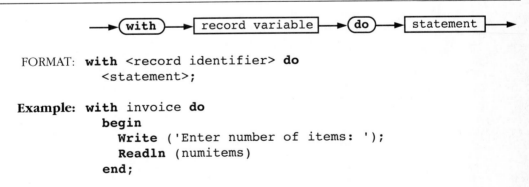

FORMAT: **while** <condition> **do**
    <statement>;

Example: **while** temp <> 0 **do**
    begin
      sum := sum + temp;
      Write ('Enter temperature: ');
      Readln (temp)
    end;

with Structure

FORMAT: **with** <record identifier> **do**
    <statement>;

Example: **with** invoice **do**
    begin
      Write ('Enter number of items: ');
      Readln (numitems)
    end;

APPENDIX F

Summary of Turbo Pascal 6.0 Functions and Procedures

This appendix lists, in alphabetical order, the system-defined functions and procedures presented in the text. Each entry gives an identifier, type of subprogram (function or procedure), what unit (if any) it occupies, the page number in the text where it is introduced, a definition, program format, and an example.

Abs Function   Returns the absolute value of a number.   p. 160

           FORMAT: `Abs ( <number> )`
           Example: `diff := Abs (value1 - value2);`

Assign Procedure   Links an external file to an internal file structure.   pp. 78, 403

           FORMAT: `Assign ( <file identifier>, <external file name> );`
           Example: `Assign (intfile, extfilename);`

Chr Function   Returns the character corresponding to an ASCII decimal code value.   p. 166

           FORMAT: `Chr ( <decimal code> )`
           Example: `ch := Chr (88);`

Close Procedure   Removes access to an open file.   pp. 81, 406

           FORMAT: `Close ( <file identifier> );`
           Example: `Close (coins);`

ClrScr Procedure   (Unit: **Crt**.)   p. 223
                         Erases an active window and places the cursor in its upper left corner.

           FORMAT: `ClrScr;`
           Example: `ClrScr;`

Concat Function   Combines a sequence of strings.   p. 166

           FORMAT: `Concat ( <string1> [, <string2>, ... , <stringn>] )`
           Example: `answer := Concat (word1, word2);`

Copy Function

Returns a substring of a given string.

p. 165

FORMAT: `Copy ( <string>, <index>, <count> )`
Example: `code := Copy (mailabel, 6, 3);`

Delete Procedure

Erases a substring from a given string.

p. 129

FORMAT: `Delete ( <source>, <index>, <count> );`
Example: `Delete (name, startpos, 5);`

Dispose Procedure

Returns a location to the memory pool.

p. 459

FORMAT: `Dispose ( <pointer variable> );`
Example: `Dispose (p);`

Eof Function

Returns the end-of-file status of a file.

p. 408

FORMAT: `Eof ( <file identifier> )`
Example: `while not Eof (intfile) do...`

Erase Procedure

Deletes an external file.

p. 410

FORMAT: `Erase ( <file identifier> );`
Example: `Erase (intfile);`

Exp Function

Returns the exponential of the argument.

p. 190

FORMAT: `Exp ( <real expression> )`
Example: `answer := Exp (power);`

FilePos Function

Returns the current position of a file pointer.

p. 412

FORMAT: `FilePos ( <file identifier> )`
Example: `location := FilePos (intfile);`

GotoXY Procedure

(Unit: **Crt.**)

p. 223

Positions the cursor at a specified row and column in the Output window.

FORMAT: `GotoXY ( < column integer >, < row integer > );`
Example: `GotoXY (24,1);`

Insert Procedure

Inserts a substring into a given string.

p. 128

FORMAT: `Insert ( <source>, <destination>, <index> );`
Example: `Insert ('xxx', answer, 4);`

Length Function

Returns the length of a string.

p. 165

FORMAT: `Length ( <string> )`
Example: `for index := 1 to Length (word) do...`

Ln Function   Returns the natural logarithm of the argument.   p. 190

       FORMAT: `Ln ( <real expression> )`

       Example: `answer := Exp (b * Ln (a));`

New Procedure   Takes a location from the memory pool.   p. 458

       FORMAT: `New ( <pointer variable> );`

       Example: `New (q);`

Ord Function   Returns the ordinal value of an ordinal-type expression.   p. 167

       FORMAT: `Ord ( <ordinal expression> )`

       Example: `if value = Ord (list)`

                 `then...`

Pi Function   Returns the value of pi (3.1415926535897932385).   p. 161

       FORMAT: `Pi`

       Example: `volume := Pi * Sqr (radius);`

Pos Function   Returns the position of the first character of a substring contained in a string.   p. 165

       FORMAT: `Pos ( <substring>, <string> )`

       Example: `while Pos (' ', value) do...`

Pred Function   Returns the predecessor of the argument.   p. 440

       FORMAT: `Pred ( < ordinal constant> )`

       Example: `before := Pred (current);`

Random Function   Returns a random number.   p. 163

       FORMAT: `Random [( <integer> )]`

       Example: `toss := Random (1);`

Randomize Procedure   Starts built-in random number generator with a random value.   p. 164

       FORMAT: `Randomize;`

       Example: `Randomize;`

Read Procedure, for files   Transfers file component into a variable location.   p. 408

       FORMAT: `Read ( <file identifier>, <input identifier> );`

       Example: `Read (intfile, name);`

ReadKey Function   Returns a character read from the keyboard.   p. 322

       FORMAT: `ReadKey`

       Example: `ch := ReadKey;`

Readln Procedure   Accepts values for variable identifiers, then skips to next line.   p. 70

FORMAT: **Readln (<identifier list>);**

Example: **Readln (age);**

Readln Procedure,   Transfers text file component into a variable location, then   p. 83
for files   skips to next line.

FORMAT: **Readln (<file identifier>, <input identifier>);**

Example: **Readln (intfile, age);**

Reset Procedure   Opens an existing file for reading.   pp. 82, 407

FORMAT: **Reset (<file identifier>);**

Example: **Reset (oldfile);**

Rewrite Procedure   Creates and opens a new file.   pp. 79, 404

FORMAT: **Rewrite (<file identifier>);**

Example: **Rewrite (newfile);**

Round Function   Returns the integer value of a rounded real argument.   p. 162

FORMAT: **Round (<real number>)**

Example: **dollar := Round (100 * value) div 100;**

Seek Procedure   Moves file pointer to a specified record.   p. 413

FORMAT: **Seek (<file identifier>, <record number>);**

Example: **Seek (intfile, recnum);**

Sqr Function   Returns the square of the argument.   p. 160

FORMAT: **Sqr (<number>)**

Example: **cube := x * Sqr (x);**

Sqrt Function   Returns the square root of the argument.   p. 161

FORMAT: **Sqrt (<nonnegative real>)**

Example: **stdev := Sqrt (variance);**

Str Procedure   Converts a numeric value to its string equivalent.   p. 130

FORMAT: **Str (<number>, <string>);**

Example: **Str (value, strvalue);**

Succ Function   Returns the successor of the argument.   p. 440

FORMAT: **Succ (< ordinal constant>)**

Example: **after := Succ (current);**

Trunc Function   Returns the integer value of a truncated real value.   p. 163

         FORMAT: **Trunc(** `<real number> )`

         Example: `boardodds :=` **Trunc** `(realodds) + 1;`

UpCase Function   Returns the uppercase equivalent of a character.   p. 294

         FORMAT: **UpCase** `( <character> );`

         Example: `cap :=` **UpCase** `(letter);`

Val Procedure   Converts a string value to its numeric equivalent.   p. 131

         FORMAT: **Val** `( <string>, <number>, <code> );`

         Example: **Val** `(gpastr, gpa, errcode);`

Write Procedure   Displays values, then stays on same output line.   p. 65

         FORMAT: **Write** `( <output list> );`

         Example: **Write** `(pay);`

Write Procedure,   Transfers variable contents into file component.   p. 405
for files

         FORMAT: **Write** `( <file identifier>, <output identifier> );`

         Example: **Write** `(intfile, taxdue);`

Writeln Procedure   Displays values, then goes to next output line.   p. 62

         FORMAT: **Writeln** `( <output list> );`

         Example: **Writeln** `('Answer is: ', answer:8:2);`

Writeln Procedure,   Transfers variable contents into text file, then goes to   p. 80
for files   next output line.

         FORMAT: **Writeln** `( <file identifier>, <output identifier> );`

         Example: **Writeln** `(intfile, name);`

Answers to Selected Exercises and Programming Assignments

Chapter 0

Exercises

1. a. The **File** menu contains options for the loading and saving of files.

   c. The Output window displays program output in the lower portion of the desktop.

   e. The Help window displays useful information on the integrated development environment or on Turbo Pascal vocabulary.

2. b. High-level languages use code that is humanlike, while low-level languages use code that is similar to the language a computer actually executes.

   d. Menu-driven systems are easier to use, and they provide on-screen assistance in executing the program. However, one may have to use additional keystrokes, making the process slower.

3. a. To print a program listing, select **Print** from the **File** menu.

   c. To get help with Pascal vocabulary, move the cursor under a Pascal term in the active Edit window, hold down the Ctrl key, and press the F1 function key (Ctrl-F1).

   e. To move the cursor in the Edit window to the beginning of a program you can either: hold down the Ctrl key while pressing Q, then release both keys and press R (Ctrl-Q/R); or hold down the Ctrl key and press the PgUp key (Ctrl-PgUp).

4. b. To delete a blocked portion of text, hold down the Ctrl key and press K. After releasing both keys, press Y (Ctrl-K/Y).

   d. To move the cursor to the position of the last error, hold down the Ctrl key and press Q. After releasing both keys, press W (Ctrl-Q/W).

Chapter 1

Exercises

1. a. The software design methodology is language independent because it can be used to design problem solutions that can be implemented in any programming language.

   c. Decomposing a problem solution into submodules simplifies the solution process by breaking a big problem into a series of smaller ones. The decomposition process also simplifies any changes that must be made.

   e. Syntax errors result from a misuse of a programming language, such as failing to place a semicolon where it is needed or incorrectly spelling a Pascal vocabulary word. Logic errors produce incorrect or unexpected results due to misinterpretation by the programmer.

   g. Documentation should take place at every stage of the design process because, if an error is detected or an adjustment has to be made, a programmer or user has some assistance in locating and correcting the error or making the change.

17. Step 1: Analysis of the Problem (See Table G1.17)
    Step 2: Modular Design of the Solution (See Figure G1.17)
    Step 3: Design of the Structure of the Modules

    BASKETBALL JERSEY
      ENTER JERSEY DIGITS
      DETERMINE IF VALID
      DISPLAY MESSAGE

    ENTER JERSEY DIGITS
      enter first digit of jersey number
      enter second digit of jersey number

    DETERMINE IF VALID
      if first digit > 5 then
        message is "invalid number"
      else
        if second digit > 5 then
          message is "invalid number"
        else
          message is "valid number"

    DISPLAY MESSAGE
      output message

    Step 5: Verification of the Solution

    ENTER JERSEY DIGITS
      enter first digit 5
      enter second digit 7

    DETERMINE IF VALID
      5 is not greater than 5
        (skip first then part)
      7 is greater than 5
        message is "invalid number"
        (skip second else)

    DISPLAY MESSAGE
      output message......... invalid number

    Also try verification process for the following pairs of values:

First Digit	Second Digit
9	3
6	7
2	1

Table G1.17
Basketball Jersey Structure Chart
for Exercise 17

Input		Output
First digit on jersey		Message
Second digit on jersey		

Figure G1.17
Basketball Jersey Input/Output Chart
for Exercise 17

Chapter 2

Exercises

1. a. Declaration statements inform the computer how to use an identifier and how much memory to reserve for it.
   c. A **type** declaration should precede a **var** declaration because a type definition has to be known before it can be used to define a variable. If the **type** declaration did not precede the **var** declaration, the definition would be unknown at the time the variable is declared and the computer would not know how to interpret the variable identifier's data.
   e. Too much documentation can make the logic of the program harder to understand, thereby making program changes more difficult.

2. b. **real**   h. **char** or **string**   n. **real**
   d. **string**   j. **string**   p. **string**
   f. **boolean**   l. **longint**

3. a. Invalid. The word **program** must be followed by an identifier.
   c. Valid.
   e. Invalid. A semicolon must follow EnterData.
   g. Valid.
   i. Valid.

4. a. **end.**
   c. **const**
        e = 2.71;
   e. **var**
        grade **: char;**
   g. **procedure** DisplayResults;
   i. { Name } or (* Name *)

5. **program** Average;
   { This program finds the average of two real numbers }
   const
     two = 2;   { number of scores }

   var
     first,   { first number }
     second,   { second number }
     average   { average of numbers }
       : real;

   procedure EnterData;
   begin
     Write ('Enter the first real number: ');
     Readln (first);
     Write ('Enter the second real number: ');
     Readln (second);
   end;

   procedure FindAverage;
   begin
     average := (first + second)/two
   end;

   procedure DisplayAverage;
   begin
     Writeln ('Average: ', average)
   end;

   begin
     EnterData;
     FindAverage;
     DisplayAverage
   end.

Chapter 3

Exercises

1. a. The **Write** statement displays output and keeps the cursor on the same line at the end of the output, while the **Writeln** statement sends the cursor to the next line after displaying its output. For example, **Write** ('Sample') produces

      Sample_

      while **Writeln** ('Sample') produces

      Sample

      _

      where _ represents the cursor.
   c. An advantage of using one **Readln** statement for each input value instead of one for all program inputs is that it allows you to use **Write** statements to supply separate descriptions for each input value, simplifying the entry of data and minimizing the chance of entering incorrect data.
   e. A Turbo Pascal unit is a collection of useful predefined procedures that can be called by any program.

2. b. Valid.   d. Valid.

3. a. **Writeln** (a:12, b:12, c:12);
   c. **Readln** (base);
   e. **Writeln** ('Rebate $', rebate:9:2);

4. a. **procedure** CreateGuestFile;
   begin
     Assign (namefile, 'guest.txt');
     Rewrite (namefile);
     Write ('Enter a name: ');
     Readln (name);
     Writeln (namefile, name);
     Close (namefile)
   end;

Programming Assignments

5. **program** DisplayRectangle;
   begin
     Writeln ('************': 42);
     Writeln ('*   *': 42);
     Writeln ('*   *': 42);
     Writeln ('************': 42)
   end.

9. **program** ReadAndDisplayName;
   var
     firstname,
     lastname
       : string[20];

   procedure EnterName;
   begin
     Write ('Enter a first name: ');
     Readln (firstname);
     Write ('Enter a last name: ');
     Readln (lastname)
   end;

```
procedure DisplayName;
begin
  Writeln (lastname, ', ', firstname)
end;

begin
  EnterName;
  DisplayName
end.
```

14.
```
program PrintsTitle;
  uses
    Printer;

  begin
    Writeln (Lst, '------------------------': 52);
    Writeln (Lst, '|                      |': 52);
    Writeln (Lst, '| Programmed for Success |': 52);
    Writeln (Lst, '|                      |': 52);
    Writeln (Lst, '------------------------': 52)
  end.
```

```
procedure FindCircumference;
begin
  circumference := 6.28 * radius
end;

procedure OutputCircumference;
begin
  Writeln ('Circumference: ', circumference:8:2)
end;

begin
  EnterRadius;
  FindCircumference;
  OutputCircumference
end.
```

Programming Assignments

1.
```
program FutureYoungMales;
  const
    percentage = 100;
  var
    futpop,
    initpop      : longint;
    growthrate   : integer;

  procedure EnterFigures;
  begin
    Write ('Number of boys aged 5 and under: ');
    Readln (initpop);
    Write ('Projected percent growth over a five-year period: ');
    Readln (growthrate)
  end;

  procedure FindFutPop;
  begin
    futpop := (initpop * growthrate) div percentage + initpop
  end;

  procedure DisplayResults;
  begin
    Writeln ('Expected population: ', futpop)
  end;

  begin
    EnterFigures;
    FindFutPop;
    DisplayResults
  end.
```

8.
```
program ComputerInfoService;
  const
    monthlyfee = 25;
    feepermin = 1;
  var
    totmin,
    totchrg    : real;
```

Chapter 4

Exercises

1. a. Some formulas require the execution of a lower-precedence operation before a higher-precedence one. For example, in finding the average of two numbers, the values must be added and then divided by 2. It is for this reason that parentheses are used to override the standard order of operations.

   c. A tracing utility provides a "window" into the computer as it executes a program, allowing a programmer to view values of variables as he or she goes through a program one step at a time. This technique is useful in detecting and correcting errors.

   e. Program stubs are temporary modules inserted in a solution for the purpose of testing program components one at a time using the top-down testing methodology.

2. b. Invalid. The left side of := must be a declared identifier.
   d. Invalid. The assignment operator is := and not =.

3. a. `top := first div second;`
   c. `float := fifth/sixth;`
   e. `temp := 3 * temp;`

4. (1) An equal sign should replace the colon in the constant declaration. (2) The variable declarations for **real** identifiers *time* and *rate* are missing. (3) In **procedure** EnterData, apostrophes should enclose the description in the second **Write** statement. (4) A multiplication operator * should follow the identifier *principal* in **procedure** FindInterest. (5) The apostrophe should follow the $ in **procedure** DisplayInterest rather than precede it. (6) The final **end** statement should be followed by a period.

6.
```
program Circle;
  var
    radius, circumference : real;

  procedure EnterRadius;
  begin
    Write ('Enter radius: ');
    Readln (radius)
  end;
```

533

```pascal
procedure EnterTotMin;
begin
    Write ('Enter total minutes customer was connected: ');
    Readln (totmin);
end;

procedure FindTotCharges;
begin
    totchrg := (totmin * feepermin) + monthlyfee
end;

procedure DisplayResults;
begin
    Writeln ('This month''s service charges: $', totchrg:5:2)
end;

begin
    EnterTotMin;
    FindTotCharges;
    DisplayResults
end.

16. program Inflation;
    const
        quarters = 4;
        percent = 100;
    var
        janprice,
        aprprice,
        futprice,
        quartincr,
        yearincr,
        pctquartincr,
        pctyearincr
            : real;
        name
            : string[20];

    procedure EnterData;
    begin
        Write ('Enter name of the item to be priced: ');
        Readln (name);
        Write ('Enter price of this item in January: $');
        Readln (janprice);
        Write ('Enter price of this item in April: $');
        Readln (aprprice)
    end;

    procedure FindIncreases;
    begin
        quartincr := (aprprice - janprice) / janprice;
        yearincr := quartincr * quarters;
        pctquartincr := quartincr * percent;
        pctyearincr := yearincr * percent
    end;

    procedure FindFuturePrice;
    begin
        futprice := (yearincr * janprice) + janprice
    end;

procedure DisplayResults;
begin
    Writeln ('Item: ',name);
    Writeln ('Price increase in first quarter: ',
             pctquartincr:4:1, '%');
    Writeln ('Price increase by end of year: ',
             pctyearincr:4:1, '%');
    Writeln ('Predicted price at this time: $', futprice:8:2)
end;

begin
    EnterData;
    FindIncreases;
    FindFuturePrice;
    DisplayResults
end.
```

Chapter 5
Exercises

1 a. Value parameters are considered one-way because a copy of the value of the actual parameter is made in the formal parameter and a change in that formal parameter is not detected by the actual parameter. Variable parameters are considered two-way parameters because both the actual and formal parameters refer to the same physical location and a change by either is detected by the other.

   c. Actual parameters are those in the calling program, while formal parameters are the local variables of a procedure that are associated with the actual parameters in the call.

   e. A side effect is a change in a variable's value in a subprogram that affects a value outside that subprogram but is not passed through a parameter. For example, a change in a global variable in a procedure is echoed throughout the program even through the new value is not returned to the call through a parameter.

2. b. Valid.   d. Valid.

3. a. Str (total, stotal);

   c. procedure FindPayment (principal, term, rate : real;
                             var amount : real);

   e. Val ('341.87', rnumber, code);

4. b. <number> is a value parameter; <string> is a variable parameter.

5. a. x before call: ford
      z before change: ford
      z after change: forward
      x after call: forward

   c. i = 3
      a = 3
      b = 33
      i = 3
      j = 33
      c = 33
      d = 8
      i = 8
      j = 33

6. a. See Figure G5.6a
   c. See Figure G5.6c

```pascal
begin
  EnterData;
  CalculateDepreciation;
  DisplayDepreciation
end.

10. program PhotonEnergy;
    const
      h = 6.63E-34;
      c = 3.00E+8;
    var
      wavelength,
      energy
        : real;

    procedure EnterWavelength (var wavelength : real);
    begin
      Write ('Enter wavelength: ');
      Readln (wavelength)
    end;

    procedure FindEnergy (wavelength : real; var energy : real);
    begin
      energy := (h * c)/ wavelength
    end;

    procedure DisplayEnergy (energy : real);
    begin
      Writeln ('Energy of photon in joules: ', energy)
    end;

begin
  EnterWavelength (wavelength);
  FindEnergy (wavelength, energy);
  DisplayEnergy (energy)
end.

18. program SphereVolumeIncrease;
    const
      c = 4.19;
    var
      oldradius,
      newradius,
      additionalvolume
        : real;

    procedure EnterRadii (var oldradius, newradius : real);
    begin
      Write ('Enter radius of original ball, in feet: ');
      Readln (oldradius);
      Write ('Enter radius of ball, in feet, after adding putty: ');
      Readln (newradius)
    end;

    procedure FindCube (r : real; var cube : real);
    begin
      cube := r * r * r
    end;
```

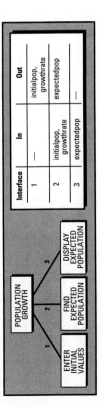

Interface	In	Out
1	--	initialpop, growthrate
2	initialpop, growthrate	expectedpop
3	expectedpop	--

Figure G5.6a
Population Growth Solution Design and Module Interface Table for Exercise 6a

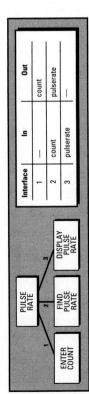

Interface	In	Out
1	--	count
2	count	pulserate
3	pulserate	--

Figure G5.6c
Pulse Rate Solution Design and Module Interface Table for Exercise 6c

Programming Assignments

```pascal
4. program FindDepreciation;
   var
     purchaseprice,
     salvagevalue,
     depreciation
       : real;
     years
       : integer;

   procedure EnterData;
   begin
     Write ('Enter purchase price: $');
     Readln (purchaseprice);
     Write ('Enter salvage value: $');
     Readln (salvagevalue);
     Write ('Enter number of years for depreciation: ');
     Readln (years)
   end;

   procedure CalculateDepreciation;
   begin
     depreciation := (purchaseprice - salvagevalue) / years
   end;

   procedure DisplayDepreciation;
   begin
     Writeln ('Straight-line depreciation value: $', depreciation:8:2)
   end;
```

535

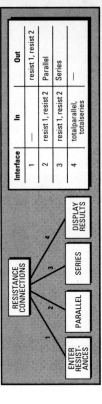

Interface	In	Out
1	—	speed
2	speed	Distance
3	brakedist	—

Figure G6.6a
Braking Distance Solution Design and Module Interface Table for Exercise 6a

Interface	In	Out
1	—	resist 1, resist 2
2	resist 1, resist 2	Parallel
3	resist 1, resist 2	Series
4	totalparallel, totalseries	—

Figure G6.6c
Resistance Connections Solution Design and Module Interface Table for Exercise 6c

Interface	In	Out
1	—	names
2	names	reverse
3	revnames	—

Figure G6.6e
Change Name Format Solution Design and Module Interface Table for Exercise 6e

```
procedure CalculateAddVolume (oldradius, newradius : real;
                          var addvolume : real);

  var
    cube,
    oldvolume,
    newvolume
        : real;

  begin
    FindCube (oldradius, cube);
    oldvolume := c * cube;
    FindCube (newradius, cube);
    newvolume := c * cube;
    addvolume := newvolume - oldvolume
  end;

procedure DisplayAddVolume (addvolume : real);
  begin
    Writeln ('Additional volume: ', addvolume:8:2, ' cubic feet.')
  end;

begin
  EnterRadii (oldradius, newradius);
  CalculateAddVolume (oldradius, newradius, additionalvolume);
  DisplayAddVolume (additionalvolume)
end.
```

Chapter 6

Exercises

1. a. Functions and procedures are called subprograms because they can be considered small programs that are called by master programs to perform specific tasks.

   c. **Ord** returns the ordinal number of its parameter. If the parameter were not an ordinal data type, its ordinal (or positional) value in a list could not be determined.

   e. To test the randomness of the random number generator, a program could be written that chooses a large number of random values and tabulates how many fall in certain predesignated ranges. For example, if 10,000 random integers between 1 and 5, inclusive, are chosen, 20% should be 1's, 20% should be 2's, etc. Any deviation from these values would show a bias on the part of the random number generator.

2. b. Invalid. **Concat** is a function; its value must be assigned to another identifier.

   d. Valid.

3. a. =   g. 3
   c. 1.69   i. 3.142
   e. 11

4. b. **Random**(37)
   d. **function** Largest (a, b, c : real) : real;

5. a. x in One: 18.39
   x in PartA: 8.19
   y in PartA: 18.39
   c. c in Three: 8
   g in Four: 8
   a in PartC: 29
   b in PartC: 8

6. a. See Figure G6.6a
   c. See Figure G6.6c
   e. See Figure G6.6e

Programming Assignments

2. **program** AstroDistances;
```
      var
        nummiles,
        numlightyears
            : real;

    procedure EnterMiles (var miles : real);
    begin
      Write ('Enter number of miles to be converted: ');
      Readln (miles)
    end;

    function LightYears (miles : real) : real;
      const
        milesperlightyear = 5.88e+12;
      var
        templightyears
            : real;
```

```
9. program Resistors;
    var
        resistor1,
        resistor2,
        resistinseries,
        resistinparallel
            : real;

    procedure EnterData (var r1, r2 : real);
    begin
        Write ('Enter resistance R1 in ohms: ');
        Readln (r1);
        Write ('Enter resistance R2 in ohms: ');
        Readln (r2)
    end;

    function Parallel (r1, r2 : real) : real;
        var
            temparallel
                : real;
    begin
        temparallel := (r1 * r2) / (r1 + r2);
        Parallel := temparallel
    end;

    function Series (r1, r2 : real) : real;
        var
            tempseries
                : real;
    begin
        tempseries := r1 + r2;
        Series := tempseries
    end;

    procedure DisplayEquivalences (rs, rp : real);
    begin
        Writeln ('Equivalent resistances for R1 and R2');
        Writeln ('Connected in parallel: ', rp:6:2,' ohms');
        Writeln ('Connected in series: ', rs:6:2,' ohms')
    end;

begin
    EnterData (resistor1, resistor2);
    resistinparallel := Parallel (resistor1, resistor2);
    resistinseries := Series (resistor1, resistor2);
    DisplayEquivalences (resistinseries, resistinparallel)
end.
```

```
        begin
            templightyears := miles / milesperlightyear;
            LightYears := templightyears
        end;

        procedure DisplayLightYears (lityears : real);
        begin
            Writeln ('Equivalent distance in light years: ', lityears:8:2)
        end;

    begin
        EnterMiles (nummiles);
        numlightyears := LightYears (nummiles);
        DisplayLightYears (numlightyears)
    end.
```

```
14. program FloorCost;
    var
        floorwidth,
        floorlength,
        tilecost,
        totalcost
            : real;
        numboxes
            : integer;

    procedure EnterData (var wdth, lngth, tilecost : real);
    begin
        Write ('Enter width of floor in feet: ');
        Readln (wdth);
        Write ('Enter length of floor in feet: ');
        Readln (lngth);
        Write ('Enter cost for each tile: $');
        Readln (tilecost)
    end;

    function AreaFloor (wdth, lngth : real) : real;
        var
            temparea
                : real;
    begin
        temparea := wdth * lngth;
        AreaFloor := temparea
    end;

    procedure FindFloorCost (var numboxes : integer;
                var totalcost : real; wdth, lngth, tilecost : real);
        const
            tilesperbox = 12.0;
            areapertile = 1;
        var
            costperbox,
            areaperbox
                : real;
    begin
        costperbox := tilesperbox * tilecost;
        areaperbox := tilesperbox * areapertile;
        numboxes := Trunc (AreaFloor(wdth, lngth) / areaperbox) + 1;
        totalcost := numboxes * costperbox
    end;

    procedure DisplayResults (boxes : integer; cost : real);
    begin
        Writeln ('To tile this area you will need ',boxes,
                ' boxes of tile.');
        Writeln ('These boxes will cost $',cost:6:2,' plus tax.')
    end;

begin
    EnterData (floorwidth, floorlength, tilecost);
    FindFloorCost (numboxes, totalcost, floorwidth, floorlength,
                tilecost);
    DisplayResults (numboxes, totalcost)
end.
```

Chapter 7
Exercises

1. a. Since the selector in a **case** structure must be an ordinal data type, any **case** structure can be written as a sequence of nested **if ... then ... else** structures, with the ordinal values becoming part of the conditions in each.

   c. Nested structures occur when one programming structure is contained entirely within another.

   e. A semicolon preceding the **else** clause in an **if ... then ... else** structure indicates the end of the structure. In that case, the term **else** stands by itself, leading to a syntax error, since it only has meaning in an **if** structure.

2. b. Invalid. ; should not precede the **else** clause.
   d. Valid.

3. a. True.   c. True.   e. False.

4. b. **if** num > 0
         then
            Writeln ('positive')
         else
            if num < 0
               then
                  Writeln ('negative')
               else
                  Writeln ('zero');

   d. **case** lettergrade **of**
         'A' :
            gradepoint := 4 * numcredits;
         'B' :
            gradepoint := 3 * numcredits;
         'C' :
            gradepoint := 2 * numcredits;
         'D' :
            gradepoint := 1 * numcredits;
         'F' :
            gradepoint := 0
      end;

6. a. 3   c. 5   e. 7   5
   b. d   d. p   3
      aooo   ooooy

7. b. d

Programming Assignments

3. **program** DriverLicense;
   const
      passinggrade = 70;
   type
      stringtype = **string**[20];
   var
      name,
      result
         : stringtype;
      grade
         : **real**;
      test
         : **char**;

```
procedure EnterData (var name : stringtype;
                     var grade : real; var test : char);
begin
   Write ('Enter name: ');
   Readln (name);
   Write ('Enter grade on written examination: ');
   Readln (grade);
   Writeln ('Enter the result of driving test ');
   Write ('(P for pass or F for fail): ');
   Readln (test);
end;

function PassOrFail (grade : real; test : char) : stringtype;
   var
      result
         : stringtype;
begin
   if (grade >= passinggrade) and ((test = 'P') or (test = 'p'))
      then
         result := ' is '
      else
         result := ' is not ';
   PassOrFail := result
end;

procedure DisplayResult (name, result : stringtype);
begin
   Writeln (name, result, 'eligible for a driver''s license.')
end;

begin
   EnterData (name, grade, test);
   result := PassOrFail (grade, test);
   DisplayResult (name, result)
end.
```

9. **program** CalculateEquivalentWeight;
   uses
      Crt;
   type
      stringtype = **string**[8];
   var
      choice
         : **integer**;
      weight,
      value,
      equivalent
         : **real**;
      planet
         : stringtype;
      valid
         : **boolean**;

```
procedure EnterData (var weight : real);
begin
   ClrScr;
   GotoXY (10,10);
   Write ('Enter your weight on earth: ');
   Readln (weight)
end;
```

```
function PlanetChoice : integer;
  var
    choice : integer;
begin
  ClrScr;
  GotoXY (25,3);
  Writeln ('Choice of Planet');
  GotoXY (10,5);
  Writeln ('Enter number preceding planet of your choice.');
  GotoXY (15,7);
  Writeln ('<1> Mercury');
  GotoXY (15,8);
  Writeln ('<2> Venus');
  GotoXY (15,9);
  Writeln ('<3> Earth');
  GotoXY (15,10);
  Writeln ('<4> Mars');
  GotoXY (15,11);
  Writeln ('<5> Jupiter');
  GotoXY (15,12);
  Writeln ('<6> Saturn');
  GotoXY (15,13);
  Writeln ('<7> Uranus');
  GotoXY (15,14);
  Writeln ('<8> Neptune');
  GotoXY (15,15);
  Writeln ('<9> Pluto');
  GotoXY (10,17);
  Writeln ('Choice ---> ');
  Readln (choice);
  PlanetChoice := choice
end;

procedure WeightValue (choice : integer;
           var planet : stringtype; var value : real;
           var valid : boolean);
begin
  valid := true;
  case choice of
    1 : begin
          planet := 'Mercury';
          value := 0.38
        end;
    2 : begin
          planet := 'Venus';
          value := 0.91
        end;
    3 : begin
          planet := 'Earth';
          value := 1.00
        end;
    4 : begin
          planet := 'Mars';
          value := 0.38
        end;
    5 : begin
          planet := 'Jupiter';
          value := 2.53
        end;
    6 : begin
          planet := 'Saturn';
          value := 1.06
        end;
    7 : begin
          planet := 'Uranus';
          value := 0.92
        end;
    8 : begin
          planet := 'Neptune';
          value := 1.20
        end;
    9 : begin
          planet := 'Pluto';
          value := 0.57
        end;
    else
      valid := false
  end
end;

procedure CalculateEquivalent (weight, value : real;
                        var equivalent : real);
begin
  equivalent := weight * value
end;

procedure DisplayEquivalent (valid : boolean;
             weight, equivalent : real; planet : stringtype);
begin
  ClrScr;
  GotoXY (20,8);
  Writeln ('Weight Equivalency');
  GotoXY (12,11);
  if valid
    then
      begin
        Writeln ('Weight on earth: ', weight:6:2, ' lbs.');
        GotoXY (12,13);
        Writeln ('Equivalent weight on ', planet, ': ',
                 equivalent:7:2, ' lbs.')
      end
    else
      Writeln ('Improper input')
end;
```

(continued)

```pascal
procedure DeterminePosition (x, y : real;
                             var position : stringtype);
begin
  case 3*Sign(x) - 2*Sign(y) + 6 of
    1 :
      position := 'in the second quadrant';
    3 :
      position := 'on the negative x-axis';
    4 :
      position := 'on the positive y-axis';
    5 :
      position := 'in the third quadrant';
    6 :
      position := 'at the origin';
    7 :
      position := 'in the first quadrant';
    8 :
      position := 'on the negative y-axis';
    9 :
      position := 'on the positive x-axis';
    11 :
      position := 'in the fourth quadrant'
  end
end;

procedure DisplayPosition (x, y : real; position : stringtype);
begin
  GotoXY (10,12);
  Writeln ('Position of Coordinates');
  GotoXY (15,15);
  Writeln ('(', x:4:1, ', ', y:4:1, ') lies ', position, '.')
end;

begin
  EnterCoordinates (x, y);
  DeterminePosition (x, y, position);
  DisplayPosition (x, y, position)
end.
```

Chapter 8

Exercises

1. a. In a definite loop structure, the number of repetitions is known by the system prior to execution of the loop; in an indefinite loop structure, the number of repetitions is determined by the value of a variable in the loop and is not known in advance.

   c. Initialization of summing and counting variables is important because arbitrary values are stored in memory locations before a program is executed. To make sure a correct answer is obtained, each of these variables must be started at the correct value.

   e. Tracing is an important technique for error detection in loop structures because, with tracing, programmers can follow the activity of variable quantities that are altered by the loop, enabling them to detect abnormal behavior if it occurs.

2. b. Valid.   d. Valid.

3. a.
```pascal
for i := 1 to 8 do
  Writeln ('That''s all folks!');
```

```pascal
begin
  EnterData (weight);
  choice := PlanetChoice;
  WeightValue(choice, planet, value, valid);
  CalculateEquivalent (weight, value, equivalent);
  DisplayEquivalent (valid, weight, equivalent, planet)
end.
```

15.
```pascal
program FindPositionOfPoint;
uses
  Crt;
type
  stringtype = string[22];
var
  position
    : stringtype;
  x,
  y   : real;

procedure EnterCoordinates (var x, y : real);
begin
  ClrScr;
  GotoXY (10,3);
  Writeln ('Coordinates of a Point');
  GotoXY (15,6);
  Write ('Enter x coordinate: ');
  Readln (x);
  GotoXY (15,8);
  Write ('Enter y coordinate: ');
  Readln (y)
end;

function Sign (a : real) : integer;
var
  temp
    : integer;
begin
  if a > 0
    then
      temp := +1
    else
      if a < 0
        then
          temp := -1
        else
          temp := 0;
  Sign := temp
end;
```

```
procedure GetNumberOfTosses (var numtosses : integer);
begin
   ClrScr;
   GotoXY (10,13);
   Write ('Enter number of coin tosses: ');
   Readln (numtosses)
end;

function Heads : boolean;
   const
      two = 2;
begin
   if Random(two) = 1
      then
         Heads := true
      else
         Heads := false
end;

procedure FindPercentages (tosses : integer;
                           var perhead, pertail : integer);
   const
      percent = 100;
   var
      numheads,
      i       : integer;
begin
   numheads := 0;
   for i := 1 to tosses do
      if Heads
         then
            numheads := numheads +1;
   perhead := Round((numheads/tosses) * percent);
   pertail := percent - perhead
end;

procedure DisplayPercentages (numtosses, perchead, perctail
                              : integer);
begin
   ClrScr;
   GotoXY (10,5);
   Writeln ('The coin was tossed ', numtosses, ' times.');
   GotoXY (10,8);
   Writeln ('Coin was heads ', perchead, '% of the time.');
   GotoXY (10,10);
   Writeln ('Coin was tails ', perctail, '% of the time.');
   Writeln
end;

procedure Continue (var answer : char);
begin
   repeat
      GotoXY (10,23);
      Write ('Do you want to play again? (y/n): ');
      Readln (answer)
   until (answer = 'y') or (answer = 'n')
end;
```

c.
```
   sum := 0;
   Write ('Enter value (-1 to end input): ');
   Readln (value);
   while value <> -1 do
      begin
         sum := sum + value;
         Write ('Enter value (-1 to end input): ');
         Readln (value)
      end;
```

e.
```
   for i := 100 downto 0 do
      Writeln (i:5);
```

5. a.

a.		c.		e.
3		9		2
4		27		4
5		81		8
6		243		16
7				32
8				64

6. b.
```
   sum := 0;
   j := 12;
   repeat
      sum := sum + j;
      Writeln ('Partial sum: ', sum:3);
      j := j - 1
   until j < 1;
   Writeln ('Final sum: ', sum:3);
```

Programming Assignments

2. program CoinToss;
```
   uses
      Crt;
   var
      tosses,
      perchead,
      perctail
         : integer;
      answer
         : char;

   procedure Greet;
      var
         ch : char;
   begin
      ClrScr;
      GotoXY (20,1);
      Writeln ('WELCOME TO IT''S A TOSS UP!');
      Writeln;
      Writeln ('You will be asked to input a number of tosses for
               a coin.');
      Writeln ('The computer will simulate these tosses, and
               display ');
      Writeln ('the percentage of the tosses that result in heads
               and tails.');
      Writeln;
      Write ('Press any key and Enter to continue -->');
      Readln (ch)
   end;
```

541

(continued)

```pascal
begin
  Randomize;
  Greet;
  repeat
    GetNumberOfTosses (tosses);
    FindPercentages (tosses, perchead, perctail);
    DisplayPercentages (tosses, perchead, perctail);
    Continue (answer)
  until answer = 'n';
  ClrScr;
  GotoXY (30,12);
  Writeln ('Thanks for playing!')
end.
```

```pascal
8. program WorthAMillion;
uses
  Crt;
var
  numdays
    : integer;
procedure FindTime (var numdays : integer);
const
  million = 1000000.00;
  two = 2;
  doublefactor = 5;
var
  bankroll
    : real;
begin
  numdays := 0;
  bankroll := 0.01;
  while bankroll < million do
    begin
      bankroll := bankroll * two;
      numdays := numdays + doublefactor
    end
end;
procedure DisplayTime (numdays :integer);
begin
  ClrScr;
  Writeln ('If you start with a cent and double it every
            five days,');
  Writeln ('it will take', numdays, ' days to become a
            millionaire.')
end;
begin
  FindTime (numdays);
  DisplayTime (numdays);
end.
```

```pascal
14. program Cryptanalysis;
uses
  Crt;
const
  numletters = 26;
  alphabase = 'ABCDEFGHIJKLMNOPQRSTUVWXYZ ';
type
  postype = 1..26;
  strtype = string[80];
  keytype = 1..26;
var
  msglngth
    : integer;
  message,
  codedmsg
    : strtype;
  key      : keytype;
  encode
    : boolean;
  answer
    : char;
procedure GetData (var message : strtype; var encode : boolean;
                   var key : keytype);
var
  choice
    : char;
begin
  ClrScr;
  encode := true;
  GotoXY (10,6);
  Write ('Enter message to be coded: ');
  Readln (message);
  repeat
    GotoXY (10,9);
    Write ('Enter E to encode or D to decode: ');
    Readln (choice);
  until (choice = 'D') or (choice = 'E');
  if choice = 'D'
    then
      begin
        encode := false;
        GotoXY (13,11);
        Write ('Enter decoding key (1-26): ');
        Readln (key)
      end
end;

procedure Encrypt (msglngth : integer; message : strtype;
                   var key : keytype; var codedmsg : strtype);
var
  index
    : integer;
  letter,
  newletter
    : string[1];
  letterpos
    : postype;
```

```pascal
begin
  key := Random (numletters - 1) + 1;
  codedmsg := '';
  for index := 1 to msglngth do
    begin
      letter := Copy (message, index, 1);
      letterpos := Pos (letter, alphabase);
      letterpos := letterpos + key;
      if letterpos > numletters
        then
          letterpos := letterpos - numletters;
      newletter := Copy (alphabase, letterpos, 1);
      codedmsg := codedmsg + newletter
    end
end;

procedure Decrypt (msglngth : integer; message : strtype;
                   var key : keytype; var codedmsg : strtype);

var
  index
    : integer;
  letter,
  newletter
    : string[1];
  letterpos
    : postype;

begin
  codedmsg := '';
  for index := 1 to msglngth do
    begin
      letter := Copy (message, index, 1);
      letterpos := Pos (letter, alphabase);
      letterpos := letterpos - key;
      if letterpos < 1
        then
          letterpos := letterpos + numletters;
      newletter := Copy (alphabase, letterpos, 1);
      codedmsg := codedmsg + newletter
    end
end;

procedure CodeMessage (message :strtype; encode : boolean;
                       var key : keytype; var codedmsg : strtype);
var
  msglngth
    : integer;
begin
  msglngth := Length (message);
  if encode
    then
      Encrypt (msglngth, message, key, codedmsg)
    else
      Decrypt (msglngth, message, key, codedmsg)
end;

procedure OutputMessage (message : strtype; encode : boolean;
                         key :keytype; codedmsg : strtype);
begin
  if encode
    then
      begin
        GotoXY (10,15);
        Writeln ('Encrypting key chosen by computer: ', key);
        GotoXY (10,17);
        Writeln ('Coded message: ', codedmsg)
      end
    else
      begin
        GotoXY (10,15);
        Writeln ('Decoded message: ', codedmsg)
      end
end;

procedure Continue (var answer : char);
begin
  repeat
    GotoXY (10,23);
    Write ('Do you want to encode or decode another message?
           (Y/N): ');
    Readln (answer)
  until (answer = 'Y') or (answer = 'N')
end;

begin
  Randomize;
  repeat
    GetData (message, encode, key);
    CodeMessage (message, encode, key, codedmsg);
    OutputMessage (message, encode, key, codedmsg);
    Continue (answer)
  until answer = 'N'
end.
```

Chapter 9
Exercises

1. a. A structured data type is one composed of two or more data types with a set
      of rules that govern its use. Arrays and records are structured data types.
   c. Locating an element in an array structure requires you to specify the name
      of the array as well as one value for each dimension in the array.
   e. An array is a static data type because its size must be declared before a
      program is executed. Once declared, its size cannot be altered while the
      program is running.
2. b. Valid.   d. Valid.
3. a. -4   c. 1   e. 0
4. b. 2   d. 2.5
5. a. ```pascal
      type
        ctype = array[0..11] of char;
      var
        c : ctype;
      ```
      ```

```
c. zcount := 0;
   for i := 1 to 7 do
     for j := 1 to 7 do
       if a[i,j] = 0
         then
           zcount := zcount + 1;

e. sum := 0;
   for row := 1 to 5 do
     sum := sum + b[row,3];
   Writeln ('Sum of third column: ', sum);
```

6. (1) *sum* is not initialized. (2) An array declaration cannot be used in a parameter listing. (3) *sum* should be a variable parameter.

```
7. b. 1   d. 3  4  5
      5      5  6  7
             7  8  9
             9  10 11
```

Programming Assignments

```
7. program Hamming;
   uses
     Crt;
   const
     maxsize = 10;
   type
     arraytype = array[1..maxsize] of boolean;
   var
     array1,
     array2
       : arraytype;
     size,
     distance
       : integer;

procedure EnterArraySize (var size : integer);
begin
  Writeln ('Enter number of elements in Boolean arrays');
  Write (' (maximum of 10): ');
  Readln (size)
end;

procedure FillArray (var matrix : arraytype; size : integer);
var
  i : integer;
  ans : char;
begin
  Writeln ('Enter T for TRUE or F for FALSE for each element.');
  for i := 1 to size do
    begin
      Write ('Element ', i, ': ');
      Readln (ans);
      if ans in ['T','t']
        then
          matrix[i] := true
        else
          matrix[i] := false
    end
end;
```

```
procedure CalculateHammingDistance (array1, array2 : arraytype;
              size : integer; var distance : integer);
var
  i : integer;
begin
  distance := 0;
  for i := 1 to size do
    if array1[i] <> array2[i]
      then
        distance := distance + 1
end;

procedure DisplayArray (array1 : arraytype; size : integer);
var
  i : integer;
begin
  for i := 1 to size do
    Write (array1[i]:6);
  Writeln
end;

procedure DisplayHammingDistance (array1, array2 : arraytype;
              size : integer; distance : integer);
begin
  ClrScr;
  GotoXY (1,5);
  Write ('Array 1: ');
  DisplayArray (array1, size);
  Write ('Array 2: ');
  DisplayArray (array2, size);
  GotoXY (20,10);
  Writeln ('Hamming distance: ', distance)
end;

begin
  ClrScr;
  EnterArraySize (size);
  Writeln;
  Writeln ('Fill First Array':30);
  FillArray (array1, size);
  Writeln;
  Writeln ('Fill Second Array':30);
  FillArray (array2, size);
  CalculateHammingDistance (array1, array2, size, distance);
  DisplayHammingDistance (array1, array2, size, distance)
end.

13. program CatalanSequence;
    uses
      Crt;
    const
      maxsize = 15;
    type
      arraytype = array[0..maxsize] of longint;
    var
      catalanarray
        : arraytype;
```

```pascal
procedure DisplayTable (catalanarray : arraytype);

  var

    index
      : integer;

begin
  ClrScr;
  GotoXY (25,1);
  Writeln ('FIRST FIFTEEN CATALAN NUMBERS');
  for index := 0 to maxsize do
    begin
      GotoXY (31, index + 4);
      Writeln ('C(', index:2, ') = ', catalanarray[index]:10)
    end

end;

procedure FillTable (var catalanarray : arraytype);

  var
    i,
    k,
    sum
      : longint;

begin
  catalanarray[0] := 1;
  for i := 1 to maxsize do
    begin
      sum := 0;
      for k := 0 to (i - 1) do
        sum := sum + catalanarray[k] * catalanarray[i - k - 1];
      catalanarray[i] := sum
    end

end;

begin
  FillTable (catalanarray);
  DisplayTable (catalanarray)
end.

20. program GameOfLife;
  uses
    Crt;
  const
    size = 15;
    aster = ' *';
    blank = '  ';
  type
    celltype = string[2];
    answertype = string[3];
    maptype = array[0..(size + 1),0..(size + 1)] of celltype;
  var

    ans
      : answertype;
    map
      : maptype;
    generation
      : integer;
```

```pascal
procedure Introduction;
  var
    ch
      : char;

begin
  ClrScr;
  GotoXY (1,7);
  Writeln ('*************** GAME OF LIFE ************':55);
  Writeln;
  Writeln ('Enter the coordinates of a living cell.':55);
  Writeln ('Coordinates must be integers between 1 and 15.':59);
  Writeln ('Enter "99" to end entry of coordinates.':56);
  Write ('Press any key to start the game.':52);
  ch := ReadKey

end;

procedure BlankMap (var map : maptype);

  var

    row,
    clmn
      : integer;

begin
  for row := 0 to (size + 1) do
    begin
      for clmn := 0 to (size + 1) do
        begin
          map[row,clmn] := blank;
          Write (map[row,clmn])
        end;
      Writeln
    end

end;

procedure GetRow (var row : integer; var EndOfData : boolean);

begin
  ClrScr;
  GotoXY (5,3);
  repeat
    Writeln;
    Writeln ('Enter a row number from 1 to ', size,'.');
    Writeln ('Enter "99" to stop entry of data: ');
    Write ('  Row -->');
    Readln (row);
    if row = 99
      then
        EndOfData := true
      else
        if (row < 1) or (row > (size + 1))
          then
            Writeln ('Error.  Row number cannot be ', row,'.')
  until ((row > 0) and (row < (size + 1))) or EndOfData

end;
```

```pascal
procedure GetColumn (var column : integer;
                     var EndofData : boolean);
begin
  repeat
    Writeln;
    Writeln ('Enter a column number from 1 to ',size,'.');
    Write (' Column --> ');
    Readln (column);
    if (column < 1) or (column > (size + 1))
      then
        Writeln ('Error. Column number cannot be: ',column,'.')
  until (column > 0) and (column < (size + 1))
end;

procedure Continue;
  var
    ch
      : char;
begin
  GotoXY (10,24);
  Write ('Press any key to continue.');
  ch := ReadKey
end;

procedure CheckNewCell (var map : maptype;
                        row, column : integer);
  var
    ch
      : char;
begin
  if (map[row,column] <> aster)
    then
      map [row,column] := aster
    else
      begin
        Writeln;
        Writeln ('Already a living cell there.');
        Continue
      end
end;

procedure StartGame (var map : maptype;
                     var generation : integer);
  var
    row,
    column
      : integer;
    endofdata
      : boolean;
begin
  ClrScr;
  Writeln ('Enter coordinates of ''live'' cells.');
  generation := 0;
  BlankMap (map);
  endofdata := false;
  repeat
    GetRow (row, endofdata);
    if (not endofdata)
      then

        begin
          GetColumn (column, endofdata);
          CheckNewCell (map, row, column)
        end-
  until endofdata
end;

procedure PrintMap (map: maptype; generation : integer;
                    var ans : answertype);
  var
    row,
    clmn
      : integer;
begin
  ClrScr;
  for row := 1 to size do
    begin
      GotoXY (23,row);
      for clmn := 1 to size do
        Write (map[row,clmn]);
      Writeln
    end;
  GotoXY (30,21);
  Writeln ('Generation ',generation);
  GotoXY (3,24);
  Write ('Type "end" to end, another key to continue --> ');
  Readln (ans)
end;

procedure CountNeighbors (map : maptype;
                          var neighbors : integer; row, column : integer);
begin
  neighbors := 0;
  if map[row-1,column-1] = aster
    then
      neighbors := neighbors + 1;
  if map[row-1,column] = aster
    then
      neighbors := neighbors + 1;
  if map[row-1,column+1] = aster
    then
      neighbors := neighbors + 1;
  if map[row,column-1] = aster
    then
      neighbors := neighbors + 1;
  if map[row,column+1] = aster
    then
      neighbors := neighbors + 1;
  if map[row+1,column-1] = aster
    then
      neighbors := neighbors + 1;
  if map[row+1,column] = aster
    then
      neighbors := neighbors + 1;
  if map[row+1,column+1] = aster
    then
      neighbors := neighbors + 1
end;
```

(continued)

546

Chapter 10

Exercises

1. a. To access an element in an array, you must specify the name of the array and all its indices; to access a field in a record, you must specify the record name and the field name.
   c. Fields can be accessed by only identifying their names if the statements containing these references are enclosed in a **with** structure.
   e. The efficiency of a linear search can be improved by sorting the list because the search need go only as far as a certain value to determine if a value is in the list or not. For example, if an integer list is sorted in ascending numeric order and 34 is the target value, you have only to compare list items until you reach a value greater than 34.
2. b. Invalid. A **do** is missing following the record name r.
   d. Valid.
3. a. alpha   c. betaalpha   e. balphaeta
4. b. **type**

```
    repairtype = record
        modelname  : string[20];
        repaircost : real;
        numrepairs : integer
    end;
    allrepairstype = array[1..100] of repairtype;
var
    repairs : allrepairstype;
```

   d. **type**

```
    salestype = record
        name : string[20];
        monthsales : array[1..12] of integer;
    end;
var
    sales : salestype;
```

5. (1) No type declared for the function. (2) Loop not primed. (3) No index indicated for zoopop. (4) No value returned through function name. (5) Count not initialized.
6. a. potato cost: $ 3.95   c. A dog has 4 legs.
7. b. Add the following subprograms to the program in the chapter after the FillTable procedure:

```
function NumberContinents (continentinfo : tabletype) : integer;
var
    index : integer;
begin
    index := 1;
    while continentinfo[index].name <> sentinel do
        index := index + 1;
    NumberContinents := index - 2
end;

procedure Interchange (var one, another : continenttype);
var
    temp : continenttype;
begin
    temp := one;
    one := another;
    another := temp
end;
```

```
procedure CopyNewMapToMap (var map : maptype;
                               newmap : maptype);
var
    row,
    column
        : integer;
begin
    for row := 1 to size do
        for column := 1 to size do
            map[row,column] := newMap[row,column]
end;

procedure BuildNewMap (var newmap : maptype);
var
    row,
    column,
    neighbors
        : integer;
begin
    for row := 1 to size do
        for column := 1 to size do
        begin
            CountNeighbors (map, neighbors, row, column);
            case neighbors of
                2 :
                    newmap[row,column] := map[row,column];
                3 :
                    newmap[row,column] := aster;
                else
                    newmap[row,column] := blank
            end
        end
end;

procedure PrintGenerations (var map : maptype;
                                ans : answertype);
var
    newmap
        : maptype;
begin
    while ans <> 'end' do
    begin
        generation := generation + 1;
        BuildNewMap (newmap);
        CopyNewMapToMap (map, newmap);
        PrintMap (map, generation, ans)
    end
end;

begin
    Introduction;
    StartGame (map, generation);
    PrintMap (map, generation, ans);
    PrintGenerations (map, ans)
end.
```

```
procedure SortTable (var continentinfo : tabletype);
  var
    pass, i, continentcount : integer;
    switch : boolean;
  begin
    continentcount := NumberContinents(continentinfo);
    switch := true;
    pass := 1;
    while (pass <= continentcount) and (switch) do
      begin
        switch := false;
        for i := 1 to continentcount - pass do
          if continentinfo[i].name > continentinfo[i+1].name
            then
              begin
                switch := true;
                Interchange (continentinfo[i], continentinfo[i+1])
              end;
        pass := pass + 1
      end
  end;

procedure NextScreen;
  var
    ans : char;
  begin
    GotoXY (1,23);
    Write ('Press any key to go to the next screen');
    ans := ReadKey
  end;

procedure DisplayTable (continentinfo : tabletype);
  var
    index : integer;
  begin
    ClrScr;
    GotoXY (28,1);
    Writeln ('Continent Inmation');
    GotoXY (1,4);
    Writeln ('Name':15, 'Area':13, '1985':17, 'Population':17);
    Writeln (('1000 sq. mi.)':33, 'Population':15, 'Density':13);
    Writeln ('(thousands)':48);
    Writeln;
    index := 1;
    while continentinfo[index].name <> sentinel do
      with continentinfo[index] do
        begin
          Writeln (name:15, area:14, population85:17,
                   popdensity:14:2);
          index := index + 1
        end;
    NextScreen
  end;
```

Change the main program to the following:

```
begin
  FillTable (continentinfo);
  SortTable (continentinfo);
  DisplayTable (continentinfo);
  GetInmation (continentinfo)
end.
```

10. d. Replace the procedure EnterRoundScores in the chapter with the following:

```
procedure EnterRoundScores (var board : boardtype);
  var
    index,
    roundnum
              : integer;
    tempname
              : nametype;
    found
              : boolean;
  begin
    ClrScr;
    Write ('Enter round number: ');
    Readln (roundnum);
    ClrScr;
    GotoXY (20,1);
    Writeln ('SCORES  ROUND ', roundnum);
    GotoXY (1,4);
    Write ('Enter golfer''s name (xxx to end input): ');
    Readln (tempname);
    while tempname <> 'xxx' do
      begin
        found := false;
        index := 1;
        while (index <= board.numgolfers) and (not found) do
          with board.golfer[index] do
            if name = tempname
              then
                begin
                  found := true;
                  Write ('Enter score ',name, ': ');
                  Readln (roundscore[roundnum])
                end
              else
                index := index + 1;
        if not found
          then
            Writeln ('Name not found.');
        Writeln;
        Write ('Enter golfer''s name (xxx to end input): ');
        Readln (tempname);
      end;
    CumulateScores (board)
  end;
```

Programming Assignments

1. program BaseballStatistics;
   uses
     Crt;
   type
     playertype = record
       name : string[30];
       numatbats,
       numhits : integer;
       batavg : real
     end;
     teamtype = array[1..25] of playertype;
   var
     team
       : teamtype;
     numplayers
       : integer;

   procedure Continue (var ans : char);
   begin
     repeat
       GotoXY (10,24);
       Write ('Do you want to add data for a player (y/n)? ');
       ans := ReadKey
     until ans in ['n','N','y','Y']
   end;

   procedure EnterData (var team : teamtype;
                        var numplayers : integer);
   var
     ans
       : char;
   begin
     numplayers := 0;
     ClrScr;
     Continue (ans);
     while ans in ['y','Y'] do
       begin
         ClrScr;
         GotoXY (1,10);
         numplayers := numplayers + 1;
         with team[numplayers] do
           begin
             Write ('Enter player name: ');
             Readln (name);
             Writeln;
             Write ('Enter number of at bats: ');
             Readln (numatbats);
             Writeln;
             Write ('Enter number of hits: ');
             Readln (numhits);
             Continue (ans)
           end
       end
   end;

   procedure FindBattingAverages (var team : teamtype;
                                  numplayers : integer);
   var
     i : integer;
   begin
     for i := 1 to numplayers do
       with team[i] do
         begin
           batavg := numhits / numatbats;
           batavg := Round (batavg * 1000) / 1000
         end
   end;

   procedure DisplayStatistics (team : teamtype;
                                numplayers : integer);
   var
     i : integer;
     ch : char;
   begin
     ClrScr;
     GotoXY (30,1);
     Writeln ('Player Statistics');
     Writeln;
     Writeln ('Player':20, 'At Bats':12, 'Hits':12, 'Average':12);
     Writeln ('------':20, '------':12, '----':12, '-------':12);
     for i := 1 to numplayers do
       with team[i] do
         Writeln (name:20, numatbats:12, numhits:12, batavg:12:3);
     GotoXY (10,24);
     Write ('Press any key to end program.');
     ch := ReadKey
   end;

   begin
     EnterData (team, numplayers);
     FindBattingAverages (team, numplayers);
     DisplayStatistics (team, numplayers)
   end.

8. program FamousPersonSearch;
   uses
     Crt;
   const
     sentinel = 'end';
     maxsize = 20;
   type
     nametype = string[20];
     persontype = record
       name : nametype;
       age : integer
     end;
     arraytype = array[1..maxsize] of persontype;
   var
     personinfo
       : arraytype;

```pascal
procedure FillTable (var personinfo : arraytype);
  var
    index
      : integer;
begin
  ClrScr;
  index := 1 ;
  Writeln ('FAMOUS PERSON INFORMATION DATA ENTRY');
  Writeln;
  Writeln ('Type "end" for person''s name to stop entry: ');
  Write ('Person''s name: ');
  Readln (personinfo[index].name);
  while personinfo[index].name <> sentinel do
    begin
      Write ('Enter that person''s age: ');
      Readln (personinfo[index].age);
      index := index + 1;
      Writeln ('Type "end" for person''s name to stop entry: ');
      Write ('Person''s name: ');
      Readln (personinfo[index].name)
    end
end;

procedure SearchTable (personinfo : arraytype; target : nametype;
                       var location : integer; var found : boolean);
  var
    index
      : integer;
begin
  index := 1;
  found := false;
  while (personinfo[index].name <> 'end') and (not found) do
    if personinfo[index].name = target
      then
        begin
          location := index;
          found := true
        end
      else
        index := index + 1;
  if not found
    then
      location := 0
end;

procedure DisplayAge (personinfo : arraytype; location : integer);
begin
  ClrScr;
  GotoXY (25,1);
  Writeln ('FAMOUS PERSON INFORMATION');
  with personinfo[location] do
    begin
      GotoXY (15,5);
      Writeln ('PERSON: ',name);
      GotoXY (15,7);
      Writeln ('AGE: ',age)
    end
end;

procedure Swap (var personinfo : arraytype; location : integer);
  var
    temp
      : persontype;
begin
  temp := personinfo[location - 1];
  personinfo[location - 1] := personinfo[location];
  personinfo[location] := temp
end;

procedure Continue (var ans : char);
begin
  GotoXY (1,23);
  Write ('Press "x" to end, another key to continue -->');
  ans := ReadKey
end;

procedure GetInformation (var personinfo : arraytype);
  var
    ans
      : char;
    target
      : nametype;
    location
      : integer;
    found
      : boolean;
begin
  repeat
    ClrScr;
    GotoXY (10,1);
    Writeln ('INFORMATION ON FAMOUS PEOPLE');
    Writeln;
    Write ('Enter a person''s name: ');
    Readln (target);
    SearchTable (personinfo, target, location, found);
    if found
      then
        begin
          DisplayAge (personinfo, location);
          if location > 1
            then
              Swap (personinfo, location)
        end
      else
        begin
          GotoXY (10,5);
          Writeln ('No information found for ',target)
        end;
    Continue (ans)
  until (ans = 'x');
end;

begin
  FillTable (personinfo);
  GetInformation (personinfo)
end.
```

```pascal
15. program PlayBridge;
      uses
        Crt;
      const
        handsize = 13;
        decksize = 52;
      type
        valuetype = string[2];
        cardtype = record
          suit : char;
          value : valuetype
        end;
        handtype = array[1..handsize] of cardtype;
        decktype = array[1..decksize] of cardtype;
      var
        deck         : decktype;
        deckindex    : integer;
        North,
        East,
        South,
        West         : handtype;
      procedure InitializeDeck (var d : decktype;
                                var deckindex : integer);
      var
        i : integer;
      begin
        for i := 1 to decksize do
        begin
          d[i].suit := ' ';
          d[i].value := '  ';
        end;
        deckindex := 1
      end;
      procedure TranslateValue (numvalue : integer;
                                var stvalue : valuetype);
      begin
        case numvalue of
          1 :
            stvalue := 'A';
          2 :
            stvalue := '2';
          3 :
            stvalue := '3';
          4 :
            stvalue := '4';
          5 :
            stvalue := '5';
          6 :
            stvalue := '6';
          7 :
            stvalue := '7';
          8 :
            stvalue := '8';
          9 :
            stvalue := '9';
          10 :
            stvalue := '10';
          11 :
            stvalue := 'J';
          12 :
            stvalue := 'Q';
          13 :
            stvalue := 'K'
        end;
      procedure TranslateSuit (numsuit : integer; var chsuit : char);
      begin
        case numsuit of
          1 :
            chsuit := 'S';
          2 :
            chsuit := 'C';
          3 :
            chsuit := 'D';
          4 :
            chsuit := 'H'
        end;
      procedure GetOneCard (var card : cardtype);
      var
        chsuit       : char;
        stvalue      : valuetype;
        numvalue,
        numsuit      : integer;
      begin
        numvalue := Random(13) + 1;
        TranslateValue (numvalue, stvalue);
        card.value := stvalue;
        numsuit := Random(4) + 1;
        TranslateSuit (numsuit, chsuit);
        card.suit := chsuit
      end;
      function GoodCard (card : cardtype; deck : decktype) : boolean;
      var
        i : integer;
      begin
        GoodCard := true;
        i := 1;
        for i := 1 to 52 do
          if (card.suit = deck[i].suit)
              and (card.value = deck[i].value)
            then
              GoodCard := false
      end;
```

(continued)

```
procedure DealOneHand (var hand : handtype;
          var deck : decktype; var deckindex : integer);
  var
    card
      : cardtype;
    i : integer;
  begin
    i := 1;
    while i < 14 do
      begin
        GetOneCard (card);
        if GoodCard (card, deck)
          then
            begin
              hand[i] := card;
              deck[deckindex] := card;
              deckindex := deckindex + 1;
              i := i + 1
            end
      end
  end;

procedure DealFourHands (var North, East, South, West : handtype;
          var deck : decktype; var deckindex : integer);
  begin
    DealOneHand (North, deck, deckindex);
    DealOneHand (East, deck, deckindex);
    DealOneHand (South, deck, deckindex);
    DealOneHand (West, deck, deckindex)
  end;

procedure DisplayOneHand (hand : handtype);
  var
    index
      : integer;
  begin
    for index := 1 to 13 do
      Write (hand[index].value:4, hand[index].suit)
  end;

procedure Continue;
  var
    ch
      : char;
  begin
    GotoXY (20,24);
    Write ('Press any key to continue.');
    ch := ReadKey
  end;

procedure DisplayFourHands (North, East, South, West : handtype);
  begin
    ClrScr;
    GotoXY (27,1);
    Writeln ('FOUR BRIDGE HANDS');
    GotoXY (1,4);
    Writeln ('NORTH');
    DisplayOneHand (North);
```
(continued)

```
    GotoXY (1,8);
    Writeln ('EAST');
    DisplayOneHand (East);
    GotoXY (1,12);
    Writeln ('SOUTH');
    DisplayOneHand (South);
    GotoXY (1,16);
    Writeln ('WEST');
    DisplayOneHand (West);
    Continue
  end;

begin
  InitializeDeck (deck, deckindex);
  DealFourHands (North, East, South, West, deck, deckindex);
  DisplayFourHands (North, East, South, West)
end.
```

Chapter 11

Exercises

1. a. A file is dynamic because it uses only the file space (disk space) it needs. There is no need to declare the size of the file in advance of its use.

   c. An internal file structure is a structure that temporarily stores a data file in main memory. Once an internal file has been established, the data in that file is transferred to a disk file or external file when an internal file structure is closed.

   e. The maximum size of an array is dictated by how much main memory is available, while the maximum size of a file is determined by the capacity of the disk that stores the file. The size of an array has to be declared prior to its use, whereas a file grows or shrinks as needed.

2. b. Valid.   d. Valid.

3. a. `Assign (repairs, 'b:\rprfile');`

   c. `Erase (carfile);`

   e.
```
Reset (intfile);
for i := 1 to 10 do
  begin
    Read (intfile, nameage);
    nameage.age := nameage.age + 1;
    Seek (intfile, recnum-1);
    Write (intfile, nameage)
  end;
```

4. b. Replace the previous AddToFile with the following:

```
procedure AddToFile;
  var
    coinrecord
      : cointype;
    intfile
      : intfiletype;
    masterfile
      : extfilenametype;
```

(continued)

```pascal
begin
  ClrScr;
  GotoXY (15,3);
  Writeln ('Add To Master File');
  GotoXY (10,5);
  GetMasterFileName (masterfile);
  Assign (intfile, masterfile);
  Reset (intfile);
  Seek (intfile, FileSize(intfile));
  EnterRecordData (coinrecord);
  with coinrecord do
    while description <> '' do
      begin
        Write (intfile, coinrecord);
        EnterRecordData (coinrecord)
      end;
  Close (intfile)
end;

5. b. procedure HighFile (source, dest : extfilenametype);
var
  temp : real;
  intfile1, intfile2 : intfiletype;
begin
  Assign (intfile1, source);
  Reset (intfile1);
  Assign (intfile2, dest);
  Rewrite (intfile2);
  while not Eof(intfile1) do
    begin
      Read (intfile1, temp);
      if temp > 30000.0
      then
        Write (intfile2, temp)
    end;
  Close (intfile1);
  Close (intfile2)
end;

7. Enter integer: 34
   Enter integer: 19
   Enter integer: 2
   Enter integer: 8
   Enter integer: 10
   Enter integer: 25
   34   19   2   25   10
```

Programming Assignments
```pascal
5. program ProgramCollection;
   uses
     Crt;
```

(continued)

```pascal
type
  categorytype = string[15];
  titletype = string[20];
  publishertype = string[20];
  progtype = record
    category : categorytype;
    title : titletype;
    publisher : publishertype
  end;
  intfiletype = file of progtype;
  extfilenametype = string[25];
var
  choice
    : char;

procedure GetMasterFileName (var masterfile : extfilenametype);
begin
  GotoXY (15,17);
  Write ('Please enter name  master file: ');
  Readln (masterfile)
end;

procedure Continue;
var
  ch
    : char;
begin
  GotoXY (1,24);
  Write ('Press any key to continue.');
  ch := ReadKey
end;

function GetCategory : categorytype;
var
  ch
    : char;
begin
  ClrScr;
  GotoXY (18,1);
  Writeln ('THE AVAILABLE PROGRAM CATEGORIES:');
  GotoXY (13,3);
  Writeln ('Press first letter of category of interest.');
  GotoXY (15,6);
  Writeln ('<E>ntertainment          <S>preadsheet');
  GotoXY (15,8);
  Writeln ('<W>ord Processing        <C>ommunications');
  GotoXY (15,10);
  Writeln ('<D>atabase               <G>raphics');
  GotoXY (15,12);
  Writeln ('<O>ther                  <Q>uit');
  GotoXY (15,15);
  Write ('Category --> ');
  Readln (ch);
  case ch of
    'E','e':
      GetCategory := 'ENTERTAINMENT';
    'S','s':
      GetCategory := 'SPREADSHEET';
```

(continued)

```pascal
'W','w' :
    GetCategory := 'WORD PROCESSING';
'D','d' :
    GetCategory := 'DATABASE';
'C','c' :
    GetCategory := 'COMMUNICATIONS';
'G','g' :
    GetCategory := 'GRAPHICS';
'O','o' :
    GetCategory := 'OTHER';
else
    GetCategory := 'NULL'
end
end;

procedure EnterRecordData (var progrecord : progtype);
begin
Writeln;
with progrecord do
    begin
    category := GetCategory;
    if category <> 'NULL'
    then
        begin
        GotoXY (15,17);
        Write ('Enter title: ');
        Readln (title);
        GotoXY (15,19);
        Write ('Enter publisher: ');
        Readln (publisher)
        end
    end
end;

procedure CreateFile (extfile : extfilenametype);
var
    progrecord
        : progtype;
    intfile
        : intfiletype;
begin
Assign (intfile, extfile);
Rewrite (intfile);
EnterRecordData (progrecord);
while progrecord.category <> 'NULL' do
    begin
    Write (intfile, progrecord);
    EnterRecordData (progrecord)
    end;
Close (intfile)
end;

procedure CreateMasterFile;
var
    masterfile
        : extfilenametype;
```

(continued)

```pascal
begin
ClrScr;
GotoXY (15,15);
Writeln ('To create a master file:');
GetMasterFileName (masterfile);
CreateFile (masterfile)
end;

procedure MergeFiles (extfile1, extfile2 : extfilenametype);
var
    progrecord
        : progtype;
    intfile1,
    intfile2,
    intmergedfile
        : intfiletype;
begin
Assign (intfile1, extfile1);
Reset (intfile1);
Assign (intfile2, extfile2);
Reset (intfile2);
Assign (intmergedfile, 'merge');
Rewrite (intmergedfile);
while not Eof(intfile1) do
    begin
    Read (intfile1, progrecord);
    Write (intmergedfile, progrecord)
    end;
while not Eof(intfile2) do
    begin
    Read (intfile2, progrecord);
    Write (intmergedfile, progrecord)
    end;
Close (intfile2);
Erase (intfile2);
Reset (intmergedfile);
Rewrite (intfile1);
while not Eof(intmergedfile) do
    begin
    Read (intmergedfile, progrecord);
    Write (intfile1, progrecord)
    end;
Close (intfile1);
Close (intmergedfile);
Erase (intmergedfile);
end;

procedure AddManyToFile;
var
    drive
        : string[1];
    tempextfile,
    masterfile
        : extfilenametype;
begin
ClrScr;
GetMasterFileName (masterfile);
GotoXY (15,19);
```

(continued)

```pascal
      Write ('Enter drive temporary data file (a-z): ');
      Readln (drive);
      tempextfile := Concat (drive, ':\temp');
      CreateFile (tempextfile);
      MergeFiles (masterfile, tempextfile)
    end;

    procedure AddSingleToFile;
      var
        progrecord
          : progtype;
        intfile
          : intfiletype;
        masterfile
          : extfilenametype;
    begin
      GetMasterFileName (masterfile);
      EnterRecordData (progrecord);
      Assign (intfile, Masterfile);
      Reset (intfile);
      Seek (intfile, FileSize(intfile));
      Write (intfile, progrecord);
      Close (intfile)
    end;

    procedure CreateReport;
      var
        targetcat
          : categorytype;
        progrecord
          : progtype;
        intfile
          : intfiletype;
        masterfile
          : extfilenametype;
    begin
      targetcat := GetCategory;
      if targetcat <> 'NULL'
        then
          begin
            GetMasterFileName (masterfile);
            ClrScr;
            GotoXY (20,1);
            Write ('REPORT: ', targetcat, '  PROGRAMS');
            GotoXY (1,3);
            Writeln ('TITLE':25, 'PUBLISHER':25);
            Writeln;
            Assign (intfile, masterfile);
            Reset (intfile);
            while not Eof(intfile) do
              Read (intfile, progrecord);
              with progrecord do
                if targetcat = category
                  then
                    Writeln (title:25, publisher:25)
              end;
```

(continued)

```pascal
            Close (intfile)
          end;
          Continue
        end;
    begin
      ClrScr;
      GotoXY (19,1);
      Writeln ('PROGRAM COLLECTION FILE SYSTEM');
      GotoXY (15,3);
      Writeln ('Press the number preceding your choice.');
      GotoXY (15,6);
      Writeln ('<1> Create Master File');
      GotoXY (15,8);
      Writeln ('<2> Add More Than One Record to File');
      GotoXY (15,10);
      Writeln ('<3> Add A Single Program Record to File');
      GotoXY (15,12);
      Writeln ('<4> Create a Report of a Category');
      GotoXY (15,14);
      Writeln ('<5> Exit Program');
      GotoXY (15,17);
      Write ('Choice --> ');
      choice := ReadKey;
      case choice of
        '1' :
            CreateMasterFile;
        '2' :
            AddManyToFile;
        '3' :
            AddSingleToFile;
        '4' :
            CreateReport
      end;
    until choice = '5'
    end.

14. program SubscriberInfo;
    uses
      Crt;
    const
      mxlst = 3;
    type
      listtype = 0..mxlst;
      strtype = string[20];
      magtype = record
        title : strtype;
        expir : string[8]
      end;
      addtype = record
        street : string[15];
        city  : string[15];
        state : string[12];
        zip   : string[5]
      end;
      maglisttype = array [1..mxlst] of magtype;
      subtype = record
```

(continued)

```pascal
    name    : strtype;
    address : addtype;
    lstsze  : listype;
    maglst  : maglsttype
  end;
  intfiletype = file of subtype;
  extfilenametype = string[25];
var
  masterfile
    : extfilenametype;
  choice
    : char;
procedure GetMasterFileName (var masterfile : extfilenametype);
begin
  ClrScr;
  GotoXY (20,9);
  Write ('Enter subscriber master file name: ');
  Readln (masterfile)
end;

procedure Error;
begin
  Writeln ('Sorry, not found!')
end;

procedure Continue;
var
  ch
    : char;
begin
  Writeln;
  Write ('Press any key to continue.');
  ch := ReadKey
end;

procedure EnterAddress(var subscriber : subtype);
begin
  with subscriber.address do
    begin
      Write ('STREET: ':30);
      Readln (street);
      Write ('CITY: ':30);
      Readln (city);
      Write ('STATE: ':30);
      Readln (state);
      Write ('ZIP CODE: ':30);
      Readln (zip)
    end
end;

procedure EnterMagazines (var subscriber : subtype);
var
  magtitle
    : strtype;
begin
  Writeln;
  Writeln ('< Press the Enter key at TITLE prompt when
            finished. >');
  Writeln;
  with subscriber do
```

(continued)

```pascal
begin
  if lstsze < mxlst
    then
      repeat
        Write ('Please Enter Magazine TITLE: ':30);
        Readln (magtitle);
        if (magtitle <> '')
          then
            begin
              lstsze := lstsze +1;
              maglst[lstsze].title := magtitle;
              Write ('(mm-dd-yy) EXPIRATION DATE: ':30);
              Readln (maglst[lstsze].expir);
              Writeln
            end;
      until (magtitle = '') or (lstsze = mxlst);
    if lstsze = mxlst
      then
        Writeln ('Magazine list ',name,' is FULL.')

end;

procedure RemoveMagazines (var subscriber : subtype);
var
  magtitle
    : strtype;
  i
    : integer;
begin
  Writeln;
  Writeln ('< Press the Enter key at TITLE prompt when
            finished. >');
  Writeln;
  with subscriber do
    begin
      if lstsze > 0
        then
          repeat
            Write ('Enter Magazine TITLE to Remove: ':30);
            Readln (magtitle);
            if magtitle <> ''
              then
                begin
                  i := 0;
                  repeat
                    i := i + 1
                  until (i = lstsze) or
                        (magtitle = maglst[i].title);
                  if magtitle = maglst[i].title
                    then
                      begin
                        maglst[i] := maglst[lstsze];
                        lstsze := lstsze - 1
                      end
                    else
                      Error
                end;
          until (magtitle = '') or (lstsze = 0);
```

(continued)

```
procedure AddMore (var ans : char);
var
    ch : char;
begin
    repeat
        Writeln;
        Write ('Add another subscriber record? y/n --> ');
        Readln (ans);
    until ans in ['Y', 'y', 'N', 'n']
end;
procedure CreateFile (extfile : extfilenametype);
var
    subscriber
        : subtype;
    intfile
        : intfiletype;
    ans
        : char;
begin
    ClrScr;
    GotoXY (20,1);
    Writeln ('CREATE FILE');
    Assign (intfile, extfile);
    Rewrite (intfile);
    repeat
        Writeln;
        EnterSubscriberData (subscriber);
        Write (intfile, subscriber);
        AddMore (ans)
    until ans in ['N', 'n'];
    Close (intfile)
end;
procedure MergeFiles (extfile1, extfile2 : extfilenametype);
var
    subscriber
        : subtype;
    intfile1,
    intfile2,
    intmergedfile
        : intfiletype;
begin
    Assign (intfile1, extfile1);
    Reset (intfile1);
    Assign (intfile2, extfile2);
    Reset (intfile2);
    Assign (intmergedfile, 'merge');
    Rewrite (intmergedfile);
    while not Eof(intfile1) do
        begin
            Read (intfile1, subscriber);
            Write (intmergedfile, subscriber)
        end;
    while not Eof(intfile2) do
        begin
            Read (intfile2, subscriber);
            Write (intmergedfile, subscriber)
```

(continued)

```
    if lstsze = 0
        then
            Writeln ('Magazine list is EMPTY.')
end;
procedure ChangeDate (var subscriber : subtype);
var
    magtitle
        : strtype;
    i : integer;
begin
    ClrScr;
    Writeln ('Magazine title whose expiration date changes: ');
    Writeln;
    Write ('Enter title: ':30);
    Readln (magtitle);
    with subscriber do
        if lstsze > 0
            then
                begin
                    i := 0;
                    repeat
                        i := i + 1
                    until (i = lstsze) or (magtitle = maglst[i].title);
                    if magtitle = maglst[i].title
                        then
                            begin
                                Write ('(mm-dd-yy) DATE: ':30);
                                Readln (maglst[i].expir)
                            end
                        else
                            Error
                end
            else
                Writeln ('Sorry, list is empty!')
end;
procedure EnterSubscriberData (var subscriber : subtype);
begin
    with subscriber do
        begin
            Write ('Please enter SUBSCRIBER NAME: ':30);
            Readln (name);
            EnterAddress (subscriber);
            lstsze := 0;
            EnterMagazines (subscriber)
        end
end;
```

(continued)

```
        end;
      Close (intfile2);
      Erase (intfile2);
      Reset (intmergedfile);
      Rewrite (intfile1);
      while not Eof (intmergedfile) do
        begin
          Read (intmergedfile, subscriber);
          Write (intfile1, subscriber)
        end;
      Close (intfile1);
      Close (intmergedfile);
      Erase (intmergedfile)
end;

procedure AddSubscribers (masterfile : extfilenametype);
  var
    drive
      : string[1];
    tempextfile
      : extfilenametype;
begin
  ClrScr;
  GotoXY (20,1);
  Writeln ('ADD SUBSCRIBERS');
  Writeln;
  Write ('Enter drive  temporary data file (a-z):  ');
  Readln (drive);
  tempextfile := Concat (drive, ':\temp');
  CreateFile (tempextfile);
  MergeFiles (masterfile, tempextfile)
end;

procedure SearchRecord (masterfile : extfilenametype;
            var subscriber : subtype; var location : longint;
            var found : boolean);
  var
    namesought
      : strtype;
    intfile
      : intfiletype;
begin
  Assign (intfile, masterfile);
  Reset (intfile);
  found := false;
  with subscriber do
    begin
      Write ('Enter Subscriber NAME: ',:30);
      Readln (namesought);
      found := false;
      while not Eof(intfile) and not found do
        begin
          Read (intfile, subscriber);
          if namesought = name
            then
              begin
                location := FilePos (intfile);
                found := true
              end
```

(continued)

```
      end;
    Close (intfile)
  end;

procedure UpdateRecord (masterfile : extfilenametype;
            subscriber : subtype; location : longint);
  var
    intfile
      : intfiletype;
begin
  Assign (intfile, masterfile);
  Reset (intfile);
  Seek (intfile, location - 1);
  Write (intfile, subscriber);
  Close (intfile)
end;

procedure RemoveSubscriber (masterfile : extfilenametype);
  var
    subscriber
      : subtype;
    namesought
      : strtype;
    found
      : boolean;
    intfile,
    tempfile
      : intfiletype;
begin
  ClrScr;
  GotoXY (20,1);
  Writeln ('REMOVE SUBSCRIBER');
  GotoXY (1,4);
  Write ('NAME: ');
  Readln (namesought);
  Writeln;
  found := false;
  Assign (intfile, masterfile);
  Reset (intfile);
  Assign (tempfile, 'copy');
  Rewrite (tempfile);
  with subscriber do
    while not Eof(intfile) do
      begin
        Read (intfile, subscriber);
        if namesought <> name
          then
            Write (tempfile, subscriber)
          else
            found := true
      end;
  if found
    then
      Writeln (namesought,' has been removed from file.')
    else
      Error;
  Reset (tempfile);
```

(continued)

```
      Rewrite (intfile);
      while not Eof(tempfile) do
        begin
          Read (tempfile, subscriber);
          Write (intfile, subscriber)
        end;
      Close (tempfile);
      Close (intfile);
      Continue
    end;

procedure ChgMagazineInfo (masterfile : extfilenametype);
var
  ch         : char;
  subscriber : subtype;
  found      : boolean;
  location   : longint;
begin
  ClrScr;
  SearchRecord (masterfile, subscriber, location, found);
  if found
    then
      begin
        GotoXY (30,3);
        Writeln ('CHANGE MAGAZINE INMATION');
        GotoXY (20,6);
        Writeln ('Press the number preceding your choice.');
        GotoXY (20,8);
        Writeln ('<1> Add one or more magazines to list.');
        GotoXY (20,10);
        Writeln ('<2> Remove a magazine from list.');
        GotoXY (20,12);
        Writeln ('<3> Change the Expiration date
                    of a magazine.');
        GotoXY (20,14);
        Writeln ('<4> Cancel');
        repeat
          GotoXY (20,17);
          Write ('Enter choice --> ');
          ch := ReadKey
        until ch in ['1'..'4'];
        ClrScr;
        case ch of
          '1' :
            EnterMagazines (subscriber);
          '2' :
            RemoveMagazines (subscriber);
          '3' :
            ChangeDate (subscriber)
        end;
        case ch of
          '1','2','3' :
            begin
              UpdateRecord (masterfile, subscriber, location);
              Continue
            end;
          '4' :
            begin
              Writeln;
              Writeln ('Cancelled...');
              Writeln
            end
        end
    else
      Error

end;

procedure ChangeOfAddress (masterfile :extfilenametype);
var
  subscriber : subtype;
  found      : boolean;
  location   : longint;
begin
  ClrScr;
  GotoXY (20,1);
  Writeln ('CHANGE SUBSCRIBER ADDRESS');
  GotoXY (1,4);
  SearchRecord (masterfile, subscriber, location, found);
  if found
    then
      begin
        EnterAddress (subscriber);
        UpdateRecord (masterfile, subscriber, location)
      end
    else
      Error;
  Continue
end;

begin
  ClrScr;
  GetMasterFileName (masterfile);
  repeat
    ClrScr;
    GotoXY (18,1);
    Writeln ('MAGAZINE SUBSCRIPTION FILE SYSTEM');
    GotoXY (15,4);
    Writeln ('Press the number preceding your choice.');
    GotoXY (15,6);
    Writeln ('<1> Create Master Subscriber File');
    GotoXY (15,8);
    Writeln ('<2> Add Subscriber');
    GotoXY (15,10);
    Writeln ('<3> Remove Subscriber');
    GotoXY (15,12);
    Writeln ('<4> Change Subscriber Address');
    GotoXY (15,14);
```

(continued)

(continued)

559

```
Writeln ('<5> Modify Subscriber Magazine Inmation');
GotoXY (15,16);
Writeln ('<6> Exit Program');
GotoXY (15,21);
Write ('Choice --> ');
choice := ReadKey;
case choice of
   '1' :
       CreateFile (masterfile);
   '2' :
       AddSubscribers (masterfile);
   '3' :
       RemoveSubscriber (masterfile);
   '4' :
       ChangeOfAddress (masterfile);
   '5' :
       ChgMagazineInfo (masterfile)
   end;
until choice = '6'
end.
```

Chapter 12

Exercises

1. a. The ordinal value of a constant identifier in an enumerated data type is determined by its position in its declaration. The first item in the list has an ordinal value of 0, the second an ordinal value of 1, and so on.

   c. The only way to access any part of a linked list is to start at the pointer that gives the address of the first node in the list. If that pointer is lost, the first node is inaccessible and, as a consequence, so are other items in the list.

   e. Although valid, the definition is unsuitable as a recursive solution to $n!$ because successive calls to $n!$ do not approach a terminating condition, since the value of n is increased with each successive call.

2. b. Invalid. Cannot output the value of an enumerated data type.

   d. Invalid. The ^ is missing following the p in $p.name$.

3. a. type
```
        flavortype = (vanilla, chocolate, strawberry);
```
   c. type
```
        ptrtype = ^persontype;
        persontype = record
            name : string[20];
            age : integer;
            next : ptrtype
            end;
var
    p : ptrtype;
```
   e. change := Pred(nickel);

5. a.
```
      9    9    8      c.   66   30
      7    9    8           36   30
      7   15    8            6   30
                             6   24
                             6   18
                             6   12
                 Answer:     6
```

6. a.
```
procedure DisplayFlag (flagcolor : flagcolortype);
begin
   case flagcolor of
   red :
       Writeln ('red');
   white :
       Writeln ('white');
   blue :
       Writeln ('blue')
   end;
end;
```

Programming Assignments

2.
```
program MovieIncomeByRating;
uses
   Crt;
type
   catetype = (G, PG, PG13, R, NC17);
   ratingtype= string[4];
   movietype = record
      rating : ratingtype;
      number : integer;
      total,
      average : real
   end;
   allmovietype = array[G..NC17] of movietype;
var
   choice
         : char;
   movieinfo
         : allmovietype;
function Category : catetype;
var
   choice
         : char;
begin
   ClrScr;
   GotoXY (20,1);
   Writeln ('MOVIE INCOME');
   GotoXY (10,4);
   Writeln ('Press number preceding movie rating of interest.');
   GotoXY (15,6);
   Writeln ('(1) G');
   GotoXY (15,8);
   Writeln ('(2) PG');
   GotoXY (15,10);
   Writeln ('(3) PG13');
   GotoXY (15,12);
   Writeln ('(4) R');
   GotoXY (15,14);
   Writeln ('(5) NC17');
   repeat
      GotoXY (15,16);
      Write ('Rating (1-5) --> ');
      choice := ReadKey
```

(continued)

```pascal
    until choice in ['1'..'5'];
    case choice of
      '1' :
        Category := G;
      '2' :
        Category := PG;
      '3' :
        Category := PG13;
      '4' :
        Category := R;
      '5' :
        Category := NC17
    end
  end;

procedure Continue;
  var
    ch
      : char;
  begin
    GotoXY (10,24);
    Write ('Press any key to continue.');
    ch := ReadKey
  end;

procedure Initialize (var movieinfo : allmovietype);
  var
    cat
      : catetype;
  begin
    for cat := G to NC17 do
      begin
        with movieinfo[cat] do
          begin
            case cat of
              G :
                rating := 'G';
              PG :
                rating := 'PG';
              PG13 :
                rating := 'PG13';
              R :
                rating := 'R';
              NC17 :
                rating := 'NC17'
            end;
            number := 0;
            total := 0.0;
            average := 0.0
          end
      end
  end;

procedure EnterRecordData (var movieinfo : allmovietype);
  var
    income
      : real;
  begin
    with movieinfo[category] do
      begin
        number := number + 1;
        GotoXY (15,20);
        Write ('Enter income received from this movie: $ ');
        Readln (income);
        total := total + income;
        average := total / number
      end
  end;

procedure DisplayResults (movieinfo : allmovietype);
  begin
    with movieinfo[category] do
      begin
        ClrScr;
        GotoXY (10,5);
        Writeln ('Movie Rating: ', rating);
        GotoXY (10,7);
        Writeln ('Number of movies recorded: ', number);
        GotoXY (10,9);
        Writeln ('Total income from these movies: $', total:10:2);
        GotoXY (10,11);
        Writeln ('Average income from these movies: $', average:9:2);
      end;
    Continue
  end;

begin
  Initialize (movieinfo);
  repeat
    ClrScr;
    GotoXY (20,1);
    Writeln ('MOVIE INCOME');
    GotoXY (10,4);
    Writeln ('Press the number preceding your choice.');
    GotoXY (15,6);
    Writeln ('<1> Enter Movie Information');
    GotoXY (15,8);
    Writeln ('<2> Display Movie Information');
    GotoXY (15,10);
    Writeln ('<3> Exit Program');
    GotoXY (15,12);
    Write ('Choice --> ');
    repeat
      choice := ReadKey;
    until choice in ['1'...'3'];
    case choice of
      '1' :
        EnterRecordData (movieinfo);
      '2' :
        DisplayResults (movieinfo)
    end;
  until choice = '3'
end.
```

```
7. program Palindrome;
   uses
      Crt;
   type
      stringtype = string[20];
      pointertype = ^nodetype;
      nodetype = record
         ch : string[1];
         next : pointertype
      end;
   var
      list
           : pointertype;
      word,
      drow
           : stringtype;

   procedure EnterWord (var word : stringtype);
   begin
      ClrScr;
      GotoXY (30,5);
      Writeln ('PALINDROME');
      GotoXY (20,8);
      Write ('Enter palindrome test word: ');
      Readln (word)
   end;

   procedure LoadWord (word : stringtype; var list : pointertype);
      var
         p
           : pointertype;
         i : integer;
   begin
      list := p;
      for i := 1 to Length (word) do
      begin
         New (p);
         p^.ch := Copy (word,i,1);
         p^.next := list;
         list := p
      end
   end;

   procedure ReverseWord (list : pointertype;
                          var drow : stringtype);
      var
         p
           : pointertype;
         i : integer;
   begin
      p := list;
      drow := '';
      for i := 1 to Length (word) do
      begin
         drow := Concat (drow,p^.ch);
         p := p^.next
      end
   end;

   procedure Continue;
      var
         ch : char;
   begin
      GotoXY (20,10);
      Write ('Press any key to continue.');
      ch := ReadKey
   end;

   procedure CompareWords (word, drow : stringtype);
   begin
      ClrScr;
      GotoXY (30,5);
      if word = drow
      then
         begin
            Writeln (word,' = ',drow);
            GotoXY (23,7);
            Writeln (word,' is a palindrome.')
         end
      else
         begin
            Writeln (word,' <> ',drow);
            GotoXY (27,7);
            Writeln (word,' is not a palindrome.')
         end;
      Continue
   end;

begin
   EnterWord (word);
   LoadWord (word, list);
   ReverseWord (list, drow);
   CompareWords (word, drow)
end.

11. program Advertising;
    uses
       Crt;
    type
       nettype = (ABC, CBS, Fox, NBC, CNN);
       pointer = ^prognode;
       prognode = record
          progname : string[25];
          income : real;
          next : pointer
       end;
       root = record
          total : real;
          rtptr : pointer
       end;
       alltypes = array[ABC..CNN] of root;
    var
       choice
          : char;
       allnetworks
          : alltypes;
```

```pascal
procedure GivingChoice (var choice : char);
begin
  ClrScr;
  GotoXY (20,1);
  Writeln ('Network Advertising Barometer');
  GotoXY (10,4);
  Writeln ('Enter number preceding choice.');
  GotoXY (10,6);
  Writeln ('(1) Add Program Data ');
  GotoXY (10,8);
  Writeln ('(2) Report on All Networks');
  GotoXY (10,10);
  Writeln ('(3) Report on One Network');
  GotoXY (10,12);
  Writeln ('(4) Report on All Networks With Revenues
                Below Entered Amount');
  GotoXY (10,14);
  Writeln ('(5) Report on One Network With Revenues
                Below Entered Amount');
  GotoXY (10,16);
  Writeln ('(6) Quit Program');
  repeat
    GotoXY (15,19);
    Write ('Choice (1 - 6) --> ');
    choice := ReadKey
  until choice in ['1'..'6']
end;

procedure Continue;
var
  ch
    : char;
begin
  GotoXY (1,24);
  Write ('Press any key to continue.');
  ch := ReadKey
end;

function FullScreen (count : integer) : boolean;
const
  screenlimit = 20;
begin
  if count >= screenlimit
    then
      FullScreen := true
    else
      FullScreen := false
end;

procedure Initialize (var allnetworks : alltypes);
var
  network
    : nettype;
```

```pascal
begin
  for network := ABC to CNN do
    with allnetworks[network] do
      begin
        total := 0.0;
        rtptr := nil
      end
end;

procedure PromptNetwork (var net : nettype);
var
  ch
    : char;
begin
  ClrScr;
  GotoXY (25,1);
  Writeln ('Network Choice');
  GotoXY (15,4);
  Writeln ('Enter number preceding choice of network');
  GotoXY (15,6);
  Writeln ('<1> ABC           <4> NBC');
  GotoXY (15,8);
  Writeln ('<2> CBS           <5> CNN');
  GotoXY (15,10);
  Writeln ('<3> Fox');
  repeat
    GotoXY (15,13);
    Write ('Choice (1 - 5) -- > ');
    ch := ReadKey
  until ch in ['1'..'5'];
  case ch of
    '1' :
        net := ABC;
    '2' :
        net := CBS;
    '3' :
        net := Fox;
    '4' :
        net := NBC;
    '5' :
        net := CNN
  end
end;

procedure CreateProgramNode (var ptr : pointer);
begin
  ClrScr;
  GotoXY (20,1);
  Writeln ('Data Entry');
  New (ptr);
  GotoXY (10,5);
  Write ('Enter Name of Program:  ');
  Readln (ptr^.progname);
  GotoXY (10,8);
  Write ('Enter Income From Ad Sales:   $ ');
  Readln (ptr^.income);
  ptr^.next := nil
end;
```

(continued)

563

```pascal
procedure Again (var ans : char);
begin
  repeat
    GotoXY (10,24);
    Write ('Add data for another program? Y/N --> ');
    ans := ReadKey
  until ans in ['Y', 'y', 'n', 'N']
end;

procedure AddProgramNode (var allnetworks : alltypes);
var
  p       : pointer;
  network : nettype;
  ans     : char;
begin
  repeat
    PromptNetwork (network);
    CreateProgramNode (p);
    with allnetworks[network] do
      begin
        total := total + p^.income;
        if rtptr <> nil
          then
            p^.next := rtptr;
        rtptr := p
      end;
    Again (ans);
  until ans in ['n', 'N']
end;

procedure DisplayANode (ptr :pointer; var count : integer);
const
  col = 35;
  two = 2;
begin
  Writeln;
  Writeln (ptr^.progname:col, '$':9, ptr^.income:10:2);
  count := count + two
end;

procedure PrintHeader (network :nettype);
begin
  ClrScr;
  Write ('THE ':12);
  case network of
    ABC :
      Write ('ABC');
    CBS :
      Write ('CBS');
    Fox :
      Write ('Fox');
    NBC :
      Write ('NBC');
    CNN :
      Write ('CNN')
  end;
  Writeln (' NETWORK');
  Writeln ('------------------------------------')
end;

procedure DisplayNet (allnetworks : alltypes; network : nettype);
var
  ptr   : pointer;
  count : integer;
begin
  PrintHeader (network);
  count := 0;
  with allnetworks[network] do
    begin
      if rtptr = nil
        then
          Writeln ('NO PROGRAMS')
        else
          begin
            ptr := rtptr;
            Writeln ('PROGRAM NAME':24, 'AD REVENUES':30);
            repeat
              if FullScreen (count)
                then
                  begin
                    Continue;
                    count := 0
                  end
                else
                  begin
                    DisplayANode (ptr, count);
                    ptr := ptr^.next
                  end;
            until ptr = nil
          end;
      Writeln ('------------------------------------');
      Writeln ('TOTAL INCOME:    $':44, total:10:2);
    end;
  Continue
end;

procedure ReportOne (allnetworks :alltypes);
var
  network
        : nettype;
begin
  PromptNetwork (network);
  DisplayNet (allnetworks, network)
end;
```

(continued)

```pascal
procedure ReportAll (allnetworks :alltypes);
  var
    network
         : nettype;
begin
  for network := ABC to CNN do
    DisplayNet (allnetworks, network)
end;

procedure GetCutoff (var cutoff :real);
begin
  ClrScr;
  GotoXY (20,12);
  Write ('Enter cutoff figure: $ ');
  Readln (cutoff)
end;

procedure DisplayBelow (allnetworks :alltypes; network : nettype;
                        cutoff : real);
  var
    ptr      : pointer;
    count    : integer;
    found    : boolean;
begin
  PrintHeader (network);
  Writeln ('The Following Programs Made Less Than $':10,
           cutoff:6:2,':');
  Writeln;
  count := 0;
  found := false;
  with allnetworks[network] do
    if rtptr <> nil
      then
        begin
          ptr := rtptr;
          repeat
            if FullScreen (count)
              then
                begin
                  Continue;
                  count := 0
                end
              else
                begin
                  if ptr^.income < cutoff
                    then
                      begin
                        found := true;
                        Writeln (ptr^.progname:10);
                        count := count +1
                      end;
                  ptr := ptr^.next
          until ptr = nil
        end;
  if not found
    then
      Writeln ('None Found':10);
  Continue
end;

procedure ReportOneBelow (allnetworks : alltypes);
  var
    network
         : nettype;
    cutoff
         : real;
begin
  PromptNetwork (network);
  GetCutoff (cutoff);
  DisplayBelow (allnetworks, network, cutoff)
end;

procedure ReportAllBelow (allnetworks :alltypes);
  var
    network
         : nettype;
    cutoff
         : real;
begin
  GetCutoff (cutoff);
  for network := ABC to CNN do
    DisplayBelow (allnetworks, network, cutoff)
end;

begin
  Initialize (allnetworks);
  repeat
    GivingChoice (choice);
    case choice of
      '1' :
        AddProgramNode (allnetworks);
      '2' :
        ReportAll (allnetworks);
      '3' :
        ReportOne (allnetworks);
      '4' :
        ReportAllBelow (allnetworks);
      '5' :
        ReportOneBelow (allnetworks)
    end
  until choice = '6'
end.
```

(continued)

```
17.  program ExponentiationFunction;
     uses
         Crt;
     var
         base,
         result
                   : real;
         exponent
                   : integer;

     procedure EnterData (var base : real; var exponent : integer);
     begin
         ClrScr;
         GotoXY (30,5);
         Writeln ('EXPONENTIATION');
         GotoXY (9,9);
         Write ('Enter value of base: ');
         Readln (base);
         GotoXY (9,11);
         Write ('Enter exponent: ');
         Readln (exponent)
     end;

     function PowerValue (exponent : real) : real;
     begin
         if exponent = 0
            then
               PowerValue := 1
            else
               if exponent > 0
                  then
                     PowerValue := PowerValue (exponent - 1) * base
                  else
                     PowerValue := PowerValue (exponent + 1) * (1/base)

     end;

     procedure Continue;
     var
         ch
                : char;

     begin
         GotoXY (10,24);
         Write ('Press any key to continue.');
         ch := ReadKey
     end;

     procedure PrintResult (base, result : real; exponent : integer);
     begin
         GotoXY (9,14);
         Write (base:8:2, ' to the power ', exponent, ' is: ');
         Writeln (result:10:4);
         Continue
     end;

     begin
         EnterData (base, exponent);
         result := PowerValue (exponent);
         PrintResult (base, result, exponent)
     end.
```

Index

Turbo Pascal
5.0 & 5.5
Supplement

John DiElsi

Table of Contents for Turbo Pascal 5.0 & 5.5 Supplement

Preface to Supplement

This supplement was created for users of Turbo Pascal 5.0 and 5.5. Since the focus of Chapter 0 in the parent text is the introduction of the Turbo Pascal 6.0 programming environment, a 5.0/5.5 version of that chapter is reproduced in its entirety in this supplement. Users of version 5.0 or 5.5 can then cover the remaining chapters in the parent text as they are, with a few exceptions. A summary of these variations from version 6.0 follows this supplemental Chapter 0; it outlines, as well, other differences between the parent text and this supplement.

Since hot-key assignments and editor commands vary slightly between versions 5.0/5.5 and version 6.0, the appendices listing these appear in this supplement, as do the Answers to Selected Exercises from the 5.0/5.5 version of Chapter 0.

CHAPTER 0

The Turbo Pascal 5.5 System

Key Terms

Break/watch	**New**
bug	object code
Change dir	operating system
Compile	**Options**
compiler	**OS shell**
cursor	output device
Debug	prn
Directory	processor
disk drive	program
Edit	**Quit**
File	**Run**
hardware	**Save**
hot key	scroll
input device	secondary storage
integrated development	software
environment (IDE)	source code
language	TOUR
Load	**Trace into**
main memory	**User screen**
menu line	**Write to**
monitor	**Zoom**

Objectives

- To introduce hardware and software terminology and fundamentals
- To present the essential components of the Turbo Pascal integrated development environment (IDE)
- To provide hands-on experience for the programming process through a step-by-step exercise

0.1 Introduction

Mention the term *computer* and you're likely to get a wide range of responses, from awe to disgust. Some people think computers can do everything, while others think they should do nothing.

A computer is nothing more than a sophisticated tool, a collection of devices—*hardware*—that can be instructed to perform a variety of tasks. It is difficult to talk to a computer on its own terms, since all it basically understands is a series of on/off states, a combination of switches whose values are either on or off. To make the task of communicating with a computer easier and more efficient, we have to write a set of instructions—a *program*—in a high-level, or Englishlike, *language* and have it translated into a low-level language, one the computer understands. The translator, called a *compiler*, takes the program's instructions (*source code*) and puts it in a form the computer can execute (*object code*). Turbo Pascal is a language presented in an *integrated development environment (IDE)* that simplifies the creation, correction, and production of programs.

This chapter introduces the fundamental concepts common to all computer systems. It summarizes the basic operation of the Turbo Pascal IDE and provides a step-by-step guide for creating and running a sample program. More detailed explanation of the IDE can be found in the Turbo Pascal User's Guide that accompanies the software.

0.2 Hardware and Software Fundamentals

Every computer system consists of both a set of devices (the *hardware*) and instructions (*software*) for using that hardware. The major hardware components of a computer system include a *processor, main memory*, one or more *disk drives*, a printer, a *monitor*, and a keyboard. Figure 0.1 shows these components and how they're interrelated.

The processor performs all the calculations and makes all the decisions. It receives data and instructions from main memory and stores results there. *Secondary storage* devices, such as disk drives, store information that is not immediately required by the processor. They hold data and instructions, which are transferred to and from main memory as needed. The printer and monitor are *output devices* that receive results from main memory; the keyboard is an *input device* that enters data into main memory. Since secondary storage devices send data to and receive data from main memory, they also can be considered input and output devices.

The most powerful hardware in the world is useless without software to tell it what to do, and the most important piece of software is the operating system. An *operating system* is a collection of programs that control all the resources in a computer system, from hardware through programming languages and service programs. Turbo Pascal 5.5 is a programming

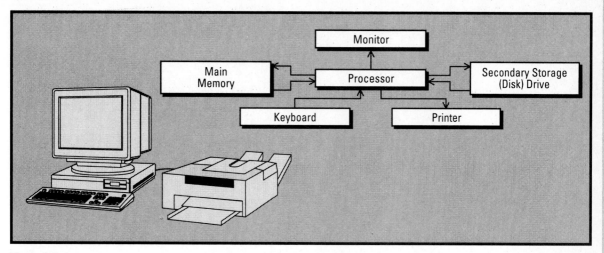

Figure 0.1
Components of a
Computer System

language that was designed to work with IBM or IBM-compatible microcomputer systems with either fixed (hard) or removable (floppy) disks, using the MS-DOS or PC-DOS operating system. Although there is also a version available for Macintosh microcomputers, that version will not be discussed here.

If the integrated development environment is not already installed on your computer, the Turbo Pascal User's Guide provides detailed instructions.

0.3 The Turbo Pascal Integrated Development Environment (IDE)

The Turbo Pascal integrated development environment consists of a text editor for entering and editing program instructions, an integrated debugger to help locate errors (*bugs*) in the program, and a compiler to translate the instructions into machine-readable form. Pull-down menus, windows, and Help facilities simplify its use.

The main screen appears immediately after you load Turbo Pascal (see Figure 0.2). Press the F10 function key to erase the version/copyright statement in the center of the screen, and move the cursor to the Edit window. The *cursor*, the blinking underscore symbol (_) in the upper left corner of this window, indicates where the next entered character will appear on the screen.

There are four sections to the main screen: the main menu line at the top, the Edit window, the Watch window, and the hot-key line at the bottom.

The main *menu line* gives you access to the commands in the IDE. If you press function key F10 to get to the main menu line, one of the seven menu choices will be highlighted. All menu titles, menu choices, and hot-key descriptions are displayed in **boldface** type. To move from one menu item to another, you can either use the left- and right-arrow keys on the keyboard or press the first letter in the menu name (for example, F for **File**). If a

Figure 0.2
Turbo Pascal 5.5
Main Screen

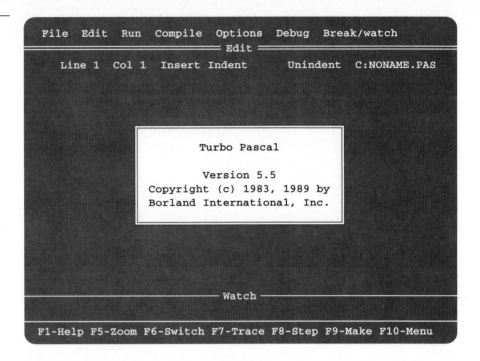

```
  File  Edit  Run  Compile  Options  Debug  Break/watch
═══════════════════════════ Edit ══════════════════════════
    Line 1  Col 1  Insert Indent        Unindent   C:NONAME.PAS



                ┌─────────────────────────────────┐
                │                                 │
                │          Turbo Pascal           │
                │                                 │
                │          Version 5.5            │
                │   Copyright (c) 1983, 1989 by   │
                │   Borland International, Inc.   │
                │                                 │
                └─────────────────────────────────┘




────────────────────────── Watch ──────────────────────────

 F1-Help F5-Zoom F6-Switch F7-Trace F8-Step F9-Make F10-Menu
```

menu item is highlighted, you can display the menu associated with that choice by pressing the down-arrow key. You can also display a menu in one step, by holding down the Alt key and pressing the first letter in the name of the menu item. To go to the **Run** menu, for example, hold down the Alt key and press R, the first letter in **Run**.

The cursor must be in the Edit window in order to enter the instructions for a Pascal program. To move from the menu line to the Edit window, use the arrow keys to highlight **Edit** and press the Enter key, or just hold down the Alt and press E (Alt-E) from any place in the IDE system. The status of the editor is shown in the first line of the window; it indicates the program line and screen column for the current position of the cursor as well as the file name for the program in the window.

The Watch window furnishes assistance in tracking down program errors, or bugs. You will learn in a later chapter how it helps to correct programs.

The hot-key line provides shortcuts for activating some of the more common menu choices. The *hot keys* change to adapt to the current activity in the IDE. Table 0.1 summarizes selected hot-key options, which also can be found in Appendix A in the Supplement.

The Output window (or User screen) is not visible, but is generated when a program produces output. You can switch back and forth between the main screen and the User screen by pressing Alt-F5. To replace the Watch window with the User screen, activate the Watch window by pressing

F6, and use Alt-F6 to make the switch. To return to the Watch window, press Alt-F6 again.

A program called *TOUR*, which is included in the Turbo Pascal 5.5 software package, guides you through the fundamentals of the IDE. To use this program, place the disk containing it in the active disk drive, type *TOUR*, and press the Enter key. Follow the directions on the screen to learn more about the IDE's features.

Hot Key	Menu Equivalent	Function
F1		Calls appropriate Help screen
F2	File/Save	Saves current editor file
F3	File/Load	Loads disk file
F4	Run/Go to cursor	Executes to cursor location
F5		Zooms/unzooms active window
F6		Changes active window
F7	Run/Trace into	Traces into subroutines
F8	Run/Step over	Steps over subroutine calls
F10		Toggles between main menu and Edit window
Alt-F1		Calls last Help screen
Alt-F3	File/Pick	Lets you pick file to load
Alt-F5	Run/User screen	Switches to User screen
Alt-F6		Switches the contents of the active window
Alt-F9	Compile/Compile	Compiles active program
Alt-B		Goes to **Break/watch** menu
Alt-C		Goes to **Compile** menu
Alt-D		Goes to **Debug** menu
Alt-E		Goes to Edit window
Alt-F		Goes to **File** menu
Alt-O		Goes to **Options** menu
Alt-R		Goes to **Run** menu
Alt-X	File/Quit	Quits Turbo Pascal and returns to DOS
Ctrl-F1		Gives language help while in editor
Ctrl-F2	Run/Program reset	Ends debugging session
Ctrl-F4	Debug/Evaluate	Evaluates or modifies variable
Ctrl-F7	B/Add watch	Adds expression to Watch window
Ctrl-F8	B/Toggle breakpoint	Toggles breakpoint
Ctrl-F9	Run/Run	Executes active program
Shift-F10		Displays version screen

Table 0.1
Turbo Pascal 5.5 Hot Keys

0.4 Turbo Pascal Menus

Making a selection from the menu line displays a lists of options related to that menu heading. All the options in any menu listing in the IDE can be chosen by displaying the listing using function key F10. Either highlight the choice and press Enter, or press the first letter in the option name, followed by Enter. Some options have hot-key equivalents, which are shown to the right of the option when a menu is displayed. You can back out of any selection by continuing to press the Esc key until you activate the Edit window. This chapter discusses a few of the fundamental menu options you will be using; others are presented later in the text.

File Menu

The **File** menu shown in the upper left corner of Figure 0.3 provides options that help load existing files and save files.

The **Load** option gets an existing file from the disk and displays it in the Edit window. It can be activated either by selecting **Load** from the **File** menu line or by pressing the function key F3 (the hot key for **Load**). The IDE then displays the Load File Name window asking for a file name (Figure 0.4). A file name usually consists of up to eight letters, a period, and the extension PAS. Often, a descriptive name is chosen to help remember the contents or purpose of a program file. If you can't remember the name of the file to load, press the Enter key; the IDE will then display a window listing all the

Figure 0.3
File Menu

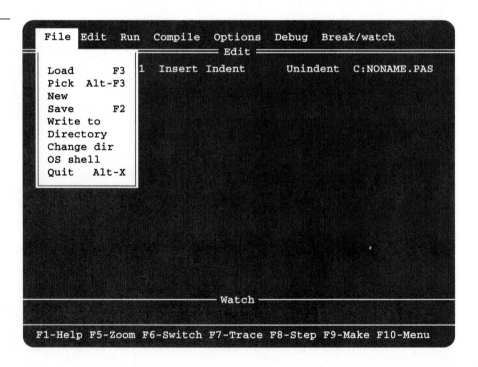

Figure 0.4
Load File Name Window

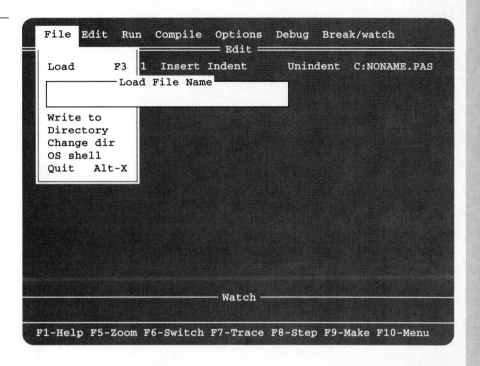

Figure 0.5
Window Listing All Current
Pascal Files

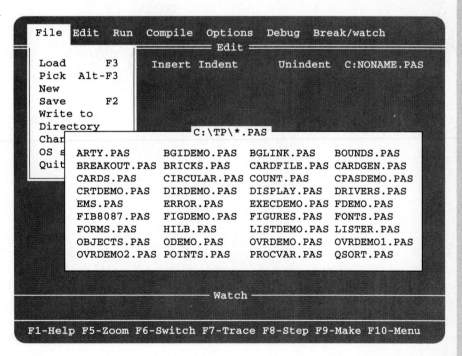

Pascal files in the current directory. See Figure 0.5. To load a file, highlight the desired file name with the arrow keys and press Enter. A copy of the file is transferred to the Edit window.

The **File** menu option **New** erases the contents of the Edit window. To choose **New**, display the **File** menu and either highlight **New** and press Enter or press N, the first letter in the option name. There is no hot-key option for **New**. If a program file is already in the window, the IDE may ask if you want to save it before it is erased.

The **Save** option copies the file in the Edit window to a disk. This option can be chosen just as the other options were or by using the F2 hot key. If the file has no name and has not yet been saved, a window on the screen asks you to supply one. Just type a descriptive name for the file (no more than eight letters), preceded by the letter designation of the drive on which the file is to be saved, including a colon and a complete directory path (see Figure 0.6). Press Enter to return to the Edit window. If the file already has a name, no windows appear and the file is saved under the current name. (Additional information concerning directories can be found in your computer's DOS manual.)

The **Write to** option enables you to save a copy of the edit file under a different file name or produce a printed copy of that file. The **Directory** option displays all the files in the current active directory. The **Change dir** option allows you to activate another directory. When you change to

Figure 0.6
Prompt to Name an
Unnamed File

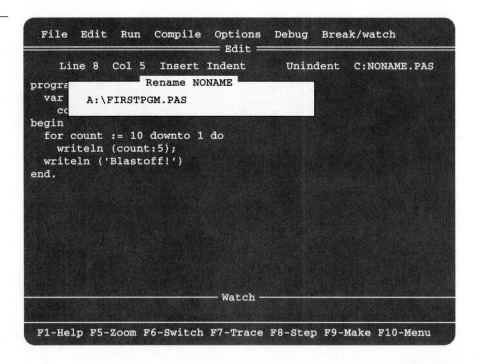

another directory, that directory becomes the default for all further file activity during that session.

The **OS shell** option permits you to leave Turbo Pascal IDE temporarily and takes you to DOS, where you can execute any DOS command. To return to Turbo Pascal, just type the word *exit* and press the Enter key.

If you select the **Quit** option, the IDE is closed for business, and you return to the operating system. The hot-key option for **Quit** is Alt-X.

Edit Option

The sole function of **Edit** is to open the Edit window for the creation and editing of a program file. There is no menu for this choice.

Run Menu

The **Run** menu contains options that let you either execute a program, move through it one step at a time, or view the User screen. As Figure 0.7 shows, each option in this menu has its equivalent hot key.

Use the **Run** option from this menu (Ctrl-F9) to translate a program in the Edit window into machine-readable form (compile the program) and execute it. If there are any errors in the compile phase, a description of the error is shown at the top of the Edit window. Pressing any key removes the description and moves the cursor to the error position.

The **User screen** option (Alt-F5) allows you to flip back and forth between the User screen and the IDE main screen.

The **Trace into** option also is very useful in finding program errors. Details of its operation are given in Chapter 3.

Figure 0.7
Run Menu

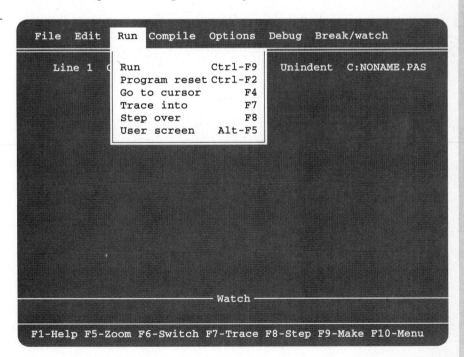

Figure 0.8
Compile Menu

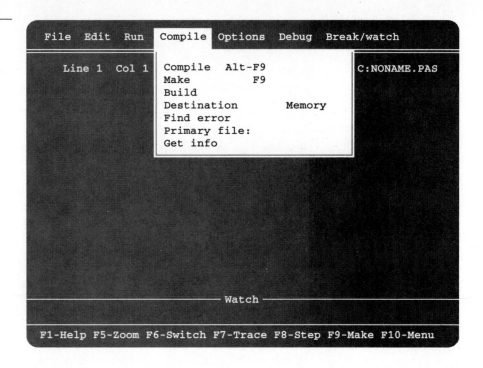

Compile Menu

The **Compile** menu shown in Figure 0.8 includes the **Compile** option (Alt/F9), which translates the source code in the Edit window to object code. The program is not executed, but relevant error messages are displayed.

Options Menu

The **Options** menu in Figure 0.9 provides facilities that allow you to specify new defaults for compiler options.

Debug Menu

The **Debug** menu in Figure 0.10 supplies options that help detect and correct errors in programs.

Break/watch Menu

The **Break/watch** menu in Figure 0.11 allows you to follow the values of program quantities in a program for the purpose of detecting incorrect action. Its use will be featured in Chapter 3.

0.5 The Turbo Pascal Editor

You must be able to move around the Edit window while it is active. Although this can be done with the four arrow keys, this sometimes proves tedious. A number of movement commands make it easier to navigate in the Edit window. For example, instead of repeatedly using the left-arrow key to move the cursor to the beginning of the existing line, you can press the Home key.

Figure 0.9
Options Menu

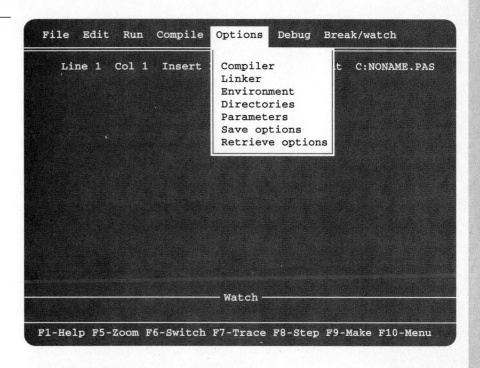

Figure 0.10
Debug Menu

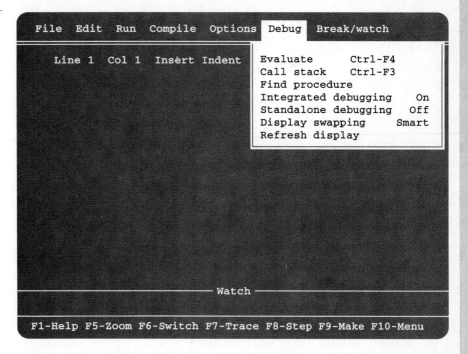

Figure 0.11
Break/watch Menu

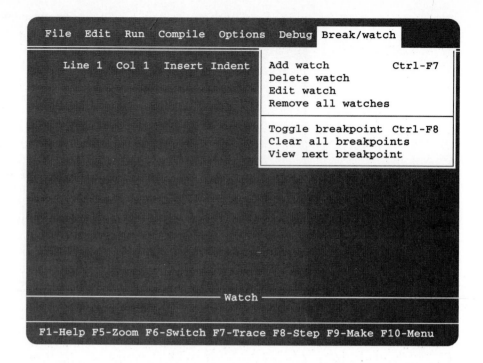

The Turbo Pascal Editor also includes commands for inserting text, deleting text, and performing operations on blocks of text. For example, to delete the character to the left of the cursor, press Ctrl-H or the Backspace key. To delete an entire line, move the cursor to that line and press Ctrl-Y.

A summary of the more common editor commands is given in Table 0.2 and in Appendix B in the Supplement. Complete detailed descriptions can be found in the Turbo Pascal User's Guide. A little practice with the more powerful features of the Turbo editor can save you many keystrokes.

0.6 Function Key Equivalents

The bottom line of the Turbo Pascal IDE main screen lists the hot-key options that are appropriate for the current programming activity. Not all of the hot keys are visible at the same time; different ones appear according to what is needed.

Pressing the F1 hot key displays a Help window that provides information on the active part of the main screen. For example, pressing F1 when the **File** option on the menu line is highlighted shows a description of the function of each of its menu choices (as in Figure 0.12). If the Edit window is active, F1 provides a summary of the cursor movement keystrokes. The bottom line of the screen would then give options related to the Help window, such as pressing the Esc key to erase it.

Table 0.2
Turbo Pascal 5.5 Editor
Commands

Function	Keystroke
Movement Commands	
Character left	Ctrl-S or left arrow
Character right	Ctrl-D or right arrow
Word left	Ctrl-A or Ctrl-left arrow
Word right	Ctrl-F or Ctrl-right arrow
Line up	Ctrl-E or up arrow
Line down	Ctrl-X or down arrow
Page up	Ctrl-R or PgUp
Page down	Ctrl-C or PgDn
Beginning of line	Ctrl-Q/S or Home
End of line	Ctrl-Q/D or End
Top of window	Ctrl-Q/E or Ctrl-Home
Bottom of window	Ctrl-Q/X or Ctrl-End
Beginning of program	Ctrl-Q/R or Ctrl-PgUp
End of program	Ctrl-Q/C or Ctrl-PgDn
Insert and Delete Commands	
Insert line	Ctrl-N
Delete line	Ctrl-Y
Delete block	Ctrl-K/Y
Delete to end of line	Ctrl-Q/Y
Delete character left of cursor	Ctrl-H or Backspace
Delete character under cursor	Ctrl-G or Delete
Block Commands	
Mark block begin	Ctrl-K/B
Mark block end	Ctrl-K/K
Mark single word	Ctrl-K/T
Print block	Ctrl-K/P
Copy block	Ctrl-K/C
Delete block	Ctrl-K/Y
Hide/display block	Ctrl-K/H
Move block	Ctrl-K/V
Read block from disk	Ctrl-K/R
Write block to disk	Ctrl-K/W
Miscellaneous	
Find	Ctrl-Q/F
Find and replace	Ctrl-Q/A
Invoke main menu	F10
Language help	Ctrl-F1
Load file	F3
Save file and remain in editor	Ctrl-K/S or F2

Figure 0.12
Help Window for the
File Menu

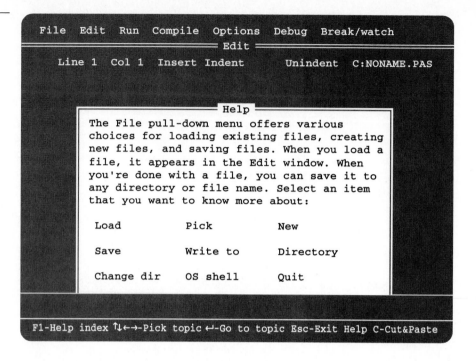

The **Zoom** hot key (F5) removes the Watch window from the main screen to provide more room for the Edit window. Pressing F5 a second time returns the Watch window. Function key F6 allows you to switch the active window between the Edit window and the Watch window, while F10 lets you activate the menu line options.

0.7 Running a Sample Pascal Program: A Step-by-Step Guide

The following exercise should familiarize you with the basics of using the Turbo Pascal IDE to create, edit, and execute a simple program. At this point you need not be concerned about understanding the Pascal code; it is discussed in later chapters.

1. Enter the Turbo Pascal IDE by typing *turbo* at the DOS prompt and pressing the Enter key.

2. After the IDE screen appears, press F10 to activate the Edit window. The cursor should be on "Line 1" and "Col 1" of that window.

3. Enter the following program exactly as written:

```
program Countdown;
  var
    count : integer;
begin
  for count = 10 downto 1 do
    Writeln (count:5)
  Writeln ('Blastoff!')
end.
```

4. Attempt to run the program by pressing Ctrl-F9. The system responds by displaying the following error message at the top of the Edit window:

   Error 91: ":=" expected

   The cursor is underlining the equal sign in the *for* statement. A program does not produce any output unless all errors of this type are corrected.

5. Press the colon symbol (`:`) to change `=` to `:=`, and the error message disappears.

6. Again, try to run the program by pressing Ctrl-F9. This time the system responds with another error message:

   Error 85: ";" expected

   Even though the cursor is under the *W* in the second *Writeln* statement, the error occurred because a semicolon was missing at the end of the first *Writeln* statement.

7. Press the up-arrow key once to move the cursor to the preceding line, press the End key to move the cursor to the end of the same line, and enter a semicolon. The edited program becomes:

```
program Countdown;
  var
    count : integer;
begin
  for count := 10 downto 1 do
    Writeln (count:5);
  Writeln ('Blastoff!')
end.
```

8. Run the program by entering Ctrl-F9. After a brief period of time (and some activity), you're back in the Edit window. It looks as though nothing has happened, but the output from the program is waiting for you in the Output window.

9. Select **User screen** from the **Run** menu, or press Alt-F5, and you'll see the following output:

```
                  10
                   9
                   8
                   7
                   6
                   5
                   4
                   3
                   2
                   1
            Blastoff!
```

10. Press any key to return to the main screen.

11. To see both the Output and the Edit windows together, first press F6 to jump to the Watch window and then press Alt-F6 to switch from the Watch window to the Output window. The cursor appears in the Output window at the end of the output. In this window, the arrow keys allow you to move through the text (*scroll*) to see all the output.

12. Press Alt-F6 again to replace the Output window with the Watch window, followed by F6 to activate the Edit window.

13. Press Alt-F9 to compile the program. This translation process does not execute the program but displays a window giving information about the file, if there are no errors (see Figure 0.13).

14. Now it's time to save the correct version of this program. Press F2 to activate **Save** from the **File** menu. A window appears on the screen asking you to name the program, since you have not yet done so, and the name **NONAME** appears in the window. Type the file name **BLASTOFF** preceded by its complete path name, for example,

    A:\BLASTOFF

    and press the Enter key. (The system automatically adds the PAS extension.) After a brief period of disk activity, the Edit window becomes active and the file name **A:BLASTOFF.PAS** appears in the upper right corner of the main screen.

15. Since a copy of the file is saved on disk, you can remove the program from the Edit window by pressing Alt-F to activate the **File** menu and *N* to choose the **New** option. The Edit window is now ready for another program.

If looking at the blank screen reminds you that you should have made a printed copy of the program before erasing it, you can quickly call up a file copy from the disk on which it was just saved.

16. Press F3 to load the file and copy it from the disk back into the editor. The system responds by asking for the name of the program to load. Press Enter, and a listing of all the programs on your program disk is displayed. Highlight

Figure 0.13
After a Successful
Compilation

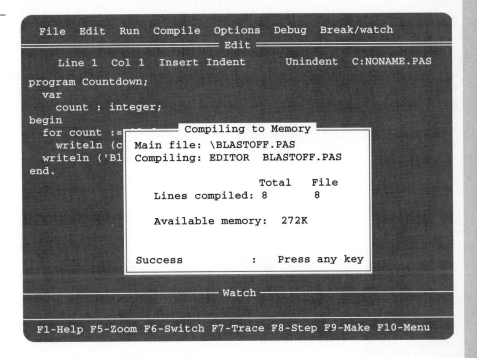

```
   File  Edit  Run  Compile  Options  Debug  Break/watch
================================ Edit ================================
      Line 1  Col 1  Insert Indent          Unindent   C:NONAME.PAS
program Countdown;
  var
    count : integer;
begin
  for count :=          Compiling to Memory
    writeln (c     Main file: \BLASTOFF.PAS
  writeln ('Bl     Compiling: EDITOR  BLASTOFF.PAS
end.
                                   Total    File
                      Lines compiled: 8        8

                      Available memory:  272K


                      Success          :   Press any key

================================ Watch ================================


 F1-Help F5-Zoom F6-Switch F7-Trace F8-Step F9-Make F10-Menu
```

BLASTOFF.PAS, press the Enter key, and the program is transferred to the Edit window.

17. Make sure the printer is turned on, then press Alt-F to activate the **File** menu.

18. Type *W* or use the arrow keys to highlight **Write to**, and press the Enter key. The IDE displays a window that asks the new destination for the file in the Edit window. At this point you can change the default output device name and save the program on another disk, with another name, or send a copy of it to the printer. Your choice here is the printer.

19. The special name *prn* indicates that the program is to be sent to the printer. Type *prn* in this window to change the default output device to the printer, then press the Enter key. A copy of your program is printed and all subsequent saves are to the printer until the default is changed.

20. To reset the default output device name to the original disk file, choose **Write to** from the **File** menu again. This time type the following in the destination window:

   A:\BLASTOFF.PAS

The IDE asks if you want to overwrite the previous copy of the file A:\BLASTOFF.PAS. Press Y, and the original file name again appears in the upper right corner of the Edit window.

Figure 0.14
Help Window Explaining
the Use of **begin**

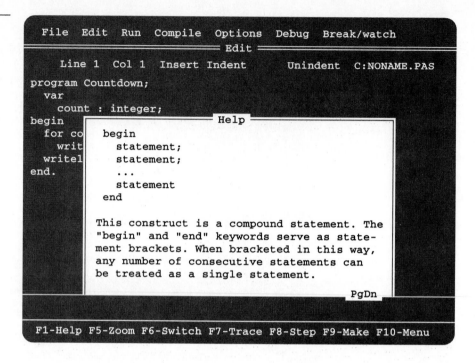

21. The IDE Help facility also gives assistance with Pascal vocabulary. Put the cursor under the Pascal word **begin** in the program, and press Ctrl-F1. The window that appears explains how **begin** is used in a Pascal program (see Figure 0.14). If the Help screen is too small to hold all the necessary Help information, press the PgDn (page down) key to display more. Pressing the Esc key erases a Help window.

22. Leave the Turbo Pascal IDE and return to DOS by pressing Alt-X or choosing **Quit** from the **File** menu.

This exercise samples the more common functions of the Turbo Pascal IDE. Additional features are discussed throughout the text. More detailed information on these and other features can be found in the Turbo Pascal User's Guide that accompanies the software.

Store and Forward

[Note: The "Store and Forward" section at the end of each chapter in this text summarizes the important points presented in that chapter and tells how they prepare you for the topics in succeeding chapters.]

A computer system has hardware components that store, calculate, display, and accept data; it also must have software to tell the hardware what to do. Because computers do not understand human languages and most humans find it difficult to understand the computer's language, compilers were developed to translate instructions from a high-level human language to the object code the computer understands.

The Turbo Pascal integrated development environment (IDE) provides the tools and a comfortable atmosphere for creating, editing, and executing programs written in the high-level language called Pascal. An elementary knowledge of how the IDE works is necessary before you can write programs.

The next step is to learn some general strategies for solving problems and apply these strategies to work out problems requiring computer solutions.

Exercises

1. Explain, in general terms, the purpose of the following components of the Turbo Pascal integrated development environment:
   a. **File** menu
   b. Hot keys
   c. Output window or User screen
   d. **Write to** option from the **File** menu
   e. Help window

2. Answer the following questions in paragraph form.
   a. What are secondary storage devices, and why are they needed in a computer system?
   b. Distinguish between high-level and low-level computer languages.
   c. What is the purpose of an operating system?
   d. Cite an advantage and a disadvantage of a development environment that uses menus.
   e. What is the difference between the **Compile** and **Run** options in the IDE?

3. Explain, in paragraph form, how each of the following tasks is performed.
   a. Print a program listing.
   b. Cancel the last command chosen in the IDE.
   c. Get help with Pascal vocabulary.
   d. Replace the Watch window on the main screen with the Output window.
   e. Move the cursor in the Edit window to the beginning of a program.

4. Users often must consult the manuals that accompany software to find out how to perform certain tasks. Using the Turbo Pascal User's Guide, describe how to do each of the following:
   a. Block a portion of text in the Edit window.
   b. Delete a blocked portion of text from the Edit window.
   c. Exit the editor without saving the current program file.
   d. Move the cursor to the last error position.
   e. Pick a file from a list of the previous eight files loaded into the Edit window.

Summary of Variations Between Turbo Pascal 5.0/5.5 and Turbo Pascal 6.0

The following list of the important differences between Turbo Pascal 5.0/5.5 and Turbo Pascal 6.0 is arranged alphabetically by function. *Text Ref.* indicates the first major occurrence of the concept in the main text.

Add watch *(Text Ref.: Sec. 4.5 Top-Down Testing with the Turbo Pascal IDE)*

In Turbo Pascal 5.0/5.5 the **Add watch** command is found in the **Break/watch** menu; in Turbo Pascal 6.0. it is found in the **Watches** submenu of the **Debug** menu. In either case, **Add watch** can be invoked by pressing Ctrl-F7.

Breakpoints *(Text Ref.: Sec. 4.5 Top-Down Testing with the Turbo Pascal IDE)*

To insert a breakpoint in your program in Turbo Pascal 5.0/5.5, select **Toggle breakpoint** from the **Break/watch** menu or press Ctrl-F8. In Turbo Pascal 6.0, **Toggle breakpoint** is found in the **Debug** menu, but still can be activated by pressing Ctrl-F8.

Closing the Watch Window *(Text Ref.: Sec. 4.5 Top-Down Testing with the Turbo Pascal IDE)*

There is no command to close the Watch window in Turbo Pascal 5.0/5.5. You can remove all the variables in that window by selecting **Remove all watches** from the **Break/watch** menu when the Watch window is active. In Turbo Pascal 6.0, select **Close** from the **Window** menu to remove the Watches window.

Dialog Box Appearance *(Text Ref.: Sec. 3.6 Text File Output)*

Although they are *functionally* similar in the different versions, the dialog boxes for many menu selections differ from version to version.

Output Window Display *(Text Ref.: Sec. 4.5 Top-Down Testing with the Turbo Pascal IDE)*

In Turbo Pascal 5.0/5.5, to view both the Output and Edit windows simultaneously, press F6 to activate the Watch window and then press Alt-F6 to display the Output window. To remove the Output window, press Alt-F6 again; the Watch window then appears. In Turbo Pascal 6.0, selecting **Output** from the **Window** menu reveals an Output window. To remove it, select **Previous** from the **Window** menu.

Previous Screen *(Text Ref.:* Sec. 4.5 Top-Down Testing with the Turbo Pascal IDE)

The **Previous** (screen) option that is used in Turbo Pascal 6.0 to erase the Output window is not available in Turbo Pascal 5.0/5.5. To remove an Output window from the screen and uncover the Watch window in version 5.0/5.5, press Alt-F6 while the Output screen is active.

Printing a Program Listing *(Text Ref.:* Sec. 3.3 Printer Output)

To obtain a printed copy of the active program in 5.0/5.5 use **Write to** from the **File** menu to change the default output device to the printer (*prn*). Any subsequent **Save** selections are sent to the printer unless you change the default output device back to a disk file. The **Print** option from the **File** menu in Turbo Pascal 6.0 is not available in versions 5.0 and 5.5.

Trace Facility Preparation *(Text Ref.:* Sec. 3.9 Tracing a Program with the Turbo Pascal IDE)

To prepare for tracing in Turbo Pascal 5.0/5.5, make sure the following options are on: the **Integrated debugging** option from the **Debug** menu; the **Debug information** option in the **Compiler** option of the **Options** menu; and the **Local symbols** option in the **Compiler** option of the **Options** menu. To set (or reset) these options, highlight the option and press the Enter key. In Turbo Pascal 6.0, these options are found in different menus and changed in a slightly different manner.

Watches Window Display *(Text Ref.:* Sec. 4.5 Top-Down Testing with the Turbo Pascal IDE)

The Watches window of Turbo Pascal 6.0 is called the Watch window in Turbo Pascal 5.0/5.5. In 5.0/5.5, the Watch window does not have to be activated; it appears on the screen when the system is initiated.

APPENDIX A

Turbo Pascal 5.5 Hot Keys

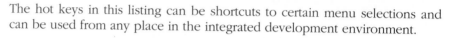

The hot keys in this listing can be shortcuts to certain menu selections and can be used from any place in the integrated development environment.

Hot Key	Menu Equivalent	Function
F1		Calls appropriate Help screen
F2	File/Save	Saves current editor file
F3	File/Load	Loads disk file
F4	Run/Go to cursor	Executes to cursor location
F5		Zooms/unzooms active window
F6		Changes active window
F7	Run/Trace into	Traces into subroutines
F8	Run/Step over	Steps over subroutine calls
F10		Toggles between main menu and Edit window
Alt-F1		Calls last Help screen
Alt-F3	File/Pick	Lets you pick file to load
Alt-F5	Run/User screen	Switches to User screen
Alt-F6		Switches to contents of the active window
Alt-F9	Compile/Compile	Compiles active program
Alt-B		Goes to **Break/watch** menu
Alt-C		Goes to **Compile** menu
Alt-D		Goes to **Debug** menu
Alt-E		Goes to Edit window
Alt-F		Goes to **File** menu
Alt-O		Goes to **Options** menu
Alt-R		Goes to **Run** menu
Alt-X	File/Quit	Quits Turbo Pascal and returns to DOS
Ctrl-F1		Gives language help while in editor
Ctrl-F2	Run/Program reset	Ends debugging session
Ctrl-F4	Debug/Evaluate	Evaluates or modifies variable
Ctrl-F7	B/Add watch	Adds expression to Watch window
Ctrl-F8	B/Toggle breakpoint	Toggles breakpoint
Ctrl-F9	Run/Run	Executes active program
Shift-F10		Displays Version screen

APPENDIX B

Turbo Pascal 5.5 Editor Commands

This appendix gives a summary of selected Turbo Pascal 5.5 editor commands. In some cases two different keystroke combinations can be used to activate the command. Notation such as Ctrl-Q/S means: hold down the Ctrl key while pressing Q, and then, after releasing both keys, press S.

Function	Keystroke
Movement Commands	
Character left	Ctrl-S or left arrow
Character right	Ctrl-D or right arrow
Word left	Ctrl-A or Ctrl-left arrow
Word right	Ctrl-F or Ctrl-right arrow
Line up	Ctrl-E or up arrow
Line down	Ctrl-X or down arrow
Page up	Ctrl-R or PgUp
Page down	Ctrl-C or PgDn
Beginning of line	Ctrl-Q/S or Home
End of line	Ctrl-Q/D or End
Top of window	Ctrl-Q/E or Ctrl-Home
Bottom of window	Ctrl-Q/X or Ctrl-End
Beginning of program	Ctrl-Q/R or Ctrl-PgUp
End of program	Ctrl-Q/C or Ctrl-PgDn
Insert and Delete Commands	
Insert line	Ctrl-N
Delete line	Ctrl-Y
Delete block	Ctrl-K/Y
Delete to end of line	Ctrl-Q/Y
Delete character left of cursor	Ctrl-H or Backspace
Delete character under cursor	Ctrl-G or Delete

Function	Keystroke
Block Commands	
Mark block begin	Ctrl-K/B
Mark block end	Ctrl-K/K
Mark single word	Ctrl-K/T
Print block	Ctrl-K/P
Copy bloc	Ctrl-K/C
Delete block	Ctrl-K/Y
Hide/display block	Ctrl-K/H
Move block	Ctrl-K/V
Read block from disk	Ctrl-K/R
Write block to disk	Ctrl-K/W
Miscellaneous	
Find	Ctrl-Q/F
Find and replace	Ctrl-Q/A
Invoke main menu	F10
Language help	Ctrl-F1
Load file	F3
Save file and remain in editor	Ctrl-K/S or F2

Answers to Selected Exercises in Supplementary Chapter O

Chapter 0

Exercises

1. a. The **File** menu contains options for the loading and saving of files.
   c. The Output window displays program output.
   e. The Help window displays useful information on the integrated development environment or on Turbo Pascal vocabulary.

2. b. High-level languages use code that is humanlike, while low-level languages use code that is similar to the language a computer actually executes.
   d. Menu-driven systems are easier to use, and they provide on-screen assistance in executing the program. However, one may have to use additional keystrokes, making the process slower.

3. a. To print a program listing, select **Write to** from the **File** menu, place the keyword **prn** in the Output device window, and press the Enter key.
   c. To get help with Pascal vocabulary, move the cursor under a Pascal term in the active Edit window and hold down the Ctrl key and press the F1 function key (Ctrl-F1)
   e. To move the cursor in the Edit window to the beginning of a program, you can either: hold down the Ctrl key while pressing Q, then release both keys and press R (Ctrl-Q/R); or hold down the Ctrl key and press the PgUp key (Ctrl-PgUp).

4. b. To delete a blocked portion of text, hold down Ctrl key and press K. After releasing both keys, press Y. (Ctrl-K/Y)
   d. To move the cursor to the position of the last error, hold down the Ctrl key and press Q. After releasing both keys, press W. (Ctrl-Q/W)

Index to Turbo Pascal 5.0 & 5.5 Supplement